THE MOAT FARM MYSTERY

The Life and Criminal Career of
SAMUEL HERBERT DOUGAL

M.W. OLDRIDGE

First published 2012

The History Press
The Mill, Brimscombe Port
Stroud, Gloucestershire, GL5 2QG
www.thehistorypress.co.uk

British Library Cataloguing in Publication Data.
A catalogue record for this book is available from the British Library.

ISBN 978 0 7524 6629 3

Typesetting and origination by The History Press
Printed in Great Britain

CONTENTS

Introduction and Acknowledgements   7

Foreword   13

Epigraph   17

Chapter One   19

Chapter Two   45

Chapter Three   77

Chapter Four   99

Chapter Five   114

Chapter Six   136

Chapter Seven   147

Chapter Eight   169

Chapter Nine   186

Chapter Ten   214

Chapter Eleven   235

Chapter Twelve   265

Chapter Thirteen   283

Bibliography   300

Notes   303

INTRODUCTION AND ACKNOWLEDGEMENTS

THE MOAT FARM Mystery was one of the most notable criminal affairs of the early years of the twentieth century, but this book is the first to be devoted entirely to the matter since a publication called the *Trial of Samuel Herbert Dougal*, which was issued during the inter-war period. In the years that followed, the case rather faded from view, and, when it did attract factual coverage, it did so chiefly in essay-length pieces, often printed in crime anthologies, and very few of these renditions relied on any original research. The turning points of the Moat Farm case ossified into legend as the story was repeated, and repeated again. This book revisits some of the accretions of Moat Farm lore, re-examining them from a fresh perspective.

In 1928, the *Trial of Samuel Herbert Dougal* was merely the latest work in the blossoming *Notable British Trials* series published by William Hodge of Edinburgh. Two earlier series – *Notable Scottish Trials* and *Notable English Trials* – had been merged in 1921 and, in addition to providing court transcripts of the famous criminal actions of the Victorian and Edwardian periods – those featuring the great Hawley Harvey Crippen, Dr Pritchard, William Gardiner, Florence Maybrick, *et al* – the series extended back to cover historical crimes – the trial of Mary, Queen of Scots, the *Bounty* Mutineers, the trial of King Charles I, and so on. Best of all, with each transcript came illustrations reproduced on high-quality, in-bound plates, timelines, appendices containing contextual material, and introductions by, as it were, guest editors. Some of these remain remarkable for their intelligence and perspicuity. It is, I suppose, possible to understand the legal world of the early 1900s without having to read Donald Carswell's introduction to the *Trial of Ronald True*, or Eric R. Watson's introduction to the *Trial of George Joseph Smith*, but it would seem unfortunate to deny oneself the experience in either case. Occasionally, the stellar

quality of the material which the *Notable British Trials* series provided would have real-time effects: William Roughead's *Trial of
Oscar Slater* was instrumental in introducing Sir Arthur Conan
Doyle to this famous miscarriage of justice. Conan Doyle would
later play a central role – not least financially – in having Slater's
conviction overturned.

The editor of the *Trial of Samuel Herbert Dougal* was Fryniwyd
Tennyson Jesse (1888–1958). Jesse was one of a handful of female
editors of the *Notable British Trials* series – others included
Winifred Duke and Helena Normanton, whose names ought
to be known to anyone with a passing interest in the true-
crime literature of the mid-twentieth century. A great-niece of
the famous poet, and with a sparkily independent personality,
Jesse investigated the darkness of the soul in several introductions for Hodge's series, and in many other works of fiction and
non-fiction of her own: in addition, she had been a war correspondent during the First World War, reaching Antwerp by the
late September of 1914. She was twenty-five years old, and the
only female journalist at the front line at the time.

In the late twenties, Jesse set exceptionally high standards
for subsequent writers on the Moat Farm Mystery with her
introduction to the *Trial of Samuel Herbert Dougal*. She had,
obviously, inherited some of her great-uncle's literary sensibili-
ties: as an encapsulation of the perverse character of her subject,
Jesse's description of Dougal as possessed of 'some of the tastes
attributed to the more dissolute Roman emperors' defied all
competition then, and, I think, still does today. The memorably
'clayey, lumpy girls' of Dougal's subsequent legend – they appear,
on their bicycles, in almost every run-through of the Moat Farm
case – originated, at least under this description, with Jesse. As an
editor of insight and sensitivity, she is practically peerless even
among those associated with the *Notable British Trials* series; her
introduction to the *Trial of Rattenbury and Stoner*, which was written a few years later, remains essential reading for any student
of crime. Here, Jesse delineates the true scale of the bridgeless
disconnect between fantasy and reality upon which murder
sometimes throws its awful spotlight, and the piece serves as a
little distillation of Jesse's genius. When, subsequently, I refer to
Jesse – 'Jesse says this', 'Jesse suggests that', and so on – it is to her
introduction to the *Trial of Samuel Herbert Dougal* that I allude.

Priced at 10*s* 6*d* upon publication in 1928, the *Trial of Samuel Herbert Dougal* is now available second-hand and in decent (but not perfect) condition for, typically, about £20 or £30, and, if anything you see in this book stimulates any further curiosity about the Moat Farm Mystery, I can only suggest that, to feed it, you obtain Jesse's work, to the surpassing aesthetic and intellectual qualities of which I can only aspire.

I have been lucky to have received the generous support of many people in writing *The Moat Farm Mystery*. It started out as an accident – I grew up in Ware, a small town in Hertfordshire with a happy history of brewing and drinking. Samuel Herbert Dougal had, for a while, been the licensee at one of Ware's many public houses and, knowing nothing in particular about the case, but intrigued by the connection, I asked my parents to find out which one. They did – they had both recently retired, and it kept them busy – and gradually my interest in Dougal's eccentric story deepened. Besides my parents, I have the honour to thank the following people for their various contributions: Joan Borrowscale, Susan Collier, Stewart Evans, Nicola Guy, Cate Ludlow, Hazel Miller, Matilda Richards, and Neil Storey. The staff of the archives and museums which I have visited have been invariably helpful – countless other people have listened to me telling them about the case, or answered the occasional unsolicited enquiry by email, without, perhaps, betraying their true feelings, and, for this indulgence, I am thankful. In addition, Nick Connell, who has helped and encouraged me throughout the process, was kind enough to agree to write the foreword.

But this book is dedicated to the memory of Nick Culpeper, who died in February 2011 without seeing this book in print. Nick was the Moat Farm expert *sans pareil*, and lived in Newport, in north-west Essex, a few miles from the infamous farm itself. He had conceived of an interest in the Moat Farm Mystery in about 1980, when he worked in Heffers bookshop in Cambridge. He was asked by a friend of his to obtain a copy of Jesse's book; he did so, glanced through it, obtained a second copy, and embarked on his own enquiries. He visited the farm in the early 1980s when it was up for sale, introducing himself to the estate agent as a 'Dougal ghoul'. He was allowed in to look around anyway, and the estate agent admitted that they had been expecting a few tourists, of which Nick was the first. In the meantime, Nick fastened on to local rumours – eighty years after the event – which described Dougal's habits, his acquaintances, his sex life, and so on. Nick pointed out to me the building in Newport, once a pub, in which Dougal purportedly drank; he showed me the yard in which Dougal parked his steam-car; he told me of local people who claimed, for better or worse, to be related to Dougal by illegitimate connection.

Nick gradually obtained an extensive Moat Farm archive, and his instinct to collect drove him to seek out books and magazines which mentioned the case. These he added to the bookshelves which lined the walls of his cottage, where his interests competed constantly for space: the Moat Farm here, the A6 Murder there, Jack the Ripper there, and, there, there and there, Aleister Crowley and his coterie of black magicians and hangers-on. Crowley had been fascinating Nick since the 1960s, although he did not subscribe to the Beast's exclusive philosophical principles: in fact, he had become interested in the man's writings after being advised that they were notoriously difficult to understand. Over forty years, Nick's unmatched collection grew to include a number of books from Crowley's own library, for example, and who-knows-how-many scarce and unique editions otherwise.

An avid bibliophile, Nick would occasionally 'customise' his books, unless they were of very obvious intrinsic value – for me, his customised edition of Jesse's *Trial of Samuel Herbert Dougal* assumes its own significance. The first edition of Jesse's book had contained, on one of its plates, a portrait of Mr Justice Wright, but it was soon realised that the image used was, in fact, a photograph of the *wrong* Mr Justice Wright. The plate was omitted from subsequent editions, but Nick obtained a photograph of the correct individual, and tipped it into his second edition copy. He particularly enjoyed the idea that the *wrong Wright* had sneaked into Jesse's first print, and that his adapted second-edition would be the only one to show the *right Wright*. Nick declined to write on the Moat Farm himself – nothing longer, at any rate, than the occasional article in the village magazine – although he was uniquely qualified to do so. He felt, quite unjustifiably, that he would be unable to do a good job.

Shortly before Christmas 2010, Nick emailed me to say that he had 'something I need to talk to you about in the near future'. When we spoke on the phone later that day, he told me that he had been recovering from cancer when I had first met him, and that he had now been advised by his doctor that the illness had returned, and that no treatment was possible. He expected to die in two or three months, and asked me to visit him in order to take possession of his Moat Farm collection. I visited him a few days after Christmas – snow lay on the Essex fields, and, in his cottage, Nick sat on his sofa trying to warm himself on a small heater; in truth, the room *was* warm, but Nick's body had stopped feeling it. He looked quite ill, but his humility, and his stoic sense of cosmic balance, had not deserted him. He was well supported by friends and neighbours, whom he disliked troubling, and whose assistance he received gratefully and modestly. As for his doctor's prognosis, Nick said that this was just 'one of those things'.

I spoke to him once more, on the telephone, in January 2011. He told me that he had stopped going to the hospital – Addenbrooke's, in Cambridge – because they could not really do anything for him. He had recently discovered a few things which had been omitted from the Moat Farm collection he had passed on to me, and, in spite of his circumstances, he made arrangements for these items to be sent to me in the post. He told me that he was 'a great believer in things being in the right place'.

A little less than three weeks later, Nick died. I was invited to attend the funeral, and the gathering afterwards at the Fleur de Lys in Widdington, one of Nick's favourite local pubs. I was able to make it to the gathering – so were, probably, a hundred other people, a mark of Nick's popularity. Rarely can such events have reflected their subject's *joie de vivre* so precisely. From the bar, a weird visage stared out at the guests – it was a cake with Crowley's face on it, and the speeches consisted in part of some ribald poetry of which Nick was especially fond, and then came the ritual disposal of a pint of a certain brand of ale, not favoured by Nick, in the lavatory, 'back where it came from'. I knew Nick less well, I suppose, than many of the other attendees, but well enough to be aware that his sense of humour had not died with him. Stories were told of Nick's younger days, when, in the sixties, in a house built on a roundabout in Cambridge, and with the top-volume Rolling Stones LPs irritating the neighbours, he would mark the arrival of the police on the doorstep with, pretty much, an invitation to the officers to either join in or stop spoiling the fun. The gathering at the Fleur de Lys made sense of Nick's approach to life – and death, too – and there was, as he would no doubt have wished, much joy expressed by those touched by his generosity and effervescent spirit.

When I last saw Nick, I promised him that I would dedicate my Moat Farm book to him – I wasn't in contract at that time, but I had brought together what I thought was an increasingly workable manuscript; I believed that I foresaw its publication, and could reasonably be confident in making the promise. He seemed pleased by the idea, although it was obvious that he would never see the book itself. It is, therefore, a privilege to be able to dedicate this book to Nick's memory, and I am grateful, and will remain grateful, to him for his interest, encouragement, and kindness. I hope he would have approved.

M.W. Oldridge
October 2011

FOREWORD

IN 1928 THE barrister Helena Normanton suggested the possibility of a criminological hierarchy. 'Criminology,' she mused, 'has its own grim forms of monarchy; and if criminals selected Murder Kings, Dr Crippen would easily rank among the first half-dozen candidates for the throne.' Another contender was surely Samuel Herbert Dougal. The Moat Farm Murderer would be no mean pretender. Unlike Dr Crippen, who at least had the virtue of good manners, Dougal was a man with no redeeming features whatsoever.

Samuel Dougal overshadowed most of his felonious Victorian and Edwardian contemporaries. He rode roughshod through an era when the most infamous criminals attained a celebrity status, which in many cases has survived to this day. This was not only because of the horrific nature of their crimes and subsequent trials with the ever-present threat of a death sentence. The extraordinary personalities of the murderers were equally responsible for their enduring fame.

As a man Dougal is simultaneously compelling and repellent. H.L. Adam, a veteran crime journalist and true crime author, considered that in his forty-year career, Dougal was 'the most remarkable criminal I ever had anything to do with.' Oft-repeated tales of him offering naked cycling lessons to country wenches in the muddy fields surrounding his Essex farm were most likely false. However, when Dougal's past eventually caught up with him and his antecedents became widely known, crowds flocked to the Moat Farm in their thousands to view the scene of his final sensational crime.

In the course of twenty-one years of reasonably successful military service, Sergeant Samuel Dougal of the Royal Engineers had served in Wales, Ireland, the Isle of Wight, Canada and all over England. He had survived two frequently betrayed wives and a dose of syphilis. Honourably discharged and surprisingly with testimonies of his good character, Dougal soon discovered that he was not cut out for honest employment in Civvy Street.

A spell as the guv'nor of the Royston Crow pub in Ware, Hertfordshire, resulted in a suspicious conflagration followed by an insurance investigation and trial for arson at the Assizes. Within the smouldering shell of the Royston Crow was found an extraordinary document. Dougal had applied for the post of hangman and a singed letter from the Home Office inviting Dougal for an interview had survived the fire.

It seems that Dougal was fortunate to have been found not guilty of arson, but the trial marked the beginning of regular appearances in various criminal courts. There was to be an appearance at the Oxfordshire Quarter Sessions for theft, forgery charges heard at the Old Bailey, an affiliation order at the Saffron Walden Petty Sessions and ultimately his murder trial at the Essex Assizes.

Besides a few brief stints in vaguely defined jobs provided by a supportive brother, and as a woefully inadequate farmer and guest house keeper, Dougal never really worked again. Stripped of his army pension for his criminal activities, Dougal determined to avoid gainful employment by exploiting and fleecing lonely and emotionally vulnerable women. His other goal in life was to satisfy his relentless sexual drive with almost every woman he came into contact with. Dougal's remarkable stamina and vitality would never desert him and he left a string of illegitimate children in his wake.

Camille Holland was an ideal target for Dougal. A chaste spinster, sixty years of age, she was a woman of independent means after receiving a substantial legacy from an aunt. Still pining for a long-lost nautical fiancé who drowned at sea, she dreaded a bleak future as a guest house resident, slowly declining alone in genteel anonymity. All Miss Holland wanted was 'someone to look after me', and so, for want of a more circumspect plan, she placed an advert in a newspaper seeking a husband.

Tragically Samuel Dougal read the plea and Camille was powerless to resist his dubious, but undeniable earthy charms. Posing as a widower, Dougal deftly shed his tangled past and persuaded Miss Holland to masquerade as his wife at Coldhams Farm, soon to be renamed Moat House Farm on the outskirts of the small west Essex village of Clavering. Here it was business as usual for Dougal. The domestics were instantly seen as fair game for sexual harassment, while every effort was made to drain the wealth of his unfortunate inamorata. Then, on 19 May 1899, the couple were seen driving away from the farm in a trap. Dougal returned alone and instructed his farm labourers to fill in a nearby drainage ditch.

There was an inevitability that Samuel Dougal's life would end on the gallows. Just as there was always the cocaine bottle for Sherlock Holmes, there was always the rope for Dougal. First the unsuccessful attempt to become a hangman. Then, when serving time at Pentonville Prison, he made a failed suicide attempt by hanging, resulting in his being declared insane and transferred to Cane Hill Asylum. Finally the fatal drop at the hands of executioners William Billington and John Ellis at Chelmsford Prison.

The Moat Farm Mystery is not only a case study of the infamous Moat Farm Murder, but a detailed biography of Samuel Dougal that seeks to explain his motives and remarkable character. It is the first full study of the crime since the 1928 *Notable British Trials* volume by F. Tennyson Jesse. Since then, it has become a popular choice for authors of true crime anthologies, but these add little if anything to our knowledge of the case and its wicked perpetrator.

While M. W. Oldridge has graciously acknowledged his debt to the *Notable British Trials* volume on the Dougal case and the quality of its contents, his book is by far the more complete and absorbing work. Starting from scratch, he has thoroughly and systematically scrutinised the surviving contemporary records of the police, Home Office, courts, War Office and other official files held at the National Archives.

The County Record Offices of Hertfordshire and Essex yielded valuable documentary evidence. Printed sources in the form of newspapers and books were scoured and private collections opened up for the author's inspection, most importantly that of the late Nick Culpeper. Recent years have seen a proliferation of digital resources and these too have been exploited to help create this thorough, detailed volume that reveals more than any crime historian previously knew about one of the great crimes and trials of the twentieth century.

Know then the story of Samuel Herbert Dougal; faithless husband, negligent father, rapacious philanderer, mountebank, sexual predator, suspected murderer, forger, suspected arsonist, thief, certified lunatic, liar, perjurer and, unforgettably, the Moat Farm Murderer.

Nicholas Connell
Hertfordshire, 2012

When the spring is come, love,
And the rippling brooklets flow –
Then we'll meet once more, love,
In our own dear vale below.
When the moon shines soft, love,
And the silvery fountains flow,
Where the rustling leaves, love,
Whisper dreams of long ago. ...

When the winter is come, love,
And the dreary night winds blow –
Then will you forget, love,
Our fond dream of long ago?
Then will you forget, love,
This fond dream of long ago?[1]

As your hair grows whiter, I will love you more;
Though your eyes were brighter in the days of yore,
Though your footsteps falter,
My love shall never alter,
As your hair grows whiter, I will love you more.[2]

CHAPTER ONE

'Guilty or not guilty?'

No answer.

The same question again. More loudly. Urgency in the voice.

'Are you *guilty* or *not guilty*?'

The hand was there, silently twitching on the fatal lever …

ᘓᘓᘓ

SAMUEL DREDGE DOUGAL, a civil engineer born in Greenwich, and Maria Josephine Thompson, who had been born in County Tipperary, Ireland, were married in Dublin on 15 June 1846. She was still in her teens; he was twenty. His unusual middle name – curiously evocative for a civil engineer, although the railways had, by now, begun to usurp the canals – came from his mother's side. It was probably Samuel Dredge Dougal's youthful enthusiasm for his profession that had first taken him to Ireland, but he may have been an independent spirit anyway; when he married Maria, he was some distance from home, with, it seems, few family members nearby. Samuel appears to have decided, fairly soon after his marriage, that Ireland would be unable to provide the sustenance to nurture his evolving professional ambitions, or even to permit him to meet his new personal responsibilities. The potato famine was reaching a terrible crescendo, and the population was becoming radicalised in their growing desperation. One rebellion, in 1848, broke out in Maria's home town of Ballingarry. By this time, however, Samuel and Maria had left Ireland, and were living in East London, and the burden of the greater distance from home had fallen, in the end, not on him, but on her.

By 1851, they were living fairly prosperously, too – not rich, perhaps, but certainly comfortable – in Alfred Street, in Bow. Three miles removed from the city itself, Bow was a middlingly salubrious suburb situated within easy reach of the commercial buzz of the docks, to the south and south west, and the markets and financial centres to the west. Not all of her émigré compatriots, however, were in Maria's position. Thousands of Irish had fled the famine, and, for many, casual labour at London's docksides, for which there was sometimes great competition, offered their only day-to-day prospect of legitimate employment. Looking up and down the road, Samuel must have been aware that some of his neighbours had clerical jobs; some carried responsibility; some had servants: these were marks of the area's quality. On the horizon, though, the comparative misfortunes of the majority were transparently obvious. Whitechapel, sandwiched between the city and Bow, festered and fumed. It was here, in the dark alleyways and squalid courts, that the social implications of want, hunger, disease, neglect, addiction and unemployment found their expression. Already, there was a suspicion that its occult influence had begun to crawl eastwards. Mile End was next to fall; after that, Bow would be exposed to the unwelcome stink of poverty.

Whitechapel, it seems, became Samuel Herbert Dougal's playground. He had been born, the first son of Samuel and Maria, on 15 May 1847 and, word had it, had already consolidated a carefree, thrill-seeking attitude by the time of his adolescence. He was not unintelligent – when motivated, he could even be scholarly – and his father, apparently at some financial cost to himself, attempted to steer his son into his own field of civil engineering. The details are lost now, but the young Dougal is said to have taken some training – perhaps an apprenticeship – in this discipline. This made him employable, and history recalls that he was a 'remarkable draughtsman' and that he had 'particularly good and clear hand-writing'.[3] But Dougal's early facility with the pen failed to fulfil him. Work was one thing, however competent one was; the company of women, Dougal's main conflicting interest in his late teenage years, was much more exciting. Viewing the matter from beneath the furrowed brow which is the prerogative of fathers, Samuel Dredge Dougal is said to have disapproved of his son's hedonistic behaviour, but his strictures can only have frustrated the errant, headstrong, free-spending young man: at this point, sex and – perhaps – embryonic experiments with alcohol became gestures of defiance, rather than mere hobbies.[4]

The East End's unabashed public temptations provided the catalyst for disharmony at home. Dougal's late adolescence has been described in thrillingly evocative, and even envious, terms: 'vainglorious', 'dissolute', 'extrovert', 'adventurous', 'erring'.[5] In fact, 'superficial' and 'pretentious' might fit equally well. He may have fraudulently adopted the habit of speaking with his mother's Irish accent, finding that women enjoyed the music of the language.[6] He may have been encouraged by his early successes with the opposite sex, each separate triumph bolstering his confidence, and he may have been selfish and, for his time, sexually uninhibited.[7] Extrovert and adventurous all this may have been; examined another way, Dougal's licentious predilections, and his glib immunity to his parents' remonstrations, simply laid the foundations for what was to come.

ஒ௸ை

But much of this is really hearsay, and the first glimpse we catch of the man, beyond the peradventure of his early years, finds him in the flush of his early adulthood: in the middle of March 1866, Samuel Herbert Dougal, R.E., 8739, stood on the Kentish coast at Chatham.[8] He had committed to the Royal Engineers for the usual term of service – twelve years. The army was not so long out of the chaos of the Crimea, and, although the public enquiry into the failures of the campaign had sometimes highlighted the lack of intellectual potential in the average British soldier, new recruits were always necessary, and liable to be found among those for whom being shot at by foreign enemies at least represented steady employment. Dougal, with his gift for draughtsmanship and clerical work, detoured naturally into the Engineers. The Ordnance Survey, in particular, was undertaking major mapping exercises across the country at the time, and Dougal's talents dovetailed neatly with these projects.

A little under 10 stone in weight, 5 feet 8½ inches in height, advertising himself as nineteen going on twenty (a little older than he really was), with grey eyes, brown hair, a fair complexion, no smallpox scars, and a visible vaccination mark: nothing in Dougal's medical examination compromised his enlistment.

Resting, his heart beat seventy-two times per minute; he inhaled eighteen times over the same period.

Superficially, for a young man to whom physical pleasure had become a transfixing goal, all of this resembled reform – or, at least, maturation – and a sustained glow of approval radiated from Dougal's family. Away from home, and subject to the improving discipline of the military, his commendable career move demanded no second glance; but the distance Dougal had put between himself and his relatives did little, in practice, to encourage self-control. In truth, much had not changed. In April 1866, a month after his enlistment, an injury – a dislocation, caused by a 'blow against a form' – forced him into sick bay, and, since full mobility may not have been regained for thirty-six days afterwards, a tedious period of recuperation seems to have followed. Boredom was Dougal's nemesis, and it may have been during this period that he reverted to his previous thrill-seeking pattern.

On 24 October 1866, he returned to the hospital, again staying for five days. This time, however, the reason was different. Dougal had begun to see no reason why his progress within the Royal Engineers should be incompatible with his ongoing quest for sexual ecstasy, and he reported to the doctor suffering from primary syphilis. He had a lesion, a chancre, probably on his penis. In the column on the medical record sheet entitled 'Circumstances in or by which Disease was induced', the medical officer generously wrote 'contagions', but there is no doubt that Dougal had availed himself of the services of one, or very possibly more, of the local prostitutes. When he left the hospital, the chancre may have begun to respond to the doctor's prescription of *lotio nigra*, a solution of mercury.[9]

It is probably the case that Dougal's sexual forays were prolific throughout his period in the Royal Engineers. He would not have been the only military man to visit prostitutes. It may also be true to say that Dougal's 'growing reputation as a sexual athlete', to use Roy Harley Lewis's phrase, meant that he could attract women as easily as he could pay for them himself, and, in fact, make a profit along the way.[10] Fryniwyd Tennyson Jesse writes that 'only his fellow-soldiers knew his private life to have been a long procession of inglorious victories over servantmaids and shopgirls, who were relieved of their virtue and their money by Dougal'.[11] The combination of sex and money continued to animate Dougal, just as it had in London.

On the other hand, divesting innocent Kentish girls of their virginity *and* their money came with a built-in escape clause. When the fact that they had been tricked, and were consequently out of pocket, hit them, they were in no position to protest, lest their own sexual morals be inquired into. Social anxieties about female sexuality provided Dougal with the scope he needed to pursue his hedonistic lifestyle. The money which he took from one victim would entice another one, if he needed one. It is fair to assume that his sexual appetite, in the blush of his youth, was enormous.

Only venereal diseases stood up for the town's female population as Dougal swept through them like fire. By 19 November, he was back in the hospital for another five-day spell, complaining of orchitis, a testicular condition which can manifest itself in intense pain, swelling, and the presence of blood in the urine and in the ejaculate. This was unpleasant, and Dougal was treated with fomentations. It was also, as the doctor must have been aware, sexually transmitted, linked to chlamydia and gonorrhoea. Dougal demurely attributed his condition to 'a strain'. On 24 April 1867, just over a year after he had joined the Engineers, Dougal again went to the hospital, this time with condylomata – a rash resulting in white lesions, and a secondary feature of his syphilis, appearing a few months after the chancre. This time, he stayed for nine days, and was treated with silver nitrate. He gave the cause of this new ailment as 'filth'.

It may not have been an entire coincidence that, at this juncture, Dougal's work began to take him away from Chatham. Of course, a surveyor was little use if he was tied to his office, and whatever training Dougal may have required had probably now been completed, but it cannot have escaped the notice of his superiors that the medical problems with which Dougal reported were, more often than not, the injurious knock-on effects of his ardent sexual adventures. He had spent nearly three weeks in the hospital with venereal complaints within the first fourteen months of his service with the Royal Engineers. It was not yet a disciplinary matter, but something had to be done.

Some time in 1867 or 1868, Dougal began a tour of duty at Cork Harbour, in Ireland.[12] If he was still affecting an Irish accent, this may have recommended him for the transfer. It is hard not to see the posting as a tactical manoeuvre on the part of Dougal's commanding officers; removing the man from the various entice-ments of Chatham may have been intended to help him settle down, and to encourage him to develop a more mature under-standing of himself and his responsibilities. One doubts, however, that Cork was entirely free of vice; Dougal, with his sixth sense for dissolution, was accustomed to tracking it down when and where he could. Eventually, he seems to have rebelled against the discipline which the Engineers were attempting to foster within him. It is not clear whether he was back in Chatham, or whether he was in Cork, or perhaps somewhere else, but, on Tuesday 21 July 1868, he failed to report to work at 8.00a.m. At 9.00p.m., having been missing the whole day, he turned up, albeit too late to participate in the regiment's formal tattoo. For this offence, he was fined three days' pay.

Then, on Saturday 8 August, Dougal went missing again. This time, he was gone until the following Thursday. On his return, from who knows where, he found himself stripped of five days' pay and, from 15 August until 21 August, he was imprisoned, the days of his absence being deducted from his service record. It is notable that, after August 1868, Dougal never again went to the military prison. The next few years were not without some excitement – the brothel and the low-grade public house could not be taken out of the man, even if the man could be taken out of the brothel and the low-grade public house – but Dougal seems generally to have known better than to court visits to the so-called glasshouse in the future.

Re-posted again, he arrived in Chester on 23 September 1868, the disciplinary infractions of the summer still not far behind him. There was ongoing Ordnance Survey work in North Wales with which Dougal was now to assist; he would be billeted with civilians when his work took him into the dark Welsh mountains, far from base. This again seems to have been intended to impose a sense of routine on Dougal's erratic lifestyle: his breaches of the disciplinary code had revealed that his resistance to the army's strict expectations remained firm; his quest for erotic transporta-tion remained undimmed. In Wales, his access to the raw materials of his private endeavours would probably be more limited. He may also have been expected to 'improve' as a consequence of the stunning and unspoiled scenery, which, it might have been supposed, could not fail to leave its impression on the depraved canvas of Dougal's soul.

This was really as innocent a hope as it sounds, but there were, at least initially, superficially positive indications of moral improvement. On Monday 8 March 1869, Dougal, the imperiously independent hedonist, married Lovenia Martha Griffith at Northop Church, near Mold in Flintshire. He was twenty-two; she was twenty. The marriage was announced in the *Liverpool Mercury* on 12 March, a public sign of the sudden and wholly unexpected leap into public respectability which Dougal was taking.[13] It is probable that Dougal's father-in-law, a stationer, made the arrangements for the announcement to be published, and met any costs involved. For Dougal, a man who was so much at the mercy of his urges, this was all very out of character, and perhaps, as Lewis suggests, a 'major error of judgement'.[14] The real cause of Dougal's sudden marriage is not known – it is possible that Lovenia Martha Griffith had become pregnant, forcing Dougal's hand; although, if she did, she would seem to have later miscarried.

For Dougal's part, there certainly seems to have been something distinctly involuntary in this arrangement. Domestic tranquillity and intolerable tedium were linked ideas in his mind. His wife – who seems to have been known by her middle name, Martha – was an encumbrance, and the situation, far from being one of emotional neatness and fulfilment, looked untidy. Martha was unrecognised by Dougal's employer: having failed to seek his superiors' permission to marry, Dougal 'only obtained military recognition as a married man on 12 May 1877', although Martha clearly lived with him at certain barracks in the meantime.[15] Of course, Dougal was in denial – Martha was, no doubt, somewhere out of the way when, stupidly, he again absconded from duty at Abergele on 12 February 1870, only returning on St Valentine's Day. The episode cost him three days' pay; he probably spent the missing time with a girl. Despite his marriage, he remained steadfastly devoted to his intemperate habits.

None of this made itself obvious to Dougal's family in London, who continued to believe that his youthful hedonism had subsided. Dougal, luxuriating in this delayed parental approval, lost little time in sending Martha down to London, and to his parents' then-home, Livingstone House, on Livingstone Road, in Battersea. In April 1871, at the time of the national census, she was listed there, with Dougal's parents, his three brothers and his sister. By now, she was twenty-one; she was also pregnant. To the onlooker, it all betokened Dougal's new-found maturity; for Dougal, it was to his advantage to keep Martha at a safe distance. She gave birth at Livingstone House on 3 June 1871. The baby was named Charles Herbert Dougal. As before, the *Liverpool Mercury* announced the happy event.[16] At the time, Dougal was probably still in Wales.

In late 1872, another child followed; this was Lovenia, named after her mother. She was probably conceived around the time Dougal received his first increment on his military salary, 1*d*, for good conduct.[17] Since his last flit without leave, in early 1870, he had enjoyed a period of settled professional behaviour which had, at last, recommended him to his superiors. He may — it seems doubtful — have developed somewhat more moderate habits; much more likely, he had simply become more cautious about hiding his misdemeanours, probably in order to sustain the useful support of his wife's family. On 1 March 1873 — St David's Day, and the day before the seventh anniversary of his enlistment at Westminster — he was, at last, promoted to the rank of Second Corporal.

Before the year was out, Dougal was transferred to the Engineers' barracks at the Tower of London. Even he may have seen the irony in this. Once the state's greatest prison, the Tower cut in where the eastern boundary of the City of London met the Thames. Whitechapel was a short walk away through Goodman's Fields, or up Leman Street. It was as if the ghosts of his early years were returning to him, or, more accurately, he to them. He moved with Martha, Charles and Lovenia into rooms for married soldiers in Martin Tower, at the north-eastern corner of the inner wall.

Then, on 24 December 1873, little Lovenia died, aged fourteen months. An inquest was conducted on Christmas Day, and the death was attributed to convulsions linked to teething. The effect on the family is difficult to apprehend. Dougal was in the midst of an extended period of relatively good conduct — would the loss affect him, tip the subtle balance? Martha was seven months pregnant. The birth of George Marmaduke Dougal on 22 February 1874 must have been framed darkly with her sadness.

Professional good tidings – Dougal received another promotion, to the rank of Sergeant and Third Class Military Staff Clerk, on 26 January 1874, and another pay increment, authorised on 14 February 1874 – conflicted with the family's loss. Martha may have prevailed on Dougal to seek a transfer away from the awful Tower, with its secrets and its spectres – considering that Lovenia had died at Christmas, the whole affair was tinged with an undeniably Dickensian sense of pathos, unbearable and suffocating. By May, Dougal was in Belfast.[18]

✦

Dougal's most recent promotion had seen him move away from surveying and into administration. As a clerk, he became an operative within the biggest bureaucracy in the world. The work may sometimes have been intellectually unchallenging, but he may already have been tiring of a lifestyle which had seen him dragged from one grim place to another. While this was typical for a surveyor, as a clerk Dougal could hope for a more prolonged placement in one locale.

This would not be Belfast, although he appears to have been there for three years. Initially, he served as Senior Military Engineer Clerk under Major-General G.S. Tilly, the Commanding Royal Engineer of the Belfast District. Writing later from his retirement in Dulwich, Tilly recalled Dougal's 'diligence and intelligence' which 'gave me full satisfaction'. Tilly left Belfast in October 1876, and Richard H. Stotherd replaced him. He, too, remembered Dougal as 'very steady, hardworking and attentive to his duties'. All this is entirely possible; Dougal's ability to complete his work never seems to have caused complaint. Stotherd also remembered that Dougal worked under him until May 1878, however, and here he was mistaken. The opportunity to settle somewhere had arisen, and, in May 1877, Dougal had taken it. He was to be billeted to Halifax, Nova Scotia, across the Atlantic in Canada.

Perhaps, after three years in Belfast, it was time for Dougal to move on, although if he had burned his bridges, or otherwise got into trouble, we do not know of it. It is difficult to know, too, why Dougal decided to look to North America for a sense of permanence, particularly as his relationship with his parents and, by extension, his siblings, had turned in his favour. There is nothing to show that he was *persona non grata* in England. However, on Monday 14 May 1877, two days after gaining belated military recognition for his marriage, he, Martha, and George sailed for the New World – Charles, Dougal's eldest son, probably stayed behind in the custody of his grandparents.[19]

The Royal Engineers were, in truth, coming towards the end of their engagement in Nova Scotia. Halifax had been established as a military garrison in the eighteenth century, but the value of a standing military force in the North-West Atlantic had diminished over the course of the nineteenth century, with the focus of British interests shifting towards Africa and India. In the meantime, the retinue of Engineers still in Nova Scotia were given the task of photographing the defence complexes of which they were in charge. A remarkable series of pictures resulted, depicting the area in all its natural beauty.[20]

It is difficult to see Dougal failing to take an interest in the photographic process. In his thirties, he became increasingly fascinated by the rapid scientific progress which was taking place around him. Electricity, which was then becoming subject to increasing human control as a power source, became a particular point of curiosity, and Dougal developed a practical knowledge of it. In 1877, he may have had almost no experience of operating the telegraph; by 1882, he was in charge of the Telegraph Office (Military) at the Royal Engineer Office in Nova Scotia, and was, according to the eventual head of the Royal Engineers' Telegraph Service in the Boer War, A.E. Wrottesley, an 'expert Telegraph manipulator ... thoroughly acquainted with the connections of the Telegraph Instruments in use at the Station (Morse Recorders, Polarized Relays and Sounders, Field Pattern, etc.)'.[21] Remarkably, he undertook his telegraphic duties in addition to his administrative duties, showing the reserves of energy which dwelt within the man, and the great feats he could achieve when he could be motivated to deploy them. He is also believed to have owned a yacht, developing an interest in sailing in the clear Atlantic waters.[22]

On 5 July 1877, not long after arriving in Nova Scotia, Dougal had been re-engaged with the Royal Engineers. The twelve years for which he had originally enlisted were nearly elapsed; now, he agreed to give a total of twenty-one years' service, due to end in March 1887.[23] He gained an additional penny on his pay for good conduct on 13 March 1878, and on 1 October 1880 was promoted again, becoming a Quartermaster-Sergeant and Second Class Military Staff Clerk. Professionally, Dougal had had a decade of practically uninterrupted, if somehow modest, success – and there had been no trips to the glasshouse, no awkward scandals, and apparently no venereal disease. Again, his commanding officers glowed with satisfaction – Wrottesley wrote that he considered Dougal 'thoroughly trustworthy'; Charles C. Carter, writing later to Dougal from India, praised 'your character and the manner in which you did your work'.[24]

The family grew again. Emily Maria Cleopatra Dougal was born in 1878, and Albert Edward Dougal followed, on 9 November 1880, though there may have been losses too – children named Oscar Lewis Dougal, Ada Beatrice Dougal, Beatrice Dougal, Samuel Dredge Dougal (named after his grandfather) and, perhaps, James Dougal all appear to have died at terribly young ages. Even these misfortunes did not seem to affect Dougal's professional equilibrium, however. In July 1881, Dougal was made Quartermaster-Sergeant and Engineering Clerk, probably in recognition of his work with the telegraph.[25] On 14 February 1884, he gained a fourth increment of a penny on his pay, reflecting his good conduct. He was now thirty-seven, within sight of the end of his military career and, as far as anybody could tell, enjoying personal and professional contentment.

✺

Suddenly, everything started to unravel. As a clerk in a fixed post, even one working amid Nova Scotia's vast panoramas, Dougal found himself forced uncomfortably closer to Martha, and the pressure began to tell – his yachting excursions came, now, with dreams of escape. He seemed to have become dissatisfied by the stability and contentment which he may have enjoyed in the 1870s. He had retained his reputation as a sexual predator: one Canadian newspaper, some time after the event, recalled that he was 'one of the finest looking men in uniform ever seen in Halifax' and a 'great favourite with females'.[26] The tactics he had developed in his days at Chatham – the dignity of the uniform, the melody of the Irish lilt – may still have been effective weapons in his compulsive pursuit of attractive but naïve women. He is widely believed to have made a crutch of drinking, and there are suggestions, made later, that Dougal had begun beating Martha. Jesse describes Martha as having led 'a very unhappy life' in Nova Scotia; she implies that Dougal would 'ill-treat' her.[27] Dougal, for his part, later claimed that Martha was 'ailing'; she had been ill, he said, since the mid-1870s.[28] In his account, this would have been the reason for her unhappiness.

There developed an almost frantic edge to Dougal's activity. His extra duties at the Telegraph Office took him in one direction; his intellectual curiosity and creativity took him in another. On Saturday 23 February 1884, Dougal and Edward Bolman, a Nova Scotian of his acquaintance, signed an indenture relating to their new invention, 'to be known as the "Dougal-Bolman Combination Automatic Break and Coupler"'.[29] Grandly, they planned to patent the device 'in the different countries which they mutually agree upon'. Financial provisions were made in case either signatory sold any part of their holdings. Dougal retained the document for years to come, but it was later said that he exploited their partnership to defraud Bolman of a substantial amount of money.

The invention was not, apparently, a success, but the episode illustrated Dougal's ready ability to survive the tides of rapidly changing technology. It seems likely that he played a role in the adaptations to the fortifications at Nova Scotia which occurred in and around 1884 – Piers, the historian of the fort at Halifax, who was writing in the 1940s, reflected that these changes had become necessary because electricity had begun to 'take a prominent part in warfare'.[30] Electricity remained Dougal's amateur specialism. Searchlights, a response to the introduction of underwater craft, may have been the area of Dougal's main involvement: years later, he would have a hand in implementing electric light systems back in England.

By the summer of 1885, Dougal's marital situation must have become untenably bad: drinking and womanising had long been the makeweights in his life. Then, on Saturday 27 June 1885, Martha died. The death was sudden, unexpected – unless she really had, as Dougal later reported, been ill for years. Unquestionably, it was rapid – Jesse says that Martha, 'after suffering great pain', died on the same day that her symptoms first appeared.[31] Some accounts concertina the duration of Martha's illness into a twelve-hour period, or even less.[32] After her demise, things went no more slowly – one version of events suggests that Martha was buried in Fort Massey cemetery 'two days later'; most suggest that interment occurred 'within twenty-four hours'.[33] Dougal, writing much later, reacted angrily to these 'insinuations'.[34] Martha was '*not* interred the next day after decease but ... kept the usual time, about four or five days,' he objected. He attributed her death to tuberculosis.

But what *had* happened to Martha? We have only Dougal's word for her chronic illness. Most observers, all of whom were writing many years later, concluded that she had been murdered. The suddenness of her death argues against a long-standing condition such as tuberculosis; but we are without any picture of Martha's health in the months and years before. Perhaps she had declined gradually, and then died rather suddenly. There is a suggestion that her final symptoms included 'pains', and the condition certainly seemed to be related to something Martha had eaten.[35] This pointed to food poisoning, or, more suspiciously, the adulteration of a meal – perhaps a dose of arsenic, the drug of choice for so many Victorian poisoners, would have done it. Martha's prompt burial (if it *was* prompt, which Dougal denied) concealed the evidence of any crime. Against these suspicions, Dougal protested that Martha had been 'attended by the Regimental Doctor', who should, if he had any doubts about the cause of death, have referred the case for further investigation.

One chronicler goes further, elucidating a financial motive for the murder. He observes that Martha did not leave a will – in the circumstances, her estate 'would have passed on to Dougal'.[36] But there is no indication that Martha had anything Dougal wanted: more to the point, it was not clear that there was anything Martha had *now* that she had not had, say, two or three years before, or whenever the relationship had begun to sour. It was true that Martha's mother, Alicia, had died in 1883 – her father, Thomas, had died in the first part of 1874, when Martha was still mourning the Christmas-time death of her daughter, Lovenia – but there is no sign of any inheritance: the Griffiths' finances were reasonably situated, but they were not wealthy. Dougal's conduct in the aftermath of Martha's death was clearly plausible enough to permit him to sidle away from any contemporary public suspicion. He announced his wife's death in ironically parsimonious terms in the *Halifax Morning Herald*: 'Died Lovenia Martha, the wife of Quartermaster Sergeant Samuel Herbert Dougal, Royal Engineers, aged 37 years'.[37]

ഇരുന്നു

In fact, Dougal's experiences over the next four months or so taught him that he could be almost careless, and still avoid detection. Approximating broken-heartedness, he applied for and was permitted 'a short furlough in England', and left Nova Scotia on an eastbound ship on 16 July 1885.[38] By 4 August, he was back, and he had another woman with him.[39]

His overseas trip gave Dougal the opportunity to distribute his children to well-meaning relatives, and perhaps to boarding schools or even children's homes, back in England.[40] He was constitutionally isolated from their feelings about their mother's death, and, in their absence, the effect upon them of his rapid second marriage – to Mary Herberta Boyd, aged twenty-eight – is difficult to appreciate. It was not unknown, and not wrong, for widowers to remarry, but it was flying in the face of convention to do so with such brash celerity. It was as if Dougal was challenging the world to see him, to judge him, and still the world would not see, and would not judge. Ever-selfish, with a nuanced view of the world which shunned balance and perspective in favour of self-gratification and bravado, Dougal began to behave as if the feelings of invulnerability which had characterised the carnival of his young adulthood had fully returned. He appeared to have resolved, whether consciously or unconsciously, to approach forty with the wilful energy of his youth.

In fact, in spite of Dougal's supposed furlough in England, Mary Herberta Boyd was Irish. She comes across well in the literature: her father had apparently been an army surgeon; Edgar Wallace wrote that she was 'tall, young and good-looking'; and, as one newspaper put it, she 'was said to have a lot of money'.[41] She also had a daughter who, like Dougal's daughter, was about seven years old and named Emily. Mary had, very likely, been widowed, and this may explain the source of her rumoured wealth. Obviously, however, Dougal could sense her aching vulnerability – the fact that he managed to persuade her to emigrate to Nova Scotia within, apparently, just a few days of meeting her probably shows that she, like many of Dougal's past conquests, had idealised him, imagining him to have become instantaneously, hopelessly besotted with her, as she had become with him. This was exactly the sort of misapprehension which Dougal, now in the midst of deepening moral extinction, loved to nurture. On Friday 14 August 1885, less than two weeks after he had stepped back onto the Nova Scotian shore with Mary, and less than seven weeks since Martha had succumbed to whatever had she had succumbed to, Dougal and Mary married, again without the leave of his superiors, 'at the home of the curate of St Paul's Anglican Church'.[42]

From the start, Mary, like Martha, and like innumerable and nameless others, was a victim of Dougal's internal *éminence grise*, the grasping hidden self which contrasted so starkly with his charming exterior. Martha, after so many years of marriage, may have begun to see it for what it was, and it is probable that his infidelities were the cause of many of their arguments. She could not tear herself away from him – where would she go, in Nova Scotia? – but she may at least have fought back for a time. One suspects, though, that Mary never saw the hypocrisy in Dougal. When she arrived in Nova Scotia in August, she was in love, and, purportedly, in 'excellent health'.[43] By the end of the first week in October, she too was dead.

This time the decline had, perhaps, been a little more drawn-out. The *Daily Telegraph*, writing later, supposed that 'fourteen days' had elapsed between the onset of Mary's symptoms and her death; but most other sources suppose that the speed of the demise rivalled that of Martha's.[44] There was an alarming sense of *déjà vu*: Mary's illness manifested itself in vomiting and coughing fits; Dougal, somewhat ambiguously, attributed the death to Mary's having 'eaten poisonous oysters'.[45] First-hand, and well after the event, Dougal again objected to rumours which were circulating about his part in the matter. Mary, he gushed in his indignation, 'was in a consumption when I married her, but we hoped the change from Ireland to Canada would be beneficial … [however] it failed to improve her condition'.[46] Apart from this, Dougal insisted that his ministrations for Mary had been of the same unimpeachable standard as had been his ministrations for Martha. Again, the regimental doctor had attended the dying woman; again, burial had not been hurried through, but had happened at the ordinary time, four or five days later.

Naturally, the retrospective sources disagree. One newspaper describes Mary's funeral as taking place on 'the day after she died, and there were two mourners – Dougal and one other'. Like Martha, Mary was laid to rest in Fort Massey cemetery, although their memories were hardly distinguished by lavish expenditure:'they are only marked by two slabs bearing official military numbers'.

Still, scarcely an eyelid batted. In Dougal's heroic version of events, he had fallen in love with and rather gallantly married a woman who was, it seems, at death's door. He had taken her across the sea to a place of crystal waters and huge, clear skies, for the benefit, he hoped, of her precarious health; but there she had sadly faded, leaving him to look after her child, which he did, equally gallantly. In all other versions, Mary's wealth is emphasised, the nature of her fatal illness questioned – 'a violent stomach upset, indicating an irritant of some sort' is a typical description – and the strange echoes of Martha's death amplified.[47] It was only hindsight which made made the latter comparison available, or even tempting; but no contemporary suspicions about the causes of Dougal's wives' misfortunes seemed sufficient to prevent him from drifting untarnished into the affections of his next inamorata – Bessie Stedman, the daughter of a local farmer. Indeed, Bessie may have been hovering on the edges of the drama for a little while: she is described in Edgar Wallace's account as having been 'a friend of both the Mrs Dougals'.[48] There is a good chance that, if the scene at Mary's funeral was accurately depicted, the 'one other' mourner, beside Dougal at the grave, was Bessie.

She was the familiar type – 'good-looking', 'young' – these were both epithets which had also been applied to Mary.[49] Bessie was about twenty-two, and deeply susceptible to Dougal's flattering attentions.[50] It would have been easy for him to play on her well-intended sympathy: he had, after all, lost two wives, and he was accustomed to mimicking the effects of grief, even if this emotion, like remorse, remained outside his affect. She was probably helpful with Mary's Emily, who was Dougal's only surviving dependant in Canada, and then only by virtue of his marriage to a now-deceased woman. In retrospect, it seems surprising that Dougal did not immediately attempt to send Emily back to Ireland, since she would inevitably be a drain on whatever profit he had made from her mother's death. The psychological effects of her traumatic experiences – a sudden emigration and the loss of her mother in not much more than a couple of months – were quite uninteresting to him; in spite of Bessie's help, it is entirely possible that they remained with Emily for the rest of her life.

⁂

Just as he turned forty, in May 1886, Dougal made ready to be sent back to England. After nearly nine years in Nova Scotia, he was being posted to Aldershot, in Hampshire, with less than a year of his contracted service remaining.[51] So what of Bessie? Would he take her, too?

Of course he would: she was, at this stage, unquestioningly loyal, probably prepared to overlook his dalliances, and inclined to attribute some of his mood swings to the shock of his bereavements. On the other hand, unless they were married, her passage to England would not be complimentary of the military. Dougal, in his typically bluff manner, but saving pennies where he could, decided that a formal ceremony would be unnecessary; he 'represented' Bessie as his wife, tempting those around him to object.[52] Unusually, someone did – the commanding officer, who was required to sign for the free pass, demurred. Dougal, unperturbed, is supposed to have forged a marriage certificate.[53] The commanding officer demurred again. Fed up, Dougal paid for Bessie's ticket out of his own pocket.[54]

And so Dougal's career in the Royal Engineers wound down towards its conclusion. At Aldershot (and without the burden of his stepdaughter Emily, who had been returned to her maternal relatives in Ireland), he continued with his clerical duties, now under the direction of Ferdinand Bedwith Mainguy, an old acquaintance from Nova Scotia who had also been posted back to England.[55] Responsibly, Dougal began writing to former colleagues, seeking their testimonials, aware that he would be required to get a civilian job when he left the military. In his private life, however, the constant pressure of maintaining the unswerving rectitude of his public image was, again, beginning to tell, and his 'marriage' to Bessie had already begun to suffer. He had started to mistreat her – again, physical measures are suspected – and she, in her naïveté, may still have been expecting the relationship, regardless of its violence, to attain permanence.[56] Dougal had no intention of marrying her, but he may very well have hinted that he would, purely to keep her interested – Bessie herself later spoke of his 'false representations'.[57] When she asked him about the marriage for which she still craved, he hit out. At least once, according to the received wisdom, he threatened to kill her.[58]

At this point, the remoteness of her home, and the real danger posed by her not-quite-husband, may have come into sudden and disconcerting focus. Bessie realised that her hoped-for marriage would never materialise, and she fled, staying for a while with an English relative before leaving for the safety of Canada. When she asked Dougal what to say to explain her position to her family in Nova Scotia, he is understood to have callously suggested that she don the black trappings of widowhood, and explain that he had died.[59] Lacking the limiting mechanism of a functioning conscience, he found the 'false representations' he made to the world to be quite ordinary, quotidian, the equal of everyone else's pretences. Mourning was simply the easiest of these to simulate, since whatever one needed to imitate authenticity – yards of crepe would do it – could be acquired from a nearby shop. Hindsight granted Bessie a sense of detached perspective on her ordeal:'He was a monster,' she said,'and I was one of his victims'.[60]

Dougal was probably unattached, then, when he finally left the army on 22 March 1887. Taking his imprisonment in 1868 into account, he had served for twenty-one years and twelve days. On 6 March 1887, he had gained a fifth and final penny on his pay for good conduct; this was, generously, meant to suggest Dougal's reliable professional qualities in time to influence his pension award.[61] He also received a gratuity of £5 and his Long Service and Good Conduct medal, silver on a dark crimson ribbon, with his name and military number etched into the rim. It was an award about which he would profess enormous pride throughout his life – in truth, though, he later exploited it for the automatic sense of authority and rectitude it suggested; and, anyway, it can have been only a partial reflection of his decadent military years.

His pension was settled at 2s 9d per day – not enough to live on, but useful all the same.[62] The pension board recorded that Dougal was forty at the end of his period of engagement. He was 5 feet 11 inches tall, 2½ inches taller than he had been when he joined the Engineers in 1866. His hair was still brown, his eyes grey, his complexion still fresh. Overall, his character was, as far as the Royal Engineers were concerned, 'very good'; he had gained a second class Certificate of Education, although, in view of the apparently effortless facility with which he acquired new skills (provided his interest could be attracted and maintained), one suspects that this may have represented an underachievement.[63] Completing the formalities of his discharge, Dougal declared himself to be, of all things, a blacksmith by trade: since he had joined the military as a civil engineer, and had latterly been a clerk, with interests in mechanical and electrical engineering, this was peculiar.[64]

He informed the military that he intended to take up residence at 21 Birley Street in Battersea, South London, and left Aldershot, turning his back on a lifestyle he had known since 1866. The address he had given was probably that of his younger brother, Frederick Henry Dougal, known as Harry, who was a next-of-kin agent, reuniting people with unclaimed inheritances. This may have been intriguing to Dougal, who was more practised in the opposite art of separating people from their money.

❧

The restless Dougal did not stay with Harry for long. He took a succession of opportunistic jobs as he attempted to reintroduce himself to civilian life – the first, with Messrs Defries and Son of Houndsditch, restored him to the very periphery of his pre-military stamping ground of the East End. But life as a travelling salesman of 'plate, cutlery, glass, and china' may have soured quickly. Dougal had alighted upon a new affection: this time, it was one Marian Paine, *née* Rogers, a young widow from Maidstone, who found herself caught in his web. Marian already had children of her own – Alfred and Gertrude, roughly nine and seven respectively – but Dougal appears to have made her pregnant again fairly quickly, as he was wont to do, while uttering his usual empty promises of marriage.[65] In 1888, Elsie, the couple's first out-of-wedlock daughter, was born. Responding almost responsibly to his increasing domestic commitments – several of his children by Martha had returned to him since his honourable discharge from the Royal Engineers, and the baby was another mouth to feed – Dougal found new employment on the Isle of Wight.

This new position – storekeeper for the *Mercury*, a training ship moored at Binstead – capitalised on Dougal's experience as a former Quartermaster-Sergeant. In other ways, though, the ethos of a charitably-run enterprise, captained by a penitent (and once controversial) figure by the name of Charles Hoare, seemed inconsistent with Dougal's own values. Hoare and his partner, Beatie Sumner, were moral transgressors whose own lives, post-scandal, symbolised the hope of forgiveness and repair. The *Mercury* itself was a finishing school for the nautically-inclined: in 1888, near the outset of his involvement, Hoare was probably only taking those who were able to pay for their education, but he rapidly steered the ship into increasingly philanthropic waters, taking 'pauper boys' with a view to ensuring that they should never again 'trouble the rates'.[66] Dougal's own interest grew as he discovered that the set-up needed a shot of electricity. Hoare wrote that, in addition to his duties managing the stores, Dougal would supervise the 'Mechanics and other workmen', made himself 'thoroughly conversant with our Electric Light Installation' and played a role 'in connection with its extension', and 'also erected a line of Telephone [*sic*]; and also an Electric Bell Connection, both of which he has maintained in an efficient manner'.[67] This appointment, and the opportunities to work with electricity, brought Dougal as close as he ever seemed to get to vocational fulfilment. When the *Mercury* sailed for the Mediterranean in the autumn of 1888, however, Hoare reduced his land-based workforce, and Dougal was one of those who had to leave. His testimonial reported that he was 'most reliable', and his work 'most satisfactory'. But on Saturday 10 November 1888, Dougal, Marian and the children were back in London, taking up residence at 14d Victoria Buildings, on the Battersea Park Road.

Dougal's next adventure took him to rural Hertfordshire. Almost impulsively, he took the licence on a public house, the Royston Crow, on Baldock Street, in the quaint market town of Ware. While the training ship had enabled him to exploit his technical interests, this new commitment could promise nothing similar. Dougal examined his finances – the cost of the goodwill, furniture and fittings of the Royston Crow came to £92 16s 3d, a not-insubstantial sum, and his pay at Binstead had been only £2 a week. There were some savings, but, in order to find the purchase-money, he was obliged to raise £17 on a £500 life insurance policy he had held with the Royal Insurance Office since September 1881. This brought the equity he had stripped from this policy to a total of £42 – he had nibbled away other small amounts over the years – although he had consistently paid his annual premium of £13 13s 9d. The bank draft was sent to him at Victoria Buildings in a letter dated Saturday 19 January 1889.[68] Dougal returned the receipt to the insurance office and, by the following Friday, he was ready to make his payment.

The Royston Crow was an old oak and lath building positioned in the middle of a row of timber-framed houses and artisans' shops on the west side of the street. Above the twin bars on the ground floor stood two first-floor bedrooms, and two more bedrooms were located in the attic above those; below the bars, accessed via a hatch, was a basement; Dougal moved his family into the living quarters and, situating himself behind the bar, started work. Things appear to have gone fairly smoothly for the first couple of months, but turnover may not have been quite what it ought to have been.

Personal satisfaction, however, was becoming harder to come by, and Dougal was becoming unsettled. It is hard to know whether there were any parts of the position he had taken – at his own cost – which really appealed to him. He had the opportunity to talk to his customers, something which must have served him well enough with Defries, but that had been a sales role, and patter and persuasion, which Dougal had in spades, clearly counted. In Ware, he was stuck behind the bar, working in the building in which his wife and family lived, and he had none of the same opportunities to exploit casual and passing acquaintances to the satisfaction of his immoral inner appetites. Even as he approached his forty-second birthday, in May 1889, his compulsive preoccupations with sex and money would not go gently into the good night, and the tedium of his situation quickly began to bite.

What he needed was a way of reopening those old points of contact – a way out of the daily drudgery of life at the Royston Crow, which had so rapidly become intolerable, and a means of meeting the increasingly urgent demands of his unfulfilled, overarching drives. In typical fashion, he thought of a plan. Examined in retrospect and from a distance, it seems ludicrous, and slightly frightening. In 1889, it could just have worked.

⤜⋆⋆⤛

That spring, a series of unfortunate episodes had brought one James Berry to the notice of Sir Edmund Lechmere. Sir Edmund sat in the House of Commons, the Member for Bewdley in Worcestershire; Berry had since 1884 been the principal public executioner – a position which demanded impeccable integrity.

By 1889, a hectic schedule and the feverish political milieu had begun to test Berry's resolve. To relax – and perhaps to make a little money – after executions, he had once or twice allowed himself to be drawn into so-called levees and smoking concerts, held in public houses, at which the horrors of his trade were probably fairly vaguely depicted, the audience's imaginations being left to dress in costumes of fantastic gore the unembellished narrative frameworks Berry constructed. These excursions into public entertainment were not the sort of thing expected of the executioner (at least by those with responsibilities towards the moral health of the nation), and Lechmere, deciding to raise the matter in Parliament, fastened onto the somewhat archaic system by which the executioner was retained. At the time, despite the national scope of the post, it nominally fell to the Sheriffs of London and Middlesex to pay the hangman's stipend; most local Sheriffs, whose task it was to see executions carried out in regional prisons, simply hired the London and Middlesex executioner when they needed him. On 11 April 1889, Lechmere rose in the House of Commons to ask whether it was not time to bring Berry under the direct control of the Home Office. This, he implied, would facilitate closer monitoring of the executioner's behaviour, and bring an end to the unseemly levees.[69]

There were other controversies, too. The voice of abolitionism was growing louder, and accidents at executions, when they occurred, added to the clamour. The long drop, a recent innovation, was an improvement on the short drop, which left its victims conscious and choking to death, but too long a drop risked decapitation. In 1885, Robert Goodale had had his head torn off at Norwich, and the howls of public protest deafened.

For the executioner, though, accidents were not only humiliating and stigmatising but, at worst, deeply shameful, and a challenge to his sense of self. Berry, after the Goodale affair, resolved to resign, and was stricken on the train home; he had, indeed, collapsed on viewing the headless body in the pit.[70] As it happened, he did not resign (not, at least, on this occasion), but his susceptibility to emotionally vigorous responses to his work caught up with him in the end. In his later years, he began to drink; when he threw that habit in, he tried almost at once to commit suicide. He failed, but other executioners would succeed in similar attempts.

The Home Secretary, Henry Matthews, in answer to Lechmere's enquiry, favoured the existing hiring system, which had the advantage of keeping central government out of the arrangements by which its citizens were executed, but he was prepared, as he put it, 'to give a partial undertaking'.[71] Since Berry was for hire, there was a theoretical market for execution-ers – in practice, however, only Yorkshire ever used a different man. Matthews agreed to look into the possibility of identifying another man, one whom the Home Office could recommend to local Sheriffs, much as Berry was recommended by the Sheriffs of London and Middlesex. This way, the Sheriffs around the coun-try could choose whom they wished to hire to perform their executions. Since this measure had the eventual aim of breaking Berry's virtual monopoly, Lechmere withdrew his motion before the House was required to vote upon it. Matthews' undertaking was indeed partial, however – he confessed that he did not know whether it would even be possible for the Home Office to iden-tify a 'fit and well-conducted' person who could compete for Berry's work.

Back at the Royston Crow, Dougal must have spent the weekend poring over the newspaper reports of the parliamen-tary debate. The gears of government may have ground slowly, but Dougal, an engineer at heart, examined them with a critical eye. How could the Home Office identify a suitable execu-tioner if men of quality, such as he, shied demurely away from writing in? This was the usual way to apply to be an execu-tioner, although, like Berry, one would normally write to the Sheriffs of London and Middlesex. Taking up pen and paper, Dougal wrote directly to the Home Office. He would be their nominated executioner.

The advantages were plentiful. Dougal yearned for the thrill-ing possibilities that travel brought: as an executioner, presuming the Sheriffs hired him, he would visit every corner of the British Isles. If in his reading he had sensed anything about the demands which the Home Office would make with regard to his behaviour, he ignored them – such complications just addled the thought process. He envisaged a thrilling life of express train journeys taken from city to distant and unfamiliar city, and he foresaw the admiration of the crowds which thronged the platform as his carriage drew to a halt; moreover, he pictured relief from the monotony of serving behind the bar in the Royston Crow, and a chance to escape Marian and the children. No executioner was full-time – indeed, many were, perhaps not quite by chance, publicans in their private existences – but the possibility of a Home Office retainer and fees and expenses every time he performed a hanging, all in addition to whatever he could make at the Royston Crow, chimed perfectly with his unsubtle, grasping love of money.

And that was not all. In 1888 or 1889, James Berry 'attended a series of experiments conducted in Manchester ... to see if electrocution represented an improvement on hanging'.[72] For the purposes of the experiments, a dog and a calf stood in for the condemned; the results were apparently 'not impressive', and Berry declined to throw his weight behind the use of electricity as a means of execution. But, looked at another way, this was all a matter of engineering. Dougal, with his experience in the field, might have reasoned that electricity was likely to be a less temperamental method of executing a prisoner than the traditional rope. In America, the experiments with dogs and calves had long since ceased – by the following summer, it had, for the first time, used the electric chair on a human being, William Kemmler. In Britain, the reports of the innovative execution carried a tone of detached curiosity – *The Times* reported that the electrocution 'does not seem to have been attended by such a measure of success as will be likely to encourage a repetition of the experiment'.[73] But, in view of the occasional frailties of the hanging system, it was not implausible that British execution methods might, sooner or later, change. If the Home Office wanted someone to lead the nation towards the electric chair, so to speak, then Dougal was obviously that man.

On Monday 15 April 1889, Dougal sent his first application to the Home Office. Just over a month later, on 17 May, he wrote again. By post, on 6 June, he received a reply:

H.M. Prison Millbank

6th June [1889]

Mr S.H. Dougal may call [at] H.M. Prison, Millbank London S.W. at 11-30 o'clock on Saturday next, the 8th instant, with reference to his applications to the Home Office of the 15th April and 17th May 1889.

No expenses will be allowed on complying with this intimation.

[Signed] C. Kirkpatrick
Governor

Mr S.H. Dougal
Baldock Street
Ware
Herts[74]

Dougal kept the appointment, and, as the summer of 1889 reached its dry height, his name was one of those being considered for the macabre duties of the chief executioner.

In an odd way, Dougal's moral bankruptcy may have served him well if he had been taken on as hangman. In less than forty-two years, his deficiencies had driven him through the lairs of London, Chatham, and the Empire, through one casual sexual liaison after another, through deception after deception, through the non-chalant murders – perhaps – of his first two wives, through the spastic violence of his relationships with Bessie and Marian and, before them, Martha, and into a trade for which he did not care, in a town whose sleepiness he had begun to abhor: they could also have insulated him from the harm sustained by the more ordinary souls of other executioners. But it seems redundant to speculate about these matters. At its heart, Dougal's application to the Home Office articulated his own irreducible core of inhumanity – the position of public executioner linked, for him, sex and money, to both of which Dougal was irredeemably addicted; and, of course, death, upon whose visage Dougal would calmly look, ever unaffected, ever remorseless. In the Isle of Wight, he had apparently acquired an ornamental human skull, a curious memento of his happiest time since leaving the army, and a graceless metaphor for its owner's own inverted perspectives on truth and secrecy, the internal and the external. Somewhere within the Royston Crow, the skull grinned fixedly at him, gazing at its enigmatic owner with its extinct eyes, while Dougal planned to make the deaths of others a professional reality.

CHAPTER TWO

ON FRIDAY 5 July 1889, half an hour before midnight, the Royston Crow burst into flames.[75] Marian and the children were upstairs, having retired for the night, but Dougal, who had closed the pub for the evening, was alone in the basement. Suddenly, fire was all around him, pushing up the hatch to the kitchen, and flickering its way into the bar, where some hanging clothes were set alight.[76] Below, in the flame-lit basement, Dougal was trying to put out the fire – he 'was very seriously burned about the arms, hands and face' in the attempt, but the blaze was becoming overwhelming. Abandoning the basement, Dougal raced up the stairs to alert his family to the danger.[77]

Smoke filled the building, clogging the stairwell, and Dougal and Marian realised that there was no way down the stairs, no way out through the main door to the street. Shouting from an upstairs window, they attracted the attention of a policeman: he fetched a ladder, and brought the family out and down the ladder to safety.

In the meantime, smoke was continuing to pour out of the basement as the fire took a grip. The town's fire brigade – founded weeks earlier – had been sent for, but they had not yet arrived, and, unused to and lacking confidence in Ware's new arrangements, those living on the buildings huddled on either side of the Royston Crow were not content to wait any longer for them. Frederick Pugh, a courageous fishmonger living two doors to the north of the burning building, took matters into his own hands, and 'went down into the cellar, where the fire originated, and dashed pail after pail into the suffocating smoke'.[78] By the time the fire engine was brought to the scene, the fire had been put out.[79]

Dougal confessed his carelessness. He had been filling a benzoline lamp in the basement, he said, when the vapour had ignited on a gas jet. This seemed plausible enough, but Granville Sharpe, himself a publican at the Saracen's Head and the newly appointed Captain of Ware's volunteer fire brigade, seemed to doubt the veracity of the explanation. The lamp was never found, he pointed out; and, when he visited the Royston Crow the day after the fire to check on its landlord's welfare, there was almost no stock on the entire premises. This seemed suspicious.

Ignorant of Sharpe's misgivings, Dougal applied for the insurance money to cover the cost of the damage to the pub: since the end of May, he had held a policy with the Royal Insurance Company: for an annual premium of 8s 9d, he had insured the household goods, linen and apparel in the Royston Crow for £150, and the stock in trade and utensils for £200. On 21 June, he took out a second policy, this one in the Phoenix Fire Office; now, he valued the stock and household goods equally, each at £150.[80] The timing was fortunate, to say the least – within weeks of taking out his policies, the fire against which Dougal had covered himself had, indeed, taken place. Dougal estimated the cost of the fire to be £4 13s 3d. This trifling sum was paid without much fuss.

Then, on the evening of Friday 3 August 1889, the whole thing seemed to happen again, but on a grander scale. At a quarter to midnight, Elizabeth Riddle, who lived in the adjoining building to the north of the Royston Crow, saw Dougal leave his pub, lock the door, and walk away in the direction of the High Street. At five past midnight on Saturday 4 August, twenty minutes after the landlord had been seen leaving the premises, a policeman saw flames flickering through the bars on the ground floor.

An urgent attempt to rescue the inhabitants was abandoned when a neighbour mentioned that the remainder of Dougal's family had departed for Ramsgate earlier that week; now, the fire brigade arrived to deal with the fire. It seemed to behave in an unexpected way, to 'rush about the room', and rapidly engulfed the entire building, with eruptions of flame occurring in the right-hand attic bedroom, and, while these outbreaks were being dealt with, new eruptions coming from the left-hand bedroom. Gradually, however, the brigade quelled the flames. The hoses were turned off at a quarter past two, and the charred remains of the Royston Crow – which was very badly burned – were boarded up. And Dougal remained away until the morning of Monday 5 August, having apparently been with his family by the seaside; and, when he returned, he stood in Baldock Street, and looked up at the wreck of his pub.

This time, charges followed. Dougal again applied for an insurance payout, but the physical appearance of the burned building invited suspicion. Charles Jackson, a fire assessor, toured round it, finding unusual heaps of combustible materials: one, in the left-hand attic bedroom, consisted of a layer of old clothes, then the back of a broken chair, then another layer of clothes, then the lid of a box, and then another layer of clothes.[81] Concealed in the centre of the pile was a child's frock – on this, Jackson detected the tell-tale smell of an accelerant: either benzoline or paraffin, Jackson thought. Other items – some rags on the first floor, the collar of a soldier's tunic – gave off the same odour. On the stairs to the attic, a chain of garments slithered like a strange animal, apparently as a means of communicating the fire to all parts. On the floor of the bar, a variegated pattern had formed, with some parts more burned than others. This, Jackson believed, showed where the liquid accelerant had been laid in streams. It also seemed to correlate with the 'rushing' movement of the fire in its early stages.

Arrested drowning his sorrows in the Lion and Wheatsheaf, Dougal was charged with arson and attempting to defraud an insurance company, and, after a series of hearings at the local police court, committed for trial at the Hertfordshire Winter Assizes, to be held in Hertford in December 1889. There was a gentlemanly feel to proceedings at Ware, where Dougal sat languidly on a chair in front of the dock while the charge was being considered by the magistrates. He maintained his agnostic stance throughout – it had all happened in his absence, he said – and reserved his defence, being bailed on the sureties of his father and his brother Harry. Marian stuck by him, and Dougal seemed to wait out the months between the police court hearings and his trial in a state of undisturbed serenity. He may well have gone to Knockholt, in Kent, where his father now lived. The atmosphere of untrammelled calm stood in awkward contrast to the potentially severe punishment which Dougal faced if he was found guilty at the Assizes. The maximum penalty for conviction of arson was imprisonment – for life.

When the trial did occur, no reference was made to Dougal's shady personal history: by contrast, Wightman Wood, a journeyman barrister who had been retained for the defence, would emphasise Dougal's reported good character in the Royal Engineers. Besides this, Dougal had no previous conviction, and was hardly likely to admit voluntarily to the rumours which had begun to gather around him. Either way, one's previous record remained, even in 1889, largely insusceptible to subsequent enquiry: no reliable means of tracing a criminal career had yet been implemented, as Forrest Fulton, one of two barristers acting for the Crown, would later discover to his cost in the affair of Adolph Beck. With Fulton was Richard Muir, whose star was ascending rapidly. Crippen, the Seddons, Steinie Morrison – all would suffer in court as their cases became porous under the glare of Muir's penetrating scrutiny. The judge was Mr Justice Denman, nearly seventy, and with his own most famous case – that of Mary Pearcey – still ahead of him.

On the morning of Friday 6 December 1889, the courtroom was full by half past ten.[82] The case was to last all day, and had obviously attracted some measure of local interest. The prosecution ran through a succession of witnesses, including many who had suffered personally in the second fire at the Royston Crow. Thomas Burgess, a shoemaker living immediately to the south of the pub, estimated that he had thrown 500 pairs of boots into the street when the fire began to threaten his property; his wife's health had suffered in the time since the inferno, apparently as a result of the stress the episode had caused her. But personal inconvenience, and even personal distress, did not prove malicious intent. Three fire experts were called to prove the signs of deliberate fire-setting with which the husk of the Royston Crow teemed. But Wightman Wood chipped away at the prosecution case in his cross-examinations. Charles Jackson, who was quite clear about what he had seen, was put in the invidious position of having to defend himself against a slur – there was no corroborative evidence for it, but Dougal recalled Jackson saying, 'Take my advice and hook it,' pointing backwards over his shoulder with his thumb. Jackson defended himself against the accusation of impropriety, but one wonders whether the damage was done. Wood's subsequent cross-examination of William Penfold, a man whose career had been built on fire, was even more successful, and significantly more orthodox. Penfold claimed decades of experience, but fell to Wood's suggestion that the distinctive patterns of burning found on the ground floor of the Royston Crow may have shown not where the accelerant was, but where sand had been, with those parts which were the more burned being those which were not covered by heaps of sand. Penfold's swift, in-court conversion to the farcical sand theory did much to damage the case of the prosecution.

Other gifts fell into Wood's lap: fourteen to sixteen gallons of paraffin had been spilled by a fireman, addressing the fire from Mrs Riddle's backyard; perhaps this had been the source of the smell, once the fluid had been trodden through the pub in the course of the battle against the flames. In his closing speech, he threw out absurdities – the snake of clothing on the stairs, and the heaps of linen in the rooms, were all the natural by-products of Dougal's wife's temporary absence at Margate. Without her civilising influence, Dougal had immediately reverted to a brutish, primitive way of living, casting off garments where he wished – any man would do the same, said Wood, deadpan. At a little past six o'clock, with these arguments ringing in their ears, and their stomachs rumbling, the jury withdrew to consider their verdict; between half past six and a quarter to seven, they were back, finding Dougal not guilty on both counts.

The case against Dougal faltered, in the end, on the uncertainties which typically plague arson cases: nobody saw Dougal torch the pub; all that was known was that he had left the building twenty minutes before the blaze was discovered. Any accidental spark might have brought the timber structure quickly down and, for a hungry jury, this must have constituted reasonable doubt. In Ware, however, some remained unconvinced of Dougal's innocence, despite the verdict. William Lawrence and Arthur Goodfellow had been Dougal's last customers, arriving at the Royston Crow at 10.45p.m. and 10.50p.m. respectively on the evening of Friday 3 August, and finding its landlord 'unusually quiet', and then, suddenly, voluble, and voluble, in particular, on the subject of fires. Dougal remarked that, since the July incident, he no longer used open fires in the house, or liquid fuel. He had a little gas stove on which he cooked his breakfast, and Goodfellow had allowed him to borrow a piece of tubing to make it work. These prudent precautions naturally contained the risk of any more fires. An hour later, the place was in flames.

Neither Lawrence nor Goodfellow, however, was called to court, which seemed like an omission. On the police's part, their sweep of the Royston Crow in the days after its immolation turned up documentation which seemed to show that Dougal was in mounting debt to his brewery; and, perhaps even better, they found Dougal's personal diary. By the time of the trial, though, these important exhibits had been lost, and the brief to the barristers had been annotated to say that 'no mention of them should be made'. Ware's police force was headed by Reginald Wymer, a man who was, by instinct, a watercolour painter, and not a fierce custodian of the law. The police themselves were unprepared for a case of any significance, being more accustomed to dealing with trivial offences and cases of public drunkenness, all of which could be summarily handled by local magistrates.

Delighted though he may have been by his acquittal, Dougal's brush with the law had come to the attention of the Home Office. On 17 January 1890, a small committee met at Millbank Prison to determine the names of potential hangmen.[83] Seven candidates were interviewed – James Billington, Francis Gardner and Robert Wade were taken on – but an eighth was not called.[84] A note in the file recorded that 'Samuel Herbert Dougal was not invited to attend, as it had been ascertained that he now keeps a public house and has recently been tried and acquitted at the Assizes on a charge of arson'.[85] The discretion of the executioner had to be beyond question, and any brushes with the law were liable to bring the position, and the Home Office, into disrepute; the recruitment process had only been initiated because of concerns over the reliability of the incumbent Berry. This decision marked the end of Dougal's hoped-for career in state executions.

Nor was Dougal permitted to return to the Royston Crow, which had, somehow, been brought back from the dead. His brewery, Phillips of Royston, had been curiously supportive of him throughout the ordeal of the arson case. Now, he wished to have his licence (which, with the pub closed, had reverted to the custody of the brewery in September 1889) transferred back to him, and Phillips cheerfully agreed to the idea. A local petition, featuring twenty signatures, however, spoke of the public alarm the proposal had caused, and Ware's magistrates blocked the return of the licence. Dougal's victory in the courts had, as it turned out, been a costly one: he had avoided prison, but he left Ware without his alcohol licence, and without his roseate vision of becoming an executioner.

⋘⊙⋙

Another period of drifting ensued. There seems to have been a short period in Southend, where he purportedly became a Freemason, but London offered a form of anonymity which the lonely, limited towns of the countryside never could. By early 1891, he was in Stroud Green, in North London, living at Stapleton Hall, a grand, spacious building, parts of which dated back to the early seventeenth century. More recently, it had been refronted, and, in the early 1890s, it presented its distinguished aspect to the south-west, its solemn sash windows neatly situated around its central porch.[86] It was also the local Conservative Club. Dougal, betraying his political sympathies, had contrived to become the club's new steward, and had taken quarters there.

Gladys, Dougal and Marian's second daughter, had been born at Stapleton Hall in February 1891, but her arrival did nothing to hasten her parents' marriage. Dougal continued to sidestep the question, and shuffled his growing collection of offspring like cards, retaining some, and distributing the rest to boarding schools. With the exception of the secret of their unmarried status, they projected an image of unmitigated normality – but it was not to last. The details are missing, but Marian, it was said later, left Dougal 'owing to his cruelty, taking with her the two children that had resulted from the connection'.[87] She may have fled 'in the middle of the night', having found her devotion exhausted.[88] By 1892, Dougal was in Ireland, single, and engaged as a quantity surveyor in the rebuilding of the Royal Barracks.[89]

Dougal had not long been liberated from Marian's attentions – and the financial burden of her children, and their children – before he married for a third time. On Sunday 7 August 1892, he married Sarah Henrietta White at St Paul's Church, in Dublin. The ceremony was performed according to the traditions of the Church of Ireland.[90] Sarah – known to Dougal as Hennie – was apparently a spinster 'of prepossessing appearance' in her early twenties at the time of her marriage.[91] She lived at 34 Montpelier Hill, on the north bank of the River Liffey. Dougal lived a few doors away, at number 13. Sarah was the daughter of William White, a laity missionary apparently connected to the church in which they were married.[92] Approximately double Sarah's age, and apparently respectable and professional, Dougal may have seemed a reliable choice of partner. Still, according to one account, something worried Sarah's family about the union: they disapproved, considering Dougal 'not a suitable person'.[93] The newlyweds moved to Aughrim Street, a few roads to the north, and then, three months after their wedding, they left Dublin, looking towards London.

They took rooms at 190 Earlsfield Road, in the south-west of the city, not far from Dougal's old stamping-ground of Battersea, but work was difficult to find. Perhaps because there was nothing else for it, Dougal and Sarah moved again five months later, in the spring of 1893, going to Biggin Hill, in Kent, where Dougal's brother Harry, spending money to make money, was developing property. Dougal probably resented the very principle of having to resort to the grace and favour of his junior sibling, but Harry had offered him a position overseeing one of his building projects, and Dougal had little choice. He moved with Sarah to a little cottage on Single Street, and here, on Monday 29 May 1893, their daughter Olive was born.[94]

Despite this, smooth waters may, once again, have been difficult to come by. Dougal's position with Harry lasted until the end of the year, when, it is suggested, the elder man's undimmed quest for illicit physical pleasure brought about another small-scale scandal.[95] There is little to show what might really have happened, however. Harry was a generous man, with some patience and a belief in charity which may well have originated with his religious convictions, but he may have reasoned that Dougal, with roughly nine months' work behind him, was now better equipped to survive by himself, and ought to be permitted, even encouraged, to do it. Released by Harry, Dougal set out for London.

∽◈◈◈∾

Sarah returned to Dublin in or around February 1894 – later, she said that she had taken umbrage at her husband's immoral ways, but there seems to have been a hint of shared planning in her move, and she and Dougal remained in contact. He found his way into a common lodging house at 150 Great Dover Street, in Southwark, south-east London. Circumstances were hard, and, without Sarah and Olive, expenses were kept to a minimum. The impoverished area of London in which he was living, however, offered Dougal little in the way of financial opportunity: the money was to the south, in the suburbs of Camberwell, Dulwich, Clapham and Brixton, and that called for a plan. By the end of March, Sarah had answered Dougal's call and travelled to London, bringing with her Olive and, surprisingly enough, Dougal's step-daughter Emily, known as Millie, the daughter of Mary Herberta Boyd. These were costs which, a month before, Dougal seemed in no position to meet; Sarah, presenting a bedraggled appearance on the evening of Wednesday 28 March, and with two children in tow, borrowed five shillings from a policeman named Patterson, and the money formed the down payment on a 'large front room at 35 Trinity Street', just to the south of Great Dover Street. The next day, Dougal repaid the loan, having found the money from somewhere after all. It seemed as if further wealth was expected to arrive before too long.

Before July, the family had moved to 44 Langton Road, in north Brixton; then they went to Maydwell Street in Camberwell, staying with 'a friend named Mrs Maxwell', to whom Dougal gave a vague and misleading impression of his movements, claiming to have just arrived in London from Dublin.[96] It was as if he was an animal circling its prey, waiting restlessly for its time to strike. Certainly, he did not spend much time lurking outside the Camberwell branch of the London and South-Western Bank before fixing on a likely victim.

ာတ်ာ

Miss Emily Maria Booty was a spinster in her early fifties, and a repository of unfulfilled dreams. She lived at 25 Denmark Hill, just off Camberwell Green, buoyed up by a private sum of money which obviated the need to work. Her leisurely existence lacked only the bliss of romance, in which area she had never had any luck. Wiping ten years off her age had been vanity, and in vain. Still nothing would bring her the happiness she so desired.

Then, in August 1894, outside the Camberwell branch of the London and South-Western Bank, she bumped into Samuel Herbert Dougal, as if by accident. His Long Service and Good Conduct medal gleamed on his chest. As Miss Booty put it, 'an acquaintance sprang up between us'.

In fact, Dougal wasted no time in worming his way into the centre of Miss Booty's unpractised affections. She felt pity for him – he was a widower, he said – and his anguish mirrored hers. As Miss Booty's fantasies rapidly approached their obvious crescendo, Dougal flitted, sweeping up Sarah (who was pregnant again), Olive, and Millie, none of whom were known to his new paramour, and vanished to Dublin. In his absence, he expected Miss Booty's ardour, which was now at critical mass, to fuel itself. From Ireland, he wrote to her, asking for money.

Dougal may have been temporarily taken aback to find his request denied. Miss Booty had been made of sterner stuff than he had first believed: she wrote back to him, complaining about his indelicate presumption. Rethinking his strategy, he fell into a cloistered silence, as if wounded by her distrust, and waited for Miss Booty's inherent longing for companionship to exert its powerful influence: she, growing fearful of losing him, soon retreated from her principled position, and sent the money anyway.[97] It was a sign that Dougal was already in control, whittling away at Miss Booty's resistance. He wrote back to her, returning the money and enclosing a note explaining that he was married, and 'in the habit of duping women and extorting money from them'.[98] The entire episode was stage-managed, not for pecuniary gain, but to ensure that Miss Booty was helplessly under his spell.

When he returned to London – alone – in September, they renewed their acquaintance. She challenged him over his admission that he was a married man: Dougal admitted it, but adjusted the story slightly, saying that he was separated from his wife.[99] She forgave him, desperate to sustain their acquaintance. He suggested that they take a house in the country together – he suggested that she bankroll the enterprise: she agreed. Her confidence had melted away. Miss Booty later revealed that she had had about £90 (in cash) to her name when Dougal inveigled himself into her affections in August; now, she set about delivering this wealth into the hands of her lover, and her torturer.

But, in single life, Miss Booty was living easily on her money. Even for a spinster of modest habits, £90 was not a substantial sum; the remainder of her fortune was tied up in shares. She had, in particular, forty £5 shares in the Grand Hotel at Brighton. On Saturday 20 October 1894, these were offered for sale in *The Times* as Dougal sought to liberate their cash value. The advertisement asked interested parties to write to Miss Booty at 19 Orchard Row, Camberwell; this, plainly, was Dougal's latest address, for he was handling the sale.[100] In the end, the shares realised only three-eighths of their nominal value, as Dougal settled for a quick return at £75.

Arthur Machen was a writer of tales of the macabre, of improving prospects, and only in residence at Northend House, near Turville, in Buckinghamshire, some of the time – when he was not, he was to be found at Great Russell Street or in a French vineyard. While his Buckinghamshire property was empty, Machen let it out through the agency of his solicitor, Alfred Montague Kennett, and it was this house to which Dougal and Miss Booty soon repaired.[101]

In late 1895, Machen published a work called *The Three Impostors; or, the Transmutations*, a novel of curious significance, with narrative layered upon narrative, its characters weaving fitfully in and out of each other's lives. One character, Richmond, *alias* Wilkins, was, Machen's biographer later claimed, based on Dougal himself.[102] While this seems unlikely – Walter Dew, the policeman who caught Crippen, met with Machen in February 1895, finding that the author 'knows nothing of "Dougal", with the exception that he took a house from him', all the transactions having been performed by Kennett – some details do indeed seem to fit. Both wore beards, although Dougal's was the fuller. Richmond is 'a bit of a coward', Machen says; this was true enough of Dougal.[103] And, like Dougal, Richmond is a stickler for appearances – 'the most scrupulous observer could find nothing amiss with the fashion or make of his clothes'.[104] Writing in retrospect, however, it was easy for Machen to overplay his connection to his tenant. In an article which was apparently first published in 1924, Machen described a meeting with Dougal (and Miss Booty, who, he appears to suggest, had a weakness for drink), but the evidence for it is lacking.[105] Like all writers, Machen imagined the scene, and then imagined it again, finally alighting on a version he found plausible.

The pair arrived at Northend House by Thursday 8 November 1894.[106] It was a grand, spacious place, built on two storeys. To the north, it looked onto a pond; to the south and east, its lawns swept gracefully around it. It was remote enough to offer Dougal and Miss Booty the seclusion they – *he* – sought. Dougal had already persuaded his victim to adopt his surname, giving the impression that they were any ordinary married couple, and had concocted a story about their having been brought into holy union by the vicar of the church of St Mary the Virgin in Henley. Miss Booty's friends, informed by letter of her sudden romance, offered their congratulations by reply.

But the nightmare soon brewed up. Far from feeling secure in Dougal's affections, Miss Booty quickly perceived that Charlotte Larner, the thirty-seven-year-old, unmarried daughter of a widowed and retired farmer who lived nearby, had begun to attract her not-husband's attention. In an effort to reduce the threat of this outsider, Miss Booty would seem to have made some attempt to make friends with Charlotte, but her territorialising was transparently amateur, and the strategy backfired. Charlotte and Dougal were brought closer together, and Miss Booty's powerlessness, and her humiliation, were revealed to be almost total.

In addition, Dougal was devouring her bank account, acquiring furniture and farm machinery; on 20 December, having stayed in London overnight, he returned to Northend House in the company of Sarah, Millie, Olive, and Herbert – his new baby by Sarah. Miss Booty's Arcadian reverie promptly dissolved – even she realised that Dougal had 'brought his wife and three children to Northend House'.[107] Sarah, abstracting herself from the matter, later claimed to have 'found Dougal living at Northend, Henley-on-Thames, with a Miss Booty as man and wife'.[108] This, though, represented a liberally-realised version of events: it is obvious that she and the children had travelled to London by prior arrangement, meeting there with Dougal (who was, anyway, going to be in the city spending Miss Booty's money) at an appointed time. This sort of obfuscation would come to characterise Sarah's later recollections of her life with Dougal.

Things worsened. Miss Booty footed the bill, but the Dougals behaved as if they were the aristocracy, and reduced the depersonalised Miss Booty to the rank of servant. Sarah restored herself to the marital bed, and Miss Booty moved into one of the spare rooms, unable to leave, but not wanting to stay. Then the thought-experiment radicalised – on Monday 7 January 1895, Herbert Bernard Dougal died in a convulsion, aged only three months, and Dougal's behaviour deteriorated. Miss Booty's utility was dwindling in line with her bank account, but she would not leave Northend of her own volition: if he – or Sarah – wished her to go, Dougal would be required to engineer her departure. With a view to the future, Dougal had apparently already advertised in the *Christian Million*, a devout newsletter, for a 'mentally or otherwise afflicted Lady or Gentleman to take charge of'. Without Miss Booty – or a suitably well-off replacement for her – he would have no money at all.

Robert Larner, Charlotte's father, was the voice of reason. Miss Booty explained her position to him, and he, sympathetically, advised her to leave Northend House, writing off her investments in it. By Monday 18 February 1895, with all her money finally spent by the profligate Dougals, Miss Booty was ready to follow Larner's advice.

According to later reports, Miss Booty spent the night in her bedroom packing her things.[109] All that she had she attempted to gather into one place, although, for the time being, she left certain items of limited value in the bottom drawer of a chest of drawers.[110] When, at half-past five the next morning, she crept downstairs from her bedroom to the sitting room, Dougal followed her. He was in an immoderate mood, frustrated by an increasingly unprofitable Miss Booty. His temper was beginning to get the better of him.

As Miss Booty looked up, she saw Dougal waving a dagger, and a gun. He told her that he would 'do for her', and stalked back upstairs. Miss Booty was terrified, and fled into the dawn, 'scantily attired', according to some reports, or only lacking a bonnet, according to others.[111] She clambered over the fence which marked the perimeter of the Larners' property, and was taken into their farmhouse, having finally broken away from the clutches of her strange ordeal.[112]

With her escape, Miss Booty seems to have recovered something of her personality. She asked her mysterious rival Charlotte
Larner to contact the police – in accordance with Robert
Larner's advice – and quickly organised for some men with a van
to remove her furniture from Northend House.[113] By the time
Superintendent Edwin Hawtin arrived, at about eleven o'clock,
the furniture was being taken out.[114]

Hawtin accompanied Miss Booty back to Northend House.
Miss Booty, her strength returning to her, made sure that Hawtin
demanded Dougal's dagger and gun (which Dougal compliantly
gave up), saw the furniture removed in the van (despite Dougal's
objections) and then scurried upstairs to check the possessions
which she had packed the previous night.[115] Dougal had told
Hawtin that, with the furniture gone, there was nothing more
in the house of Miss Booty's.[116] But she found that her boxes had
been 'ransacked and the things put in their proper place again'.
She opened the bottom drawer of the chest of drawers in her
bedroom. The items she had put there on the previous evening
were missing.

Miss Booty reported the absence of the items – one linen duster,
two tea cloths and four yards of dimity, a cotton fabric which its
owner would probably have turned into bedsheets or curtains – to
Superintendent Hawtin.[117] He led the way to Dougal's bedroom,
procuring a key to Sarah's box from Sarah herself.[118] Opening
the box, Superintendent Hawtin revealed the missing items. He
asked Dougal to account for the relocation of the items, from Miss
Booty's room to his own. Dougal said nothing.

'I did not take them,' said Sarah, who was watching events. 'My
husband gave them to me to put in my box.'[119]

Miss Booty charged Dougal with stealing the duster, the tea
cloths and the dimity, and Hawtin removed him to the station.[120]

လာတတ

Dougal was fortunate not to have been charged with a more serious offence, but nobody had witnessed him menacing Miss Booty
with weapons. By contrast, the discovery of the fabrics in Sarah's
box had been widely witnessed, and this charge, paltry though it
was, seemed likely to stick. Miss Booty, when she came to put a
cash value on the contested articles, thought that they were worth
about 5s 2d.[121] It was a petty amount of money, and clearly not

commensurate with the abuse she had endured over the course of six months. Dougal was committed for trial at the Easter Quarter Sessions, to be held in Oxford, and liberated on a £50 bail. It is not clear whose money he used to pay the bond, but he returned to live in Northend House with Sarah and the children. He still had not paid a penny in rent on this property. Miss Booty, who had, stayed on in nearby Watlington.

Prior to his trial at the Quarter Sessions, Dougal, thinking things over, settled on a pre-emptive strike. On 8 March 1895, he put Miss Booty in the dock at Marlow, stating that, when she returned to Northend House after fleeing to the sanctuary of Robert Larner's farmhouse, she had taken 'an incubator and other articles value £8'. The other articles to which the claim referred included a wheelbarrow, a spade, a shovel, and a garden fork. But the case folded when it became clear to the magistrates that Dougal had not paid for these items, and could not pretend to be their owner. It seems unlikely that Dougal had wanted the disputed tools returned to him for the purpose of doing any work around the farm – he never troubled himself with that, and the effect of the hearing, brought up on frivolous grounds, was, ultimately, to humiliate Miss Booty. But if Dougal had hoped that the experience would cause her to withdraw her complaint – a much more serious trial was, of course, pending, and the public interest in this tribunal was likely to be greater, and the potential embarrassment more widespread – then he was to be disappointed.

On Tuesday 9 April, Miss Booty stood up at the County Hall in Oxford, and actively contested her case. Dougal blustered his way through his own defence, jabbing artlessly at Miss Booty in cross-examination, and highlighting her willing acquiescence to a bizarre lifestyle which seemed to have ended in personal animus. She accepted that he had returned the money she had sent to him in Ireland – she accepted that he had admitted that he was married and in the habit of duping women – she had followed his lead anyway.[122] No charges had been laid with regard to Dougal's frightening exhibition of weaponry, but Miss Booty had not forgotten her experience. 'I did not take proceedings against you for this,' she said, 'but I hope you will be prosecuted'. Laughter rang around the court – Miss Booty's attempts to find a higher pitch of objection as the *ex post facto* martyr sounded forced. But still she persisted with her humiliating task: she had written to her friends about a non-existent marriage, yes, but she had done so, she told Dougal, 'at your dictation'. Dougal was fiercely undeterred, and pressed on into increasingly personal territory, until interrupted by the Chairman of the Oxfordshire Quarter Sessions, Sir William Anson, who characterised Dougal's intrusive enquiries as 'cruel'.

In his defence, Dougal called two witnesses who were known to be well-disposed towards him – his stepdaughter Millie and Charlotte Larner. Millie told the court that she remembered 'her mother' – Sarah – saying that 'she had some of Miss Booty's tea towels in her room'. This was at breakfast on 18 February.[123] Millie also remembered that 'her father was out of the house when they were put in her mother's box'.[124] This evidence did not seem to rule out the possibility that *someone* had taken *something* that belonged to Miss Booty, but, if Millie was right, then Dougal, out and about, could not have been the culprit. Charlotte, on the other hand, readily assented to Dougal's suggestion that Miss Booty had conceived of a personal vendetta against him. When she had fled to the Larners' house, Charlotte told the court, Miss Booty had told her that she would 'like to see the prisoner with handcuffs on'.[125]

Dougal then spoke 'at considerable length' in his own defence.[126] His case was a convoluted one, lacking the focus and vision which a barrister could have given it. He approached and retreated from his various arguments haphazardly, veering away from the charge, and finally alighting on a trusted motif – his military background, and the futility of risking his pension, which could be forfeited in response to a conviction, for the purpose of stealing household articles worth a few shillings.[127] He denied that a crime had taken place, since Miss Booty had bought the cloths and the dimity from 'a traveller from Henley' under his name; but he also insisted that the bill for the items had not been paid until *after* she had brought the charge against him. These were not matters upon which he had tested Miss Booty in the course of his cross-examination.

The jury retired, and were out about a quarter of an hour.[128] When they returned, they were asked for their verdict. They found Dougal not guilty.

The foreman added that the jury's view was that 'the prisoner's conduct towards Miss Booty was bad in the extreme', but Miss Booty cannot have been cheered by their useless sympathy. Jesse, writing long after the event, supposed that the jury's decision probably turned on Dougal's 'excellent Army record'.[129] Perhaps it was so. The case ended in farce, with the much-wronged Miss Booty wronged once again.

By May, she had returned to Camberwell, taking lodgings at 27 Station Road, with little left of her personal wealth. Dougal, similarly badly off, had returned to Northend House, where he was determinedly withholding the rent, before seeking the return of the incubator and the other garden tools which remained in the custody of the police. Like his attempt to regain his licence at the Royston Crow, this seemed to torture the logic of acquittal beyond local tolerances. The Buckinghamshire constabulary forced him through a legal process, but Dougal, perhaps already sensing that he was *persona non grata* in the courts of the Thames Valley, did not attend the session at Wycombe on Tuesday 7 May 1895. The costs of the frivolous case were set against him *in absentia*, and, with no way of paying, Dougal abandoned the growing arrears at Northend House – 'a final superb gesture', in Arthur Machen's words – and fled.[130]

He, Sarah, Millie and Olive returned to Ireland, taking rooms at 2 Liffey Street, in Inchicore, just outside Dublin; and Millie faded once again into the care of her maternal family.

For the first time in about eighteen months, Dougal was forced to find paid employment. Despite his recent flirtations with the law, his military pension and his air of military rectitude remained intact. He had not been convicted of an offence, and his somehow-unchanged circumstances neatly recommended him for an appointment as a messenger in the Commander of the Forces Office, at the Royal Hospital in Dublin, the Irish branch of the better-known Chelsea Hospital in London. He had applied for the post while still on bail and awaiting trial at the Oxfordshire Quarter Sessions.

It would not be long, however, before Dougal's behaviour put him into disfavour with his employers. On Tuesday 24 September 1895, his employment at the Royal Hospital ended (as he later acknowledged) 'in consequence of a threat used towards a clerk in the Adjutant-General's office'.[131] A short period of suspension preceded the formalisation of his dismissal on Sunday 29 September. Dougal responded to this apparent setback with practised nonchalance.

He had, in fact, been unable to resist the temptation of a memento or two, glimpsed as he passed through the offices of his superiors. Captain Smithson, aide-de-camp to Lord Wolseley (the Adjutant-General), had had the misfortune to leave his chequebook in plain view; Colonel Childers, Assistant Military Secretary, kept a chequebook issued to his wife in an unlocked drawer. Dougal removed a few blank cheques individually, complete with their counterfoils, from each book. Then he engineered his own dismissal, threatening a clerk for the purpose. It appears that he hoped to be rapidly forgotten; and, since nobody had suspected the theft, and no charges had been brought, and no conviction handed down, his pension remained unaffected. In his diary, Dougal recorded the payment of the quarterly sum of £12 11s 1d on 3 October 1895.

Even then, there remained the task of realising the value of the stolen cheques. On Wednesday 16 October, at about half past two in the afternoon, Dougal, back in London, walked into Messrs Cox & Company's Bank, Charing Cross branch, in Craig's Court.[132] Approaching a cashier named Frederick William Hodges, he asked to cash a cheque. Taking the cheque from his pocket, Dougal apparently tore it. Hodges gave Dougal a piece of gummed paper to stick the cheque back together, and told him to write 'accidentally torn' on the cheque, and to sign it, all of which Dougal did. Hodges noticed that the cheque, for £35, was made payable to someone by the name of Greenfield, and had been signed by Lord Frankfort. Frankfort was the Commander of the Forces in Dublin.

Inspecting the repaired cheque, Hodges observed that the tear and the gummed paper had indeed been marked and signed by Greenfield, and so he cashed the cheque, giving Dougal three £10 notes, numbers KI 74333, KI 74334 and KI 74335, and £5 in gold. Dougal left the bank, and, at three o'clock, arrived at the Bank of England – about half an hour away from Charing Cross, across the city, at a strolling pace. Entering the bank, Dougal went up to William Richard Percy Lawrence, a cashier in the

Issue Department, and asked to change the three £10 notes he had received from Hodges. He endorsed the notes in the name of Greenfield, and received £30 in coins, contained in a brown paper bag. He now travelled back westwards, in the direction whence he came, to Bedford Street, running north off the Strand, and went into the Civil Service Supply Association.

Dougal had not been a working civil servant for just over three weeks, but he may still have been in possession of the membership card permitting him to buy from the Supply Association. At about five o'clock, Miss Florence Tapp, a seventeen-year-old assistant in the boot department, wrote Dougal a receipt for his order of a pair of lady's boots and a pair of lady's shoes. He instructed her to send them on to 2 Liffey Street, addressed to his wife.[133] He paid in cash, and took the receipt with him.[134]

Back in Dublin, another suspicious cheque came to light. It had been cashed in the Bank of Ireland, before Friday 18 October, in favour of one Colonel Stockwell, of the Royal Hospital Military School. The value of the cheque was £47 10s 0d, and it had been made out in the name of Lord Wolseley. The Bank of Ireland had realised, some time after cashing the cheque, that it was a forgery, taken, along with another cheque which had not yet surfaced, from Captain Smithson's chequebook. The Dublin police sent the dubious cheque to Scotland Yard, in London, where the Metropolitan Police received it on 19 October. A letter accompanying it requested that it be shown to Lord Wolseley, who was in London at the time, to find out whether he recognised it. Initial suspicion, the letter said, attached to 'Private C.R.W. Crook, 13th Hussar who was then servant with Captain Smithson, but who is now with his regiment at Dundalk'. On the morning of 27 October, Wolseley was shown the cheque by Inspector Frank Froest. Wolseley declared it a forgery, and stated that he could not recognise the handwriting.

On Friday 25 October, according to his diary, Dougal paid 3s rent 'and gave notice to leave 2 Liffey Street on the following Friday'.[135] In fact, he left on Tuesday 29 October, going to a small village called Prosperous, in County Kildare, to the west of Dublin. This reinforced a layer of anonymity which Dougal had engineered at Inchicore: according to one later police report, he 'did not associate with any person in the neighbourhood of his former residence'.[136] Where Sarah, Millie and Olive were at this time is unclear: the Dublin police wrote that Dougal's 'wife's relatives reside at Chapelizod, but ... they cannot be approached directly'. The reason for the Whites' immunity to even the politest police enquiries is not known.

In the meantime, Crook's image had faded from the vision of the investigators in Dublin and London, to be replaced more firmly by Dougal's distinctive form – Colonel Childers's information with regard to Dougal's dismissal from the hospital had turned the detectives' heads. On 4 November 1895, a letter marked 'Pressing' was sent to Scotland Yard by the Dublin police. Lord Frankfort had checked his incomings and outgoings, and he noticed the withdrawal, by cheque, of £35, a transaction for which he could not account. He contacted Cox's Bank, and they sent Greenfield's cheque to him.[137] Immediately realising that it was a forgery, he informed the Dublin police of the offence, and took them the cheque in question. They were now able to compare the Frankfort cheque with the Wolseley cheque, finding certain similarities in the writing.[138] In their 'pressing' letter, they communicated these findings to the Metropolitan Police, providing Dougal's name, but admitted to 'a difficulty in tracing him'. Nobody seemed to know where he had gone.

In London, thirty-nine-year-old Inspector Charles Richards had been attempting to unravel the knot. With the case against Dougal improving with every new discovery, and with Colonel Childers in tow, Inspector Richards hurried down to the Bow Street Police Court on the morning of Monday 11 November and asked the magistrate Franklin Lushington to grant a warrant against Dougal over the matter of the Frankfort cheque. Lushington did, and, back at Scotland Yard, Richards filed an urgent request 'to proceed to Dublin'. By one o'clock that afternoon, news arrived to the effect that Dougal had been spotted in County Kildare. Richards caught the 8.20p.m. train from Euston that same evening, heading for Holyhead, and a boat to Dublin.

In the company of two Irish policemen, Gaffney and Walsh, loaned to him by the local force, Richards arrived in Prosperous at four o'clock the next day. He clutched the arrest warrant. They found Dougal at home.

'Your name is Dougal,' said Walsh.

'Yes,' said Dougal.[139]

'I arrest you on a warrant for forging and uttering a cheque,' said Walsh.[140]

'All right,' said Dougal.[141]

'Dougal,' said Richards, 'I am an inspector from Scotland Yard. If you listen, I will read the warrant to you.' Richards read the warrant, and Dougal made no reply.

With the suspect in custody, Inspector Richards combed the house, searching without success for the missing cheques, or 'any traces of Lord Wolseley's or Lord Frankfort's signature'.[142] After five minutes, Dougal had a question.

'Who is bringing the charge?' he asked Richards.

'Messrs Cox & Co.; it is for forging the signature of Lord Frankfort to a cheque,' Richards replied.

'All right,' said Dougal, again.

In fact, although direct evidence of the forgery itself was not discovered, Richards found a wealth of evidence which offered support to the stories told by the cashiers and store assistants Dougal had encountered in London on 16 October. The receipt, handed to him by Florence Tapp, was uncovered (with Dougal's former address written on it). A brown paper bag containing seventeen sovereigns was also found.[143] Beyond this, Richards seized a Post Office savings bank book, a case containing a Masonic apron, an agreement for renting a house, three memo books, one photograph, two marriage certificates, one birth certificate, three pension papers and some other, miscellaneous, testimonials and memos.[144] Presumably in one of the memo books, Dougal had been keeping his diary.

Richards flicked to the date of 16 October 1895. There, Dougal had written, 'At home most of the day – went into town and made a few small purchases and called in at the Institute and read the papers'. Part of the entry for the next day, 17 October, was 'carefully cut out', Richards said, the remaining part reading: 'Attended Masonic Lodge in evening with Brother Shore; no business'.[145] These humdrum accounts of a life lived within the parameters of the law were, Richards knew, not entirely genuine.

Then Richards and Dougal started on the journey back to London. They caught the train from Sallins to Dublin, and Dougal spent the night there in a cell. The next morning, they boarded the boat for Holyhead, transferred to the railway, and arrived back at Euston at 6.00p.m. At 6.30p.m., Dougal was ushered into an identity parade at Bow Street Station. Hodges, Cox's cashier, peered at Dougal and the eight innocent men alongside him. He concluded that Dougal was 'like the man who presented the cheque', but he could not swear to it. His recollection was of a clean-shaven man. It is likely that Dougal had removed his trademark beard before uttering his cheque – since then, it had grown back.

A series of hearings at the police court upheld the charge of forging and uttering, and Dougal's trial was set for the Central Criminal Court on Monday 9 December. He was remanded to Holloway Prison in the meantime.

క్రాఠⁿ

Sarah now ghosted into view. She (and, presumably, Olive) had found lodgings at 39 Grafton Road, a short walk from the prison, and from here she wrote to Richards at Scotland Yard:

> 39 Grafton Road
> Holloway
>
> Monday
>
> Dear Sir,
>
> Would you have the kindness to send my Husbands [*sic*] pension papers to the Governor of Holloway prison. They should have been be sent in the 1st of Dec & unless they are sent in (if fortune favours us) he will be unable to draw it.
>
> Believe me
> Yours sincerely
>
> S. Henrietta Dougal[146]

Richards did not receive the letter until Tuesday 3 December, by which time the papers should, apparently, already have been sent in, but the lack of a more precise date of writing than 'Monday', and the carelessly scored-out mistake, converting a past participle into its future equivalent, suggest that the letter was not written until 2 December anyway. Dougal and Sarah may originally have been hoping for his release, and the abandonment of the charge. Now, they realised that they would have to apply for the pension – payable on New Year's Day – through the prison, provided they could get hold of the papers, which were in Richards's custody. The handwriting on the letter – including the signature – closely resembled Dougal's: he had, presumably, sought permission to write the letter on her behalf during one of her visits to the prison, although, years on, Sarah is said to have had the ability to write by herself. Whichever way one looked at it, for Dougal to approximate someone else's signature while remanded in Holloway Prison on a forgery charge seemed like remarkably cool work. Richards, the irony of Dougal's actions apparently eluding him, simply recommended that Sarah be told that the papers could not be given up at the moment. John Summers, a police sergeant from Y Division (Holloway), called round to 39 Grafton Road to pass on Richards's decision. Sarah told Summers that she would inform her husband when she next visited him in prison.

In the meantime, Sarah's role in the affair of the forged cheques refused to come into clearer view. Richards had taken from Dougal's house at Prosperous a letter 'showing that a banking account had been opened in the name of [the] prisoner's wife since the forged cheque was cashed'.[147] Here was another little hint, hardly picked up at the time, of Sarah's shadowy complicity in Dougal's crimes – perhaps, while at Northend, she had appropriated some of Miss Booty's possessions while her husband was out of the house; in Dublin, she had been the recipient of the footwear he had bought with the money realised on the forged cheques; now she held a bank account with, one supposes, what remained of the profits of the forgery still sitting in it. But perhaps she was thought to be at Dougal's mercy. The case against him had formed gradually, piece by piece; but there was no sign of the same process occurring with Sarah.

Even on the morning of the trial, Dougal refused to hire counsel. Pleading not guilty to the charge, but without any witnesses to call, or any obvious idea of how to conduct his case, he presented an aimless figure to the Old Bailey. Sir Charles Hall, Recorder of London, and the judge in the matter, appointed William Hamilton Leycester to watch the case on Dougal's behalf.

While Dougal looked passively on, Henry Hamilton Lawless, acting for the prosecution, knitted together the separate strands of evidence against him. Lord Frankfort – the supposed signatory of the disputed cheque – noted that Dougal had seen his signature on countless occasions: Frankfort's mark was on all sorts of documents which passed through the Royal Hospital. There was an inconsistency, too, on the disputed cheque. 'I generally sign, "Frankfort, Major-General"', he told the court, all on one line: but the cheque showed the 'Major-General' below the 'Frankfort'. Frederick William Hodges began to see differences between the feigned hand of the body of the Frankfort cheque, and the genuine hand of Dougal's endorsement of it, which the day-to-day demands of work in a busy bank had not permitted him to detect at the time. William Lawrence, from the Bank of England, looked at Dougal and failed to identify him as the felonious customer; then he looked at the brown bag, removed by Richards from Prosperous, and failed to identify that, too.

In the end, however, the prosecution case was somehow greater than the sum of its parts. *The Times*, which reported on the case the next day, described some of the evidence as 'circumstantial', and the mass failure of the key witnesses to identify the forger remained a difficulty, but, at the heart of the case, the handwriting evidence remained solid.[148] The last witness to be called, one Thomas Henry Gurrin, a handwriting expert resident at 59 Holborn Viaduct, was a regular turn at the Old Bailey, frequently employed by Scotland Yard, the Home Office and the Director of Public Prosecutions to give his opinion on the provenance of dubious documents. He had compared the cheque, the correspondence list, the diary and the bank notes, and had come to the conclusion that all were written by the same person. He pointed out the similarities he had detected.[149] Backing Lord Frankfort, he saw the signature on the cheque as an 'imperfect imitation' of the original. He told Lawless that he had had nearly twelve years' experience in handwriting analysis. Leycester cross-examined, finding that Gurrin had been consulted after the case had been presented to the magistrate, but Gurrin denied that the existing doubts about the cheque's authenticity had in any way affected his investigation. In eleven years, he said, some juries had disagreed with his evidence, 'but not very often; I think in about three cases out of about eight hundred'. When they did, 'it does not mean that in those three cases they meant to diametrically oppose me', but that 'sometimes my evidence requires corrob-oration'. As it happens, Gurrin added, 'I have not changed my opinion with regard to those three cases'. His integrity seemed unimpeachable.

∽∾∾∽

When the case went to the jury, Dougal's first conviction in a criminal court was practically assured. There was a vacuum where the evidence for the defence should have been – Leycester had had no time to prepare a case; Dougal had been inertly unin-terested throughout his remand. Examined from a distance, the only irony in the inevitable guilty verdict was the jury's recom-mendation to mercy, 'on account of [Dougal's] previous good character'.

Before sentencing could take place, however, Lawless spoke up for the prosecution, advising Sir Charles that another forged cheque – the Wolseley cheque – had come to light in Ireland. Dougal's past indiscretions may have been obscure, but his recent penchant for forgery was fair game. Inspector Richards was recalled and asked whether the police intended to prosecute Dougal over this matter. Richards told Sir Charles that 'as he [Dougal] had been convicted [on the present charge] I did not think it likely that a further charge would be preferred against him'.[150] There was little doubt – based on the appearance of the handwriting – that Dougal was responsible for this forgery, too. Sir Charles decided to postpone sentencing until the plans for the Wolseley forgery could be determined: if there had been only one charge against the prisoner, he said, he should have felt inclined to give effect to the jury's recommendation of mercy; but, if there were a second charge, it would 'alter his mind'. The court adjourned, Dougal returning, guilty but unsentenced, to Holloway Prison, while Richards collated the evidence of Dougal's other forgery.

This took a month. Richards had a letter sent to the Dublin police, who responded, frustrated, that the Bank of Ireland's cashier – predictably enough – 'is unable to identify him [Dougal] as the person who cashed the cheque'. 'The Bank authorities do not intend to take any further action in the matter,' they wrote. There was:

> no moral doubt but [that] Dougal is the person who stole and forged
> the attached cheque as he had access to the cheque book at this time,
> but he cannot be prosecuted for want of proof.

Suddenly, too, Dougal's good fortune of recent years – and the silence surrounding him – began to dissipate. Hawtin had already written to Scotland Yard about the Miss Booty incident; on 12 December, Reginald Wymer wrote from Watford, where he was Deputy Chief Constable and Superintendent of C Division of the Hertfordshire Constabulary, mentioning the Royston Crow affair. He also wrote to Superintendent William Wood, his successor at Ware, who sent on a newspaper clipping from December 1889. By 17 December 1895, the official picture of Dougal's desperate habits was more complete than it had been at any time in the past. Richards was clear that Dougal 'has not been getting his living honestly since he left the Army'.

This bore on another issue, that of Dougal's pension. There was now a conviction against his name, although, following an exchange of letters, the Commissioners of the Chelsea Hospital eventually confirmed that the 'gravity or lightness' of Sir Charles's sentence would influence their actions. It lay within their power to cancel, reduce or suspend a pension, but they scaled their responses to the behaviour of ex-military felons against the impartial measure of the law.

On Monday 13 January, Sir Charles, Richards, Lawless and Dougal reconvened at the Central Criminal Court.[151] The evidence from Hertfordshire and Oxfordshire, although it refined Richards's opinion of Dougal, and although both cases showed Dougal in the throes of economic crime, was inadmissible – he had twice been found not guilty. On the subject of the Wolseley cheque, produced for Sir Charles's inspection, Lawless explained the Dublin police's unwillingness to proceed with a prosecution. But the handwriting evidence had underpinned Dougal's conviction, and Sir Charles's consideration of the Wolseley forgery clearly convinced him that Dougal was the culprit. When he heard that there was no intention to prosecute him further, Dougal's spirits must have lifted. He may even have anticipated his release, driven by the jury's plea for mercy. Sir Charles, turning to the dock, made it clear that he considered the offence a serious one. He gave Dougal a twelve-month sentence, with hard labour.

❦

Dougal was removed to Pentonville Prison to officially begin his sentence. His release date was set for 8 December 1896 – a year from the date of his conviction, rather than a year from the date of his sentencing. There was no remission for the time he spent in custody before his trial.

Upon his arrival at the prison, Dougal 'appeared depressed' and was placed under observation.[152] His hard labour apparently began with oakum-picking – the dreadfully dull and frequently painful task of pulling apart used ropes to separate the strands within them. Within two weeks, he had had enough of this.

At about 4.30p.m. on Sunday 26 January 1896, Dougal was discovered to have attempted to hang himself from the bell handle in his cell. He was promptly removed to the prison hospital and contained in a 'loose restraint jacket' – put simply, a straitjacket. Charles Bowyer, Principal Warder at Pentonville Prison, seemed sceptical about Dougal's suicidal intentions. He was not certain whether Dougal had 'made, or feigned to make' a genuine attempt on his own life. Examining him in the hospital, Bowyer found 'no marks visible around his neck'; indeed, Dougal 'did not appear to be in any way injured'. Bowyer supposed that the length of rope Dougal had used to undertake his 'attempt' was given to him to be picked apart in the course of his labours. Dougal's bell handle, Bowyer noted, was 'about 5ft high from the floor of his cell'. Dougal was a little under six feet tall – he would have had to contort himself, crouching, kneeling, only in order to draw the rope taut. Starting from the vertical, it would have been practically impossible to generate enough tension to pull the rope into the trachea. Even if Dougal had spread himself out on the floor, drawing the rope as tight as possible, he could only have experienced an unpleasant death by strangulation, unless the force of the rope on the vagal nerve had caused a sudden cardiac arrest.[153] But the undamaged skin of Dougal's neck suggested that he had not, in fact, tightened the rope at all.

Wrapped up in his straitjacket, Dougal spent the rest of Sunday and the whole of Monday in the hospital. He slept 'on and off' on the night of 26 January, and slept well the next night. Bowyer noticed that he ate well.[154] On 28 January, the straitjacket was removed, and Dougal was moved to an Association Ward, where he was observed to behave appropriately. He continued to sleep well.

On Wednesday 29 January, Charles A. Innes, the doctor in charge of the prison hospital, applied to Pentonville's Visiting Committee to have Dougal certified insane and removed to an asylum. The Committee were satisfied with Dr Innes's evaluation of Dougal, and countersigned the certificate.[155] Bowyer remained dubious – he noted that, except for a disturbed night on 30 January, Dougal slept soundly, betraying no sign of acute mental crisis, but, by Monday 3 February, arrangements had been made to transfer Dougal to the Cane Hill Lunatic Asylum, in Surrey. John Manning, the Governor of Pentonville Prison, completed the paperwork, recording Dougal's illness as 'acute melancholia'.[156] The prison had noticed his symptoms 'on reception'. The prisoner's state of mind at the time he committed his offence was 'unknown'.

Charles Bowyer accompanied Dougal to Cane Hill. Dougal, Bowyer remembered, gave him 'no trouble whatever'.[157] When they arrived, they were required to wait in the reception room. Dougal was peering at the institution's regulations, posted on a wall. He turned to Bowyer.

'I see, Mr Bowyer,' he said, 'that I shall be able to see my wife here every week.'

༄ఠ

On admission at Cane Hill, the proximal cause of Dougal's suicidal ideation was assumed to be his 'adverse circumstances, loss of pension &c'.[158] He was regarded as having been insane for '21 days' (according to one document), or 'since about 14 Jany 1896' (according to another). No attempt was made, however, to ascertain Dougal's state of mind prior to his arrival at Pentonville. His inactivity in November and December, seeming to sit idly by while the state prepared its case against him, could, perhaps, have been linked to the onset of a mood disorder, although the alternative interpretation, in which Dougal hubristically awaited an emancipation which did not come, remains persuasive. The lack of information about Dougal's psychology in the last months of 1895 is perhaps best understood to represent the absence of official concern – none of his behaviours made anyone think that he was mad.

Nor had the Chelsea Hospital actually rescinded Dougal's pension by the time of his suicide attempt. As a letter to Inspector Richards had made clear, the Pension Commissioners had considerable discretion, although the fact that Dougal had been sentenced to hard labour may indeed have put his case beyond the pale.[159] In fact, the Commissioners only withdrew the pension on 30 January 1896, informing the War Office of their decision on the following day. Word of the decision might not have reached Dougal until February, by which time he had been declared insane and his transfer to Cane Hill was *fait accompli*.

In the light of all of this, it is easy to be cynical about Dougal's rapid progress at Cane Hill. He was in fine health at his initial medical, conducted by Dr James M. Moody. Dougal stood 5 feet 11 inches, and weighed 11 stones and 9 pounds. He was of clean habits, Moody wrote, with no family history of phthisis or intemperance. Dougal was not thought to be a risk to others. Moody found him well-nourished, with dark hair and a greyish beard, equal pupils, a clean tongue, grey-blue eyes, no bruises, and a healthy heart and lungs.[160] He also seems to have been sensitive to his new charge's peculiar character:

> Depressed and desponding. Answers in a low voice. Admits that he has attempted to hang himself but says he cannot remember much about it. Says he feels all kinds of impulses which he can hardly control. Evasive and furtive. His memory is fair. Very reserved. Shifty and strange.

Dougal was issued with a red ticket, marking him out to the asylum's attendants as a patient who needed to be watched closely.

Given into the care of Dr Arthur Norman Boycott, the Assistant Medical Superintendent working under Dr Moody, Dougal continued to conduct himself with the apparent serenity which Bowyer had observed in the hospital at Pentonville. A note

made by Boycott in the institution's Case Book on Thursday
6 February said that Dougal slept well, behaved quietly and took
his food. He had, Boycott remarked, a 'reserved manner'. The following Saturday, Boycott was required to make a statement to
the Commissioners in Lunacy with regard to his new patient. In
view of Dougal's calm temperament, good appetite and consistent sleep patterns, Boycott's assessment sounds rather forced:

> Melancholia. He is depressed and desponding. Admits having
> attempted to hang himself. Gives a confused and disconnected
> account of the affair. Moderate health.

On 14 February, less than two weeks after he had been issued
with it, Dougal's red ticket was withdrawn. He was no longer
thought to be at risk of suicide.

Dougal seems to have enjoyed his time in the asylum, which
operated on humane and progressive grounds, steadily finding
relief from his melancholic symptoms. By 20 February, Boycott
was able to write that his patient was 'not so depressed'. By
3 March, he was 'going on well', able to work (presumably at
tasks which in no way resembled the hard labour to which he
had been sentenced), 'more cheerful' and even 'rational'. In April,
Boycott said Dougal was 'improving slowly'; in May, that Dougal
exhibited 'no depression'. He had been moved to a different ward
– a sign that the doctors thought that he was getting better –
but Dougal was careful to illustrate the fragility of his emerging
sanity. He quarrelled with one R.J. Lloyd – the notes do not say
what about – as if to emphasise the fact that his convalescence
ought not to have been gainsaid. He feared removal to prison if
he betrayed rapid signs of recovery.

Even this amateurish pretence of vulnerability proved difficult
to sustain, however. Moved to a third ward in June, the relaxed
Dougal behaved 'exemplarily'. Boycott noted a 'nervous twitching of the face', but still there was no sign of the depression
which had afflicted him before. Dr Moody was increasingly ready
to confirm that Dougal was, once again, sane.

There was one more contemporary hint, though, that Dougal
had been shamming. Dr Moody picked up a rumour that Dougal

had admitted to 'hanking with the Prison Authorities'. When he asked around, seeking to discover the source of the story, nobody was able – or willing – to say from whom he had heard it. Dr Moody eventually settled on the idea that the rumour had originated with another patient, a man named Harrison, who was, unfortunately, helplessly mad, delusional, and, by 1903, when his condition was inquired into by the Home Office, in 'a very bad state' in Hanwell Asylum.

On Thursday 10 September 1896, Moody and Boycott signed a Certificate of Sanity, confirming that Dougal was safely returned from his journey into madness. With nearly three months of his custodial sentence remaining, however, there remained the problem of what to do with him now. Moody sent a letter to the Home Office, reporting Dougal's recovery, and requesting that they sanction 'his free discharge from the Asylum'. The prospect of returning to prison, he said, may cause Dougal 'worry and anxiety' sufficient to 'cause him to have a relapse of his illness'.

The Home Office found the letter on the following Tuesday, bound to other papers. Passed to a civil servant for consideration, the idea of immediate release left an unpleasant taste – Dougal had only served a fortnight of the sentence given to him – but his removal to prison, against medical opinion, would have been undiplomatic (and, if the doctors were right, possibly injurious to their patient's gossamer mental health). A letter of 21 September informed Dr Moody that Dougal was to remain in the asylum until the expiry of his sentence.

Moody was invited to write back in disagreement with the decision, if he thought it was the wrong one, and on Friday 9 October he did so. Presenting the Home Office's judgement to Cane Hill's Visiting Committee, the inevitable objection was raised: as a sane man, why should Dougal be detained in a lunatic asylum? Moody's letter expressed the Committee's opinion, although he may have guessed that the Home Office would be immovable on the matter. A cursory note on the Home Office docket reads, 'I still think this man had better remain'.

Dougal does not seem to have been greatly put out by the decision. He would be required to stay at Cane Hill until December, but, being *compos mentis*, he was under few restrictions. He was transferred to the nominal care of one Dr Donaldson, whose case notes were of the briefest kind – on 21 October, he found that Dougal 'continues better mentally' and was 'quiet and well behaved'. Dougal had begun working with the fireman in J Ward, a man named George Roberts, but this casual, social labour can scarcely have resembled the spirit-breaking toil to which he had originally been sentenced. By 30 November, with little more than a week until his release, Dougal had become the model of sanity. Donaldson again:

> Quite rational and seems in every way better mentally. Well behaved and quiet. Takes an intelligent interest in his surroundings. In good bodily health.

And so, on Tuesday 8 December 1896, Dougal was released, *mens sana in corpore sano*, and returned to the land of the living, none the worse for his experience, largely unpunished for his crimes, and fundamentally unreformed.

⤜๑๑๑⤛

Some time after his release from Cane Hill, Dougal was heard to say that, 'once you get into the asylum, you can keep there by breaking a plate or two occasionally'.

CHAPTER THREE

ON THE OUTSIDE again, with his affliction, his madness, officially gone, Dougal set about demonstrating that it had truly been there in the first place. His pension had been withdrawn by the Commissioners of Chelsea Hospital upon his conviction, and Dougal, jobless and otherwise penniless, planned to petition for its restoration on the grounds that he had, at the time of his offence, been unconscious of the nature and quality of his actions. As if to suggest his penury – or his baroque relationship with sane norms – he inscribed his argument 'on a piece of grocer's wrapping paper'.[161] The text stood alongside a 'rough woodcut of a Chinaman and a legend to the effect that T. Patey, grocer, sells the best sugar and tea'.[162]

'We, the undersigned,' Dougal's petition begins, his clerkly formality returning, apparently, automatically to him in his moment of need; and he maintains a similarly official tone through a snapshotted, rather one-sided recollection of his military career, which was, he says, full of 'extra zeal' and 'excellent work', and a similarly slanted version of his civilian life after his discharge ('*vide* testimonial', he writes, with reference to the halcyon days aboard the *Mercury*). His illness, if that is what it was, is described with, perhaps, a little added emphasis here and there: his suicide attempt, he believes, was a 'very determined' one, which it was not; he states that he was 'under treatment' at Cane Hill until 8 December 1896, although he had been pronounced sane nearly three months before, and the asylum was quite prepared to have him discharged without further treatment at that time. Would a sane man have risked his pension for the sake of a few forged cheques? Dougal thinks not, and hopes that others will agree:

Your memorialists therefore suggest that the mental aberration from which he afterwards suffered had already shown itself, and therefore they think that he was certainly not responsible for his actions at the time the forgery is supposed to have taken place ...[163]

The petition then ends in more obsequiousness and feigned humility, emphasising Dougal's straitened financial position, and, of course, 'his previous thirty years' uninterrupted good character'.[164] But the dissimulation and the lies ultimately compromised the plan, never allowing it to develop into something with which the Commissioners could be troubled. Dougal abandoned the petition before the grocer's paper had attracted a single signature. No 'memorialists' were, apparently, to be found; Dougal's pension was lost forever.[165]

⤷◈⤶

Thomas Patey, the grocer on whose wrapping paper Dougal wrote his petition, was a widower with a shop on St Philip's Road in Battersea. This reflected the fact that some form of salvation, in the usual figure of Harry, had indeed emerged – Dougal may, indeed, have gone from Cane Hill to stay with his brother in Wandsworth. Sarah – whose whereabouts during the year of her husband's incarceration are obscure – remembered that Harry felt that he could 'start him [Dougal] in the world again'.[166] Dougal, for his part, may have been stripped of his army pension, but he had no intention of going without money.

Harry offered Dougal a supervisor's position at Biggin Hill, where he was still developing a suburb of his own. The former incumbent, Jesse Terry, had been sequestered to work on another of Harry's interests at Worthing, and Harry probably knew that a position of relative seniority would resonate with Dougal's supercilious thinking about the quality of his work in the Royal Engineers. In the early part of 1897, together with Sarah, Dougal moved into a 'small cottage at Biggin Hill facing the Village Green'. It is not clear whether Olive was with them or not. If not, she was probably in Dublin, being cared for by her grandmother.

Dougal's level of remuneration was a matter of some discussion among the local community. It was 'generally understood', according to Charles Wood, living and working at the Black Horse, that the new manager was on 30s per week. Terry, asked later what he thought about this, supposed that Dougal's job 'I daresay would be worth £2 per week' – and there is a hint of bitterness here. Sarah later recollected that Dougal's weekly wage had indeed been £2. At the time, however, it was apparently she who broadcast the figure of 30s; Elizabeth Whiting, licensee at the Black Horse, had heard her say so 'frequently'.

This boastful approach to her private financial affairs did not preclude Sarah from asking Elizabeth Whiting's mother Mary for money. Mary was a widow, in her mid-seventies, her husband George having passed away in 1892. Examined cynically, she was almost as defenceless as Miss Booty. Elizabeth's instinctively cautious supervision of her mother's dealings with Sarah ensured that the loans were never for more than what Elizabeth called 'small sums'.

On the other hand, the fact that Sarah, the leisurely beneficiary of her husband's apparently notable salary, would ask for money at all seemed rather strange. Another version of Sarah's self-publicising behaviour has her telling her neighbours that she and Dougal were in 'poor circumstances'. But although they were probably defaulting on a hire-purchase agreement by which they had acquired their furniture, neither Dougal nor Sarah were ever given to paying out money if they thought they could get away without doing so: it was hardly a measure of their penury. After the couple had been living at Biggin Hill for 'a few months', Charles Wood was approached at his pub by a man who wished to remove the Dougals' furniture. Wood allowed the man ('whose name I never knew') to hire his van, and engaged a neighbour named Batchelor to help shift the furniture. As they were doing this, Dougal returned home, and he seems to have settled his debt, for Wood and Batchelor were told to put the things back. Wood was paid half a sovereign for his trouble, about which he may have been rather pleased: Dougal's ready ability to settle his outstanding debts without very much notice probably speaks of the genuine liquidity of his financial situation. In 'poor circumstances', apparently, he was not.

Sarah's strange inconsistencies had begun to catch the attention of her neighbours. Terry, who had returned from Worthing and moved in next door to Dougal, remembered that Sarah and Dougal 'used to disagree. I think she used to drink.' In fact, according to Charles Wood, such quarrels were 'frequent'. The Black Horse was a short distance away from the Dougals' cottage – Wood himself had 'frequently interposed between them'. He had seen enough to know that Dougal would 'ill-use' Sarah, resorting to violence when their tempers flared: valiantly, Wood, in his twenties and, perhaps, already falling in love with Elizabeth Whiting's younger sister Maria, stood between them when he had to.

Elsewhere, Dougal was attracting his own enmity. Terry, who had been aware of Dougal in 1893, during his first stint at Biggin Hill, found that he did not enjoy living next door to his employer's immoderate brother. 'I did not like the man and had nothing to do with him,' he said, bluntly. Nor did Terry work under Dougal. Indeed, it was difficult to know what Dougal's duties were, especially once Terry had returned to Biggin Hill. As he had before – for example, at the *Mercury*, and at Nova Scotia – Dougal created a diverse role for himself, working 'at anything that was required to be done', according to Charles Wood, and 'sometimes with the horses'. This was a nebulous position for a manager to occupy, and perhaps one of the causes of the more-responsible Terry's resentment with regard to Dougal's level of pay. It also had the potential to become embarrassing to the patient Harry.

It was probably the noisy marital rows which hastened Dougal's departure from Biggin Hill, however. On one occasion, Charles Wood and Charles Smither, the village postmaster, decided that they had better both go round to the Dougals' cottage to intervene. 'I threatened to enter his cottage and bring him out,' recalled Wood, 'and he stated that if I did so he would shoot at us'. Wood looked into the house, perhaps through a window, or through a partially open door. 'I saw the gleam of a barrel of some weapon and we went away for a time,' he recalled.

꧁꧂

As he had at Northend, then, Dougal had arrived at a situation of stress which, it seems, only the exhibition of weapons could relieve. What could have happened?

On Sunday 3 October 1897, Dougal's eldest surviving daughter, Emily, had died at his house in Biggin Hill. She was eighteen years old at the time. Dougal registered her death the following Wednesday. He had been present at the death, he said.

It was all very odd. Emily, at eighteen, was hardly a candidate for serious illness in the way that little Herbert Bernard, for example, who had died in Northend House, had been. Nor was her cause of death – given on the death certificate simply as 'coma' – necessarily insightful. What had caused the coma? At this distance, it is probably impossible to say. But there remains the suspicion that the death certificate masks something darker. It is possible that Emily had, finally, decided to confront her father about her mother's death, the trauma of which she is unlikely to have forgotten, and the realities of which may have become unavoidable. Dougal may have taken what for him must have seemed to be the only way out of an uncomfortable line of questioning.

Poor Emily. The good folk of Biggin Hill, when they were asked for their recollections of Dougal, did not mention her death, which in itself seems strange, for Dougal would ordinarily have milked any such misfortune for whatever public sympathy it could give up. It is as if some secrecy had attached itself to the matter, although earlier incidents, such as Olive's birth in 1893, remained available to some individual memories.

Nor did Sarah recall Emily's death when she, later, described her life with Dougal. However, she remained confused – or deceptive – in her sequencing of events. 'He was as cruel to me as before,' she complained of her time at Biggin Hill, and, by her own description, in the January or February of 1898, she fled once more to her mother in Dublin. Again, there is no apparent recollection of this in the memories of her neighbours at Biggin Hill. Elizabeth Whiting, whose mother was still owed money by Sarah at the time of the Dougals' departure (and who therefore had a motive for following their movements) stated that 'they lived at Biggin Hill for 18 months or two years,' never mentioning an estrangement. In truth, a year and a half was the more accurate end of Elizabeth's estimate – other sources place Dougal elsewhere at the end of 1898. Sarah, perhaps coming closer to the mark, added that she returned from Ireland in March 1898, and took a cottage on Coombe Road, in Croydon, Surrey, with Olive.[167]

Dougal may have shuttled back and forth between Croydon and Biggin Hill over the ensuing months. When he travelled to work from Croydon (where he spent his weekends), he went by bicycle, a measure of his fitness, his visceral energies uncompromised as he hit fifty. But, if Sarah is to be believed, Dougal remained 'very immoral with women at Biggin Hill', and word of this may have reached Harry.[168] In the late summer of 1898,

according to Charles Wood, Dougal 'quarrelled with his brother
who was said to have given him £10 to get rid of him'. Even the
honourable Harry's tolerance had its limits. Dougal's behaviour
had once again ruined a fairly lucrative opportunity.

Opinions were split as to Dougal's financial circumstances
upon his dismissal. His £10 payoff was cursory, but the fact that
Dougal accepted it apparently without much argument suggests
that a degree of financial pressure had, perhaps, begun to build
up around him. He had probably been immune to rent at Biggin
Hill – Harry had apparently built the house in which Dougal
lived: the lease on the house at Croydon, though, clearly ate into
his wages. Jesse Terry recognised Dougal as a 'very careful man',
which was very likely a euphemistic gloss on its subject's ultra-
parsimonious habits, and thought that he had saved some money
from his generous wages; but Charles Wood thought that Dougal
was genuinely 'hard up when he left Biggin Hill', pointing out
that he had (unsuccessfully) sought employment with William
Blake, a farmer, and James McCaig, a breeder of racehorses, before
retreating from the area. Sarah, ignoring the evident fluidity in
her domestic arrangements, claimed that Dougal was giving her
15s per week during their 'split' – she at Coombe Road and he
at Biggin Hill – but it is hard to see this as a significant additional
expense. Still, she insisted, 'at this time I know he was poorly off
and had not a penny to help himself with'.

꧁꧂

It is the autumn of 1898, and Dougal has 'suddenly disappeared'.[169] To her neighbours, Sarah claims destitution – but they
are 'well-to-do', and they help her financially. Explaining her situation, she tells them that her husband, who had resided with her
in Coombe Road at least since he had lapsed into employment
at Biggin Hill, has 'gone off with a rich lady'.

꧁꧂

She was appalled by the very idea, but Camille Cecile Holland
was now sixty. She had been born on 4 February 1838, in
Chandernagore, in India.[170] At the time, this was a French colony,
although it had been intermittently won and lost in battles with
the British over the years; Camille's mother, Marie, was indeed
French, an offshoot of the Henrique family, and clearly the deci-

sive influence upon her strikingly Gallic appellation. Her father
William, however, was from Merseyside, a cotton merchant and
the ambitious scion of an established mercantile family. His
own father, also called William, had been a renowned grocer in
Georgian Liverpool, and the city itself boomed as transatlantic
trade moved through its gears. The cotton and sugar grown in
the humid, rural south of the United States of America were
moving eastwards in vast convoys, arriving at port in Liverpool,
and soon encountering new mass-production techniques in the
Lancastrian factories which grew up as a result of – and whose
output served to perpetuate – the Industrial Revolution. Once
an insignificant estuary settlement, Liverpool had expanded to
become a focus of Britain's global economy. The Hollands would
not be the only ones to make their fortune on the back of this
phenomenon.

India was, of course, the second front of the cotton merchant;
along with his brothers, Charles and Henry, William began to
forge a multinational interest in the lucrative trade, its reach
extending across vast oceans as the increasing potential of their
enterprise opened up new commercial vistas. Charles and Henry
went to New Orleans; Camille, for her part, may have been
schooled in Paris – or so it was said – reflecting not only her
heritage on her mother's side, but also the financial advantages
her father had accrued through his business. Her elder brother
George, who, less exotically, married in Kent in 1866, and resided
in middle-class Bermondsey in 1871, nonetheless followed his
father in the administration of Anglo-Indian business, working
for the East India Company.

By 1891, however, Camille had not married. Her maiden aunt,
Sarah Ann, a former schoolteacher, with whom Camille then
lived at 12 Kilburn Priory, in Hampstead, had provided a virtual
exemplar of the Victorian spinster's life, and other women in the
Holland line may have had similar difficulties in love. In Camille's
case, meanwhile, an unforgotten sadness apparently lurked in the
background – the details are lost to us, but, in her youth, she is
understood to have formed an attachment to a 'young Naval officer', perhaps 'the brother of a school friend of hers'.[171] Roy Harley
Lewis, and at least one contemporary journalist, suggest that the
young man was Camille's fiancé.[172] Whatever the truth, the story
went that the object of Camille's affections met his death, sud-

denly, by drowning in the sea.[173] Camille was heartbroken. Since then, she had devoted herself to his memory, constantly wearing his ring, which was retrieved when his body washed ashore, and had remained unmarried, and *virgo intacta*.

She is an enigma in the hands of those who, later, attempted to describe her. Devoutly religious, a member of the Catholic Apostolic Church and obediently passive in the face of what she perceived to be life's divine narrative, she nonetheless paid considerable attention to her appearance, and invariably, even in her later years, attracted what Jesse refers to doubtfully as 'the gentlemen'.[174] Like Miss Booty, Dougal's former prey, Camille felt that she could get away with claims of untruthful youthfulness, knocking off a decade here and there – white lies which scarcely concealed the yearnings within her.[175] Committed as she was to the memory of her mysterious, long-deceased lover, she remained compelled by the prospect of romance. In her poetry – in truth, dismal stuff, for an English Emily Dickinson she was not; despite the artistic potential inherent in her isolation and her loss, Miss Holland knew the art but not the mystery – she recorded, dully, the transience of joy, and hoped for a 'more permanent bliss' in the afterlife.[176] But despite all her protestations, Camille's urgent desire for terrestrial fulfilment manifestly outweighed her ostensible resignation to the perfections of the beyond. She belonged to that class of spinsters whose early romantic disappointments had made them vulnerable, even much later, to the gentlest male persuasion: the emotional cargo of the innocent, sadly thwarted young woman she had been remained the dominant force in her personality, decades on. Like Miss Havisham, she was cobwebbed, cocooned inside her dreams. Of course, again like Miss Havisham, the fact that she was financially buoyant put her at special risk. Jesse, who is sympathetic towards Miss Holland, and even speaks fairly kindly of her doggerel, nonetheless calls her *The Predestined Victim*.[177] Nothing could be more apposite.

Her aunt died in August 1893, and Miss Holland found herself comfortably off, deriving an inheritance of something between £6,000 and £7,000 from Sarah Ann's will.[178] This conferred certain freedoms upon Miss Holland, and she pursued a leisurely and peripatetic lifestyle untroubled by monetary worries. Already she had been through India and France; she had lived with her aunt in Hampstead; she had taught in Paddington, where she is visible in the 1881 census, a 'Professor of Music' at a girls' school. Now, she drifted from place to place, opening an account with the National Provincial Bank in Piccadilly while she was living at 58 Kenilworth Road, in Willesden, in May 1895; writing to her nephew Edmund from her lodgings at 4 Rue Espagnole, Place Van Eyck, in the Belgian city of Bruges, in November 1895, and mentioning that she intended to travel on to Brussels.[179] In May 1896, she wrote to a long-standing friend, Thomas Charles Cartwright, from 1 Guilford Street, off Russell Square in London's West End; then, in June, she wrote to him from Brighton.[180] In January 1897, she was living at 42 Cornwall Road in Bayswater: George Mold, a shoemaker whose shop on the Edgware Road Miss Holland had patronised since 1884, delivered a pair of boots to her at this address, and she continued to stay here until at least December 1897. Immediately prior to 17 June 1898, she was thought to have resided at Langham Place, just north of Regent Street, in London.

This nomadic existence may already have begun to pall, however. The lodging houses in which she stayed were phantasmagorical halls of mirrors, crammed full of financially comfortable, emotionally unfulfilled spinsters and creaking, gnarled bachelors. Miss Holland saw awful iterations of herself at every turn. She moved again, to 37 Elgin Crescent, in Notting Hill, to a house run by Florence Pollock, a young widow (although, perhaps predictably, not quite as young as she pretended to be). At, it seems, about the same time, Miss Holland 'advertised in some paper for a husband'.[181]

❧

It was a difficult summer for London Exhibitions (Limited), the proprietors of the Earls Court Exhibition. On Monday 18 July, a series of explosions had taken place in a specially erected storeroom at the venue, killing Edward Davis, who was sixty-eight years of age, and injuring several others.[182] At the inquest hearing, it was found that the contents of the storeroom on the fateful day had included large quantities of gunpowder and sodium, and the basic ingredients for creating colourful smoke displays: these were among the military-themed attractions of the Exhibition. Some of the sodium – but by no means all – had been stored under petroleum to prevent its reacting with moisture in the air. But the temperature that Monday had been 75 degrees in the shade, and the storeroom was airtight. When the petroleum vapour went up, sparked, it was thought, by some loose sodium, the gunpowder was bound to follow. The building, now burning furiously, was promptly soaked by the fire attendants, and the subsequent explosions were probably those of the unprotected sodium, reacting to the water.[183]

This, perhaps, was trouble enough for the company but, days later, on Friday 29 July, they were in court to hear the protests of one Mr Bolton, a photographer, who claimed that his work had been unlawfully appropriated. The case referred in particular to the advertising posters for the Exhibition, which boasted a lithographed image of a lion. Bolton had identified the image as, originally, one of his own – he even named the lion in question, which was called Prince, and drew attention to certain features which distinguished Prince from other lions. The posture which Prince had adopted in Bolton's original photograph, and which had been replicated on the poster to which Bolton objected, had, the plaintiff said, taken him three days to achieve. Alert with his camera at the very moment of Prince's inspiration, Bolton now found that his property had been plastered across the walls of the city, diminishing the value of his image. Mr Justice Mathew, adjudicating, found that the fault lay with the agency which had produced the poster, although he advised London Exhibitions (Limited) to be more careful in the future.[184]

Unseen, through the carnage and the red tape, strolled Miss Holland and, at her side, the man who had responded to her newspaper advertisement.

⋘☙⋙

Shortly after Miss Holland had moved into 37 Elgin Crescent, Miss Emma Wharton, one of the other residents, had repaired to the coast for her annual holiday.[185] This left Miss Wharton's dressmaker, Annie Whiting, aged about twenty, at a loose end. Miss Holland asked Annie to work for her, retaining her for 4s 6d a day. Before long, Annie had become Miss Holland's *confidante*, as well as her hired help.

Annie began to notice that Miss Holland was receiving telegrams. By the time Annie asked her about them, Miss Holland must have been at an acme of excitement, bursting to tell. They were from 'her sweetheart', she said, who was 'a widower with one son who was afflicted and unable to get his living'. Annie committed the details to memory. 'On one occasion she said the son was either 13 or 15 years of age and that she was very fond of him,' she remembered. Miss Holland regularly met her sweetheart at the Earls Court Exhibition, assignations which Annie deduced to have been arranged by telegram.

Then, between Friday 15 July and Friday 5 August, Miss Holland was away from Elgin Crescent altogether. The absence of the guests from the house, particularly in peak season, was little to be remarked upon, although Mrs Pollock, for the purpose of calculating Miss Holland's bill, recorded the dates in her day book. Annie, however, was suspicious, and, when Miss Holland returned, Annie persuaded her to tell her where she had been. Southend, Miss Holland said, with her sweetheart. They had stayed at the Royal Hotel. Annie cautioned Miss Holland to say nothing of her escapade to the other residents, 'or she would get a bad name'.

'Oh, his son was there with us,' replied Miss Holland. But the effectiveness of this dubious chaperone was inevitably limited. Miss Holland asked Annie to make her 'a nice dressing gown as she said when at Southend her sweetheart came into her bed-room and she was ashamed as she was wearing an old dressing jacket and an old nightdress'. So, they had been in each other's bedrooms – or at least, he had been in hers – and now Miss Holland, a committed Catholic, devoted to the memory of her chaste, youthful relationship with the deceased Naval officer, and described by Jesse as 'timid, precise' and, not least, 'elderly', had begun to wonder whether her nightwear was sexy enough.[186] Annie, thinking liberally about the matter, went ahead and provided Miss Holland with 'a new dressing gown and 3 or 4 new pink nightdresses'.[187]

Justifying her out-of-character behaviour, Miss Holland no doubt felt that her insistence on separate hotel rooms reflected her unimpaired moral integrity, but it is clear that she had, in her early sixties, embarked on a sexual relationship for the first time. This was a voyage into the unknown for which she was scarcely prepared. Another absence from the lodging-house was recorded by Mrs Pollock between Thursday 1 September and Friday 16 September – evidence of Miss Holland's whereabouts is lacking, but, within ten days of her return, she had been to visit her nephew Edmund, telling him that she intended to take a holiday in Brighton. Perhaps betraying an underlying anxiety about her serial flits with her sweetheart, she asked to take Edmund's daughter May with her. Edmund and his wife Esther refused her request.[188] Like Miss Holland's sweetheart's afflicted son, May, sickly herself, could not have been much use as an escort, even if she had been allowed to go.

Back at Elgin Crescent, Annie was the middleman in Miss Holland's still-secret liaison. She would, at Miss Holland's behest, stand by the window of her first-floor room, watching for Miss Holland's sweetheart to cycle up the road. Then she would inform Miss Holland, who would make it to the front door before her sweetheart had had a chance to knock.[189] Only with Annie would the true depths of Miss Holland's nervousness emerge: on one occasion, Miss Holland told her that she intended to take a house at Sydenham or Brighton – a story partly reflecting that she had told Edmund – and begged Annie to go with her, 'as she thought it would mean her death'. Annie's wisdom was being pressed into increasing action. 'I pooh-poohed this but she repeated it several times.'

'Why do you marry the man if you are afraid of him?' Annie asked her.

'I am sick of boarding houses,' said Miss Holland, 'and as I am getting old I want someone to look after me'.

But Annie 'again pressed her as to what she was afraid of'.

'I have been told,' replied Miss Holland, *sotto voce*, 'that I can have a baby up to the age of fifty-two.'

'You are too old, Miss Holland,' said Annie, straightforwardly.

'I am only forty-seven although they think downstairs I am only forty-five,' said Miss Holland.

Annie was unconvinced. 'I knew she was older,' she remembered. She was also aware that Miss Holland's 'menses had left off'. Miss Holland herself apparently had no appreciation of the significance of her menopause.

'I am afraid if I have a baby I shall be allowed to die slowly,' Miss Holland confessed. 'I shall have no one to care for me unless you come to live with me.'

But Miss Holland's unfitness for a sexual relationship was already obvious. Annie's superior understanding of the female anatomy and its processes, and her modern and liberal perspective on what was, by anyone's standards, a strange and rather undignified extra-marital fling, could only paper over the cracks. Annie saw that Miss Holland's anxieties had begun in the uncharacteristic choices her elderly charge had made. Who was this sweetheart who had mesmerised her so?

One afternoon a short while after this, with Annie in position by the window awaiting the sweetheart's anticipated visit, Miss Holland asked her to call upon her early the next morning. She was going to Brighton by the 10.20a.m. train, she told Annie, 'to take a house'.

The next morning, Annie called early, as she had said she would, and was surprised to find Miss Holland still in bed. 'You won't catch that train,' Annie said.

'I am not going,' replied Miss Holland. 'Miss Whiting, we have entirely parted. I have found out that he does not want me, only my money. What do you think! He wants me to withdraw all my money and let him invest it in his name, but I won't do it, so we have entirely parted.'

Miss Holland, as a woman of leisure, was hardly short of money, but she may have inherited something of her father's fiduciary sense all the same. When she was in Belgium in 1895, she had written to Edmund:

> Bruges is rather a primitive place, but there are such beautiful things in some of the shops & so cheap that one feels inclined to buy a whole heap and sell them again in London where they would fetch double the price, although perhaps the duty would be a disadvantage.[190]

To Annie, however, she seemed simply to have been 'very close with her money'.[191] The mysterious sweetheart had, Annie assumed, finally touched a nerve. And, for a 'short time', the lovers saw nothing of each other; but then there was a reconciliation, and, to Annie's dismay, the whole thing began once more, and with an added veil of mystery thrown over it. No longer did Miss Holland speak to Annie of her fears of childbirth – no longer did she ask her to join her in the dreamed-of-and-feared house at Sydenham or Brighton. Indeed, Annie was piqued to find that Miss Holland

no longer told her where she was going at all. Becoming more
and more concerned, Annie even accused Miss Holland of being
about to marry her sweetheart, firmly implying that to do so
would be a grave mistake, but Miss Holland 'did not reply'.

On Friday 4 November 1898, Miss Holland set off, at last, for
Brighton. She was away until the following Tuesday, according
to Mrs Pollock's notes, and, according to Jesse, on the Monday
of her trip she called on a house agent in the town.[192] Returning
to London, and now apparently divested of the qualms she had
once had about her sweetheart's inappropriate interest in her
bank account, Miss Holland seemed to have resolved to make
her relationship an increasingly public one. On two occasions,
both probably in the last week of November or the first week of
December, her sweetheart was invited into the house.[193] Once,
Annie saw the man; from the doorway of the drawing room, she
heard Miss Holland address him as 'Dougal'. To Mrs Pollock,
Miss Holland had described her paramour as 'the Captain', saying
his name was 'McDougal'. Mrs Pollock recalled him as a 'tall
military-looking man with a short trimmed beard and of rather
elderly appearance'.

Of course, Dougal would have been appalled by the suggestion
that he was elderly, but, in truth, he did what he could to prevent
Mrs Pollock seeing him too clearly. On his first visit, standing in
the hall at 37 Elgin Crescent, he turned his face from her view and
made no reply when Mrs Pollock asked him, 'For Miss Holland?'
Already annoyed by this, Mrs Pollock, when she saw him for the
second time a few days later, and he again turned his back on her,
decided to say something. Posterity has unfortunately failed to
record exactly what, but, shortly after this, Miss Holland mentioned to Annie that Mrs Pollock had been 'abrupt' with her
visitor, and that he was no longer allowed to visit her there.

In spite of Mrs Pollock's well-meant intervention, in spite of
Annie's sensible counsel, and in spite of her own serious misgivings, Miss Holland's time at Elgin Crescent was winding down.
She was increasingly firmly in Dougal's clutches. A lease on a furnished house – Parkmore, in the village of Hassocks, just outside
Brighton – was due to commence on 5 December, at a cost of 30s
a week.[194] On 3 December, she wrote to her nephew Edmund,
who had been looking after her dog, Jack. The letter, slightly disingenuous, slightly portentous, is worth quoting in detail:

37 Elgin Crescent,
Notting Hill, W.

3rd Decr. 1898

My dear Edmund,

I do hope that you are much better by now & that dear little May is feeling also better it must be nice to be with you again poor child I must see what she could fancy for Xmas do you think a large doll? I did so want to send her something but I have been so busy getting ready to go away to Brighton I was not at all well and I ran up there for a week & felt the air quite revived me. I want to take Jack along with me – could you get some one to bring him to Victoria Station ~~on Thursday next or~~ rather on Tuesday whichever day would be more convenient to catch the 2 p.m. train – he must be there before that time to allow for his ticket to be taken 1/6 and I would be pleased if he could be well washed and combed so as to look very nice. Of course dear Edmund I shall always try to be good to you, you may depend upon me for your kindness & attention I don't know how long I may be away for some time I think but I will write you when I'm settled. If you could manage to send Jackie on <u>Tuesday I would prefer it</u> as some one will take him for me. I shall be at the station about 2 p.m.

My fond love & to the children & Esther

Yours very affectly

C. Holland[195]

Further demands with regard to Jack followed in a postscript; Edmund sent his wife with Jack to Victoria Station on Tuesday 6 December 1898, where she handed him over to Miss Holland. Then, for Edmund, a dark silence descended. As he later remembered:

That is the last time any member of my family saw her. We knew nothing of her connection with Dougal.

⁂

Dougal's narrative was riddled with his usual lies. Although he had been debarred from drawing his army pension, this only reflected his behaviour since leaving the military: he was allowed to keep his medal for Long Service and Good Conduct, which had been awarded for his (still unquestioned) behaviour while he was actually serving. As he wandered around the Earls Court Exhibition, he must have seen veterans with rows of medals pinned across their chest, very likely men who had ventured out from the Chelsea Hospital for the military-styled entertainment on offer. But for Miss Holland, in her innocence, Dougal's single award, which he still wore, must have spoken volumes about his trustworthiness and integrity. Forever chained to the memory of a young man whose own military career must have been cut tragically short, the sudden interest which this stentorian, impressive character − a Captain, no less − had begun to take in her must have thrilled Miss Holland on levels to which she had little conscious access. This rendered her additionally vulnerable, and Dougal can hardly have been able to believe his luck.

The identity of the afflicted teenage chaperone − the 'widowed' Dougal's 'only' son − need not be sought too forcefully. Dougal had no son of the right age − no child of that age whom he recognised, at least − and the invention of the unfortunate boy was merely a symptom of Miss Holland's rapid loss of autonomy. One can almost hear Dougal's affected Irish lilt: 'It is to be regretted, Cecily dear, that those who have not found love are often envious of those who have. Of course, back in London, you cannot say that you spent these weeks alone with me, by the sea in Southend: the jealousy of the other residents would have its repercussions for you. No, I shall not ask you to do it, although one day, my love, we will be free of their prejudices. You may depend upon it ...' Cloying and sentimental though it may seem now, this was all inspirational stuff for an elderly woman whom life had passed by. The addition of the child to the mix simply muddied the waters: it was hardly the done thing to ask about the precise nature of an upstanding widower's son's affliction. The image of the unreal boy had been invented to arrest any potentially uncomfortable conversations before they had a chance to begin.

Secrecy and dissimulation were, naturally, the foundations upon which Dougal built his deceptions, the architecture of pretence. As Miss Booty had, Miss Holland participated in the ruses, one after the other, for a time disclosing her fears only to Annie, and then disclosing no more. Blinded by the sudden possibilities of contentment, and the loving relationship she had longed for, the risks she took became greater and greater. In the end, she even overcame her instinctive parsimony, committing to meeting the rent on Parkmore, although the cheques she made out – one in December 1898, and one in January 1899, were only for £6 each.[196] She made them out payable to Dougal, whose name, presumably, was on the lease, although he had already made it clear to Miss Holland that he had no money. There is no doubt that she was already masquerading as Mrs Dougal, a troubling affectation justified by further soothing words from her sweetheart. How desperately familiar it all was.

Back at Elgin Crescent, opinions were apparently split. Florence Pollock noted that Miss Holland had not only had 'a large quantity of new clothes made' shortly before her departure, but had 'left most of her old things behind'.[197] 'We formed the opinion,' she said, 'that she was going away to get married'. But some of the residents – particularly, apparently, the spidery old gentlemen whose senescence was doomed to be spent in the very boarding-house *ennui* to which Miss Holland had become averse – 'thought not'.[198] They, perhaps, sensed the illicit, erotic element in Miss Holland's sudden, intense relationship, and saw that marriage was hardly integral to any such dynamic. Annie Whiting, who knew more than Mrs Pollock, and more than the old men, took Miss Holland a nightdress on the day she was leaving, although she did not help her to pack. She asked Miss Holland to write to her, which Miss Holland promised to do, and Annie was saddened when 'she did not keep her promise'.[199]

❧

Life in Hassocks, a small village to the north of Brighton and separated from it by patchwork fields and rolling hills, stood in stark contrast to that of the Notting Hill boarding-house. In the darkness and chill of the Sussex winter, Dougal and Miss Holland seemed to make a point of avoiding society, even though their flight from London had granted them an anonymity which would have withstood all but the most determined of examinations. Only Annie Waddington, an eighteen-year-old servant of another couple, Mr and Mrs Crone, who were either the previous occupants of the premises, or who simultaneously occupied another part of it, seemed later to remember them.[200]

But Dougal had no intention of renting long-term. Cheques for £6 – sums which he may or may not have paid on to the letting agent, as he was supposed to – were small beer: Miss Holland was worth a thousand times as much. Before the end of 1898, Dougal had been in contact with Lysaght John Rutter, a land agent of Messrs Rutter and Rutter, of 10 Norfolk Street, off the Strand, in London, expressing an interest in purchasing 'a house and some land in the country'.[201]

Rutter's first suggestion was a property in Basildon, Essex. He went with Dougal to view the house, but Dougal was unimpressed. It was not large enough, he thought. He was about to marry a lady of 'considerable means', he said, and he 'did not think she would like the house'. Undeterred, Rutter equipped Dougal with the details of several other properties, and one caught Dougal's eye. Having inspected it, discussed the transaction with Rutter several times, and exchanged copious correspondence, Dougal offered to buy the hundred-odd acres of Coldhams Farm, near Clavering in Essex.[202]

This property had been put up for its sale by its owner, William Savill, earlier in 1898. On 13 December, Savill died, slightly complicating the sale, since there was now a probate consideration; but, shortly after the turn of the year, Rutter drew up a contract of sale, naming Dougal as the purchaser.[203] Dougal had requested that this be done, although he had admitted to Rutter that he had no money himself. Miss Holland, he said, would be providing the necessary capital.

The contract was sent down to Hassocks on 5 January 1899; within a week, it had been returned to Rutter's office, signed, with an accompanying letter, and a cheque for £200, made out by Miss Holland, as a deposit. All this seemed perfectly normal, but, shortly afterwards, on or about 12 or 13 January, Miss Holland arrived, alone, in the Norfolk Street offices, demanding to see the land agent. For the second time in a couple of months, Dougal's conduct had offended her sense of financial propriety.

Miss Holland asked Rutter to draw up a new contract of sale in her name. Since she was bankrolling the purchase – it was her name on the deposit cheque – she would like her name on the agreement. Rutter complied, amending the terms of the contract in Miss Holland's presence, and producing a new copy which she returned to the office to sign on 19 January.[204] The previous contract Rutter tore up.[205] Dougal must have been dismayed: he too turned up at Rutter's door, shortly after Miss Holland had had the contract redrawn, eager to have the conveyance, at least, drawn up in his name. But this was a job for the solicitors, Ingram, Harrison and Ingram of 67 Lincoln's Inn Fields, and, as it turned out, they had their own problems: the conveyance would not be completed for some months to come.[206]

This new display of autonomous thinking on Miss Holland's part was another warning shot for Dougal. One commentator writing later – Leonard Gribble – perceived a pattern of disputes that had sprung up between the pair in their isolation at Parkmore: 'a sequence of squally storms that were little more than lovers' tiffs'.[207] The evidence for this is lacking, and, in fact, Miss Holland is known to have been largely compliant in many things; but even Dougal must have spotted that she was unbending where money was concerned. He trod a fine line, ensuring that her gaze remained fixed on the romantic fulfilments of the future she had conceptualised, attempting to keep his furtive financial machinations out of her peripheral vision.

On 26 January, Dougal and Miss Holland left Hassocks, and travelled to Saffron Walden in Essex, a short distance away from Coldhams Farm.[208] On the recommendation of Ruth Parnwell, the sister of William Savill's widow and joint executrix, they applied for and took rooms at 4 Market Row. Their landlady was Henrietta Wisken, a widow in her late forties, and their new accommodation charming, if modest. They had only a bedroom and a sitting room to themselves, and the house itself – 'it juts into a sort of little square, over which its old-fashioned bow window, cut into little square panes, looks out' – possessed an antiqued, cloistered ambience.[209] Dougal and Miss Holland, as they had at Parkmore, affected to be married, although, on their first night in the place, Dougal came downstairs to ask Mrs Wisken to pass on any mail which arrived addressed to a Miss Holland. This, he reassured her, would be 'all right'.[210] The very next day, a letter addressed in this way did indeed arrive: Mrs Wisken pushed it under the door to the couple's bedroom.

William Savill, in his old age, appeared to have let Coldhams Farm run to seed, and Dougal, now that he had arrived in Essex, oversaw the operation to return it to something of its former glories, and to make it liveable.[211] He would journey there on his bicycle, returning to Saffron Walden in gushing, extrovert displays of affection for the beloved 'wife' he had left alone all day, 'ringing his bell at the other end of Market Row' to announce his homecoming.[212] In the nearby offices of land agent Benjamin Thurgood, meanwhile, the machinery of the sale of the property continued to jam.[213] Thurgood was acting as a valuer for Dougal, who had perhaps persuaded Miss Holland to allow him to seek a second assessment to compete with Rutter's. Covering the transaction, Miss Holland had asked her stockbrokers, Messrs W.H. Hart & Co., of Old Broad Street, to dispose of a £515 bond in de Beer's diamond mines, and forty shares in the Liverpool Bank, which realised £1,587 18s 0d.

The delay to the sale, and a shared affection for little Jack, who had accompanied his mistress north from Sussex, brought Miss Holland and Mrs Wisken closer together. At home together through the ensuing weeks, Mrs Wisken had the opportunity to study her new tenant quite closely, recalling her – 'Since a child I have been known to have a remarkably good memory' – as a small woman 'about 5 feet 2 or 3 inches in height', with 'a good figure for an aged person'.[214] She had 'golden hair, grey or blue eyes, powdered face'. But, despite the comprehensive overhaul of her nightwear at Elgin Crescent, she had still been unable to transfer her presentable daytime appearance to the sexually charged atmosphere of the bedchamber: 'the lady I knew as Mrs Dougal when dressed looked about fifty years of age, but when in bed ten or fifteen years older,' Mrs Wisken remembered. This aside, there was much which recommended Miss Holland to Mrs Wisken – her 'very small feet' (she wore size 2½ boots), her 'very small hands', and her 'very nice set of teeth' all spoke of a daintiness and understated grace befitting of an educated woman of her class. She was, all in all, 'a very nice lady'.[215]

Mrs Wisken was similarly impressed by Dougal's assiduous devotion to his 'wife'. He would take her breakfast in bed, on a tray, and, in the evenings, when he returned home from Coldhams Farm in what could only be assumed to be delirious paroxysms of love, the couple would 'exchange an affectionate kiss', and walk together into the sitting room, his arm around her.[216] Dougal must have been on especially fine form, since even

Mrs Wisken considered him pleasant company, with a 'friendly manner', and a charming habit of chatting away to her canary.[217] The only cloud on the horizon seemed to be Dougal's occasional habit of staying away overnight in London, detained, he said, by business.[218] This annoyed Miss Holland, who muttered darkly, 'I don't believe he need stay up at all; he could have come back if he'd wanted to'.

Things went along in this generally jolly fashion until it came time for the Dougals to leave, in April 1899. Mrs Wisken, when she came to look back nostalgically, from a distance of some years, at her brief acquaintance with the couple, could afford to lay it on rather thickly. Miss Holland – Mrs Dougal, as she knew her – was 'one of the sweetest, kindest, and gentlest of women', and Dougal 'a big, fine man, five feet ten and a half inches high and weighing sixteen stone' and 'as pleasant as you like'.[219] She recalled Dougal bringing home two sizable goose eggs, which he was carrying in his coat pocket, and for which he had paid a crown each, from which he hoped to start a flock; she recalled Camille sharing with her the story of the tragic Naval officer of her youth, and allowing her to try on the dead man's amethyst ring, which she wore next to her 'wedding ring'. Miss Holland would call her 'Mother, dear', although Mrs Wisken was actually the younger by some years, and would speak dreamily of taking her to Coldhams Farm as a housekeeper.[220]

Of course, retrospectively, the clues were there. The farmhouse to which the Dougals were to move was 'a very quaint old place, dating from the time of Elizabeth, and as lonely a building as you will come across in a day's walk,' Mrs Wisken said. There was a hint of paganism about this, of the occult and the chthonic, of the natural rhythms of the earth and the sun, of Essex as it was once, a dark, godless kingdom of its own. The very building was eccentric, 'full of all sorts of odd corners and nooks and queer rooms and recesses', and cluttered with bizarre, esoteric objects, 'amongst them a grinning skull, which was used as a candlestick'. In truth, there was no such thing, at least until Dougal moved in, and brought with him the skull he had picked up in the Isle of Wight in 1888.[221] But this fact can hardly have delayed the progression of Mrs Wisken's gothic recollections. A mythology accreted around the old farm, 'many mysteries and romances', as she put it, without naming any.[222] Suddenly, the simple optimism of this apparently devoted couple, and their excitement as they prepared to move into their splendid new home, dripped with portentous irony.

ത്ര

But all this was invisible at the time. On the day Miss Holland left Saffron Walden, Thursday 27 April 1899, the weather was gloomy, but no colder or more windswept than was typical in that part of the country at that time of year.[223] Mrs Wisken enveloped Miss Holland in a fur cape, and Miss Holland promised to visit her 'in a fortnight or three weeks'.[224] Henry Pilgrim, a labourer who had worked for Savill, and who had been assisting Dougal in readying the farmhouse for habitation, pulled on the reins of the horse, Prince, and Miss Holland, in the trap behind, set off for her new home.[225] Seven miles of flat, cheerless countryside later, she saw Dougal standing at the gate of what he now called Moat House Farm; he assisted her as she climbed out of the trap, and, together, they went into the house.

CHAPTER FOUR

MRS WISKEN'S PANDEMONIUM of East-England gothic may have been a trifle overcooked, but the Moat House, as it was now called, *was* a forbidding, remote property. It stood steepling over the unremarkable, even land around it. On the ground floor, a pair of bay windows bookended the front door; a row of three sash windows was set into the white exterior walls of the first floor, and three more windows looked out from the tiled roof above this. Jesse found that it evoked something of the Brontës in its impassive symmetry and its solitude; an alternative view was that it more closely resembled 'a product of Poe's diseased imagination'.[226] Its twelve rooms may have suggested space to Miss Holland, who was an ardent collector of trinkets; they may have suggested isolation and privacy to Dougal.[227] Before the house, there was a lawn, and, surrounding it on all sides, the moat, perhaps a dozen yards wide, in some places more, after which Dougal had renamed the farm.[228] Around the edges of the moat, tall, twisted trees – overgrown, the legacy of William Savill's previous tenure – writhed in an awful 'ecstasy of contortion'.[229] And then, outside this, there was another wooded island, in an offshoot of the moat, and acres of pasture, vast fields, interrupted only by a pond, a drainage ditch which ran from it, and by a track which led to the nearest road, running roughly south and west to Clavering and roughly north and east to Newport. Here and there, there were farm buildings – barns, cow sheds, and so on. Prince was stabled near the little bridge at the front of the house; and, for his owners, this bridge was the only means of crossing the dark, cold moat to the house, the last ligature of contact with the world beyond the water.

Dougal had spent days, and probably nights, at the house over the previous months, but there remained much to do to make the place habitable. Miss Holland's furniture had been taken out of storage in London – Old Pilgrim, as he was universally known, had helped Dougal unload the delivery van, noting the arrival, among other items, of a black grand piano, a sideboard, a whatnot (a set of display shelves), a suite of dining room furniture and an Arabian bedstead.[230] Pilgrim and Dougal set up the piano in the dining room. Dougal mentioned, in his usual casual manner, that it had cost £100, but it is likely that he had never seen it before, and certain that he had not paid for it.

With Miss Holland's arrival came Naomi Reed, a widow in her mid-fifties living in Hill Green, in Clavering, and her near-neighbour Emma Burgess, the thirteen-year-old daughter of an agricultural labourer named Charles Burgess. They were detailed to assist in unpacking the boxes and arranging the furniture, and, for two days, the Moat House seems to have been a hive of industry as Miss Holland shaped her domestic vision within the imposing walls of her new domicile.

Outside, Dougal and Old Pilgrim had begun to gaze into the drainage ditch which, with the water table in the locality being particularly high, kept the farmyard dry. Dougal expressed his intention to have the ditch filled in.

'Dougal was a stranger,' Old Pilgrim said, later. The new owner of the Moat House Farm – which soon came to be known, more simply, as the Moat Farm – could not have appreciated the secrets of the drains and culverts, ditches and channels of the property in the way that Pilgrim did. Pilgrim pointed out that filling in the ditch would flood the farmyard.

'I shall have another drain made across the road,' said Dougal, 'through the cart shed, into the ditch down by the side of the field. Where can I get the rubbish to fill in the ditch?'

Old Pilgrim told him that there was rubbish in the lane past the house. Dougal instructed Pilgrim to start work on this project 'at once', and Pilgrim did so, although, over the next few weeks, he would return to the task only from time to time. Sometimes, looking up from his toils, Miss Holland – 'Mrs Dougal' to Pilgrim, of course – would be seen strolling around in the fields near the house. Pilgrim's other duties included taking the eggs and water into the house, and, when he went there, he would speak to 'Mrs Dougal'. He seems to have struck up a polite but passing acquaintance with her, talking to her 'daily', by his own account.

Naomi Reed and Emma Burgess were released on or about Saturday 29 April. Dougal and Miss Holland had advertised for a full-time servant, and one Lydia Faithful had responded. Lydia's background is scarcely elucidated by the fleeting impressions she made on the historical record. She had been born in 1866 in Bromsgrove, in Worcestershire, to James and Maria Faithful, but, by 1891, she was a patient at the Queen's Hospital in Birmingham. Plainly, there was something very badly the matter with her, for she was in the General Hospital, a short distance away, in 1901, and her recollections of her time at the Moat House are mediated, quite oddly, through the voices of others – eventually, Lydia's personal memories cloud over, and the detached first-person plural of the Victorian official replaces them.[231] Her position at the Moat House seems to have been arranged as part of a rehabilitation programme, for whatever illness she had. A fragile character, she could hardly have been unluckier in her choice of destination.

The pretence which tied Miss Holland to Dougal was evolving as their deceitful narrative span on. Lydia arrived at Saffron Walden Station on 30 April to be met by Miss Holland and, presumably, Old Pilgrim in the trap.[232] The letters of introduction which had been sent to Lydia named the elderly lady as Mrs McDougal. Lydia climbed into the carriage with Mrs McDougal, but she became alarmed when Pilgrim steered out of Saffron Walden. She had expected to be engaged at a house in the small town, but Mrs McDougal told her that, since Lydia's arrangements had been made, 'McDougal [had] concluded to take the farm'. When the trap arrived at the Moat House, Dougal took Lydia's luggage. Mrs McDougal introduced him as her husband.

Lydia was 'very down at finding herself in such a lonely place', and, looking around the farmhouse, she discovered that many of her employers' boxes remained unopened. All was inchoate, in flux, and the place itself so desperately isolated. Initially, Lydia took Mr McDougal to be a carpenter, but later Mrs McDougal told her that he was an engineer. Letters arrived, addressed to Miss Holland, and Lydia realised that her employers were unmarried. The sense of disorientation must have been almost unendurable.

Dougal was an early riser, finding his way downstairs at about five in the morning to make the fire and get breakfast. In contrast,

Lydia remembered, Miss Holland would not come downstairs until eleven. This left several vacant hours in which Lydia, also up early, would be alone with her strange new master. On the morning of 1 May 1899, Dougal found Lydia going about her duties somewhere in the house, and 'attempted to assault her'. Even in his fifties, Dougal's libido refused to release him from its stranglehold.

Lydia fought him off, and complained to Miss Holland later that day, finding Dougal's conduct 'dreadful'. Miss Holland, however, who was dramatically out of her depth, and hardly in a position of moral authority since she had abandoned her years of virginity to Dougal and conspired with him in creating their collage of lies, 'made light of it'. Unable to summon the wherewithal to actually defend Lydia against Dougal's arrant misbehaviour, she instead planned regular strolls in the grounds, taking Lydia with her and making 'more of a friend of her than a servant'. Lydia remembered Miss Holland as 'kind and good', even though she could provide no real protection against Dougal's urgent desires.

That same evening, Dougal made a second attempt to 'seduce' Lydia. Her rejection of him had taught him nothing. This time, he went into her bedroom after she had retired for the night, and 'used her shamefully'. Again she fought him off, but Dougal, frustrated that his approaches were not meeting with willing reciprocation, seems to have been more forceful than he had been before. Later on, when a doctor examined her, Lydia was found to have been 'greatly' bruised in the encounter; but, small mercy, 'she did not allow him' – the savage Dougal – 'to get advantage of her'.

Things did not become calmer. At some point in the next couple of days, Dougal 'threatened to throw her [Lydia] into the moat', telling her that no-one would be able to find her, since all her arrangements had been for a position at Saffron Walden. The frightened Lydia, however, pencilled a note to a friend, asking to be sent some money, and this soon arrived, in the form of a postal order. On Friday 5 May, on a trip into Clavering with Miss Holland, Lydia cashed the postal order; the next day, she crossed the moat, returned to Saffron Walden Railway Station, and left Essex.

Back at the hospital after her week-long ordeal, Lydia's bruises were examined, and communication made with the Vigilance

Society, in London. What sort of operation were the McDougals running? There certainly seemed to have been a breach of trust, not only between Lydia and her erstwhile employers, but between the employers, or their agents, and the well-intentioned officials overseeing Lydia's mysterious, almost covert reintroduction to society. Lydia herself was, obviously, a vulnerable woman whose narrow escape may well have saved her from something much worse. The information and misinformation of Moat House Farm circled around her head, such that she was able to recall it years later – the idea that the bizarre couple had met on a cruise (false); the idea that they were to take in paying guests in the summer (probably false); the idea that Mrs McDougal, or Miss Holland, was paying for the farm (true, as Lydia had been there when a gentleman, perhaps Savill's son and executor, had arrived to discuss the agreement on the property). To the disappointment of the hospital authorities, however, the Vigilance Society did not investigate the Moat House or its strange occupants.

Miss Holland had 'seemed very unhappy' when Lydia told her of her decision to leave. Ineffectual and spineless though she may have been, she had depended on Lydia for her company, as much as for her assistance around the house. The prospect of living alone with Dougal, in that house, in the vast emptiness of the Essex countryside, must have terrified Miss Holland. By Tuesday 9 May, through an advertisement placed with Ingold's Registry Office in Bishop's Stortford, another servant had been engaged – Florence Havies.[233]

❧❧❧

Florence was a local girl, nineteen years of age, and until 9 May she had been in service at the Nonconformist School in Bishop's Stortford. At the end of the previous month, her parents had moved from Rye Street in Bishop's Stortford to 18 Swanfield Road, in Waltham Cross; as her time at the school came to its end, and with her new appointment arranged, Florence went to stay with her parents there. On Saturday 13 May, she travelled to the Moat Farm.

Like Lydia Faithful, Florence had been led to believe that her new employer was a married woman. Dispensing with the Scottish affectation, Miss Holland again called herself 'Mrs Dougal'. She and her husband, Florence recalled, slept in a first-floor bedroom at the front of the house: Florence spent her first night in the house in another first-floor room, at the back.[234]

In the morning, Florence rose at six in order to begin her work. She went down to the scullery, and there, in a scene which seems unsettlingly familiar, Dougal pounced. 'Mr Dougal came quite unawares, clutched me round the waist and kissed me,' Florence recalled. 'I objected' – vociferously, Jesse thinks – 'and complained to Miss Holland'. Florence was astonished by the audacity of this man – the master of the house in which she was to act as the general servant – whose acquaintance she had made less than twenty-four hours before. She told Miss Holland that she intended to leave the farm, but, for the time being, and to Miss Holland's undoubted relief, she stayed.[235]

Dougal, accelerating towards total behavioural abandon, nonetheless contained his ardour for a couple of days. Relations between him and Miss Holland cannot have been cheerful – Miss Holland remained impotent, rendered immobile in the moral no-man's-land which lay between the undoubted honesty of her servant and the nonchalance of her *faux*-husband. Then, on the evening of Tuesday 16 May, Dougal enacted the predictable second part of his strategy for deriving sexual satisfaction from the domestic staff. Miss Holland, if only thinking about the issue had not been so painful, may have guessed what was going to happen.

Both Miss Holland and Florence retired to bed at about nine o'clock, leaving Dougal downstairs. Ten minutes later, Florence heard a whisper at her bedroom door.[236]

'Florence!'

Florence froze. It was Dougal's voice. She did not reply.

'Florence!'

Again, she did not reply.

'Florence!'

'What do you want?' Florence cried, and she screamed for Miss Holland. Dougal, from the other side of the door, grabbed the handle. The door opened outwards, towards him, but Florence had sensibly bolted it from the inside. Florence pulled the door from her side as Dougal attempted to tear it open. 'The bolt,' Florence remembered, 'was nearly wrenched off'.

In the best tradition of Victorian melodrama, Florence's terri-fied exertions ended in a swoon. Florence recollected seeing Miss

Holland, roused from her bedroom, before she lost consciousness, 'and nothing after'. Dougal had probably broken the door down, but, with Miss Holland now awake and coming to Florence's aid, he had had no time to gorge his appetite on the poor young woman he had so terrified. Perhaps simulating concern for Florence's health, he went downstairs to fetch some whisky – his evening drink of choice, which he had been observed to take in moderation while he and Miss Holland had stayed with Mrs Wisken – and used it to revive the stricken girl.[237] When she returned to consciousness, however, Dougal had gone away, and Miss Holland was alone with her.[238]

'I made a complaint to Miss Holland,' Florence recalled, but the cause of her distress must have been all too obvious anyway. The two women went together to the bedroom which Dougal and Miss Holland shared, there to confront the beast. Dougal was lying on the bed, affecting a peaceful, unconcerned slumber.[239] 'It's no use pretending to be asleep,' began Miss Holland – but it is likely that her wellspring of upbraiding remarks ran dry at this point – how *does* one go about resolving the problem of one's pseudo-husband serially forcing himself on the servants? – and Miss Holland and Florence retired quietly to the spare room, where they spent the night sleeping, for safety, in the same bed. Again Florence told Miss Holland that she wanted to leave, but she remembered that she 'yielded to pressure from Miss Holland' and 'agreed to stay on'.[240] Through the following day, a Wednesday, Miss Holland cried very much; Florence spent the day with her, and, at night, they again went together to the spare room.[241]

By Thursday 18 May, Dougal is known to have been going about his business as if nothing had happened. He went, probably with a numbed Miss Holland, into nearby Quendon and opened an account with a grocer named Thomas Mumford.[242] Clearly, he could see no circumstances in which his conduct, regardless of how brutal it became, would prompt the emotionally denuded Miss Holland to ask him to leave the house – *her* house. In the meantime, a grocery account seemed like the thing to have.

Florence and the marginalised Miss Holland went on occupying the spare room. However emptily, Miss Holland had promised Florence that her terrible mistreatment 'should not occur again', and Florence still found herself torn between a nascent loyalty to her unhappy mistress and her natural instinct to flee to her parents.[243]

❦

Friday 19 May 1899 dawned, and the day apparently passed quietly. There may have been a thaw in the stand-off between Dougal and Miss Holland, however, for, at about 6.30p.m., Miss Holland found Florence in the kitchen, and asked, 'Do you mind my going into the town to do a little shopping?'[244]

'No, not as long as Mr Dougal goes with you,' replied Florence.

'Yes,' said Miss Holland. 'He is going to drive me.' She would be gone no more than an hour or so, she said.

Miss Holland had already dressed to go out, wearing a distinctive costume which Lydia Faithful had also seen her in. This consisted of 'a very dark navy blue dress, almost black', in Lydia's words, and, perhaps a little tastelessly, a white sailor hat and a lace 'fall' at the throat.[245] The skirt, which had a matching jacket, had been dyed and relined by Annie Whiting while Miss Holland was at Elgin Crescent.[246]

Florence saw Prince and the trap standing on the other side of the bridge over the moat, and Miss Holland, from the front step, called back into the house as she left, 'Goodbye, Florrie – I shan't be long'.[247] And then, perhaps thankful for some time without her overbearing employers, Florence saw Miss Holland and Dougal drive away.[248]

❦

The success of Dougal's enterprise relied, partly, on his disconcerting propensity for intercepting the mail. Certainly, this had attracted Florence's attention – 'Mr Dougal used to go out and meet the postman, and he returned with the letters about eight o'clock, as a rule'.[249] Under the sweep of this surveillance, the fact that Lydia had got her pencil-written letter out to her friend, and had actually received the postal order in return, seems remarkable. Two letters which had arrived for Miss Holland from her nephew Edmund had met with gruff, uncharacteristic responses. The second of these, announcing the sad death of May, Miss Holland's favourite great-niece, elicited nothing more than 'a short sympathetic letter but cold compared with the past correspondence between us', in Edmund's words.[250] He expected her 'to send a wreath or to attend the funeral but she did neither'. A third letter, 'in April or May', got no response at all, and, apparently concerned lest his continued attempts to contact his aunt should begin to look like a surreptitious plan to win her favours, enhancing his eventual inheritance in her will, Edmund, at length, gave in. 'I thought that I should probably hear from her again when she wanted me,' he reasoned. This display of *politesse* may have left Miss Holland wondering why her nephew no longer showed any interest in her: there is little doubt that the replies which Edmund *did* receive were secretly forged by Dougal, who was purposefully widening the gap between Miss Holland and the society in which she once lived.

With Miss Holland and Dougal out of the house, Florence had little to do but consider the fate of her *own* letter. Despite her reluctant promises to Miss Holland, Florence had that day written to her mother in Waltham Cross, describing Dougal's immoderate behaviour and her own growing unhappiness.[251] But could Dougal have seized it – or perhaps he would seize the reply, if there was one? Thoughts like these can drift and thicken to fill the empty time. Already, an hour had elapsed since Miss Holland had left the house, and there was no sign of her return.

While at the Moat Farm, Dougal had received a letter from Sarah, his wife, saying that she had become unwell.[252] He had written to her, before this, with his new, remote address, and, supposedly, a cock-and-bull story about managing an estate for an old lady; now, he travelled to Croydon to see Sarah, and, she recalled, 'said I was looking very ill and suggested I should take a Cottage near him in the Country, and arranged with me to go and stay in a Village for a day or two'. She went on:

> I was to go on Bank Holiday 22nd May 1899. He said I could not stay at the house as the lady he was managing the estate for was there herself. ... I suspected he was co-habiting with a woman at this time. He had not told me her name.

Neither Lydia nor Florence could recollect Dougal's excursion to Coombe Road, but it perhaps accounts for one of the quieter days in the house through this period. And, in fact, Dougal went out again, probably on Tuesday 16 May, driving Prince into Stansted Mountfitchet.[253] He noticed a 'To Let' card in the

window of 4 Lower Street, and, finding that the house was being
let by one Daniel Robinson, a builder whose premises were just
a little further along the same road, Dougal promptly made his
inquiries. The rent, Robinson's clerk Sidney Lancet Butler told
him, was 6*s* per week.[254] Butler took Dougal on as a tenant without a reference; the tenancy was agreed to begin on 22 May.

∽ᴑᴑᴑᴖ

Two hours had now elapsed since Miss Holland and Dougal had
left the house, and Florence was busying herself in the kitchen.[255]
Dougal entered. He was alone.

'Where's the mistress?' asked Florence.

'Gone to London,' said Dougal.[256]

'What! Gone to London and left me here all alone?'[257]

'Yes,' said Dougal, quite unaffectedly. 'Never mind, she is
coming back in a little while. I am going to meet her.'[258]

Dougal muttered something about going out to feed the horse,
and left the house. He returned again at about nine, stayed for
about ten minutes, and then left again saying that he was going to
meet Miss Holland; Florence assumed that he was off to Newport
Station, although she did not hear him drive away. He was back,
alone, at twenty to ten.[259]

'No, she has not come,' he explained to Florence. 'I suppose she
will come by that train something after ten o'clock.'

Again he waited in the house, apparently aimlessly, for a short
period, and with Florence's nerves worsening all the while. Then
he left, again with the purported goal of collecting Miss Holland
from the station. Shortly after ten o'clock, he again returned
alone.

'No, she has not come,' he announced. 'I suppose she will come
on the twelve o'clock train. That is the one I expected her on.'[260]

Once more, Dougal went out. Once more, he returned without Miss Holland. By now, it was a quarter to one on the morning
of 20 May.

'No, the mistress hasn't come,' he said. 'You had better go to
bed.'

Florence scurried upstairs to the spare room, content just to
break the strange choreography of Dougal's coming and goings,
'and stayed there all night without undressing'. Nor did she sleep,
preferring to sit by the window, perhaps so that she could try to

escape through it should Dougal, in one of his fits of lust, break down the door.[261]

⁂

At half past six in the morning, Dougal knocked on Florence's door to wake her.[262] Not asleep, and unrested, Florence rose anyway, and at seven o'clock she went downstairs. Dougal was in the kitchen, having prepared breakfast.

'I have had a letter from the mistress,' he said, 'and she is going to have a little holiday and is going to send a lady friend down.'[263]

Florence's heart sank. She 'saw no letter', as she later recalled, and, besides, she already knew that the post did not come until later in the morning.[264] Any decision Miss Holland had made to take a holiday had been sudden, to say the least – there had been no luggage on the trap the previous evening – and, now, what of the promise that she had made to Florence, the assurance she had given that Dougal would not abuse her again?[265] She was entirely alone with him, with acres of unpeopled land all around them.

In Swanfield Road, in Waltham Cross, however, Florence's mother Martha was almost at that very moment reading the letter which her daughter had sent to her. Dougal had not stopped it, just as he had not stopped Lydia's letter to her friend. Now, Martha hurried by train to Newport and, going into the Elephant and Castle public house, hired the landlord, William Jackson, who had a pony and trap, to drive her to the Moat Farm.[266] When they arrived, it was not yet twelve.

Apparently letting herself in, Martha found Florence in the kitchen, sitting at the table, weeping. Letting herself back out, Martha found Dougal, dissociating himself from his servant's distress, in the farmyard. By her own description, she 'abused him' but, in the torrent of her anger, she could not later recollect all that she had said. She knew, though, that she had told him that 'I had come to fetch my daughter away as he had behaved improperly to her by kissing her and trying to break into her bedroom'. To Dougal, there must have seemed little point denying it; in fact, faced with this display of assertiveness – from the female of the species, no less, an event to which he was quite unaccustomed – he preferred to say nothing at all. Martha demanded that Dougal pay 'a month's wages for my daughter and her railway fare back to Waltham Cross [and] also my railway fare from and back to

Waltham Cross'. Dougal went into the house 'and laid the money down on the kitchen table alongside of Florence who picked it up,' Martha recalled.

'I have not hurt your child,' said Dougal, breaking his silence; but Martha and Florence went upstairs to pack, and he was left alone with his awkward denial ringing in his ears.

A few minutes later, Martha went back downstairs to speak to William Jackson, who was waiting outside with his pony and trap, when she saw Dougal drive away, seated on his own trap, pulled by Prince. With the house now otherwise deserted, Florence's luggage was brought out, and she, Martha and Jackson drove away.

On the road to Newport, they saw a familiar figure driving towards them. This was Dougal – whom Florence must have wished she had already seen for the last time – returning to the house from wherever he had been. But Dougal must have known that his situation could hardly be improved by any last-minute attempt to placate the enraged Mrs Havies, or to cajole the trauma-tised Florence into returning with him. 'He did not acknowledge or speak to us,' Martha said, 'but whipped the horse up.'

Florence Havies married a man named Alfred Blackwell in 1900, and they went to live in the satellite suburbs of the metropolis, first at 44 Elm Road, in Leyton, then just doors away from her parents at 7 Swanfield Road, in Waltham Cross, and then at 5 Grove Place, off Grove Road, in Enfield.[267] Florence, however, was long affected by her experiences at Dougal's brutal hands. Within a handful of years, she was saying that she was no longer angry with him ('I was at the time,' she admitted), but Martha could see the effects of her daughter's ordeal.[268] 'Up to the time Florence went to the Moat House,' she remarked, 'she was a strong healthy girl, but, since then, whenever she has anything to upset her, she has been subject to hysterical fits'.[269] There exists an unflattering line drawing of Florence, a picture in which she is aged about twenty-three, and looks much older: perhaps this was the whim of the artist; perhaps not.[270] By April 1911, Florence had given birth to six children by Alfred, of whom only two remained alive. Things cannot have been easy for her.

Meanwhile, Dougal's destination on his solo journey on the morning of Florence's departure remained a mystery largely unexamined. In fact, he had probably been to send a telegram to Sarah. She was not due to join him until the Monday, a bank holiday, but, in his message, Dougal asked her 'to go to the Moat House that day, by a [*sic*] afternoon train'.[271] Obediently, Sarah went, arriving at Newport Station in the afternoon to be met by Dougal and Old Pilgrim on the horse and trap. When they reached the house, Dougal made his 'confession', telling Sarah, as she recalled, 'that he had been living there with the lady as his wife and that she left there the previous morning to go to London to find a servant and would be back in a few days'. He also mentioned that Florence had, that very morning, left with her mother. He asked Sarah to pretend to be his daughter, 'as I want to avoid a scandal'. Asked to recall her response, Sarah, with the perfect clarity of hindsight, stressed her scepticism and her independence of mind, but, as was so often the case with her, the pieces of the jigsaw would not quite join together: 'I did not intend to remain with him,' she sniffed; but she went along with the charade he had proposed.

Sarah looked around. The house was well-furnished, and the beds made. To whom did all this belong, she wanted to know? Dougal told her that everything belonged to 'Miss Holland' and that 'she would return in a few days and I was to take a Cottage where I could go if she returned'. Sarah went back to Croydon and packed her things, sending them on to the cottage in Lower Street, in Stansted. Then she returned to the Moat House.

⁂

Outside, Old Pilgrim continued to fill in the drainage ditch, working along from the end nearest the farmyard.[272] At about the end of May or the beginning of June, Dougal hired Alfred Law, in his early twenties and living with his parents on Middle Street in Clavering, to work on the farm, and Law, Pilgrim and another farmhand named Flitton began to discuss Miss Holland's disappearance. She had not been seen since riding away with Dougal on the horse and trap on 19 May – Law had seen her, once, he thought, months before, in his previous capacity at Coldham's, working for the previous owner – she and Dougal had visited the farm together as they were preparing to buy it. But since he had been re-engaged, Law had seen no sign of this woman. Instead, the current lady of the house advertised herself as Dougal's daughter.

The child with her, just turning six, was Olive – Law understood *her* to be Sarah's daughter, and, therefore, Dougal's granddaughter. In contrast to these embryonic attempts to unravel the logic of Dougal's strange, shifting domestic relations, the task of blocking the drainage ditch and diverting the drain through the cart shed must have seemed cheerfully straightforward. One day, Pilgrim recalled, 'Dougal set all three of us to work filling up that top portion of the ditch. That morning, Dougal superintended the work nearly the whole of the morning, but he was not there so much in the afternoon. We worked at it all day that day.' Dougal's sudden interest in overseeing the filling in of the ditch seemed to vanish as quickly as it had arrived.

In Stansted, Fanny Haggerwood peered out through the sixteenth-century windows of the Dog and Duck, where her father-in-law was the licensee, and where she and her husband John were living at the time, and fixed her gaze on 4 Lower Street, opposite. The new occupant's habits were irregular – Fanny would see the lady there, apparently, at breakfast, and as late as nine at night, and the lady would receive visits from a horse-and-trap-driving man whom Fanny later recognised as Dougal, but Fanny was fairly sure that he never stayed the night. Inside the cottage, Sarah's boxes, as Fanny knew, and as Sidney Lancet Butler saw when he went to collect the weekly rent, were unopened, still as they had been when they were moved from Coombe Road. Occasionally, Sarah would cross the road to buy beer, holding evasive conversations with Fanny, saying that, although she could get on well enough with her father, she was out of favour with her stepmother. Despite these oddly-timed appearances in the village, Sarah admitted later that she had never spent much time there, preferring the Moat Farm, and the company of Dougal, 'as he treated me so much kinder than he had ever done before'.[273]

There was a gradual change in personnel at the Moat House Farm as May became June. Old Pilgrim, still no closer to resolving the mystery of Miss Holland's disappearance, gave Dougal a week's notice on 1 June, and left the farm on 8 June, as his wife was unwell and wanted to go to live at Anstey, in Hertfordshire, to be near their daughter, Mary Elizabeth Driver, and their phalanx of grandchildren.[274] And, on Friday 2 June, young Emma Burgess, who had helped Dougal and Miss Holland to settle into their new home, returned as Dougal and Sarah's servant.[275] She had been sent for by Sarah, and, observing that this was not the lady whom she had assisted in April, Emma asked what had become of the *other* lady. Sarah told her that she had gone to Europe, and Emma neither asked Dougal about this, nor heard him say anything about the matter.[276]

But how were Dougal and Sarah to pay Emma's wages, or the wages of Law and Flitton, who were still outside attending to the drainage? They had no money – Sarah was known to have been destitute at Croydon, relying on the kindness of neighbours to keep her afloat, and Dougal had nothing to his name.[277] They were, for the first time, employers of others, a tremendous leap up the social scale for an aspirant couple whose previous highpoint had been Dougal's fleeting foray into the lower reaches of Dublin's civil service. The farm itself was perhaps some time away from being truly profitable – Lydia Faithful remembered Miss Holland paying a family from Clavering for planting potatoes somewhere in the wet, clay earth of the fields around the lonely house; for a landholding of the size of the Moat House Farm, a few potatoes looked like small return.[278] But, already, something had happened to alleviate their growing despondency. On Thursday 25 May 1899, on the account-holder's authority, the National Provincial Bank in Piccadilly cashed a £25 cheque on Miss Holland's account, the sum payable to Dougal.

CHAPTER FIVE

WHERE WAS MISS Holland, nearly a week absent from home and signing cheques in favour of her antic part-spouse?

Never before had the National Provincial Bank had reason to doubt the authenticity of Miss Holland's occasional missives to them; nor did they on this occasion. Miss Holland appeared to wish to draw £25 for the benefit of Samuel Herbert Dougal, and all seemed perfectly normal. There was a precedent: Dougal had been advanced a small sum at the end of 1898, covering the rent on the house at Hassocks in which they briefly stayed.[279] The bank paid the money.

Within a week, however, another letter had been received, this one dated 29 May 1899 and written, rather stiffly, in the third person:

> Miss C.C. Holland presents her compliments to the manager and will be glad if he will forward her a new Cheque Book.
>
> The Moat House,
> Coldhams, Quendon,
> Essex, 29th May 1899.[280]

This was out of character for Miss Holland – her letters to the bank generally adopted a slightly warmer tone, at least referring to herself in the first person and concluding 'Yours faithfully' or 'Very truly'. It was not widely known that Miss Holland had been personally referred to the National Provincial by one Henry Mountcastle, the son of a jeweller, and he himself an actuary with experience in stocks and shares, and a customer of the bank's head office.[281] Clearly, the bank could be expected to be discreet and professional, and Miss Holland had placed her implicit trust in them.

This new letter seemed not to have been written in Miss Holland's usual cheerful manner. On closer inspection, it did not even seem to be in her handwriting, but the bank, wary of offending an important and long-standing client, sent the chequebook, retaining the peculiar letter of request, just in case.

Before long, another third-person letter arrived at the bank. This one was dated 6 June 1899, and contained a cheque for £30 to be paid, in the form of six £5 notes, to Dougal.[282] Comparison with the previous letter showed that both were in the same unfamiliar handwriting.[283] This time, their suspicions raised, the bank wrote back, returning the cheque and asking Miss Holland to sign it again, 'in your usual manner'.[284] Promptly, it came back, with an accompanying letter explaining the perceived irregularity:

> The Moat House
> Coldhams
> Quendon
> Essex
>
> 7th June 1899
>
> Dear Sir,
>
> Cheque to Mr Dougal quite correct. Owing to a sprained hand there may be a discrepancy in some of my Cheques recently signed.
>
> Yours truly,
>
> Camille C. Holland[285]

On Thursday 8 June, the bank forwarded the six banknotes, numbered consecutively from 65070 to 65075.[286] A polite letter of 9 June – which, like those before it, was addressed from the Moat House Farm – acknowledged the banknotes' receipt; and there the matter rested.[287]

❧

But Miss Holland was not at the Moat House, and the letters to the bank, and the dubious cheques, were forgeries. Dougal had fabricated cheques for sums little greater in the past: the suggestion that the variation in handwriting was attributable to a sprained hand was his conceit, covering the as-yet imperfect development of his art. The adoption of a less stultified tone in the later correspondence certainly seems to have owed something to careful study – Dougal must have been working from a template, and, since all Miss Holland's papers had remained in the house since her sudden disappearance, there was plenty of raw material to guide him. Dougal appears to have perceived the discrepancy between his rigid early impersonations of Miss Holland and the gentle and slightly more personal letters with which the bank was familiar. Although the truth was probably lost forever in the mists which lay low on the clay earth of Essex, it is not unreasonable to suggest that Dougal may have needed some assistance to sustain this level of emotional insight.

Sarah denied it, of course, claiming later that 'I never saw him commit one of the forgeries'.[288] But her agnostic stance is difficult to defend – did she never wonder, though it would have been quite reasonable to do so, about the source of the money on which they were living, or doubt the sincerity of Dougal's evasive explanations? ('He told me he had sold some Hay and got it in that way,' she recalled.) Even worse, Sarah seemed unable to give a consistent explanation of Miss Holland's absence from home. It was true that Dougal himself was vacillating rapidly in his multiplying versions of events. Imminently expected on 19 May, as Dougal supposedly shuttled back and forth between the farm and the railway station, Miss Holland's reappearance was apparently deferred indefinitely by a seemingly non-existent letter on the morning of 20 May, and then dependent on some new, unstated contingency by the afternoon ('I was to take a Cottage where I could go *if* she returned,' as Sarah remembered it). The easiest way to account for this eccentric mishmash of conflicting statements is to suppose that all were lies. Working from this platform, Sarah's own mythopoeia looks equally bad. She had initially been told – so she said – that Miss Holland had gone to London to find a servant, and would be back within days. This was a new variation on Miss Holland's absence, but, within about a fortnight, Sarah had decided to take on Emma Burgess, apparently not prepared to wait any longer for Miss Holland to return from her own servant-seeking expedition. At Stansted, she told Fanny Haggerwood the fairy-tale about her fabulous 'stepmother'.[289] When Samuel Morton, the vicar at Clavering, and his wife Frances visited the farm in June, Dougal introduced Sarah as his widowed daughter, 'Emily', but this time, apparently, nobody mentioned the stepmother.[290] Unsurprisingly, none of Dougal and Sarah's varying explanations of her absence did anything to hasten Miss Holland's homecoming.

The idea of fraudulently dipping into Miss Holland's bank account, too, seemed to depend upon certain prevailing preconditions. Dougal, and others, knew how possessively Miss Holland felt about her money; she was bound to be angry, and to take preventative action, if she were to discover that Dougal had been drawing, unauthorised, on her account. Although he was not averse to committing frauds for relatively small profits, the possibility of killing the goose that laid the golden egg for the paltry initial gain of £25, the sum paid to him on 25 May, must have seemed a risk loaded against its taker. Put simply, Dougal's frauds, with or without Sarah's knowledge and assistance, must, by necessity, have begun when he was *sure* that Miss Holland would not be able to find him out.

In early September, Dougal gave up the rent on the cottage in Stansted, and sent his farmhands to collect Sarah's furniture and to bring it up to the Moat House.[291] Sarah was more and more settled at the farm, and Miss Holland was nowhere to be seen. On looking over the house, Sarah had found bed linen marked *C.C. Holland* and *S.A. Holland* (Miss Holland's deceased aunt and benefactress, Sarah Ann), and, intrusively, had decided to open Miss Holland's boxes too.[292] She found a 'complete ladies [*sic*] outfit' and, in a jewellery box, a variety of expensive-looking rings and pendants, one of which seems likely to have been the amethyst ring which had once belonged to Miss Holland's childhood sweetheart, and another of which, a 'ring containing Hair', as Sarah recalled it, had obvious, even cloying, sentimental value as a personal reliquary. Unmoved by this, Sarah kept hunting through Miss Holland's private and personal possessions, locating a cheque book and some counterfoils which, she said, 'some time afterwards, I cannot remember how long, I frequently saw … in my husband's writing desk'. She also found Miss Holland's private correspondence, apparently including the fateful advertisement for a husband which had alerted Dougal to his prey in the first place, and burnt it, later attributing her actions to a fit of jealousy.

Dougal, in his new feminine persona, had embarked upon a correspondence with Miss Holland's stockbrokers, William H. Hart & Co., of 26 Old Broad Street, in London. This was another company upon whose discretion Miss Holland had cautiously staked her financial affairs, and another to which she had been personally introduced, in this case by one Allen Schofield Caine.[293] Through their agency, Miss Holland had become the owner of hundreds of diverse stocks and shares: she had liberated some of their value in purchasing the Moat House Farm; now, she wrote, she wished to dispose of more of them. In particular, she wished to realise the value of forty-three shares in the Great Laxey lead mine, on the Isle of Man; 400 preference shares in George Newnes Ltd, publishers; and a £500 debenture in the United Alkali Company.

W.H. Hart & Co. returned £1,008 1s 9d on these commodities, and, duly, they forwarded the transfer certificates to Miss Holland at the farm. Dougal wrote back under his *nom de plume*, enquiring as to how many witnesses the brokers would require to witness the signature, and on which line the transfers should be signed. Later, Thomas Gordon Hensler, who looked into the forgeries, considered this letter to be 'somewhat extraordinary'. Miss Holland had offloaded stocks and shares before, without halting at the signature: it was as if she had suddenly forgotten what was, for her, an entirely familiar procedure. Perhaps assuming that she was becoming senile in her old age, the agency sent her some instructions, and the transfers, relating at least to the Newnes and United Alkali holdings, were signed and returned shortly afterwards.

In a letter of 20 September, however, 'Miss Holland' apologised for having mislaid the certificates pertaining to the Great Laxey shares. She wondered whether duplicates could be sent to her; Hart & Co., replying, confirmed that they could, provided that the proper assurances were undertaken.[294] This would require Miss Holland to swear, before a respectable witness, that she had simply lost the certificates, and had not embezzled them somehow. Of course, seeking the guarantee of a respectable witness was, for Dougal, quite out of the question. Instead, he wrote again to Hart & Co. on Friday 29 September, making all the appropriate declarations: there was the *mea culpa* for mislaying the certificates, and the observation that, though the certificates had been looked for, they had not come to light, and seemed unlikely to do so, '[a]nd I make this solemn Declaration conscientiously believing the same to be true'.[295] At the bottom, Dougal had signed the assurance from Camille C. Holland, and countersigned it thus:

Subscribed and Declared at Saffron Walden this 27th day of Septr., 1899, before me

Joseph Bell,

Justice of the Peace for the County of Essex.

Bell was a senior figure in Saffron Walden's civic administration, but he knew nothing whatsoever of the declaration he had supposedly underwritten.[296] The forty-three shares to which this particularly elaborate forgery related were, as was so typical of Dougal, the least lucrative component of the grand sale he was arranging – altogether, when the cheque for the Great Laxey shares arrived at the Moat Farm in the first week of October, they realised only £67 3s 9d.[297]

All told, though, Dougal was over £1,000 better off. He put the money into Miss Holland's bank account, sending an accompanying letter which, predictably enough, went uncontested by the National and Provincial.[298] It seems redundant to say that he had never been so wealthy.

Sarah, in the meantime, continued to see nothing, to know nothing, and to doubt nothing, if her later account is to be believed. Her behaviour at the time of the windfall, however, was unpredictable, as if the instant riches had thrown the scale of the fiduciary deception into sharp and uncomfortable relief. Even the persona she had adopted, as Dougal's widowed daughter, began to slip; another visit by the Reverend and Mrs Morton in October ended, appropriately enough, in revelation.[299]

For reasons which will never be properly ascertained, Sarah had decided to show Miss Holland's left-behind clothes to Mrs Morton. Given that this consisted of 'a complete ladies' wardrobe' of abandoned garments, some of which were monogrammed in

ink, and plainly not with Sarah's name, this gesture inevitably pro-
voked Mrs Morton's curiosity.[300] Where was the owner of these
clothes now? she asked Sarah. Sarah suggested that Miss Holland
was away 'on a yacht'.[301]

This was the first Mrs Morton had heard of Miss Holland, a
Roman Catholic who apparently escaped the radar of the local
Anglican hierarchy. Sarah, however, had had a protestant religious upbringing of her own, her father being a minor official
in the Church of Ireland, and her unsolicited confidence in Mrs
Morton perhaps reflected a troubling sense of guilt, a burden that
she felt that she could scarcely carry. She admitted her own identity to her guest, showing Mrs Morton her marriage certificate.[302]
Following this discomfiting visit, Mrs Morton and her husband
called at the house 'only … occasionally'. Something was not
right, and Sarah later recalled that Mrs Morton said she believed
that Dougal had 'done away with' Miss Holland.[303]

On 14 October, Dougal opened an account with the Birkbeck
Bank, in Southampton Buildings, off High Holborn in London,
depositing two sums totalling £55.[304] Since the inception of his
spree of imitations, he had been using Miss Holland's money to
fend off local bills. In July, he had paid eight guineas to Sworder
& Sons, auctioneers of Bishop's Stortford, for a bicycle. Henry
Sparrow, the company's managing clerk, recalled that the cheque
had been signed by 'Camille C. Holland'.[305] Further (and dearer)
transactions with Sworder & Sons, for the sale of farm stock, were
funded by the disposal of the shares at the end of September:
on 3 October, Dougal forged a cheque for £31 9s 0d, and on
12 October, another, for £153 5s 6d.[306] A cheque for £14 13s
0d was sent to Thurgood & Sons, another auction company, on
18 October; there were other forgeries along the way.[307] Then, at
the end of the same month, Dougal requested that £670 be transferred from Miss Holland's account to his own.[308] Since he was
writing as Miss Holland, and since he had created a smokescreen
through which the National Provincial's security policies were
unable to peer, the transfer went through without a hitch. Dougal
had established a comprehensive cash-flow mechanism, inscrutable to the authorities. He could sell stocks and shares through one
agency, have their retail value placed in Miss Holland's account,
switch the value to his own account, have it cashed and sent to
him in the form of banknotes, and, if he wanted, sink the num-

bered notes – more or less without trace – into the swirling mass of the currency system when he made purchases. Years later, local people, local businesses and local banks would pore through their records trying to isolate Dougal's notes, with varying success.

In the shadow of his early autumn glut of forgeries, Dougal seemed to rest, forging only occasionally, as if out of restless habit. Once, in November, he wrote to the bank in the guise of Miss Holland, observing that a document she had received from them, probably in relation to the stocks and shares he had sold, required a correction made to it.[309] For an unluckier man, this fastidious attention to detail would have chimed badly with Miss Holland's previous, perhaps geriatric, behaviour – losing the share certificates, forgetting where to sign them for transfer. His letter could have returned the bank's own attention to their previous suspicions, and to the conceit of the sprained hand. In the event, so dulled had the edge of their scrutiny become, there was no cutting through the tangled skein of Dougal's fraudulent dealings. The corrections were made, and the forger remained undetected.

Life at the Moat House Farm became almost embarrassingly simplistic. By virtue – though that is hardly the right word – of his web of deceit, Dougal had placed himself in a position in which he could be the master of (and, where necessary, the slave to) his ceaseless whims. Sarah's memories, if they can be believed, suggest that the tipping point may have been reached before the end of 1899: 'I was not there many months before my husband commenced his cruelty to me,' she said, although, notably, this was not the signal for her to leave him.[310] Clearly, something was compelling her to stay.

Against the drift of the evidence, she insisted on her wide-eyed, law-fearing innocence. At the end of November 1899, she thought, a letter arrived addressed to Miss Holland. This was not the first such letter, but Sarah's attempts to question Dougal about the ongoing absence of the mysterious lady of the house seemed never to bear fruit. When she accused him of 'getting his money dishonestly', she explained, 'he would up with his fist and knock me down and frequently not speak'. Now, Dougal opened this letter in Sarah's presence, and she saw him take out a postal order for £2, which he secreted in his desk. Sarah said nothing more about it until another letter, which she believed to be from the same address, perhaps in Manchester, arrived 'a few weeks later'. This requested that the postal order be returned, as it had been sent in error. Sarah asked Dougal 'what had become of it, and he told me he had cashed it'. Supposedly panicking, she purchased a £2 postal order and sent it away, hoping that, by making up its monetary value, the whereabouts of the original order would not be enquired into. Her luck was in: 'I heard no more about it'.

Artificial though this story now sounds – all this anxiety over a £2 postal order seems disproportionate, given the opulence and lavishness which had suddenly descended on the otherwise penniless couple – it is typical of Sarah's recollections of the early period at the Moat House. Again and again, she claimed to be oblivious to the grand scale of the criminal activity which Dougal performed in the very rooms in which they lived together. Another letter to Miss Holland, from her niece, Mary Laura Mann (*née* Holland), arrived at the farm, apparently before the end of May 1900. As her father George had done, so now Mary's husband Henry threatened to die at a terribly young age, and Mary wrote of 'distressed circumstances'. Sarah described herself as 'upset' by the letter, riven by her strengthening conviction of Dougal's wrongdoing; moved by her pity, she anonymously sent two £1 postal orders to Mary. But even this simple gesture came garbed with suspicion. 'I am unable to say whether or not it was sent through Miss Holland's Bank,' Sarah reflected, and, on reflection, to send a soon-to-be widow just £2 of her aunt's money, a drop in the ocean compared to the vast sums which Dougal had seized from Miss Holland's account, seems parsimonious, to say the least. Other letters which arrived at the Moat House – they were 'nearly always' collected by Dougal, who still seemed loath to let the postman too near the house, and would meet him in the lane instead – similarly caught Sarah motionless, despite her apparent misgivings. 'I saw plenty of the Stockbrokers Circulars addressed to Miss Holland but I never saw any of their closed letters,' she said. 'I never saw any letters from Miss Holland's Bank. I am convinced now they came.' Even if this is to be believed, the enduring wealth of the household could not, even remotely, have been generated by the farm, and one is forced to wonder why Sarah did not sense at least the moral imperative to cease living on a missing person's money. If she had, then she could have had little moral choice but to leave. If she suspected that 'something serious' had taken place, she could have reported to the police a man who must, it follows, have been dangerous to live with, and capable of great wrongs. Sarah asserted that Dougal was 'too artful a man to let me see them [the private letters from the stockbrokers and the bank] or trust me with matters like this'. But her protests seem empty – she was continuing to enjoy the good life, backed by Miss Holland's fortune, and seemingly more unwilling than unable to desist.

Similarly buoyed up on unprecedented funds, Dougal was merrily landscaping his farmland. On 21 October 1899, he had written, under his own name, to Daniels Bros., of Norwich, enclosing an extensive list of trees and shrubs with which he hoped 'to improve the general appearance' of what he referred to somewhat loftily as the 'estate' which he had 'recently purchased'. They wrote back, providing a quote for the order, but Dougal, impatient and unwilling to wait for his trees to grow, wrote again, specifying that they be 'of the best stock and largest kind'. Eventually, the flora he ordered cost him £25 6s 0d; he sent a cheque to this value on 13 November, signed by Miss Holland. The list itself is striking, running to 342 plants of twenty-five different sorts; the vivid array of colours – purples, golds, reds, pinks, silvers – was in terrific contrast to the daguerreotype shades of the Essex countryside which surrounded the house. To make sure that the trees were planted as quickly as possible, Dougal had the holes dug in advance. The filling-in of the drainage ditch had been completed by Law and Flitton after Old Pilgrim had left the farm, and, when the trees he had asked for were delivered, this was one of the areas to which Dougal paid special attention, sprinkling it with new vegetation.

In moments of leisure, which were probably plentiful, Dougal prowled around the farm, apparently clutching a rusty American 'rook rifle' – a gun particularly designed to control animal and bird populations on farms – which he loved for its 'almost noiseless' action.[311] The use of weaponry to compete with the attentions of rabbits and rooks hardly marked Dougal out as a farmer of unusual habits, but, as time had gone on, there remained a strange lack of saleable stock rolling off the hundred-acre holding. At the back of the farmhouse, Dougal had erected some beehives and, according to Jesse, he 'kept a few cows and pigs and fowls, apparently more for the sake of appearances than anything else'.[312] But none of these seemed liable to make his fortune: in fact, much of the farm may have been given over to pasture, and the pasture turned to hay. Beyond this, Dougal was 'a splendid shot', shooting for pleasure in a rural society in which this was still a popular pastime, and in which proficiency with the gun could still confer a measure of social respect. Writing in retrospect and with the use, seemingly, of Dougal's diary (he still had not given up this habit), Jesse supposed that, by dint of his sporting prowess, Dougal was 'extremely popular' within the community, and, later, he was recalled as a generous, intelligent man; but he must, too, have spent much time stalking the fields alone, keeping the potentially nosy locals at a safe distance from the farmhouse. As he went, he hummed a tune, murmuring its lyric – 'As her hair grows whiter, I love her more' – but this simple, romantic evocation of ordinary love in the middle years juxtaposed awkwardly with the curiosity which now began to attach to the strange occupants of the Moat Farm.[313] It seems likely that, with Sarah's sudden, perhaps guilt-ridden confession to Mrs Morton, the groundwork had been laid for the construction of a massive edifice of gossip and innuendo around the Moat House's peculiar inhabitants, with Miss Holland – or the previous Mrs Dougal, as she had, of course, been known – invisible through any of its windows.

Other caprices could also be indulged, now that money permitted. Dougal had always enjoyed technology, and, before long, his acquiring gaze settled on a locomobile, a primitive form of automobile. These were, at the beginning of the twentieth century, rare items indeed; Dougal bought one, which he went on to keep in the stable near the bridge, supplanting Prince. In theory, Dougal fancied himself quite the sophisticate as he drove the locomobile around the local villages, but in fact he seems to have been largely oblivious to its grace, its charm or its grand message: in a love letter he wrote some time later, the locomobile's recalled technical novelty seems quickly to have distracted him, pen-in-hand, with amusing results:

> The farm where young Bowyer lives, 'The Bonhunt', is offered for sale; you know the house, where we ran up the carriage drive in the locomobile and where I put a new gauge glass in when waiting there. Oh! for those times over again ...[314]

As an afterthought, Dougal went on to remind his correspondent that 'we had a nice little run that day if you remember?'; but, plainly, the heady, carefree days of touring around the quiet lanes of Essex with a loved one seemed to him as nothing compared to the time when, thrillingly, he replaced his gauge glass.

Back in the house, Sarah's curiosity was still tantalised by the clothes Miss Holland had left behind when she went away. She showed them to Emma Burgess, and then, together, she said, they 'packed them up, and put them away until she returned'.[315] But Miss Holland showed no sign of reappearing, and Sarah's patience, like that of her husband, was in short supply. The clothes 'remained there [unworn] about two years', Sarah claimed later.

This conflicted with the recollections of Elizabeth Whiting, however. When the Dougals had left Biggin Hill in 1898, Sarah had owed money to Elizabeth's mother Mary.[316] The Whitings must have given up hope of having the debt repaid, but, to their surprise, 'some months after they [Dougal and Sarah] went away', a letter arrived, from Sarah, containing a postal order for 10s. Even more surprisingly, shortly after the arrival of the letter, Elizabeth said, 'she visited us'.

The Whitings wondered at the appearance of their some-time acquaintance. Sarah had claimed straitened circumstances throughout 1897 and 1898, but now she appeared before them 'beautifully dressed', as Elizabeth put it. Where had she got these clothes? Dougal had 'sold a patent', Sarah explained, and had purchased a farm with the money; the lady from whom he had bought it 'had sold him a box of clothing with the furniture at the house'. This was nonsense, but the Whitings were not to know. Sarah dripped with jewels, too, and seemed to have 'plenty of money'. It was, at the very least, a striking change of fortune.

The very idea of visiting Biggin Hill was obviously demented. One suspects that it had originated with Dougal, who may still have been feeling stung by his brother Harry's summary rejection of him in the summer of 1898. The opportunity to flaunt his sudden wealth in front of his doubting brother may well have been too tempting to ignore. Sarah's role, as the sudden social mover, was ridiculous. In later years, she and Miss Holland would merge and entwine in the confused memories of the locals of Biggin Hill, such that she herself was meant to be 'about 50 years of age and her hair ... dyed a golden hue'. This was a description entirely better-suited to Miss Holland than it was to Sarah. But Miss Holland had not visited Biggin Hill. The macabre possibility that Sarah had actually approximated her appearance for the purpose of the visit remains open. She was certainly swanning around in her clothing and jewellery, and, to judge from Elizabeth's Whiting's description, may well have been using Miss Holland's luggage while Mary Whiting remained alive – 'she visited *us*'. But Mary Whiting died in the late spring or early summer of 1900, and, in turn, this suggests that Sarah's story of packing up Miss Holland's clothing and, for two years, leaving it untouched was, itself, fiction. In fact, tellingly, she paraded about in the missing woman's dresses.

Sarah, when she began to appreciate the gravity of the situation, claimed that Dougal had often told her that he had given Miss Holland £50 for her clothing, and that 'it was alright'.[317] While this tallied – in part – with the story she had given Elizabeth Whiting, the tale of Dougal's having sold a lucrative patent was entirely new, and probably her own creation. Sarah may have learned from her husband that he had once made abortive attempts to profit from his inventions; she may have clung to the idea, unearthing it for the convenient purpose of explaining her unexpected appearance and unabashed wealth to the Whitings. All in all, it was, no doubt, a thrilling role-play, albeit one which cannot have made much sense. Sarah simply made herself remarkable, fixing herself in the memories of those she visited. She might have been better advised to stick to sending out serial postal orders from the outpost of the Moat Farm.

※

The protracted sale of the farm to Dougal remained unresolved. Dougal had been in correspondence with the executors of William Savill's estate, wishing to have the property's conveyance, which had been left uncompleted, finally finished.[318] A series of delays had interrupted the process, however: initially, William Savill's death had caused some confusion, needing the interventions of solicitors to push the sale through. Then, on 17 November 1899, Dougal's solicitors, Ingram, Harrison and Ingram of 67 Lincoln's Inn Fields, collapsed under oppressive debts.[319] Cartmell Harrison, the senior partner, committed suicide on 27 November, and, in the wake of all this, Harrison's serious mismanagement of his affairs was detected. The scandalous bankruptcy of the firm occupied the courts, from time to time, through 1900, and in 1901, *The Times* reported on a convoluted case brought to the Chancery Division to decide 'which of two innocent parties, the beneficiaries or the trustees, were to suffer from the frauds of the late Cartmell Harrison, the solicitor'.[320] Evidently, Harrison's deceptions – he had appropriated some of his clients' money, telling them that he had actually invested it – had serious consequences for many people; for Dougal, they could hardly have been more convenient. He, personally, had not lost out financially to Harrison, and now the matter of the conveyance fell, as the business wound up, to Reginald Tuffley Harding, who was Ingram, Harrison and Ingram's clerk. Harding was unfamiliar with the case, and Dougal quickly perceived that, in his hands, the absent Miss Holland could become anything he wanted her to be. As Harding later reflected, throughout his dealings with Dougal, his client had given him the mistaken impression that 'Holland was a man'.[321]

George Coote, the Savills' solicitor, working at 191 Fleet Street, was having difficulty completing his side of the conveyance, too. The money Miss Holland had paid for the Moat Farm had, it seems, gone through Harrison's hands, and Rebecca and Henry Savill – William Savill's heirs – had instructed Coote not to approve a draft conveyance, prepared by Harding, until it reappeared, in full. By 2 March 1900, Dougal's tolerance had run to a low ebb, and he had a writ of summons issued, which Coote received at his office. This forced the matter, and a compromise was gradually developed which would lead to the conveyance being finalised. There was only one problem: in June, Coote wrote to Harding to say that, if Dougal wanted the conveyance made out in his name, rather than that of the original purchaser, Holland, then Holland would have to provide written – and signed – permission.

Harding wrote to Dougal to explain the situation on 14 June. Four days later, the necessary permission was sent back to him, signed by 'C.C. Holland', and witnessed by Dougal.[322] Harding countersigned the letter, validating Dougal's signature, and went to Coote's office to deliver it.[323] By mid-August, the conveyance had been completed; in line with the compromise with the Savills, Dougal had paid a mere fifteen guineas – £15 15s – to

have the work done. In return, Miss Holland's £1,500 investment
had been transferred, *in toto*, to his possession.

Dougal continued to risk detection throughout these negotiations: unmoved by the irony of the idea, he actually sought
the assistance of the law in resolving a dispute, quite illegally, in
his favour. Any further inquiry might have made Miss Holland's
absence apparent; but, between the chaos at Ingram, Harrison and
Ingram, and the financial anxiety of the Savills, nobody was in a
position to recognise either the fraudulence of Dougal's demands,
or the nonchalant forgery that propped them up. Harrison, from
the world beyond, absorbed any doubts which might have arisen
– there was no way of knowing the extent of his misconduct,
and it therefore seemed almost limitless, and the root cause of
any and all of the hitches which had ever caused the sale to drag.
The Savills must eventually have been paid their money, but not
before Dougal had escaped with a hundred acres of Essex farmland, none of which had cost him a penny.

Neither Dougal nor Sarah, to judge from the picture we have
of them in the first three-quarters of 1900, were any better than
they had ever been at conducting themselves with discretion or
caution, but only carelessness seemed likely to upset their unde-
servedly lavish lifestyle at the farm. Sarah continued to exhibit
her uncharacteristic wardrobe far more widely than was sensible,
showing it to her niece, Alice Brett, 'who stayed with us'.[324] Alice
also saw Miss Holland's chequebook, Sarah said. An array of witnesses to Dougal and Sarah's odd circumstances had begun to
gather around them.

⁂

In or around August 1900, Mrs Wisken and her daughters
Susanna, Kate and Henrietta were apparently delighted and
surprised by the sudden arrival in Saffron Walden of Jack, Miss
Holland's dog.[325] Mrs Wisken hoped that Miss Holland – Mrs
Dougal – was somewhere behind, finally visiting and making
good on the promise she had made when they had parted some
sixteen months before. Jack's owner did not turn up, however,
and Jack himself 'would not leave us'; the family took him to the
Common, expecting to find Miss Holland there, but there was
still no sign of her. At a loss as to what to do next, Mrs Wisken
took Jack home with her.

It seems remarkable that, in the midst of their crimes and deceptions, Dougal and Sarah had continued to care for Jack in Miss Holland's absence. Perhaps, if others became curious, Dougal could point to Jack as proof of Miss Holland's intention to return – why would she abandon the dog she loved so much? – but, this aside, Jack could not have been of any physical use to him. A brown and white creature, accustomed more to the lapdog lifestyle than to the toil of assisting on the farm, Jack was probably already beginning to suffer, anyway, from the arthritic condition and progressive deafness by which he was, some time later, to end his life afflicted.[326] Mrs Wisken kept Jack for three weeks, and then wrote to his mistress at the Moat Farm, saying where he was.[327]

Dougal wrote in reply, suggesting that Mrs Wisken put Jack out and allow him to find his own way home. But Mrs Wisken would not do it, fearing that Jack would get lost *en route*, and so she kept him with her. A few days later, Dougal arrived at her house, knocking furtively on her side door for attention. 'I was surprised at this,' Mrs Wisken remembered, 'and asked him if he would not go to the front door; but he said that he would rather not, and that he was quite all right where he was'.[328]

'Have you got little Jacko still?' asked Dougal.

'Yes,' Mrs Wisken replied.

'Will you let me have him?' asked Dougal.[329]

Mrs Wisken said she would, and Dougal entered the house, calling Jack back into his possession with an ostentatious display of apparent annoyance: 'Come along, Jacko. You have no business to run away from your mistress like this! How much do I owe you, Mrs Wisken?'

Although Mrs Wisken refused to take his money, Dougal left a shilling on the table, and went out, taking Jack with him and terminating his first meeting with his former landlady in nearly a year and a half with an abrupt flourish. Awkwardly, though, he had dropped a glove in the house, and had to return to get it, although Mrs Wisken 'fancied that he was very unwilling to do so'.

⸎

Gradually, Dougal had come to realise that he would have to relinquish further stocks and shares, the profits of the frauds of

the autumn of 1899 having begun to taper away as he and Sarah
continued to luxuriate in heaps of Miss Holland's money. On
Wednesday 5 September 1900, he paid himself a cheque of £100,
forging it in Miss Holland's name; on Friday 19 October, he
supplemented this with another cheque for £64.[330] Still, these
sums were insufficient to sustain their careless lifestyles, and on
31 October, Dougal wrote to the National Provincial to have Miss
Holland's share certificates in the City and West End Properties
Limited sent through.[331] This was done, and, on 2 November,
Dougal wrote to W.H. Hart & Co. asking that they sell sixty
preference shares in this company, and, additionally, fifty preference shares in the Central Uruguay Railway Eastern Extension.
These holdings returned £546 3s 0d; Dougal sent the cheque he
received from Hart & Co. to the National Provincial on Saturday
17 November, and then, on Monday 26 November, paid £550
into his own Birkbeck Bank account, from Miss Holland's.[332] Just
as before, no hint of suspicion rose against him.

Already, however, the idleness of wealth had begun to have its
debilitating effect on Dougal and Sarah, leading to restlessness
and, perhaps, attempts to flee reality in drink and illicit sex. In
the early months of 1901, Dougal wrote to Lysaght John Rutter,
through whose agency Miss Holland had originally acquired the
farm, and asked him to sell it.[333] Dougal may already have tried to
offload his property himself, through the Classified section of *The
Times*; but neither of these methods seems to have worked.[334] He
may not have liked it, and he may, for the purposes of resale, have
'improved' the property – he made a point of mentioning in his
letter to Rutter that he had had 'a pond or part of the moat' filled
in, as the land agent later recalled – but no buyers were found,
and Dougal was stuck with the Moat Farm.

Any attempts Dougal made to turn the farm's vast fields into
something proportionately profitable continued to fail. Although
he remained a man of considerable energy, even he could not
convert his acres of wet, sticky soil into a fertile seat of valuable
crops. The water hovered at a level just below the surface of the
earth, and, when it appeared above ground, it was diverted here
and there into the network of culverts and gullies which laced
the property.

While he had lived with Miss Holland at Saffron Walden, Mrs
Wisken had approved of Dougal's politely abstemious habits,

knowing him only to take a little whisky with his dinner.[335] In distant retrospect, though, she assumed that he had really been spending his leisure hours 'in the hotels and public-houses and in bad company'. Which establishments these were she did not – probably could not – say. Saffron Walden itself was not short of pubs, but the fact that Dougal's carousing, if this is what it was, failed to reach the ears of either his landlady or his 'wife' seemed to suggest that the clandestine drinking sessions were occurring further afield. If so, he could have driven out of town on his bicycle.

It was all supposition, but, if he really *was* leaving Saffron Walden in pursuit of the dubious company of the *bon vivants* of turn-of-the-century public houses, then perhaps Dougal was going to Bishop's Stortford, just across the county border in Hertfordshire. This was a round journey of something approaching twenty-five miles, the second part of which would not have been easy, tipsy and on a primitive bicycle; in terms of the distances involved, he would have been little worse off going to Haverhill, or Royston, or even Cambridge; but yet the idea that he had been drinking in Bishop's Stortford stuck. And if he had been going to Bishop's Stortford, perhaps he had been visiting the Grapes, on South Street, at that time owned and managed by one George Chapman.[336]

The rumoured acquaintance between Chapman and Dougal was notable only in retrospect. Chapman, a Polish immigrant whose real name was Severin Klosowski, dispatched three 'wives' – whom he had, *à la* Dougal, failed to marry – by way of poisoning. The last of these, Maud Marsh, died in 1902 in the Crown in Borough High Street, but the suspicions of the medical men in this case had the effect of bringing Mary Spink and Bessie Taylor, Maud's predecessors, back to the surface of the earth. Their coffins were opened, and they were remarkably well-preserved, the by-products of their chronic poisonings. Chapman was hanged at Wandsworth in April 1903, and his case generated considerable public excitement.

But did Dougal meet Chapman at the Grapes? It remains distantly possible that he did, but hardly, as Jesse's editor, the venerable Harry Hodge, later thought, 'extremely likely'. Even if Dougal had patronised Chapman's public house, both were rigidly in character, and neither could really have known that his aggressively misogynistic tactics towards women were – in so many ways – remarkably mirrored by the other. It remains a tantalising (if an unrealistic) vision, however: Bessie, the pit of her stomach burning from her not-quite-right dinner, nonetheless attempting to soothe the tense atmosphere behind the bar, selflessly reminding a momentarily wistful Chapman of his beloved old launch, the *Mosquito*, which he bought during a previous existence at Hastings; and Dougal, overhearing them from behind his mug of beer, thinking of his own boat, in which he once passed his lonely, unhappy days off the remote shoreline of Nova Scotia.[337]

If his diabolic acquaintance with Chapman was unlikely, the rumours of Dougal's sexual heroism which got abroad – and which have been repeated, often without scepticism, by subsequent authors – must be considered generally hyperbolic. Jesse, consulting with one of Henrietta Wisken's daughters in the 1920s, found that there were 'strange tales ... of bicycling lessons given in the field to girls who rode machines in a state of nature'.[338] The image this created was, perhaps, evocative enough, but Jesse embroidered it, fixing it forever in the tapestry of Dougal's dissolute life:

> What a picture – in that clayey, lumpy field, the clayey, lumpy girls, naked, astride that unromantic object, a bicycle, and Dougal, gross and vital, cheering on these bucolic improprieties ...

Her (mostly male) followers repeated the allegation, sometimes imparting an emphasis of their own. Jesse had not said that the girls would arrive at the Moat Farm in groups for their lessons, but Gordon Honeycombe, who additionally assumed that the event was a one-off, thought that she had.[339] Robert Church, perhaps transported by the image, put the lumps of the 'lumpy girls' into a very specific anatomical context, repeating the 'rumours of strange happenings' with a particular twist:

> ... for instance, it was said that [Dougal] derived considerable entertainment from watching buxom country wenches peddling [*sic*] bicycles furiously across his fields. A mere eccentricity of the wealthy the locals at first thought, until one evening a farm worker told his disbelieving young companions that earlier he had suddenly been

confronted by the young women who to his astonishment were in a state of complete undress.[340]

To be fair to Church, Jesse herself had initially suggested that Dougal's tastes tended particularly towards 'buxom country wenches', although it is difficult now to suppose that he was ever particularly choosy.[341] Only Roy Harley Lewis, writing in the late 1980s, seemed inclined to doubt the veracity of all the gossip, suspecting that Dougal's 'deeds were exaggerated by the legend that had begun to be associated with Moat Farm'.[342]

It was true, of course, that Dougal had purchased a bicycle from Sworder & Sons in July 1899. He was also known to have had one while at Saffron Walden – the vehicle on which he made his putative flights to Hertfordshire, and the unpleasant company of the landlord of the Grapes. Perhaps, therefore, by the beginning of the 1900s, Dougal had at least two bicycles. But this is hardly proof of the grand, Dionysiac rituals which were supposedly the bread and meat of local rumour. Something was wrong at the Moat Farm – Mrs Morton, at least, must have been aware of that much – but the stories of the nude cyclists seem likely to have arisen later, predicated on practically nothing.

Many authors, too, have been misled by Jesse's slightly overwrought language, invoking the classical past in an attempt to trace the dimensions of Dougal's appetites:

> In his vulgar, gross way he had some of the tastes attributed to the more dissolute Roman Emperors. He liked a touch of an orgy about his doings ...[343]

Church took this literally, repeating a story which had become attached to Dougal's legend over the years, to the effect that 'at one Bacchanalian orgy [Dougal] reputedly seduced three daughters and their mother'.[344] Lewis, abandoning Rome and heading for the near-East, remarked that, 'at one stage, [Dougal's] "harem" included three sisters and their mother'.[345] But whether one assumes that Dougal was (Honeycombe's word, ripped from the pages of the top-shelf publications of the 1970s, when he wrote his account) 'pleasuring' these ladies one by one, or all at the same time, one is probably incorrect.[346] The purported orgies and the hypothetical harems are misunderstandings of the truth, conflated with rumours, misrememberings and, probably, lies. We will meet the sisters, of whom there were actually four who became involved with Dougal in one way or another, and we will be introduced to their mother; and, of course, Dougal's behaviour towards them was execrable. But they were not swarming together in Dougal's bedroom in paroxysms of unselfconscious erotic bliss.

cಎಲ

Emma Burgess remains a mystery in the story of the Moat Farm. Perhaps, at the outset, childishly excited by the prospect of entering domestic service, she lived with the Dougals from June 1899 until April or May 1901; she appears, with them, on the 1901 census, taken on the evening of 31 March, still aged only fifteen, and Dougal noted in his diary on 11 April that he had given her a month's notice.[347] With hindsight, and in view of the treatment Dougal had shortly before meted out to Lydia Faithful and Florence Havies, this remote appointment seems a terrible risk for a child to be allowed to take, but, at the time, Dougal's civic reputation remained more-or-less intact, and Emma herself never complained about Dougal's conduct towards her. At some point shortly after the census (even she could not be sure precisely when), Emma moved out, and two years later she was in service in Highgate.[348] Her replacement at the Moat Farm was Hannah Cole, who was (apparently) the cognitively impaired single daughter of a local agricultural labourer, and, by now, in her mid-thirties.[349] Sarah remembered that Hannah was only at the house 'for a short time', and, indeed, in July 1901, Dougal was writing politely to a 'Miss L.' (Jesse suppresses the full surname), who had advertised for a position in some publication:

> I am in want of some one to look to my wants during the absence of my wife who is frequently away from home, should like one of a cheerful disposition and young, and, judging from your advertisement, you might perhaps like to try the duties. ...This is a farmhouse and a jolly English home.[350]

This description of the place was, perhaps, rather flattering: both Lydia and Florence had reacted to its austere remoteness with dismay. Of more interest was Dougal's casual observation that

Sarah was 'frequently away from home'. As Jesse says, with just a little venom, it seems that Dougal 'did not contemplate Mrs Dougal being with him much longer'.[351]

CHAPTER SIX

SAMUEL DREDGE DOUGAL had died on Tuesday 2 October 1900.[352] At the time, Samuel Herbert Dougal, his lawless son, stood midway between the resolution of the Moat Farm's conveyance difficulties and his next major foray into Miss Holland's portfolio of shares. Samuel *père* had held life assurance with the Prudential Insurance Company of Holborn, and, shortly after his death, a cheque for £184 16s 0d was paid to his executrix, Dougal's sister, Emily Mary Dougal, living out her unmarried middle age in rural Hampshire. Other policies and property holdings were to be divided between Dougal and his four siblings, and, in May 1901, to facilitate the financial arrangements written into their father's will, they opened a joint deposit account with the Birkbeck Bank. Dougal already used the Birkbeck for his own banking, which, for him, chiefly entailed moving money every so often from Miss Holland's account to his own. The family's joint account swelled to £698 12s 0d in July 1901, but Dougal must have been painfully aware that any attempt he made to cannibalise it would be subject to the scrutiny of the others. His relationship with Harry had already become strained; with uncharacteristic self-control, he resisted any temptation he may have felt to snatch the money.

Displacing his frustration, Dougal instead tore through an array of Miss Holland's holdings in September 1901. Between them, a £500, 4½ per cent stake in the Cape of Good Hope Diamond Mining Company; a £300, 6 per cent stake in the Manila Railway Company; a £300, 5 per cent stake in the Inter-Oceanic Railway of Mexico; and £250-worth of 10s ordinary shares in the Palace Theatre brought in £1,454 10s 6d.[353] Dougal paid the enormous cheque into Miss Holland's bank, and then, on 25 September, he transferred £1,400, a little less than the total sum of these most recent frauds, to his own account.[354] The only

significant problem with this glut of dealing was that it permitted no others: Miss Holland's stocks and shares were now spent,
her portfolio empty.

Sarah seemed to have developed a certain sense of calm, having,
perhaps for as many as a few consecutive months, contained her
overwhelming urge to exhibit Miss Holland's wardrobe to female
visitors. But if, as Dougal suggested, she had been absenting
herself from the Moat Farm, before and after July 1901, she had
entirely forgotten about it when she gave her own version of
events not very much later. As had happened before, however, the
memories of others continued to function where her own had
inconveniently failed her.

At some point towards the end of 1901, Sarah had relocated,
semi-permanently, to Tatsfield, in Surrey, to board at the home of
the widowed Emma Singleton.[355] Despite being over the county
boundary, Tatsfield lay within a mile or so of Biggin Hill, in Kent,
and here Sarah again began to develop a profile which defeated
her later attempts to secrete herself in shadows. She moved, probably some time before Christmas, to Nightingale Cottage, in
Biggin Hill, where she came to the attention of John Thomas
Drew, a fruit grower and traction-engine contractor living at the
grandly entitled Parkville Villa. Shortly after the new year, Dougal
joined her, and they acquired, in her name, a bungalow 'at the
top of Stock Hill'. This was Ballingarry Cottage, named after
Dougal's mother's home in Ireland – a rare display of sentimentality on Dougal's part, if indeed it was he who thus renamed
it, the object perhaps being to impress the still-sceptical Harry
with his sober, respectful choice of appellation. Now, Sarah was
seen widely in the community: by Robert Thorpe, a builder from
Hampstead who was staying in the area; by the long-suffering
Elizabeth Whiting; and, most notably, by a local labourer by the
name of George Killick, known to his friends and workmates,
Drew among them, as Dusty.

While Sarah now seemed to make Biggin Hill her home,
Dougal's presence in Kent was occasional and intermittent,
and sprinkled with strange, almost symbolic incidents which
seemed to resist easy interpretation. John Thomas Drew said that
Nightingale Cottage, in which the Dougals had stayed, burned
down after they left. Then, at Ballingarry Cottage, Dougal was
rumoured to have dug a well, filled it in and built a shed over

the top of it. What – if anything – did it all signify? Sarah, mean-while, remorselessly bothered Elizabeth Whiting, getting her to cash small cheques 'drawn on the Birkbeck Bank and signed by her husband'. Indeed, with Dougal's bank balance booming as a result of his disposal of Miss Holland's shares, Sarah spent money with careless, guiltless abandon.

⁓⁂⁓

As yet, it was hard to see what this new excursion to Kent was intended to achieve, but Sarah's absences from the Moat Farm did, probably, permit Dougal to indulge his whims – at least, to an extent – while he remained there. His craving for young women, while not, perhaps, quite expressed in the carnivalesque bicycle lessons and orgies of later rumour, nonetheless continued to inspire him, even as he approached his mid-fifties.

In particular, he had developed a recent taste for the Cranwells, a local family consisting of, among other individuals, the sisters (and mother) of his sexual legend. In November 1901, Kate and Eliza Cranwell went to the Moat Farm, meeting with Dougal and Sarah, who was there at the time, in their conservatory.[356] Sarah spoke to Eliza, a twenty-three-year-old dressmaker, about some garments she wanted adjusted; Kate, just seventeen, aimed to take over from Hannah Cole as housekeeper. After a satisfactory inter-view, it was arranged for Kate – who came with 'jet-black hair and blue, lustrous eyes – she might have come straight from the pages of Thomas Hardy' – to move to the Moat Farm to take up domestic duties on Monday 9 December 1901.[357] Hannah Cole did not leave until 'about a week later', and, when she did, a third Cranwell sister, Emily, known as Millie, and at the time a mere fourteen years of age, moved to the Moat Farm to help Kate with her tasks.[358] Suddenly, Cranwells busily filled the rooms of the Elizabethan house.

Sarah later attempted to compress her recollections of her resi-dence at Biggin Hill, squeezing it into a timeframe – all after the turning of the year – which the evidence awkwardly outsized. At the Moat Farm, she claimed, she had implored Dougal to unburden himself, to reveal what had happened to Miss Holland, but to no avail: when she spoke of Miss Holland, she said, they would quickly descend into a quarrel, and she would end up being beaten by her violent spouse.[359] Eventually, with her attempts to force the truth from Dougal having resulted only in a series of assaults, she escaped, she said, 'frightened and terrified', to Ballingarry Cottage, which, luckily for her, Dougal 'had previously given me the money to purchase'. She omitted to mention the spell at Mrs Singleton's, or even the spell at Nightingale Cottage, despite the independent evidence for them.

She also neglected to recall George 'Dusty' Killick. Killick was an engine driver, in his early thirties, single, and subject to the vacillating temper of the rural economy of the area. Born locally, and having lived locally for most of his life, he took employment where he could find it, even going so far as to say so on the 1901 census form, where his occupation is listed as 'odd work with a traction engine'. In early 1902, he and the engine had been contracted to produce bricks for Robert Thorpe, who was building a house in Biggin Hill for a Mr Abbott.[360]

Killick's quotidian professional duties left him enough time to scan the village in search of interesting company, and the free-spending Sarah caught his eye. It seems entirely possible that her acquaintance with Killick had originated in one of the local hostelries, perhaps the Blacksmiths' Arms, with Elizabeth Whiting watching on disapprovingly from behind the bar. Without attachments of any other sort, Killick probably felt at liberty to steer the affair towards its natural conclusion; Sarah, for her part, seems not to have put up too much resistance. With Dougal out of the way for extended periods, she could entertain Killick at home, and, challenging the modesty of the small community, visit him at home, too. It was probably at his house, on Saturday 15 February 1902, that Sarah and Killick first made love.[361]

Restlessly, the cuckolded Dougal would come down to Kent, an apparently oblivious impediment to his wife's fling, and then go back to Essex, his absence permitting the glowing embers of Sarah's covert romance with Killick to reignite, fuelled, very likely, by great doses of alcohol. She and Killick rapidly began to play-act domestic and even *faux*-marital roles: beginning on Saturday 1 March, and continuing for two days afterwards, the lovers 'lived and cohabited and habitually committed adultery', immersing themselves in each other in Ballingarry Cottage. Then, on or around Wednesday 16 April, with Killick truly drawn in and readily prepared to desert his job making bricks for Robert Thorpe, the couple fled.[362]

After a while, with the bricks he needed having failed to arrive, Thorpe made enquiries of his own. Some of 'the natives', as he put it, as if rural Kent were a tropical jungle to be hacked through with a machete and civilised, if necessary, by force, informed him that the man with the traction engine had gone away with the woman who lived with Dougal. Since the traction engine was, in fact, John Thomas Drew's – Killick was only the driver – Thorpe assumed that Drew was the eloper. A local scandal had apparently erupted over the lovers' conduct, but Thorpe had got hold of entirely the wrong end of it. When Drew subsequently turned up, a few days later, to complete the brick-making which Killick had abandoned, Thorpe decided not to speak to him about the affair, believing the situation to be painfully sensitive. (Years later, Thorpe, who had since repaired to his own native Hampstead, still believed Drew to have been the errant labourer. Drew was affronted by the suggestion, and objected vociferously, pointing out that he had a wife, had been married twenty years, and had five children. 'I ... have never been away from home with any woman,' he said; 'I was not absent from home one night in either April or May 1902'.) Thorpe looked on, a couple of weeks after Sarah and Killick's flight, as Dougal removed the furniture from Ballingarry Cottage. Still he hesitated to become involved in something which was really none of his business, but which obviously intrigued him considerably; he heroically waived the opportunity to commiserate with Dougal, and never spoke to Dougal's brother Harry, with whom he was acquainted, about the matter.

✦

Although the illicit couple had now been away for two weeks, and although Dougal had fairly promptly decided to take back his furniture from the cottage at Biggin Hill, he was slow to formalise the end of the relationship. The grounds to sustain a divorce action were undoubtedly manifest: everybody had seen Killick and Sarah together; everybody knew that they had run away together; they had hardly been discreet; this was a breach of the usual marital protocols, and, in theory, Dougal was quite blameless, the wronged party. Normally, all this might have been expected to have forced prompt action. In fact, however, except for his urgent concerns for his furniture, Dougal did little to avenge himself on his missing partner, sitting back passively while Sarah went footloose with another man. Generous onlookers might have assumed that his apparent composure was a delayed shock reaction to the trauma of Sarah's betrayal, or even the inaction of a man still hoping that his wife would return to him. More likely, it simply reflected the fact that he was now being kept joyfully busy entertaining the clutch of Cranwells with whom he now lived. Besides, there was no hurry.

Eliza Cranwell, in particular, had become the object of Dougal's libidinous interest. Sarah had a typically tortuous story to tell about Eliza – she had, she confessed, shown Eliza the dresses which had been left behind by Miss Holland (as she was wont to do to ladies visiting the house), although she claimed not to have said whose they were.[363] It was true, of course, that Sarah had wanted some garments adjusted, but she claimed that she had had this done by a Miss Whitehead of Bishop's Stortford. 'I do not remember Miss Cranwell renovating any,' she said; at least, not any belonging to Miss Holland.[364] Eliza, of course, had a different tale. She had indeed altered dresses for Sarah, and the ones she had altered had been removed from a trunk, and on the lid of the trunk was the name *C.C. Holland.*[365]

Dougal's adulterous relationship with Eliza developed rapidly. Nobody doubted the quality or finesse of her work, but one wonders whether it was really necessary for Eliza to remove herself to the Moat Farm for 'a week at a time' to 'do work'.[366] Dougal himself must have capitalised on the opportunities which his new abandoned-bachelor status afforded him, squeezing the sympathy out of his young admirer, although it is fairly certain that he did not wait for his wife's desertion to become complete with her flight from Kent before he embarked on his own fling with Eliza. By the time Dougal managed to coax himself into doing something about Sarah's behaviour, Eliza was mesmerised by him.

Of course, this augured badly for Eliza. Worse still, Kate Cranwell, Eliza's sister, resident elsewhere in the same house, and on the cusp of her eighteenth birthday, was already pregnant, although she did not know it yet.[367] Dougal was the father of her child.

At length, however, Dougal lurched into life, going to Bishop's Stortford on Thursday 8 May 1902 to initiate divorce proceedings through Alfred Nockolds, a local solicitor and Commissioner for Oaths.[368] Complaining hypocritically of Sarah's adultery with Killick, Dougal signed his petition, and swore an affidavit stating, among other things, that 'there is not any collusion or connivance between me and my wife Sarah Henrietta Dougal in any way whatever'. The assurance was one required by law – divorces were only permitted if they were genuine showdowns between, on the one hand, the petitioner (in this case, Dougal) and, on the other, the respondent (Sarah) and any co-respondents the petitioner cared to identify. Dougal provided the name of the unfortunate Dusty Killick in the latter capacity. On 9 May, the petition was filed with the civil courts by Sandars and Harding, solicitors, of 56 Lincoln's Inn Fields, London.

Dougal came away from Alfred Nockolds's office on Market Square – a stone's throw from the Grapes – with two citations in his hand. These were to be delivered to Sarah and Killick, and contained the civil charges to which they were to answer. But where were Sarah and Killick?

As it happened, they were in Tenby, in Pembrokeshire, Wales, and probably having a miserable time. Sarah may have been enjoyable company when she was drunk at Biggin Hill, but Killick may have begun to realise that, marooned with her in springtime South Wales, her sober, twenty-four-hour persona was not so much fun. He could be forgiven if he had started to feel that her interest in him had never been entirely genuine. He was probably grateful that Lady Llanover's baroquing influence had not extended as far west as Tenby – a temperance advocate with money on her side, she had closed all the pubs on her nearby home estate and turned them into quaint tearooms. Drink may have brought Killick and Sarah together, and, by the time they reached Tenby, it may already have been all that they had left to prevent them from falling apart.

It is therefore regrettable that Sarah omitted to mention any of this in her account of her life with (and without) Dougal. It was not Paris, probably, or New York, or Rome, but one would have expected her to have recalled her excursion to Tenby with her lover; besides, others knew where she was, so the story could hardly be kept under wraps. Within about a week of his visit to

Nockolds, one of the people who knew where Sarah was, was Dougal. This was convenient, as he had the citations to deliver.

⚜

The Friday of the Whitsun weekend dawned, and Dougal prepared to take a train westwards to Wales.[369] He preferred not to go alone.

According to Jesse, Eliza asked her mother's permission before setting off with Dougal; apparently, her mother, Emily Cranwell, readily gave it.[370] Leaving Kate and Millie to take care of the house, Eliza and Dougal travelled to Wales, finding Killick and Sarah in Tenby, and serving the citations.[371] For Killick, this was the rotten summation of a deeply eccentric period of his life. In a few short months, he had gone from casual labourer, lazily floating on the breezes of life in the Kentish countryside, to co-respondent in an acrimonious divorce case. Both couples must have passed nights of misery in Tenby's guest houses. Eliza later insisted on the chaste propriety of her sojourn with Dougal: 'we stayed at some hotel but occupied separate apartments,' she explained.[372] She was strictly in an impartial role – accompanying Dougal as his – what? – official dressmaker? – and was, slightly awkwardly, 'paid for [her] services'.[373] They returned to the Moat Farm on Tuesday 20 May 1902, where Kate, busy getting the tea, and Eliza, entering the room at just that moment, saw Dougal disposing by fire of three letters to Miss Holland which had arrived at the house in his absence.[374]

Sarah and Killick's fling folded with the citations. He was next heard of in September 1902, when he again began working for John Thomas Drew, but Biggin Hill may well have become too hot for him, and it seems unlikely that he could have recaptured the casual, stress-free existence he had once enjoyed. Nine months later, he was working in Crockenhill, near Swanley, a short distance away from the community he had known most of his life.[375]

There had already been signs that Dougal and Sarah were in happy accord throughout these trials and tribulations. Her leave of absence from the Moat Farm was hinted at by Dougal in his letter of July 1901; when, in April 1902, she fled hundreds of miles to the west, Dougal was able to locate her within about a week. This was either an extraordinary feat of deduction or inestimably unlikely guesswork on Dougal's part, unless one took the view that Sarah had written to him to inform him of her whereabouts. If she had, well, he continued to monitor postal deliveries at the Moat Farm (the letters addressed to Miss Holland had only been seen by Kate because Dougal was not there to intercept the postman; she had received them in his absence and put them on his desk); consequently, there was no substantive reason for the charade to be exposed.[376] His statement on the affidavit, averring that the divorce had not been cooked up between himself and his wife, was manifestly false.

In this analysis, Killick emerges as the patsy, easily duped by Sarah in a style much resembling that refined by her husband. In some senses, he was her Miss Holland; his utility was spent by the time Dougal arrived with the citations, and Sarah promptly jettisoned him, confident in the knowledge that society would see him as the wrongful party. Who would ever have believed his story – a man such as he, tricked by a woman? And even if any opprobrium had attached itself to Sarah for her behaviour in the affair, there remained the balancing feeling that Killick should have known better than to get involved in the first place.

On Friday 6 June 1902, Millie Cranwell left the Moat House Farm for her next appointment. This was at Ballingarry Cottage, in Biggin Hill.[377] Post-Tenby, Sarah would return to Kent, with some of her husband's nonchalance. There is no evidence that Sarah had previously met Millie – she had not attended the interview with her sisters Kate and Eliza in November 1901. In turn, this perhaps implied that Sarah had returned to Biggin Hill via Essex, selecting Millie for herself from Dougal's coterie of domestic staff. Of course, Millie was also the only Cranwell Dougal was prepared to give up: Kate was pregnant, and, for the time being, he was still sleeping with Eliza.

Sarah's cool, fleeting return to the Moat Farm may have tipped the balance for Eliza, however: she had been all the way to Wales with Dougal, believing his propaganda, which, no doubt, included among its features the implication that, once the divorce came through, he would be able to marry whomever he wished. She had assisted him in serving citations to a woman for whom, it now appeared, he had no real antipathy, no lasting resentment, nothing which would normally drive the cuckold to seek a divorce. He clearly had no intention of terminating the relationship, even if the marriage itself dissolved. Devoted to him at Whitsun, Eliza was gone from the Moat Farm by the time Millie left; Kate remembered that it was from this date that she was 'left alone in the house with Mr Dougal'.

There remained the almost-unanswerable question of the couple's motive. What advantage they saw in contriving the grounds for a divorce cannot now be known for certain. If the whole thing was planned from the first, with Killick the unwitting victim, then Dougal's lethargic response to the carefully wrought crescendo which ended in the flight of Sarah and her lover was probably extemporary. Sarah's performance in her role as the adulterous temptress might have been a little *too* convincing, briefly piquing Dougal's deformed sense of moral outrage – this must have been an interesting journey into the unknown for him – before he returned to the script and sought the citations. Since Killick was, in the eyes of the law, the one in the wrong, the way was theoretically open for Dougal to sue him for the costs of the case. But, in purely financial terms, Dougal and Sarah never stood to gain financially from the divorce; the best they could hope for was to break roughly even.

One possibility remains: Dougal had finally exhausted Miss Holland's residual financial resources with his transactions of September 1901, and, although the profits from the sales were substantial, Dougal and Sarah's tastes had become lavish and somewhat pretentious. The money they had would not last forever. He had never had much difficulty persuading old ladies to surrender their bank balances to him, but (his hypnotic effect on the female Cranwells aside) he was becoming older himself, and his upright and military deportment, which had worked its magic with Miss Holland, was perhaps beginning to fade into something more age-appropriate and, similarly, less enchanting. Sarah – younger, still eye-catching – now seemed to hold the key to future schemes. Dougal had few chances left to exploit his own vital force in the malevolent attempt to exploit another, but Sarah's attractions remained intact. For her, though, adopting Dougal's role in forging new, prosperous relationships with the lonely and wealthy may have meant having the freedom to marry, if necessary, with the windfall options of subsequent divorce or, perhaps, widowhood then becoming available. A full divorce of their own permitted them to dangle the prospect of legitimate marriage before their as-yet-unidentified, unmarried, male target. By consensually splitting, Sarah and Dougal maximised her eligibility. They surveyed London's scuttling population of doddery old bachelors as if they themselves were giants, looming hungrily over the city in search of their immoral sustenance.

CHAPTER SEVEN

A **GAINST THIS BACKDROP,** Dougal rather surprisingly decided that the time was ripe for paying guests to join him at the Moat Farm. The previous year, to no apparent response, he had placed an advertisement in the Great Eastern Railway *Farmhouse and Country Lodgings* guide to this effect, offering sanctuary to 'tired dwellers in London'.[378] According to Jesse, however, a Mr and Mrs Gill took up the offer in the August 1902.[379] They wanted a fortnight in the country shooting at the fauna, and arrived at Newport Station optimistically, only for their woozy nightmare to begin almost immediately. Dougal, arriving on the trap, played Dracula to their Jonathan Harker, sweeping them through the descending gloom 'without lights' and driving 'extremely fast', until they arrived at the lonely house in pitch darkness. Mr Gill helped Dougal to stable the pony, and then Dougal ushered them inside, where supper consisted of bread, cheese, beer and some putrefying meat which nobody touched.[380] This was evidently a bachelor's lifestyle – Dougal explained that his wife 'had gone away with one of his labourers'.[381] It was not the ideal preparation for the launch of his guesthouse.

In fact, he went on, his errant wife had turned up at the house the previous night. Concerned that he would not get his divorce if he were thought to be collaborating with her, he had left, spending the night elsewhere. When he returned to his property, earlier on the day of the Gills' arrival, his wife was no longer there.

❧

As so often happened, Sarah told what seemed to be the same story, but viewed through a prism of her own, and with the detail adapted to suit. The pre-arranged divorce, the unlawful course of which had previously run smoothly, had by now begun to gnarl and snare. This was particularly disconcerting since it was the aspiring divorcees' fault. On 5 June, Sarah had appealed for leave to appear at court, ostensibly to challenge Dougal's petition.[382] In truth, she had no such intention, but expressing the urge to do so at least conferred a sense of authenticity on the matter: it was what people would have *expected* her to do, whereas, by contrast, uncontested divorces could sometimes look like conspiracies. It also kept Killick, who was, potentially, a loose cannon with his own version of events, out of the picture. Smarting from his rejection by the capricious Sarah, there was no way he would stand up in court as the named co-respondent and back her position. He feared further shame and humiliation, preferring to disdain his former beau's appeal to the law as a last, useless gesture of his independent spirit. Sarah must have been delighted.

She was represented by Henry Porter, a solicitor working out of New Broad Street House, a stone's throw from the London terminus of the Great Eastern Railway line. Further exchanges of petitions and affidavits – for alimony and, disingenuously, for 'answers' – kept the juddering process alive through the months of June and July 1902. But then, on Friday 1 August, in Court Two of the Royal Courts of Justice, situated on the Strand, Sarah permitted the case to go undefended. Whatever resistance she had put up in advance had diminished instantly to nothing. On the bench sat the moustachioed, bearded Sir Francis Henry Jeune, GCB, a veteran of the notorious Tichborne case, but more recently known for his assiduous attitude to the cases which came before him in the Probate, Divorce and Admiralty Division.[383] In divorce cases, in particular, he was 'dignified and serious, discouraging flippancy and vulgarity', and he was disposed to give 'an attentive hearing to counsel on both sides' – but since Sarah did not wish to defend the suit, and since Killick had not attended, Jeune simply ruled the *decree nisi* into effect.[384] Poor Killick picked up the costs of the case, a measure of the blame which attached to him for his role in the misunderstood affair.[385]

A *decree nisi* was a staging post on the track towards a full divorce. It verified, theoretically, that the petition was legal and substantial, and it initiated a statutory interim period of six months, at the end of which a *decree absolute* would normally be issued, terminating the marriage. If, however, in the interim period, the grounds for divorce were shown to be insufficient, then the *decree absolute* would be withheld, and the divorce cancelled. For six months, at least, he would need to protect the secret of his collusion with Sarah.

But Sarah's story was different to that of her co-conspirator. 'A few days after he had obtained the *decree nisi*,' she said, 'I went to the Farm, where I saw Kate Cranwell'.[386] Dougal was not there, 'absent from home'. Sarah decided to stay, sleeping there for one night. As was her wont, she chanced upon various incriminating items, including 'a number of receipted Bills to Miss Holland from the Stock Brokers'. As if suddenly realising the significance of it all, she showed them to Kate, 'and I believe I said he had killed Miss Holland'.

Kate Cranwell never confirmed the veracity of Sarah's heart-to-heart story, however, and it is easier to believe that the women's sudden and terrible epiphany never happened. There were other ways in which Sarah's rendition of events refused to dovetail with Dougal's – although he recalled that she had left by the time he returned, she remembered seeing him the next morning. He was violent and angry. 'He turned me out of the house,' she said, 'and knocked me down with his fist and broke my teeth'.

The Gills' holiday went ahead anyway. They would find their letters, collected by Dougal, who continued to anticipate the postman's daily arrival, waiting on their breakfast plates when they came downstairs in the morning.[387] Dougal was visible in the nooks and crannies of the house, and was glimpsed kissing Kate, which the Gills must have considered an aspect of his marital difficulties he had neglected to grumble about over their beer and cheese on their first night in the house. By night, he schooled them in poker, remaining steadfastly sober; his guests supposed that he was recovering from a previous weakness for drink. When they retired to bed, they left him still awake at the card table; by the time they awoke, he had been to bed and risen again with the sun. Despite the strangeness of it all, Mr and Mrs Gill apparently conceived a kind of sympathy for Dougal's situation. 'They could see that he was worried', Jesse wrote, and the legal wrangles of his divorce seemed the obvious reason why.

They had also noticed two servants in the house. Kate was one; the other, perhaps, was Millie, Dougal's stepdaughter by

Mary Herberta Boyd, and thereby a relic of a past which seemed, by now, astoundingly distant. In the springtime of 1901, Millie had been a nurse at the Brunswick House Lunatic Asylum in Mistley, by the Essex coast, giving her place of birth as Clavering, and her age as twenty-three. The attachment between her and Dougal had not dimmed, despite the undulations of the years since she resided with him at Northend in Buckinghamshire. Sarah, seasoning her retrospective inventions with a rare pinch of truth, explained that Millie had gone to stay with Dougal in early 1902, acting as housekeeper (in addition to his assortment of Cranwells); she may have stayed until the autumn.[388] When Millie Dougal left, Sarah said, 'a quantity of Miss Holland's clothing and her Jewellery' went with her. Sarah did not suggest a destination for these items, however, or for this shadowy, sad figure on the periphery of Dougal's tale. Millie's childhood trauma and rootless oscillation in and swiftly out of her stepfather's life had evolved into an adult existence which took place at least partly within the walls of an asylum. Admittedly, she was not a patient, but one senses that Millie derived a measure of comfort from the thera-peutic surroundings. Things may have been even worse for Millie – in July 1901, one Emily Winifred Dougal, an asylum attendant, gave birth to a daughter, Gladys Maud Dougal, in Marylebone; no father was named at the baptism. Sarah, examining things with the benefit of hindsight, hinted that the child may have been Dougal's, conceived on some prior visit Millie had made to the Moat Farm.[389]

With the Gills having returned to London at the end of their sojourn, Dougal's life plateaued into dull familiarity for a few weeks. He had continued to use Miss Holland's account for small purchases, and on 28 August 1902, he casually signed a cheque to the value of £28 15s 0d in Miss Holland's name.[390] This was payable to one J. Heath. It was one of Dougal's finest efforts, the signature looking 'exactly like' the real Miss Holland's signature, held on file at the National Provincial Bank.[391] But expenditures of this sort simply diminished a fund which, apart from the scant return given up by the sodden fields, could grow no larger. In Kent, Sarah waited impatiently for Dougal to unearth a new source of income.

☙◦❦◦❧

Kate grew larger. Now months into her pregnancy, her condition must have been unavoidably obvious, although she and Dougal had skirted around the subject so far. It is fairly clear that, in early September, she demanded that Dougal stand by her, even marry her when his divorce came through. He, fearing the financial burden of another child, refused to do so. Kate contacted her mother, and Emily Cranwell *mère*, rendered furious by her daughter's predicament, 'at once went to the Moat Farm to see Dougal and to take her daughter away'.[392] As he had with Florence Havies's mother over three years before, Dougal reacted with studied indifference to Mrs Cranwell's rage, even when she apparently threatened him with a poker. She may 'rave' all she liked at him, he said, 'provided she said nothing to her daughter Kate'. This demand – ostensibly that of the caring father-to-be, determined that nothing shall upset the mother of his unborn child – was more likely a response to certain unsettling accusations made by the angry Mrs Cranwell about Miss Holland's unexplained absence. Emily *fille*, back at home after the implosion of her own relationship with Dougal, may well have given voice to her increasingly dark suspicions which chimed, anyway, with the gossip which had begun to circulate in the area many months before.

The distraught Kate left the Moat Farm under her mother's protection, but 'immediately afterwards [and] against her parent's wish', Kate's elder sister Georgina, nearly twenty, travelled in the other direction. This was the fourth Cranwell to enter domestic service under Dougal and, in next to no time, Georgina fell under his spell. They had their photograph taken together. Dougal looked his age – his hair was thinning, his waistline bulging – but his posture spoke of his enduring visceral strength. A horseshoe pin adorned the knot of his tie, and Georgina lovingly hooked two fingers of her left hand into the *v* at the top of his buttoned waistcoat. Dougal placed his great hand on her shoulder, drawing her towards him and dwarfing her all at once. She wore her hair pulled back from the centre and tied at the sides. Her eyes were sharper than his, but her expression less self-assured. She had dressed in a long skirt and a fancy blouse, and she wore what seemed to be a watch at her left breast. Each exhibited a ring on the fourth finger of the left hand; they both looked past the camera at something in the distance.

Family loyalty seems to have been in short supply among the Cranwell sisters, but, perhaps for no better reason than to persuade Georgina of his determination to take responsibility for his actions, Dougal began to throw cash and resources at Kate as she approached the last months of her pregnancy. He gave Mrs Cranwell 'one or two sums of money' which were intended to offset the inevitable costs of caring for the expectant mother and the expected baby, and he sent 'hares and rabbits which he shot upon the farm' to the Cranwells' residence. The apathetic and almost insulting nature of these gestures was presumably ignored by Georgina, if she had any interest in them at all. Beyond the impersonal financial and farm-pest-related offerings Dougal made, there was clearly a moral void which the birth of a child could not fill. Dougal supposed that his cash and rabbits would make adequate recompense for his sexual promiscuity, but this hardly suggested that he was prepared to take on the more fundamental aspects of fatherhood when the baby arrived. In truth, he was hoping, as usual, to avoid the force of the law – if he were named on a birth certificate, or summoned to court to answer an affiliation charge identifying him as the parent of an illegitimate child, this would undermine the moral position he had adopted in his divorce proceedings. Cuckolded he may have been, but faithful to his wife he was plainly not. His *decree absolute* depended not only on the secrecy of his complicity with Sarah, but also on the details of his recent sexual history remaining firmly behind the closed doors of the bedchamber.

Of course, given the situation, Dougal's superficial displays of duty towards Kate were unlikely to obscure the bizarre truth of his remorseless philandering. In fact, he seems to have become quite distracted at this time, immersed in Georgina's sexuality in the serene seclusion of their farmhouse, to the detriment of whatever scheme he had cooked up with Sarah.

His inaction finally drove Sarah into taking a nursing job at the Barming Heath Asylum, near Maidstone.[393] She affected the sobriquet of Etty White and, perhaps somewhat surprisingly, was considered to be 'in all respects efficient' in the discharge of her duties. She cannot have been used to employment, however, and it is not easy to know whether she was eventually compelled to work by a pressing lack of money. Sarah herself tantalised with the hint of an alternative explanation when she mentioned, a little

while later and quite out of the blue, that Dougal's former partner Marian had '2 aunts living at Maidstone'.[394] Sarah had never
met Marian, but the detail she was able to recall about her – in
passing, and without concerted effort – was consistently striking. One wonders whether Sarah had not moved to Maidstone
to establish whether the two aunts in question could be use-
fully coerced, either by Dougal, who may not have been visually
familiar to them despite his appalling treatment of Marian in the
late 1880s and early 1890s, or, perhaps, by Sarah herself. Maiden
aunts were frequently the repositories of significant funds; Sarah's
knowledge of these particular aunts resonates with retrospective suspicion. There is no evidence that either of the aunts lost
money over the matter. If they had, however, there is little doubt
that Sarah would never have mentioned them.

∽∾⊙∾∾

The scent of something wrong reached what J.H. Baker called
the 'prying nose' of the relevant authority later on that autumn.[395]
The inconsistency of Sarah's response to Dougal's petition, which
had swung from vehement opposition to meek acquiescence, had
attracted suspicion, and the King's Proctor, whose duty it was to
protect the public interest in divorce cases, decided to investigate.
A cadre of detectives was retained to examine the antecedents
of divorcees, and one of these, a gentleman named Giles, was
engaged to delve into the circumstances of the Dougals' case.[396]
He was put into contact with Ackland & Son of Saffron Walden,
a firm of solicitors led by the unusually named Bryans Ackland,
who could assist with finding the local inside track. With his
arrival in Clavering in October 1902, Giles shone an unwanted
light upon the deliberately shadowy human mechanics of the
Moat Farm, although his work, for the time being, remained a
secret.[397]

Dougal continued to indulge his collector's passion for servant
girls, adding Mary Elizabeth Nichol, a fourteen- or fifteen-year-
old girl originally from Newcastle-upon-Tyne, to his household
on 6 November 1902.[398] She found Georgina and Dougal
ensconced in their insular existences. Dougal went on receiving letters addressed to Miss Holland – Elizabeth, as his new
employee was generally known, saw three of them, although
she could not say what was in them. The atmosphere of secrecy

and transgression was becoming pervasive. Domestic service in a remote country house was typically a lonely existence; for Elizabeth, who had been launched into her position with this strange, apparently superannuated man – Mr Dougal – and his young wife – illogically identified as Mrs Cranwell – the isolation came tinged with the disturbing eccentricities of her employers.[399] It must have been frightening, and there is evidence that Elizabeth's suspicions were raised not long after her appointment.

On Monday 22 December 1902, at her parents' home in Clavering, Kate Cranwell gave birth to a baby boy. 'As soon as he heard of the birth of the child,' it was later said, Dougal 'gave Mrs Cranwell [Kate's poker-wielding mother] a certain sum to pay necessary expenses and drove Georgina in his motor car to Bishop's Stortford when she purchased the baby's "layette".'[400] These cursory gestures, like those of September, did little to endear the new father to his estranged former lover. The idea that Georgina, rather than Dougal himself, had purchased her nephew's layette – a set of clothing for newborns – signalled the half-heartedness of Dougal's interest in his own son. As if to spite him, Kate named the boy Herbert George, a clear indication of the child's paternity, and a direct threat (especially with Giles sniffing around) to Dougal's *decree absolute*. Would the consequence of his promiscuity be to undermine his divorce?

By the end of the month, his anxiety must have been reaching new levels, but Dougal had never been one to avoid the public theatre of the courts, taking suits out almost as often as he was called to account by the actions of others. Three years earlier, in December 1900, Dougal had summoned Frederick Gunn and William Monk, aged about twenty and twenty-two respectively, to the Saffron Walden Magistrates' Court on a charge of trespassing.[401] At 1.30p.m. on Tuesday 13 November of that year, he alleged, he had spotted the two men, who were local labourers, in one of his fields 'where there was no public footpath'. They were standing on either side of a ditch, using sticks to disturb the soil below them, and they had a small dog with them. Plainly, they were trying to catch rabbits, and the bank itself was full of rabbit holes, dug by rabbits which had been successfully removed from other parts of the farm and made to keep to this particular field. Dougal approached them, but Gunn and Monk ran off, 'and their pockets were bulky'. Examining the banks of the ditch, Dougal found that they had been interfered with. A dead rabbit lay at his feet. He calculated that Gunn and Monk had been thirty yards from the footpath; he himself had been forty yards from Gunn and Monk when he first saw them.

Gunn and Monk denied the charge, offering the simple defence that they had never left the footpath, and the case was duly dismissed for lack of evidence. In retrospect, Dougal could never have proved the case, which pitted his word against theirs; but he must have hoped that the nuisance of a court hearing might have deterred the rabbit-hunters from returning to his property. For three years, perhaps it did. But then, on New Year's Eve 1902, Monk reappeared.

❧☙

Elizabeth Nichol had been shopping in Clavering, and at about 4.30p.m. on 31 December 1902, she was crossing the dark fields on her way back to the Moat Farm.[402] Behind her trailed Jack, once Miss Holland's loyal companion.[403] She was about four fields from home when she encountered William Monk.[404] He said, 'Hello', and asked her whether he should accompany her home, but she resolutely 'did not answer him or give him any encouragement'.[405] Walking on, she crossed two fields and then turned round to call Jack. To her alarm, she found that Monk was following her, ten yards behind.[406] She began to run, but before long she found that the footpath she had been using had turned to mud; she picked her way through the grime, but Monk caught her up, telling her not to be in such a hurry. Thoroughly frightened, Elizabeth asked him 'what he was following her for', but Monk did not respond.[407]

She went on again, but once more Monk followed. Again, she objected, saying that she could go across the fields by herself, but this time Monk 'touched her dress twice, and pulled the dress'. She warned him that 'she might meet Mr Dougal, who sometimes came to meet her, and that she would tell him what [Monk] had done'.[408] But Monk was not to be dissuaded, and he touched her again, and asked her to give him 'one sweet kiss', and put his arm out towards her. This time she fled, getting over a stile into an adjacent field, where Monk gave up his pursuit. But even here, Elizabeth ran into 'four young fellows', perhaps friends of Monk's, who, to her relief, left her alone, although, apparently for their own entertainment, they imitated her merrily when she again called for Jack. When she at last got inside the house, Elizabeth was in tears, and her hair was unkempt and hanging down at the back.[409] She told Georgina what had happened.

Elizabeth decided to complain to the police, and, on 7 January 1903, PC James Drew of the Essex Constabulary accompanied Monk to the Moat Farm so that Elizabeth could identify him. She was instantly sure that this was the man who had followed her, but Monk averred that she had made a mistake. 'No, I have not,' she replied. 'You are dressed the same and you speak the same.'[410] Later on, as Drew and Monk returned from their visit, Monk asked gloomily, 'Well, what are you going to do with this?'[411] Drew told him that he would have to report it, and Monk said, without conviction, 'You need not do that'.[412] He did not want to bother with it, he said, 'for it would be alright'.[413] Unsurprisingly, this tepid reassurance was insufficient to still the wheels of the law, and Drew charged Monk with the assault of Elizabeth Nichol. To this, Monk said, 'I will tell you the truth, Mr Drew. I did go up the field a little way with her that Wednesday night, and I did ask her for a sweet kiss. She told me she was going to meet Mr Dougal, and went off. She said I had better go back.'

When the case came to the Saffron Walden Petty Sessions on Tuesday 14 January 1903, Monk was defended by Bryans Ackland – Giles's contact in the King's Proctor's enquiry – and eventually acquitted by the bench (among whom sat Joseph Bell, whose signature Dougal had once forged) on the grounds that, although he had behaved in 'a very stupid way', the charge, and, presumably, the local opprobrium which had followed it, had been punishment enough.[414] This was a deflating end to Elizabeth Nichol's ordeal, although she accepted in cross-examination that Monk had not been 'indecent'.[415]

Georgina's role in the case was a most curious one. Summoned to the Magistrates' Court as a prosecution witness under the sobriquet of Mrs Cranwell, and describing herself as 'housekeeper to Mr Dougal', she gave a brief account of Elizabeth's distressed state as she arrived home on the evening in question.[416] She herself had been Dougal's housekeeper since September, she said. More intriguingly, however, she appeared in the testimony of both Nichol and Monk, who agreed that Nichol had said, out in the fields, mid-harassment, that 'Mrs Cranwell would not be her mistress much longer'. The significance of this remark was not explored in court, but, in retrospect, it seems ominous, accommodating a variety of different interpretations. Perhaps Elizabeth was announcing her intention to seek new employment elsewhere – her encounter with Monk may not have been a one-off, and she may already have been tiring of his clumsily expressed and inappropriate affection before he took things a step too far by touching her dress and asking for a kiss. She may have resolved to go away, abandoning Monk to the rabbit field, and putting the heady, paranoid atmosphere of the Moat Farm down to her imagination, or the otherwise harmless idiosyncrasies of her employers. But, if this were her meaning, it would have been more straightforward, and more hurtful to the artlessly amorous Monk who insisted on troubling her four fields from home, if she had said, 'I will not be living here much longer. I am going to work somewhere else.' Instead, she made Georgina, who had not, at that time, entered into their dialogue, the subject of her ambiguous remark, as if *her* status should have been expected to change. Would Georgina walk out on Dougal, perhaps, finally, unsettled by the knotted, atavistic effect upon her family structure which he, in his sexual dissolution, had wrought? Or would Dougal dispose of Georgina? The mysteries of Elizabeth's remarks remained unresolved, although they hung tantalisingly over the case.

Eventually, with the hearing concluding in a whimper, the consequences of the affair were probably further-reaching for Dougal than they were for either Nichol or Monk. Nichol would go about her ordinary domestic business at the Moat Farm; Monk was probably rendered a minor and temporary social pariah in Clavering; but Dougal had been forced to open his front door to the police. This was a prospect which, with his divorce still in the balance, he cannot have relished. From the distance of a century and more, the vision of James Drew appearing in the fussy, slightly unfashionable rooms of Dougal's home, while Dougal himself with apparent nonchalance rested one hand on the dark lid of the grand piano, appeals greatly. Elizabeth Nichol's legal action was over, and there was no immediate prospect of a policeman returning for further enquiries, but gradually Dougal's secrets were creeping into view. The structure of his household, with Georgina performing multiple roles, blurring the boundaries of class and intimacy, may not have been exposed utterly, but he was now under greater public scrutiny than he had been at any time since he first made Miss Holland's acquaintance all those years before. The eyes of the community were turning towards him, and his plans, and Sarah's plans, depended on his ability to ensure complete discretion. He could afford no more scandals, nothing which would divest him of the layers of deliberate misdirection and disinformation which cloaked the truth. It is one of the pleasant ironies of Dougal's blustering story, however, that the first individual to throw back the shutters on the secrets of the Moat Farm was an eighteen-year-old country girl, determined and resolute in spite of her situation, rejected by the man whom she once loved, and now the mother of his illegitimate son.

⁂

Kate Cranwell, nursing young Herbert at home in Clavering over Christmas 1902, was a young woman of more substance than Dougal had suspected. She had not yet registered the birth of her son, and it seems that she had decided to force Dougal to face his paternal responsibilities. An affiliation order, naming him as Herbert's father, was presented to the Saffron Walden court.

Dougal could now choose whether to contest the order; but, given the circumstances, he had little choice. He was without significant income, surviving on the proceeds of his past frauds, but still unable to really contain the desire to live lavishly; to resign himself to alimony arrangements without argument would be to invite further burdens upon his limited purse. Equally, the rumours about his adultery and promiscuity which had begun to circulate locally might, by themselves, have compromised his divorce case, had they ever hardened into certain proof; but to decline to defend himself against the affiliation order was tantamount to a confession of sexual impropriety, and his divorce action would then be all but sunk. Therefore, on Tuesday 27 January 1903, Dougal attended the hearing before the Saffron Walden magistrates, hoping, somehow, to disrupt Kate's pursuit of fairness and the truth.[417]

The hearing lasted over two hours and, decorously, local newspapers were restrained in their coverage of the intensely personal details of the case. Bryans Ackland was retained by Kate, who, as an unmarried mother, courted public disapproval with great courage, sustained by her conviction that she was in the right,

and entitled to financial support despite Dougal's dismissive attitude towards her and her son. Dougal himself was represented by
Philip Bartlett Morle, a barrister at the outset of his career and
practising as a junior on the South-Eastern Circuit.[418]

Morle cannot have been accurately briefed – Dougal can
hardly have told him his true motivation for contesting the order
– and Ackland made substantial ground, profiting, too, from his
own client's simple honesty and, no doubt, the discussions he had
held with the detective Giles. The bowdlerised press accounts
hint at the scandals brought out, to Dougal's great embarrassment, in court. For the first time in Essex, Miss Holland's
name was uttered publicly (by Ackland, perhaps via Giles), and
the mask Dougal had once given her – that of his legal wife –
dropped away.[419] Dougal was in no position to deny that he had
lived with her 'in furnished apartments' in Saffron Walden; nor
could he pretend that he had not been stripped of his army pension after being convicted of forgery, and he admitted his shame
under pressure from Kate's relentless solicitor. Sensation followed
sensation, and even Dougal's usual optimism in legal matters must
have been challenged by the damagingly one-sided nature of the
revelations. The decision of the magistrates, who ordered Dougal
to pay 5s weekly for young Herbert's upkeep – the maximum
rate permitted under the law at the time – and £1 11s 6d costs,
the alimony to be maintained until the child reached the age of
fourteen, was predictable enough in view of the evidence, and
reflected the stark imbalance in the combatants' positions.[420]
Dougal was stymied by his lies and his deceptions, going back
years.

According to Jesse, Eliza Cranwell, who, like Kate, had eventually seen Dougal for what he was, found herself inspired by her
sister's determination. 'You have had twelve months for forging
cheques,' she exclaimed. 'You will be hung next for the killing
of that woman.'[421] Dougal's reaction to this remark is not known.

From the bench, Edmund Birch Gibson's words were more
considered. Gibson was a committed church-goer, and he
found that the evidence in the affiliation case 'revealed a terrible state of things', one which challenged the precepts of his
religion.[422] Entering into the familiar rhetorical territory of
pagan – or Eastern – polygamy, a stereotype of savagery to which
Victorian England clung, Gibson told the court that, had he not

heard the facts of the case with his own ears, it 'would have been almost incredible to believe that such a state of things existed in a Christian country'. Kate's candour – and Eliza too must have admitted sleeping with Dougal – confronted typical social attitudes about the sexuality and behaviour of women. But yet she was victorious, since any decent society ought to have expected Dougal to conduct himself with more dignity and self-control. It was clear who was at fault in the case, layettes, rabbits and such doing nothing to balance Dougal's misbehaviour towards the Cranwells. It was a matter of bitter irony, therefore, that Georgina remained transfixed by him. Emily and Kate had escaped his clutches, but she stayed loyal, still thinking of a future which, had love not clouded her vision, she should have seen crumbling into dust.

Elizabeth Nichol threw in her job on 30 January, days after the court case.[423] It is hard to believe that she was not collected – or maybe rescued – by her uncle, John Burlinson, of Netteswell, near Harlow, which suggests the rapid transmission of Dougal-related gossip across the Essex countryside. In the immediate vicinity of the Moat Farm – in Clavering, Rickling, Newport, Quendon – the rumours certainly swelled. Some of these followed the terms of Eliza Cranwell's startling allegation very closely.[424]

It was increasingly obvious that all kinds of information had got abroad, the fruit of Giles's clandestine labours. He sent his findings back to headquarters, adducing five separate reasons for preventing Dougal's divorce proceedings from going any further.[425] The fourth in the list – that Dougal 'from January 1902 to September 1902 ... habitually committed adultery with Kate Honor Cranwell at the Moat Farm' – had now been demonstrated in court. It would be difficult for Dougal, who still had the right of appeal over this matter, to argue that this, at least, was immaterial or groundless. He must have been rational enough to know that his divorce proceedings were dead in the water. He wrote to Sarah, still nursing at Barming Heath, by telegram, urging her to decamp to London and await further instructions. She did so, pleading for the train fare from her erstwhile asylum colleagues, and taking rooms in her old haunt of Camberwell. Here, it was said, she agreed, at least initially, to nurse an old, blind lady with whom she lived for a while, and she spent a fortnight, subsequently, making mantles with Gertrude Schinzing at

1 Samuel Herbert Dougal, RE 8739, in Canada, perhaps drawn from an original photograph, now lost. (*Famous Crimes*, Vol. 2, no. 27)

Smyth
1895

2 Dougal in 1895, at the time of his conviction at the Old Bailey for forgery and uttering. (Author's collection)

3 Sarah Henrietta Dougal, *née* White, in 1903; this image may have been drawn from life on or after Wednesday 25 March 1903. (Author's collection)

4 Detective Inspector Alfred Marden, depicted in a thoughtful pose. His actions and inactions would strongly influence the character of the Moat Farm Mystery. (*The Moat Farm Mystery* [Daisy Bank])

5 The Royston Crow, in Ware, Hertfordshire (on the left side, with its sign appearing above and to the right of the street lamp), in less fiery days. (Author's collection)

6 Camille Cecile Holland exhibiting her youthful public countenance. (*Trial of Samuel Herbert Dougal*)

7 Henrietta Wisken, pictured in her mourning attire. (*The Moat Farm Mystery* [Daisy Bank])

8 The Moat Farm, almost hidden from view among the overgrowth. (Author's collection)

9 The dining room at the Moat Farm. Its décor was to Miss Holland's taste, and Miss Holland's taste was twenty years out of date. (*Trial of Samuel Herbert Dougal*)

10 Jack, Miss Holland's dog, on the bridge which stood across the moat. (Author's collection)

11 Florence Blackwell, apparently trapped in her grief. (*The Moat Farm Mystery* [Daisy Bank])

12 Lower Street, Stansted. Here Sarah would seem to have waited for *something* to happen. (Author's collection)

13 Henry Pilgrim, whose forename had been popularly supplanted by the epithet *Old* some years before the Moat Farm Mystery brought him to wider attention. (*The Moat Farm Mystery* [Daisy Bank])

14 Love and trust in a one-way mirror, *c.*1903: Georgina Cranwell clings to Dougal, her eyes alight with optimism; he stares blankly into the middle-distance. (Author's collection)

15 An evocation of the quotidian patterns of life which had begun to wash over the Moat Farm by the turn of the century. The carting of manure; the shooting of partridge; the purchasing of cruet from Harrod's; and falling on one's face in the road and 'damaging same'. (Author's collection)

16 Kate Cranwell, perhaps Dougal's chief local nemesis, in late 1902 and early 1903. Note Kate's pugnacious deportment. (*The Moat Farm Mystery* [Daisy Bank])

17 Eliza Cranwell, less passionate than Kate, less idealistic than Georgina. An unflattering depiction of a young woman of twenty-five. (*The Moat Farm Mystery* [Daisy Bank])

18 Thursday 19 March 1903: Dougal is escorted to Saffron Walden by DI Marden, to his left, and PC Field, to his right. This shot was taken outside the railway station at Audley End. (Author's collection)

19 Amid the great dig, a photo opportunity. With Jack, from left to right, PC Fell, DS Scott, PC Field, PC Lindsey. (Author's collection)

20 The corpse of Miss Holland, her head tilted towards the camera, her much-admired teeth exposed. (*Trial of Samuel Herbert Dougal*)

21 In the trench where the remains were discovered. Scott is visible centre-left, with Lindsey part obscured to his left, and Field part-obscured to his right. The bearded gentlemen to the right of shot may be Old Pilgrim. (Author's collection)

22 Thursday 30 April 1903 – having been charged with murder and attended the first hearing of the inquest into Miss Holland's death, Dougal is escorted away from the Moat Farm by Alfred Marden. (Author's collection)

23 The locomobile, and four cheerful, stationary motorists – Field on the left and Lindsey on the right at the back, Fell on the left and Scott on the right at the front. (*Trial of Samuel Herbert Dougal*)

24 An indication of the public interest in the Moat Farm Mystery: a crowd gathers outside Newport Parish Hall, anticipating Miss Holland's inquest. (Author's collection)

25 Miss Holland finds her final place of rest in Saffron Walden Municipal Cemetery. (Author's collection)

26 While the mystery dominated the newspapers, crowds flocked to the Moat Farm, examining for themselves the scenes which had been depicted in so many thousands of words. (Author's collection)

27 Dougal consults with his solicitor, Arthur Newton. (*The Moat Farm Mystery* [Daisy Bank])

28 The Shire Hall, in Chelmsford – scene of the trial. (Author's collection)

29 Mr Justice Wright, a fair man, well-regarded. Would his trademark compassion for the accused rescue Dougal from his predicament? (Author's collection)

30 Charles Frederick Gill, KC: lead barrister for the Crown. (*The Strand*, Vol. 25, No. 146, February 1903)

31 The Moat Farm as it looks today. (Author's collection)

150 Camberwell New Road. Later, she would move to quarters 'nearly opposite' the Schinzings, according to Gertrude's husband, Adolf. This was a low-grade, repetitive, unfulfilling existence – perhaps worse than the asylum – and one only to be tolerated temporarily. But Dougal's telegrams had reflected the necessity, in the absence of a divorce, to change the plan. Something was in the offing.

⋘⋙

PC James Drew had decided that the local rumours had gone far enough. He had been to the Moat Farm with Monk, he had spoken to the occupants, he had followed the affiliation action, and he had made up his mind to write to Superintendent William Barnard at the Saffron Walden police station. This he did, if Honeycombe is right, 'at the end of January 1903'.[426] 'Sir,' he wrote,

> I have the honour to report, for your information that is a talk in this Village Clavering about Mr. Herbert Samuel Dougal of Moat House Farm Clavering since last October a Detective named Giles was about Clavering Making enquiries respecting Mr. Dougal and a Miss Holland, which was thought to have been Dougal wife, but about 4 years ago Mr. Dougal wife lived at Stansted as his Daughter and Mr. Dougal lived at Saffron Walden till he came to the Moat House Farm Clavering with Miss Holland. After a time Miss Holland was missing. Mr. Dougal told People she had gone in the Continent and he was Expecting her back, but she has not been seen in Clavering since. Great many things are reported to be in Mr. Dougal's House marked C.C. Holland. Since the last two Cases at the Bench from Moat House it roused people to talk again and it is now said it was Miss Hollands Money that bought Moat House Farm and People think now he must have done away with her and buried her. Dougal about 6 months ago applied for a Divorce from his wife who had misbehaved herself with a man Named George Killick Engine driver somewhere Nr. Maidstone in Kent and Dougal split on him Killick has been heard to say there will be an Essex Mystery Mr. Gaylor Farmer of Clavering was talking to me one day said his cows got into the old Castle Grounds he saw a Piece of Ground had been Moved the shape of a grave. I am now told that letters has come to Moat House addressed Miss Holland and have been answered by Dougal's wife.

I have the honour to be, Sir,

Your obedient Servant

(Signed) James Drew, P.C. 124

Mr. Supt. Barnard.[427]

It was breathless stuff, sentence spilling into sentence in Drew's urgent prose, but perhaps also a skilled distillation of the untamed, demented gossip which filled the countryside. Killick, cut off from the story after Sarah's rejection of him, suddenly reappeared in Drew's letter spouting supernatural, prophetic wisdom, warning obliquely of an 'Essex Mystery'. Somewhere near the Moat Farm, the very earth seemed to have risen, grave-like, pregnant with its secrets, in the fields where the cowmen roamed. Superintendent Barnard sent the letter on to Captain Showers, the Chief Constable of the Essex Constabulary.

Edward Maclean Showers was an ex-soldier who, like his father, grandfather and great-grandfather, had served in India.[428] Abandoning this career and moving to England, he studied to become a senior policeman, being given initial responsibility for the Exeter force.[429] In 1888, he became Chief Constable of the much larger Essex Constabulary, and, by 1903, he had attracted the esteem of his public and the attention of his superiors. In 1902, he had been in the early running for the high-profile appointment of Commissioner of the City of London Police.[430]

In 1888, the Saffron Walden Division – within the jurisdiction of which the Moat Farm lay – had been overseen by one Superintendent, one Inspector, one Sergeant and eighteen Constables, and was one of the smaller divisions in the county.[431] It remained so in 1903, and Showers, ruminating on Drew's letter, detailed Detective Inspector Alfred Marden, based at Romford, to look into the matter. Marden travelled to Clavering on Saturday 28 February.[432]

Marden was in many ways a remarkable man. He had garnered praise and notice as long before as 1885, when he went with Inspector Simmons to arrest David Dredge, James Lee and Jack Martin, an unsavoury triumvirate who were better known to the Metropolitan and City forces than they were to the Essex police.[433] Henry Smith, Commissioner of the City Police until 1901, knew that Lee and Martin 'always carried six-shooters', and, when Simmons and Marden apprehended the gang in a field off the Romford Road, Marden discovered that Dredge did, too. Dredge waved his revolver in Marden's face, but Simmons, detaining Lee and Martin nearby, fell, shot through the abdomen, the bullet lodging in his spine.[434] Marden ran to his stricken colleague, who encouraged him to pursue the miscreants, at that moment fleeing across the fields. Courageously, Marden went after them, but lost them, returning to assist the wounded Simmons, who succumbed to his injuries four days later.[435] Later, Lee was executed for Simmons's murder, although James Berry, his executioner, had doubts over the validity of the conviction.[436] Dredge was acquitted of murder – it was plainly evident that he had not fired the shot, although the prosecution argued that the consequences of collaborative crimes ought to fall on the whole party – but he was later convicted of threatening Marden and given a short custodial sentence with hard labour.[437] Martin was picked up for a separate murder some time afterwards, and hanged for this offence.[438] Marden was awarded a Star of Merit, and began his progress through the higher echelons of the Essex Constabulary.[439]

Further acclaim arrived when Marden, by then a Police Sergeant, helped to solve the 1894 murder of Florrie Dennis by James Canham Read at Prittlewell, and a step sideways to Detective Sergeant followed shortly afterwards. He was made a Detective Inspector in 1901, and his star was in its ascendant when Captain Showers asked him to investigate the rumours surrounding Dougal.

Marden's initial enquiries in north-west Essex led him to the conclusion that the Moat Farm ought to be visited. To this end, Superintendent Charles Edwin Pryke was detailed to call on Dougal. Pryke had been Superintendent of the Saffron Walden Division (and, before that, an Inspector in the same division) until he had departed for the larger Epping Division in the summer of 1902.[440] Pryke knew Dougal's locale like no other senior policeman – he had been inundated with flattering compliments at his testimonial, held at Saffron Walden Town Hall on Tuesday 29 July 1902, a function attended by Joseph Bell, Bryans Ackland and Captain Showers, among many others. On Wednesday 4 March 1903, in plain clothes, he travelled up to the Moat Farm.[441]

Dougal recognised him: 'He knew I was a police officer,' Pryke recalled.[442] Dougal invited his visitor into the house, and, Pryke said, 'I went in with him and told him I was instructed by my chief constable to make enquiries with reference to a scandal in the village and vicinity respecting the missing Miss C.C. Holland'.[443] No doubt, he said, you are aware of the rumour about her?[444]

'Yes,' said Dougal, 'There is a lot of talk caused by my divorced wife and my late servant, Kate Cranwell.'[445]

Pryke warned Dougal that he had been told to write down his responses; Dougal 'did not raise any objection', and Pryke got out a pencil and some paper.[446]

'Can you give me any information with a view to tracing the missing Miss Holland?' asked Pryke.

'I know nothing about her,' sniffed Dougal, 'and have not seen her since I left her at Stansted Railway Station about three years ago.'[447]

Pryke persisted. Dougal told him that Miss Holland had taken some luggage with her to the train station, 'which I believe consisted of two boxes'. But the details of Dougal's acquaintance with Miss Holland were proving difficult to recall. Pryke asked the names of the missing lady's relatives. 'I know none of her relations or friends,' said Dougal.

Pryke asked whether any of her possessions remained in the house, but Dougal said that they did not. Then he appeared to take Pryke into his confidence. 'We had a tiff a few days before she left me,' he admitted, ashamed, 'in consequence of my servant, a girl of about eighteen years of age, telling her that during the night I tried to enter her bedroom, which was false, as the knocking was caused by the weight of the clock striking against the wall when I was winding it up.'[448]

So she had left him – but it had all been a misunderstanding, precipitated by an ill-timed decision to wind the clock. Pryke asked for more information about Miss Holland.

'Miss Holland was a woman of about forty years of age,' said Dougal, dramatically underestimating her real vintage.[449] By her nature, she was 'reticent and penurious'. When they met, 'four years ago at Camberwell Green, London, she stated she was secretary to a ladies' club somewhere in the West End of London'.[450] This sounded like Miss Booty, except for the detail about the ladies' club; but this distant episode in Dougal's criminal career was as yet unknown to Pryke. 'She [Miss Holland] lived with me in London, Saffron Walden and here,' Dougal went on, again failing to tell the real truth. 'I never heard her say she had been in India, but she told me she had travelled on the Continent.'

Dougal's memory was letting him down, but Pryke continued his interrogation. Did Miss Holland have any financial assets?

'If she had any money or any railway shares or stocks, I was not aware of it,' said Dougal.

Did Dougal receive letters addressed to the missing woman?

'I have never received any letters here addressed to Miss Holland, but I have received a number of circulars.'[451]

'There is a rumour that your late servant, Kate Cranwell, when here signed several papers in the name of C.C. Holland,' said Pryke.

'That is false,' snorted Dougal, animated enough by the suggestion to slip into a less formal register. 'She never done such a thing for me.'[452]

But the rumours were there, as Pryke pointed out. Had Dougal profited from her absence; had he forged her signature, or asked anybody else to do so?

'I have never sent any papers away signed in the name of Miss Holland, and I have never received any money or anything else belonging to her.'[453]

'Is it a fact,' said Pryke, 'that the Moat House and the lands belong to her?'[454]

'No, it does not,' said Dougal. 'I purchased them with my money and they were transferred to me by Messrs Harris & Ingram, solicitors, Lincoln's Inn Fields, London, who will no doubt give you full particulars of the same if you see them.'[455] By now, Pryke had probably begun to get the impression that Dougal would have liked him to go. 'Harris,' Dougal went on, as if seeking to help Pryke avoid a social mishap when he departed to make his enquiries with the solicitors, 'I believe committed suicide since.'[456] This much was true, but Dougal had misremembered, or Pryke had misheard, Harrison's name.

Pryke was not deterred by Dougal's dark undertone. He began to ponder the question of Miss Holland's grounds for leaving – all over a clock being wound? Surely her misapprehension could have been easily corrected?

This nudged Dougal into another disclosure, one as unreal as the first had been. 'During the time Miss Holland lived with me,' he said, 'she used to receive letters from a man who represented himself to be a Sea Captain. She received one from him two days before she left for good.'

In Dougal's new reading, the incident with the clock had merely furnished Miss Holland with a convenient excuse; the love-letters from the Sea Captain were what had really motivated her to leave the Moat Farm. Pryke must have found the machine-gun discrepancies of Dougal's account difficult to reconcile, but he continued to prod his interviewee towards a more coherent sequence of events.

Miss Holland's flouncing departure for the preferred affections of the Sea Captain had left Dougal in the house with the unnamed servant. The day after Miss Holland took flight from the farm (or 'about three days after' – both versions exist in transcript), Dougal went on, the servant's mother turned up with the intention of removing her daughter, who was still shocked by her employer's vigorous, midnight clock-winding.[457] 'She abused me,' Dougal complained, 'and alleged that I had been interfering with her daughter. She said she should go and tell the police at Newport. A publican from Newport drove her away. I don't know the servant's name or where she came from, but I believe Waltham.'[458]

Before he had come to Essex, Dougal said, he had lived at Biggin Hill 'for seven or eight years'. And when was the last time he left the farm? 'On Tuesday, the 24th of last month, I went from here to visit my sister, Miss Emily Dougal, at Upham, Bishops Walton [sic], Hampshire. I returned home the following evening, where I have been ever since.'

Pryke was beginning to examine the room they were standing in. 'It is alleged that Miss Holland is supposed to be shut up in a room in this house,' he said. This was one version of Miss Holland's whereabouts that had been sweeping through the community, the idea apparently being that the poor woman was occasionally coerced into signing the cheques which funded Dougal's lifestyle. 'Do you mind me having a look round?'

'Certainly, go where you like,' said Dougal, and they went through the house together. Reaching what Dougal called a 'lumber room' – a room for storing unwanted furniture which was too good to throw away – he pointed to the grand piano and some other items which stood near to it, and said, 'I brought these from Kent, and some I bought at an auction sale. All the furniture in the house is mine.'[459]

'Is it correct that some of the clothing, dresses, and so on, left behind by Miss Holland, you gave to your wife and servant, and they had them altered and wore them?' Pryke asked.

'I could not do that,' Dougal replied, 'because she left nothing behind her. My late wife is lying and trying to do me all the harm she can; she knows as much or more about Miss Holland than I do.'

This statement must have given Pryke something to think about, but he pressed on nonetheless.

'Your present servant' – Georgina, whom Pryke saw as he and Dougal walked around the house – 'has been seen wearing a gold watch and chain. Did they belong to Miss Holland?'

'No,' said Dougal. 'That was in pawn; I bought the ticket from a man, and took the watch and chain out of pledge. You can see them if you like.'

'He fetched them and showed them to me,' Pryke remembered. 'They were a lady's gold watch and gold Albert chain, apparently new.'[460]

'Was your son here last week?' Pryke asked.[461] This may have referred to George, who had followed his father into the Royal Engineers, and who had returned to native shores at the end of January 1903 after serving for several years in Mauritius.

'Yes, for a few days, and he is now in London,' said Dougal.

Pryke intimated that he would try to look for the clock-frightened servant. Did Dougal have any idea where he could find her?

'Miss Holland hired the servant,' he said, 'and that is the reason I do not know her name or where she came from.'

Pryke left the house prepared to assume that he had been told the truth, disjointed and bizarre though some of Dougal's explanations seemed. Later, he would justify his credulity – 'I did not know he was lying. It was all rumour at the time.' – and admitted that he had shaken Dougal's hand as he left the farm.[462] But the very circumstances of his mission must have suggested to him that something substantial was in the air. Before travelling to Clavering, he had been summoned to Captain Showers's office in Chelmsford and, with Showers's brother-in-law and second-in-command Raglan Somerset also present, briefed on 'a number of points upon which I was to seek information' from Dougal. He was acquainted with the outline of the scandal then in transmission across the Essex countryside, and presumably saw Drew's letter.[463] The briefing took three quarters of an hour.[464] He was aware that the police had been making enquiries for 'some days'.[465]

Pryke wrote up his notes on Thursday 5 March and submitted them to Captain Showers. The same day, Dougal fled.

CHAPTER EIGHT

BY THE EVENING of Thursday 5 March, Dougal was no longer in Essex. That morning, he had visited the London & County Bank, in Bishop's Stortford, where he had held two accounts since 22 December 1902.[466] One was a current account, the other a deposit account. From his deposit account, he removed £300, its total contents. Then he went to London, where, it seems, he withdrew £305 from his account with the Birkbeck Bank, leaving behind only 16s 7d.[467]

Jesse supposed that Dougal spent a week in the capital, laden with money, staying at the London Central Hotel at 23 Long Lane, Smithfield, until 12 March, but the hotel's proprietor, John Vincent, explicitly denied it.[468] 'I am sure he did not stay here during the whole of that period,' he said, although he confessed that it was possible that Dougal may have slept there on 'any one night'. The hotel's rudimentary record-keeping systems did not permit him to trace the identities of his guests, and George Beves, the hotel's night porter, could say no more than that Dougal 'has occasionally slept at the hotel for a night, not more, at any one time'.

Other reports depicted Dougal out and about in the West End, 'certainly not appearing to be hiding from the police', but perhaps making himself anonymous in the vast crowds, and always moving.[469] This entropic, extemporary existence defied the scrutiny of the public and police alike: Dougal was ostensibly free, although he had his fears for company, alarmed by Pryke's visit and the ratcheting-up of official misgivings that this represented. Sarah's arrival in London from Kent, 'summoned' by his telegrams, may have done something to calm his escalating fears, but she may also have demanded the adoption of a more focused approach. Massive withdrawals of money were all very well, but, in the circumstances, they were liable to attract attention.

But so too was panicked flight; and, after the relief of a week in the facelessness of London, Dougal returned to the Moat Farm on the evening of Thursday 12 March.[470]

⚬⚬⚬

Superintendent Pryke's mind was changed on Sunday 8 March, when Inspector Marden hinted at evidence of wrongdoing which, he wrote to Captain Showers, undermined any lingering belief in the plausibility of Dougal's story of clockwork abandonment and seductive Sea Captains.[471] Marden had been delving into the secrets of the Moat Farm, matching each rumour against the emerging evidence, and a case of an increasingly compelling nature was coming together.

It was becoming clear that Dougal's fortune had originated with Miss Holland. The £5 note numbered 65070 – one of six sent to Dougal on 8 June 1899 – had left a trail, finally reposing in the London & County Bank after being deposited there by Thomas Mumford, the grocer from Quendon whose business Dougal used to frequent, and who himself had grown accustomed to the fact that, every so often, the newest in a retinue of 'different females' would arrive from the Moat Farm to make purchases on Dougal's behalf.[472] None of these females resembled the 'elderly lady' with whom Mumford had first seen Dougal. If the banknote had been the product of a forgery – which Marden suspected it had – the evidence would be found at the Piccadilly branch of the National Provincial Bank, where Miss Holland held her account. On Wednesday 11 March, he travelled to London, stopping at Scotland Yard on his way up to Piccadilly.

Marden called at the Yard at 1.00p.m., and his enquiry was directed to Police Sergeant Alfred Ball. Ball listened with, no doubt, growing astonishment as Marden outlined the case against Dougal, which concluded with the local rumours of Miss Holland's murder. Marden asked Ball to accompany him to the National Provincial Bank; Ball sought permission from Chief Inspector Arthur Hare to do so and, gaining it, the two men set off towards Piccadilly Circus.

At the bank, Ball and Marden learned that Miss Holland had held her account since 1895, that she had paid £1,800 for the Moat Farm, that she had never given a different subsequent address, and that 'about £3,070 had been drawn from her accounts up to the end of 1901'. As they expected, the records showed that a number of the cheques extracted from Miss Holland's funds had been made payable to Dougal. Ball recorded that a balance of 'about £1,500' remained in the account – this was probably a mistake, since Francis Manley Bird Ashwin, an accountant at the Piccadilly Branch, would later find that the balance was in fact £207 19s 4d.[473]

All the cheques which been signed in Miss Holland's name in the previous four years had been returned to her at the Moat Farm – except one. The bank produced the cheque to J. Heath for £28 15s, signed on 28 August 1902, and eventually paid via Dougal's account, ensuring dull anonymity at the vendor's end.[474] This cheque and its controversial endorsement would now form the centrepiece of the police's forgery case. However, the raft of correspondence which made up Miss Holland's file at the bank included other evidence of a highly suspicious character. It cannot have evaded Marden's attention that the £5 note he had traced in Essex had been issued the day after Miss Holland had apparently sent written reassurance to the bank, apologising for the fact that her signature might not be as good as it usually was, owing to a sprained hand.

Contact had already been made with Ernest Legrand Holland. Camille's nephew – the brother of the similarly neglected Edmund George Holland and Mary Laura Mann – had admitted to Inspector Marden on Saturday 7 March that he had had no interaction of any sort with his aunt since 1899. Marden mentioned his suspicions with regard to the fraudulent emptying of her bank account.[475] On Monday 9 March, Ernest went to the National Provincial Bank at Piccadilly, accompanied by Marden, to examine the paperwork in question. Seeing the Heath cheque produced by Ashwin, Ernest immediately denounced it as a forgery.[476] Then more of Miss Holland's signatures were produced, on bank forms and in letters, and, amid emotional scenes, Ernest denounced them, too, crying, 'They are all wrong'.[477] Marden seemed to concur with Ernest's opinion, but Ashwin was more circumspect. From his perspective, Miss Holland varied her signature 'considerably, but not unusually so'.[478] Creeping senescence might have accounted for her diminishing ability to replicate her mark. Even more tellingly, Ashwin knew that some of the documents he had shown Ernest had been signed by Miss Holland, in person, at the bank – these dated from 19 September

1895 to 30 April 1899, during which period she was known to have been alive and moving around in society.[479]

Ernest's shock and indignation had obviously got the better of him – Ashwin went on to say that Ernest did not look at the documents closely 'as far as I remember ... except the cheque'.[480] Ernest later denied that he had misfired, claiming that Ashwin's rendition of the scene was 'quite inaccurate' and 'absolutely untrue'.[481] He claimed not to have been overtaken by his emotions, saying that the police's interest in the mystery of his aunt's disappearance did not upset him, or, at least, 'not a great deal'. But, regardless of the shakiness of Ernest's opinion, the incident provided Marden with the imprimatur to interest Lord Desart, the Director of Public Prosecutions in the affair. He presented his evidence to Desart, probably on Tuesday 10 March, leaving copies with Seward Pearce, a solicitor working for the Treasury; on the same day, Captain Showers had been talking to Melville Macnaghten, who within a week would be promoted to the exalted office of Assistant Commissioner of the Metropolitan Police. Showers's view, Macnaghten wrote on 12 March 1903, was that 'there may be nothing in it – or it *may* develop into a really big thing'.[482]

∾∾∾

Back at home after his excursion to London, Dougal made plans with Georgina which paralleled those he had made with Sarah. Georgina seems not to have accompanied him on his travels, and instead probably spent a lonely week by herself in the old Elizabethan house, surrounded by the blank fields. If, wanting entertainment, she had picked up a copy of *The Times* on Tuesday 10 March, she would have found that Dougal's petition for divorce had been swiftly set aside the day before. In a hearing at the Royal Courts of Justice on the Strand, Sir Francis Jeune heard the objections of the King's Proctor. Since neither Dougal nor Sarah was present to respond, the *decree nisi* was quashed, and Dougal made liable for the costs.[483]

It was a remarkable coincidence of events. While the police hunted for Dougal's forgeries at the bank, the barristers tore down his tapestry of lies in the divorce courts. Dougal himself manoeuvred silently between them, invisible in the city's labyrinth, somewhere with Sarah.

His return to the Moat Farm on Thursday 12 March, and the sudden promise of a holiday to the coast, must have restored a forlorn Georgina's confidence in her impulsive beau. Certainly, she swiftly returned to her obedient habits. Even the peculiarities of the travel arrangements upon which he insisted seemed to escape her notice – she passively agreed to them, failing – or declining – to see them in their context. Georgina was to wait until the Saturday before taking the train to London; but Dougal would go the next morning.[484] This he did, stopping only to give Charles Burgess, one of his farm labourers, his wages of 15*s* before being driven away by a man named Livings (described unflatteringly as 'a true born Claveringite, not quite a weak intellect') in the pony and trap.[485] Hours later, he was in London, making himself indistinct again in the blur of traffic and people. PC Philip Fell had been detailed to watch the farm, but, for some reason, he had not seen Dougal go.

Georgina, however, drew more attention to herself than was good for Dougal. On Saturday 14 March, she caught the 10.00a.m. train from Newport to Liverpool Street Station.[486] With her she had 'a box and a portmanteau', both of which she left in the cloakroom at the latter station, retaining the ticket the clerk gave her. The portmanteau was marked with the letters *C.C.H.*, but only 'very faintly'.[487] Georgina handed them in using her own name. Dougal met her, and from there they travelled briskly across the City, crossing the Thames and making for Waterloo Station, and a connection for Bournemouth. Dougal had already sent a telegram to William Barkas, the proprietor of the Coburg Boarding House:

Please reserve double room, lady and self. Dougal.

They arrived in Bournemouth that evening, a world away from the chaos of their lives at the Moat Farm. It was a feeble way by which they attempted to render themselves oblivious to their impending ruin. For Dougal, the south coast evoked memories of Binstead, and his last moments of happiness and serenity some twenty-five years before. Then, he was at the summit of his abilities, his lively mind alighting on new and specialised technical subjects with ready facility. Georgina had been just a child at the time.

What they did on Sunday is not recorded, but on Monday 16 March, they took a steamer trip along the coast to Swanage. It was the archetype of Edwardian tourism – a man and his young wife enjoying the English shoreline, albeit at the wrong time of year. The weather forecast was for strong winds leading to gales, and overcast and squally conditions.[488]

Perhaps it was too difficult to ignore the inevitable; more likely, Dougal had an appointment with Sarah. Dougal and Georgina caught the train back to London on Tuesday 17 March and went to the London Central Hotel in Smithfield.[489] Dougal paid 3*s* for room 5 and they slept there overnight.

✧✦✧

Georgina's departure from the Moat Farm had alerted the Essex Constabulary to Dougal's absence. Marden returned to Scotland Yard on Sunday 15 March, telling Inspector Elias Bower that Dougal was missing.[490] Bower had been detailed to follow the case at the request of Lord Desart, although Marden, after his previous visit of 11 March, had requested that the Metropolitan CID take no action unless directed to do so by the Treasury or by Captain Showers. Bower's track record had regularly taken him into the territory of forgery, fraud and deception, which suited him to the Moat Farm case. Marden explained that he had sent two Essex officers to watch Georgina's deposited luggage at Liverpool Street Station; Bower, approvingly, sent PC Charles Backhurst and Police Sergeant James Cunningham to support them.

Marden went straight to Chiswick, meeting Seward Pearce at his home and, the next day, Pearce, Marden, Bower and Ernest Holland met at the Treasury, on Whitehall. Holland's conviction that the cheque he had seen was a forgery remained intact. He recorded his feelings, and with the police officers' suspicions written up, Marden and Holland raced to Saffron Walden Police Court, where a warrant was issued for Dougal's arrest on a charge of forgery.[491] Marden sent a telegram to Scotland Yard, handing it in at the Post Office at Saffron Walden at 5.42p.m. It was received in London just before six o'clock: 'Warrant granted no trouble'.[492]

After their meeting at the Treasury, the policemen and the Director of Public Prosecutions had agreed 'that we should concentrate our efforts to secure his [Dougal's] arrest', as Bower put it. As yet, however, there was no indication as to his whereabouts. On the morning of Tuesday 17 March, Captain Showers sent a memorandum to Bower asking him to have Dougal's photograph reproduced in the *Informations* and the *Police Gazette* – publications which would distribute his details to the police forces across the country. Marden had found a copy of Dougal and Georgina's portrait in the box at Liverpool Street Station. Showers offered to meet the costs of the exercise; Bower requested permission to go ahead with the plan, and Superintendent Donald Swanson, a veteran of the Jack the Ripper case who was now only months away from retirement, authorised him to do so. Dougal's physical description had already been circulated in edition 318 of the *Informations*, published on 16 March. He did not know it, but, when he checked into the London Central Hotel on Long Lane on Tuesday 17 March, all of London's police officers were looking out for Samuel Herbert Dougal.

⟣⟨⟩⟢

Dougal and Georgina awoke on the morning of 18 March and went to their hotel reception desk. John Vincent was there.[493] 'Will you kindly take charge of my luggage?' asked Dougal, and he handed Vincent 'a portmanteau, [a] bag and I think something else'. Vincent put them securely in the office.

He then asked Dougal whether he would want the same bedroom that evening. 'I am not quite sure,' replied Dougal. 'My movements are very uncertain.' Dougal and Georgina left the hotel, Dougal carrying a dressing bag, at about 10.00a.m.[494]

They went first to Liverpool Street Station.[495] They did not seek to take their luggage out of storage; in fact, Dougal deposited his dressing bag in the second cloakroom at the station.[496] He saw Georgina onto a Great Eastern Railway train for Essex, no doubt promising to rejoin her later that day. For reasons which are not immediately clear, she did not arrive back at the Moat Farm – although it was a journey of less than two hours – until the evening.[497]

In going to the station, Dougal was lucky to avoid the notice of the police. He was perhaps more fortuitous than clever to have used the second cloakroom, rather than returning to the cloakroom where Backhurst and Cunningham and their brother officers from the Essex Constabulary kept guard. The vast city offered the anonymity of thousands of bodies, all twisting and heaving in the rapid crush of Edwardian life, but matched it with the threat of thousands of pairs of eyes. This time, the crowd had screened Dougal from his pursuers. He may have reflected, as Georgina's train pulled away from the platform, that he would need similar good fortune if he were to escape the country unseen. He had no intention of returning to Essex.

Down Bishopsgate and Gracechurch Street, across the river, and in the cloakroom at London Bridge Station, there lay a trunk, registered in the name of White.[498] It was marked with the initials *C.C.H.W.*, but closer observation showed that 'the "W" had been recently added; it was of a different coloured paint'. The trunk's owner's whereabouts were not clear – somewhere in London, Sarah awaited the rendezvous which would take them out of England.

Back at the Moat Farm, Dougal's plans lay in blueprint. He apparently 'contemplated a trip to Ostend, and thence into Germany' – a flight into the unknown, and a mark of his urgent desperation.[499]

He had only to muddy the trail of his recent cash withdrawals – then they could flee. On 5 March, after he had drained his Birkbeck account, Dougal had gone to the Bank of England, presented five £20 notes and one £10 note, and asked for them to be changed for twenty-two £5 notes.[500] The man had nerves of steel – behind the counter sat William Richard Percy Lawrence, who had testified against Dougal when he processed his Dublin frauds through the Bank of England in 1895. Nearly eight years on, would Lawrence identify him – and what if he did? The notes were endorsed in the name of 'S. Herbert Dougal, Quendon, Essex'. Lawrence saw nothing amiss, handing over the £5 notes.

But Dougal was still carrying around the other notes he had been given on 5 March, and on 17 March Bower had visited the Birkbeck Bank in an attempt to ascertain which ones they were.[501] He was given the serial numbers, recorded in the ledger, and sent Sergeant Ball to the Bank of England to register the notes as the proceeds of a suspicious transaction – if the cashiers saw them, they were to alert the police. Dougal's visit of 5 March was appreciated when a glance at the counter cash book showed that notes numbered 90513-90517 (the £20 notes) and 84571 (the

£10 note) had indeed passed through Lawrence's hands.[502] The trace of a second visit, on 6 March, was also found. This time, Dougal dealt with Leonard Clarence Brookes, another cashier. He handed in two £100 notes, numbers 93178 and 93179, exchanging them for twenty £5 notes (numbers 96767-96786), eight £10 notes (numbers 99435-99442) and £20 in gold coin. Note 93178 bore an endorsement which matched those of the notes given over on the previous day. The total exchanged over the two visits — £310 — was greater than the sum withdrawn from the Birkbeck, alerting the police to the possibility that Dougal had drawn on more than one account. Nor did all the notes match the serial numbers given to the police by the Birkbeck bank. Somewhere, there were some £10 notes from this withdrawal which Dougal had *not* changed — at least, notes which he had not changed at the Bank of England. It was a convoluted operation, but Ball asked the bank to look out for any of the notes which were unaccounted for from the original Birkbeck withdrawal, and any of the smaller denomination notes into which Dougal had had his money changed by Brookes and Lawrence.

At about 1.30p.m. on Wednesday 18 March 1903, Dougal strolled into the Bank of England.[503] He approached the unfortunate Lawrence, who showed no signs of recognising his customer despite Ball's instructions of the previous day, and handed over fourteen £10 notes. These were numbered 13856-13860 and 84572-84580; one (number 13860) was endorsed in the name of Sydney Domville, Upper Terrace, Bournemouth. Lawrence checked his list. Finding that some of the notes matched the serial numbers mentioned by the police, Lawrence said, 'I am sorry, but I shall have to ask you to accompany me to the secretary's office.'

'Why? Are the notes stopped?' said Dougal.

'Some of them are,' said Lawrence. 'They will give you any information in the secretary's office, and it will be a question which will detain you for a few moments.'

Lawrence showed Dougal into the secretary's office, where the clerk, Ronald Clement George Dale, was working.[504] Dougal took a seat, and Lawrence asked Dale whether they might speak privately. Dale stood up, and accompanied Lawrence out of the office: Lawrence handed him the fourteen £10 notes, and Dale checked them against the police's list. He, too, found that the serial numbers corresponded, and he sent for Detective

Inspector Harry Cox, of the City of London Police, who was on duty at the bank.

In the meantime, Dale went back into his office where a docile Dougal had been waiting patiently for him. 'Where did you get these notes from?' asked Dale.[505]

'I got some of them from the bank,' muttered Dougal, meaning the Bank of England, as if it were Lawrence's fault – or, perhaps, Brookes's – that he had been encumbered with suspicious banknotes after a previous transaction. But Dale pointed out that some of the notes were marked with the stamp of the Birkbeck Bank, so it was obvious that they had not come from the Bank of England. Dougal's response to Dale's observation is not recorded.

Dale gave Dougal a slip of paper. 'Please write your name and address on that,' he said. Dougal took a pencil and wrote, *Sydney Domville, Upper Terrace, Bournemouth.* This matched the endorsement on the note Lawrence had seen.

At this point, Detective Inspector Cox arrived at the office. Later, writing in retrospect, Cox would recall having seen Dougal entering the bank – he was 'a tall, handsome man with sparkling blue eyes', Cox remembered, perhaps slightly romantically.[506] Now, Dale gave Cox the £10 notes marked with the Birkbeck stamp and the slip of paper with Domville's name on it.[507] Cox turned to Dougal, who continued to wait more-or-less good-naturedly.

'I am Inspector Cox, of the City of London Police,' he announced. 'I am informed that these nine £10 notes are part proceeds of a forgery. How do you account for the possession of them?'

'I would rather not say anything now,' said Dougal.[508]

Cox examined the slip of paper, and the banknotes. 'Is this your name?' he asked, pointing to the paper.[509] 'Sydney Domville?'

'No,' confessed Dougal.

'Your name is Dougal?' suggested Cox.

'Yes,' said Dougal.[510]

Cox told Dougal that they would have to go to the Detective Office at 26 Old Jewry, a short walk away from the Bank of England. 'All right,' said Dougal.

Later, Cox's memory made the events in Ronald Dale's office into something rather more stylised – Dougal became a mannered, bluff swell, 'rising and bowing' when Cox entered the room, and describing himself as 'at your service' when Cox mentioned the trip to Old Jewry.[511] In contrast, Cox portrayed himself as intuitive, self-confident, and scrupulously fair. It was true that there was now the problem of getting Dougal to the police station. Cox was not the only policeman of his era to consider the use of handcuffs unnecessary and undignified provided the arrested man promised to behave himself. According to his recollections, Cox sought Dougal's word on the matter.

'Now, Dougal, I have no wish to hurt your feelings in any way,' he said, 'and if you will walk quietly with me no one shall know you are with a detective!'

'Very well, Mr Cox,' Dougal replied.

Cox defended his decision to trust Dougal, observing that 'I knew absolutely nothing about my prisoner' who was, as far as he was aware, wanted only for the forgery of a cheque for less than £30. Cox had not charged Dougal with an offence: under the circumstances, Cox felt confident that they could walk to the station together. Just in case of trouble, Cox had taken the precaution of requesting that a colleague of his, Detective Williams, act as chaperone.[512]

Dougal's calm manner quickly convinced Cox that his decision had been a good one. The three men strolled casually towards Old Jewry, aiming to enter it at its northern end: the police station stood nearby, through a gateway and passage on the west side of the road. With a little distance to go, Cox sent Williams on ahead: he was concerned not to leave the bank unmanned, and asked Williams to hurry to the station to request that another detective attend the bank to cover for him. Williams promptly disappeared around the corner of Old Jewry and Gresham Street. Dougal's steady pace remained the same, shoulder to shoulder with Cox.

They turned into Old Jewry, yards from the gateway, when Dougal suddenly broke into a sprint. He fled south towards the crucible of Poultry and Cheapside and the knot of London's ancient streets.[513] Cox, initially taken by surprise, sped after him.

Dougal skipped nimbly around a clutch of men who were standing on the pavement. 'Stop him!' shouted Cox, but the bystanders 'took no notice of me'.[514] Dougal ran on, and Cox 'knew that unless I kept my wits about me he would succeed in escaping'.

From the gates of the police station, PC George Padgham joined the pursuit.[515] The policemen saw Dougal turn suddenly right, before the junction with Poultry, into Frederick's Place.

'A feeling of intense relief o'ercame me,' wrote Cox, poetically. 'I knew he was safe, for he had turned into a cul-de-sac.'[516]

Cox reached the mouth of Frederick's Place and saw that Dougal, a few yards ahead, had realised his mistake. Dougal turned and sprinted towards Cox. Cox kept his position. Dougal 'endeavoured to spring past me', Cox remembered, but as he did so, 'I shot out my fist and, striking him on the jaw, felled him to the ground'. Other accounts describe different measures, with Cox 'catching [Dougal] by the neck' and even, agriculturally, 'gripping him by the neck [and administering] a professional twist which felled [Dougal] like an ox'.[517] Cox conceded that the chase had been an exhausting one – he fell upon Dougal and, with Padgham racing to his assistance, 'you may be sure that once I had him secure he did not escape a second time'.[518] They dragged Dougal to his feet and took him, dazed and spent, to the police station.[519]

❧

At the station it was discovered that, underneath his greatcoat, Dougal glistened with jewels. The police's list of the items found about his person represented a stunning trove of charms and valuables, not all of which were obviously their prisoner's:

> ... an 18 ct. massive double open curb Albert with 15 ct. gold English lever keyless watch, centre seconds, No. 40096; 1 silver English lever watch, No. 12484, makers Kendal and Dent, 'A.J.W.' in monogram on back; 1 silver keyless Waltham watch, No. 1479052, 'S.H.D.' in monogram on back; 1 lady's 9 ct. gold guard; 1 lady's 18 ct. gold English lever watch, No. 65587, maker R. Roskell, Liverpool; 1 lady's 10 ct. gold Waltham keyless demi-hunter watch, No. 4122208; 6 unset stones, viz., 5 moonstones and 1 amethyst; 1 18 ct. horseshoe pin, set 8 diamonds and 9 pearls; 1 do. double-headed snake ring; 1 lady's gold ring, set pearl; 1 do. set in coronet fashion with 9 small and 1 large pearl; 1 lady's gold charm ring, clasped hands; 1 lady's gold ring, set large amethyst, claw setting; 1 lady's gold brooch, set 20 pearls, photograph in centre, hair in box at back, gold safety chain attached; 1 gold brooch, originally set 8 amethysts around edge, 1 large amethyst in centre, 1 small

stone missing; 1 gold oval portrait brooch; 1 lady's 18 ct. gold keeper ring; 1 15 ct. do., 'ASTORE' thereon; 1 22 ct. gold ring, set diamond, claw setting; 1 plain gold oval locket; 1 lady's 18 ct. gold Geneva watch, No. 81768; 1 bird's claw, mounted as brooch, in silver, set amethyst; 1 round gold brooch with carbuncle in centre, small pearl set therein; 1 small oblong silver vinaigrette; 1 oval granite do., mounted in silver; 2 foreign beetles, mounted in silver as earrings; 1 silver Oriental earring; 1 gold earring, turquoise in centre; 1 pair amethysts, mounted in silver as earrings; 5 silver bangles; 1 wedding ring, thin; 1 silver bookmark, shape of trowel, with onyx handle; 1 lady's silver Albert, Prince of Wales pattern, made with 3 balls therein; 1 silver gilt strap bracelet, with oblong bloodstone set near buckle.[520]

In addition, Dougal possessed eighty-three £5 Bank of England notes; eight £10 Bank of England notes; £63 in gold; two postal orders for 4s each, two more for 5s each, and one worth 7s 6d; postage stamps to the value of 2s 3½d; one £5 gold coin; a pocket case and memo; a pawn duplicate for a ring; a cigar cutter; a knife; two pairs of eyeglasses; a railway cloakroom ticket; a walking stick; a fountain pen; and a pipe and a pouch of tobacco.[521]

This was astonishing, decadent wealth – the man bulged with money and finery. Superintendent James McWilliam, who was also at the station, must have realised that this vast array of jewellery was not all for Dougal's own adornment. 'Where is the lady?' he demanded, referring to Miss Holland. Dougal calmly 'denied all knowledge of her'.[522]

Inspector Marden arrived in the city towards midnight.[523] Following his initial examination at Old Jewry, Dougal had been transferred south across the city to the police station at Cloak Lane. Here, Marden charged him with forging the Heath cheque.[524]

'Where is the warrant?' asked Dougal.[525]

Marden did not have it, but pointed out that 'its production was not necessary'. He asked Dougal whether he understood the charge.[526]

'Yes, that is quite right,' said Dougal. 'I understand perfectly well what you mean.'

Marden realised that it was too late to get his man back to Essex, and so Dougal was kept in the cells at Cloak Lane overnight. But the next morning, by the 8.40a.m. train from Liverpool Street

Station, Marden and PC James Field of the Essex Constabulary accompanied Dougal back to Saffron Walden, where, in a brief hearing before the Mayor, Dr Henry Stear, Dougal was remanded in custody for eight days on the forgery charge.[527] 'You stand committed to Cambridge gaol until March 27th,' said Stear. 'Have you anything you wish to say?'[528]

'Nothing, sir,' replied Dougal.[529] That afternoon, he was taken to Cambridge Prison by the 2.20p.m. train, escorted by PC Smith of Saffron Walden and PC Field.

The arrival of Dougal, Marden and Field's train from London that morning had attracted no little local attention. The passengers had alighted at Audley End, taking a cab into Saffron Walden and concealing themselves within the police station until the Magistrates' Court hearing. A crowd had gathered to meet them off the train, however, and Dougal's upright, military progress down the slope away from the station was recorded for posterity by an opportunistic photographer. The prisoner was walking without handcuffs, although he had apparently been handcuffed in London on the way to Liverpool Street.[530] To his right was Field; to his left, Marden: all three men had draped their greatcoats over their left forearms, such that, at the moment the shutter closed, they presented strangely similar figures. Only Dougal betrayed any hint of anxiety, glancing suspiciously to his right, perhaps in response to something shouted from the throng. Around them were the expectant in all their shapes and forms: a little girl with a straw hat; boys, their eyes trained on the countenance of the prisoner; the driver of a pony and trap, from the vantage point of his vehicle; a dog; and women, running the gauntlet of compulsive curiosity and terrible, hysterical horror, and reproducing in miniature – and at a safe remove – the fearful, fetishistic paradox at the heart of Dougal's past interactions with females. He had always attracted devotion, even blind trust, despite his unsympathetic brutality and selfishness. Now, the female population turned out to gaze upon the subject of their recent gossip, attracted and repelled in equal measure by this most unlikely career criminal.

On the evening of Wednesday 18 March, Georgina had arrived at the Moat Farm to be met by a police guard.[531] She had been prevented from entering the building, and, apparently unwelcome in her parents' home, she went to stay overnight with a friend.[532] At length, news of Dougal's apprehension in London seeped back.

'He was always so good to me,' cried Georgina, distraught.

'Was he ever good to me?' asked Kate, her sister, looking on, and nursing little Herbert. 'He did not leave you like this.'[533]

But Georgina said nothing in response. She was already pregnant with Dougal's child – little Herbert's half-sibling, and, at the same time, his cousin.

ꙮ

The Moat Farm itself was now the centre of police enquiries. On 19 March, Detective Sergeant David Scott, a thin, austere-looking gentleman, and under normal circumstances based in Chelmsford, who had been detailed to scour the immense grounds of Dougal's erstwhile home, moved himself in.[534] The ghastly place would become his home for months to come.

With Dougal in custody, an early flurry of physical evidence swept in. Superintendent Alexander Daniels of the Saffron Walden Division was sent Dougal's possessions from Liverpool Street Station – Marden noted that the portmanteau and the tin box, deposited in the cloakroom by Georgina the week before, contained an assortment of clothing, some hers, some Dougal's.[535] Among Dougal's apparel were shirts, underwear and socks. There was also a jewel case in the portmanteau which Marden considered 'identical' with one known to have been owned by Miss Holland. Inside the jewel case were 'several trinkets of jewellery'.

In Dougal's dressing bag, deposited in the second cloakroom at the station, Marden noted 'toilet appliances and [a] night shirt', but these were unremarkable alongside the deeds and conveyances to the Moat Farm and Ballingarry Cottage in Biggin Hill. These were improbable inclusions in one's holiday luggage. In farmhouse itself, Marden recorded that he could find no clothing of any value, locating only 'a few worn out articles, unwearable'.

The raking-in of Dougal's material accoutrements by the police was matched by an insatiable public hunger for more details about the case. Crowds at local railway stations were one thing: on a much broader level, the inscrutable fulcrum of the case – Miss Holland's disappearance – appealed to newspaper readers nationwide. One report, carried on Thursday 19 March, suggested that the absent lady's friends had actively hunted for her 'all over the world' since she vanished four years previously.[536] This overstated the case, since, until the visit of the police earlier that month, even Miss Holland's nephews had been too reserved to enquire into her whereabouts since 1899, but it suggested the general appeal of the mystery. Perhaps it would cross continents. Where could she be?

The groups of police officers who stood in Dougal's fields looking grimly at the thick, clinging mud beneath their feet revealed the suspicions of the official mind. Scott, Marden, PC Fell and others had certainly been there on the evening of Thursday 19 March, examining the farmhouse and the outbuildings in the gathering gloom, hoping for a discovery which would stay the shovels.[537] If digging had to begin, there were scores of acres to turn – the ordeal would be a substantial one.

Judging from the distinctive appearance of the inside of the house, Miss Holland's lifestyle seemed to have been suddenly interrupted, but also preserved in aspic. The police officers peered at the collateral of her years on the planet:

> ... her personal and household linen bearing her name; the grand piano on which she had been wont to play the little songs of her own composition; the large pictures in oils and water-colours of languishing ladies and pretty landscapes. Her music was in the music chest, and her books with her name written on the fly-leaf were in the bookcases. Her silver and electro-plate, her masses of china ornaments, the photographs of her family; in short, everything that she was known to have prized, was found there and identified as hers.[538]

However, an early discovery, made by PC Fell, scrabbling around among some 'miscellaneous rubbish' in one of the outhouses, threw Dougal's dark shadow across their quest.[539] Fell turned up a skull, *sans* its lower jaw, which could not be located, although, energised by this 'grim encouragement', the officers 'sifted every ounce of dust in the place as eagerly as miners seeking gold'. Marks of burning on the skull prompted suggestions that Miss Holland had been boiled down in a great copper cauldron which stood in the same building; other interpretations offered included the dismemberment and widespread dispersion of the body, its constituent parts separated from another by macabre human agency. Marden certainly thought the discovery an exciting one: he dashed into the house and, seizing upon Dougal's own headed paper, scrawled news of the find to Elias Bower at Scotland Yard, signing himself, 'Yours in haste, A. Marden'.[540] The excitement turned to deflation just days later: it was quickly realised that this was the candlestick-skull which Dougal had owned for years.[541] Its more recent use might have accounted for its singed appearance, but Dr Stear, a former surgeon, examined it microscopically, and decided that it bore no marks of burning by either acid or fire, and that 'as a clue to anything it was useless'.[542] This dead end exhausted the possibility that Miss Holland's body – if it were to be found at the Moat Farm at all – may yet have reposed on the surface of the earth. The only other place to look was under the ground.

◌◦◎◦◌

Mrs Wisken, Dougal's one-time landlady, suddenly realised that she was at (or, perhaps more accurately, near) the centre of a great scandal. The police had spoken to her and advised her not to comment on the case to the press, but the secrets within her were bursting to escape.[543] A newspaper found her struggling to maintain her oath of silence, describing her – with deep irony – as 'very reticent'. 'But for the fact that she had been prohibited by the police,' they wrote, 'she practically confessed that she could a tale unfold'. With gentle encouragement, and with the roseate tint of hindsight, Mrs Wisken described Miss Holland as 'a perfect lady', kind and well-meaning. Even Dougal had 'behaved as a gentleman', she said; but the journalist observed that 'her whole sympathies were obviously confined to Miss Holland, and she was distressed about her mysterious fate'. Mrs Wisken was at pains to point out that the couple's original deception – pretending to be married – had fooled her utterly, 'or,' she indignantly cried, 'they would not have come there'. Half-heartedly, given that she was enjoying her walk-on role in the drama of the Moat Farm so much, Mrs Wisken even claimed that she now wished that Dougal and Miss Holland had never stayed with her at all. But what of the simple detail of the missing lady's age? Mrs Wisken pronounced herself stumped. She could not tell.

'You never can,' she added.

CHAPTER NINE

MRS WISKEN'S REMARKS in the newspaper democratised the Moat Farm Mystery, whitewashing Miss Holland into the sort of non-existence which invited her recreation in the popular mind. The case was becoming more and more public anyway: the police rapidly began to receive letters from concerned citizens seeking to identify Miss Holland. One correspondent, Frances Swift, was an unemployed domestic servant who had once been employed by a family named Holland.[544] She became nervous when she realised that the Mrs Holland of her acquaintance *could* have been the Miss Holland of the Moat Farm. Excited by a £100 reward offered by the *Sun* newspaper to anyone who could unravel the 'strange and startling' mystery, but equally concerned that it might appear that to know something was to betray one's own involvement in the scandal, she wrote to the police under the name *X.Y.Z.*, enclosing a letter she herself had written and apparently sent to Mrs Holland:

> The way the letter came into my hands is as mysterious as the lures of the letter. The words abt 'wire' and 'sorry for my poor master' sound so Moat Farm like that it is at any rate puzzling. I do not think that the letter refers to the missing lady Holland, but sometimes the clou is coming forward in a peculiar way and so it could be as well here.[545]

Neither Mrs Holland nor Frances Swift had any connection with the case, however; in Miss Swift's case, her imagination had no doubt been fired by newspaper reports, and the sudden prospect of lucrative rewards. The police investigated the misidentification and returned Miss Swift's letter to her, perhaps soothing her festering, uncomfortable feeling (animated by who-knows-what) that she was somehow involved in the mystery.[546]

This Mrs Holland was not the only one to be pointed out by a public keen to isolate the 'clou' in the case. Some correspondents thought that they had known Miss Holland in life: Mrs Frances Howell, of West London, identified a Catherine Maynard Holland as a possible match, but, after enquiries, Captain Showers dismissed the idea. Some correspondents thought that they had known *someone* in life who might also have been known as Miss Holland: Mrs Prudence Brady of East Ham recalled a Miss Rollf who, four or five years before, had been a resident in a home for incurables in Norfolk, suffering from tumours and paralysis. The 'clou', in this case, resided in the fact that Miss Rollf was 'frequently visited' by a gentleman 'from a distant farm'. In addition, one of the nurses in the home had been named White, and she had a child named Dolly whom Mrs Brady once heard call Miss Rollf by the name 'Miss Holland'. This all sounded very compelling, but it quickly led nowhere. Some correspondents thought that they had met Miss Holland since the time of her disappearance: Percy Selby, of Bowes Park, believed that she had taken 'a suite of rooms' at 19 King's Parade, in Cambridge, in October 1899, and that she had later gone to Massachusetts. But this information, too, failed to take the police any further.

Sometimes, Miss Holland was spotted, very much alive. A telegram to Saffron Walden from PC Trefrew of the Caernarvonshire Constabulary gasped, 'There is a lady here same description as Miss Holland she refused to give her name she is slightly eccentric'.[547] But this was not much to go on, and, four days later, a letter from Trefrew's Superintendent, William Rees, confirmed the misidentification – the Essex force had sent through papers and a photograph to permit the identity of the eccentric lady to be properly checked, and she had not matched up. In another example, Dr Thomas Barnardo, the renowned philanthropist, wrote to Scotland Yard reporting his wife's idea that she had seen Miss Holland, down and out, in Eastbourne the previous winter. Barnardo himself seemed somewhat reluctant to vouch for his spouse's identification, however. 'I rather pooh-poohed the whole story,' he wrote. 'I feel almost ashamed at sending you this, because I have no proof of any sort to send you, and I daresay you are deluged with such suggestions.' In the end, Barnardo's scepticism proved justified, and his wife's candidate (known in

Eastbourne, suggestively, as Mrs White, but probably only because that was her actual name) faded into the ether.

As might be expected, some correspondents had engaged the assistance of the paranormal in the hunt for Miss Holland. Jesse describes the fervour of the spiritualists 'who had received messages from another world (one of them most unaccountably written in French) giving various accounts of where Miss Holland was if alive, and where her body was if dead'.[548] The transmission of these accounts from Heaven to Earth had obviously gone awry, though, since, *in toto*, they too came to nothing but a tangled and corrupted mess. Some people – glossed by Jesse, perhaps not unfairly, as 'cranks' – offered to comb the grounds of the Moat Farm with divining rods, hoping to determine the location of the body, but the police declined the proposals.[549] One gentleman named Bunce, who resided at Brighton, wrote angrily to the police when they had ignored his psychically-derived solution, costing him the chance of a financial 'reword' for solving what he called 'the mistry'.[550] He demanded the return of his proposal, stamped by Scotland Yard, as 'I want it for an other mistry there is £1,000 reword oferd'. As if it added to his overlooked credentials, Bunce mentioned in passing that he was 'not a profational Clairvoyant'.

Science, too, was seen by some as providing the means of solution. One correspondent wrote to ask, 'If X rays will find out where a bullet is in a human being [as they were then doing in a London murder case, in which William Platel was accused of shooting Walter Frederick Booker] why won't X rays tell you where the body of Miss Holland was buried (if ever it was) on the Moat House estate?' Another, one William Heald, had veered off into a discipline all of his own – chromoscopy. His letter is worth quoting at length:

Sir,

In the last few years I have been experimenting with Colours, and have arrived at many remarkably accurate conclusions in my deductions therefrom. I have, by way of TEST, been working out 'The Moat Farm Mystery,' and I get, from the imperfect DATA I possess somewhat remarkable deductions. I send them on to you for what they are worth.

I read that [*sic*] early in March 1899 of a slow process of poisoning in which pigments used for purposes of Art figure very prominently. Also the Spectrum gives Arsenic as a probability. The process is seen to affect the mentality adversely and Miss Holland appears to become most susceptible to the WILL–SUGGESTION of another. April of the same year marks a stage of DEEP DEPRESSION in which Miss Holland realises that her Position with Dougal is likely to undergo a great Change and she feels he will prove himself to be NOT THE MAN SHE FONDLY THOUGHT HIM.

The month following (May) gives most decidedly an INCARCERATION, as if it were in some Private Asylum, or in a small room situated near a river, or near water. I deduce from this showing that Miss Holland was incarcerated, for a time, at Moat Farm as there are NO INDICATIONS of a SUDDEN VIOLENT DEATH, and, if death has occurred it was a very slow process. Granting that death has occurred some indications of the fact will be discovered by searching beneath, or behind some Statue, Picture, or Work of Art that is in, or about Moat Farm.

Whatever you may think respecting the above I would like to add that the Spectrum gives most strongly and very decidedly the following two points: Nothing of a really satisfactory Character will be ACTUALLY KNOWN during April, but, the MONTH OF MAY WILL BRING A CLEAR, DEFINITE SOLUTION OF THE WHOLE PROBLEM, and then it will be seen how near, or how remote my deductions given above are.

Should like CHROMOSCOPY to be TESTED with more detailed DATA not only in the Case in Question, but in other Cases, as I feel sure that the System will be helpful in criminal investigation.

Trusting that I shall not be considered too presuming in sending these deductions to you, for they are drawn in perfect good faith, I am,

Sir,

Your obedient Servant,

William Heald.[551]

ഏලൂ

Occasionally, the public provided the police with information which was sensitive and sympathetic to their mission, untainted either by forays into new and doubtful sciences or into the confused hubbub of the world beyond. In the absence of x-rays and divination, Detective Sergeant Scott had to decide for himself where his subterranean search for Miss Holland ought to begin. James Bolton, a farmer living at Bassingbourn Hall near Stansted, contacted Scotland Yard with the view that Miss Holland might have been interred within one of the outbuildings. It was 'common knowledge', he said, 'that if from swine fever or some similar cause a farmer wants to secretly dispose of the dead body of an animal he usually buries it inside one of his farm buildings where the spot can easily be covered over with hay or straw etc., and entirely out of view of any other person'. Thoughtful though this was, it was the kind of inside knowledge which might have been useful to the police only if Dougal had been a skilled or successful farmer. The absence of any indications of legitimate profit or fecund abundance emanating from the Moat Farm probably ruled out Bolton's logical suggestion. Scott bowed instead to the weight of local opinion, and, on Saturday 21 March, he started to drain the moat.[552]

The scene was described by the *Herts and Essex Observer* – Marden and Scott, wearing rubber gaiters to try to keep some of the moisture out, widened an existing outlet from the moat which connected, via a gully, with a stream at Rickling. As they did so, the gentle trickle of the overflow became 'a torrent of muddy water, wherein astonished fish could be seen carried away'. Over the course of three hours, the waterline dropped by a foot, and the police continued to widen and deepen the sluice.[553] By Sunday morning, they confronted a scene which anticipated the battlefields of the First World War. The moat was mostly empty of water, and gallons of opaque slime remained. Occasional puddles sustained the minnows, but other fish flapped about aimlessly, marooned and desiccating in the air.[554]

Since at least Saturday, crowds had been arriving to watch the hunt. Superintendent Daniels had already excited public speculation when he had, it was said, removed two trunks containing human remains from the farmhouse on Friday evening. The mundane truth turned out to be that he had removed two sugar boxes containing Miss Holland's silver plate ornaments. On Saturday, he and some fellow officers had scurried across a ladder, laid horizontal, onto the island behind the house, which was separated from the living quarters by the then-full moat. Some loose turf beneath an apple tree caught their eye, and the crowd watched silently while they dug into the ground. Hitting the roots of the tree, they gave up. Disappointments such as these merely fuelled the crowd's restless anticipation of a find of great importance.

On Sunday, the public turned up in vast numbers. Some came on foot from the nearby villages, and some others from 'distant towns'. They traipsed across the damp fields, stopping to peer at the implacable house, and to watch the policeman who gazed disconsolately at the filthy bed of the moat. Whole families, apparently, arrived on expeditions from the country, driven by horses; some, of whose modernity Dougal would have approved, arrived on bicycles or even in motor cars. Captain Showers arrived by the latter means in the morning, and left again in the afternoon. 'What is the use of the police draining the Moat at Clavering so long as they keep taking Showers with them?' it was sardonically asked. The circumstances of the search were difficult and upsetting ones, and the occasional sortie into dark humour was the inevitable result.

On Monday 23 March, Fell and Scott began dredging the mire that was once the moat. They balanced on planks of wood and ladders 'half sunk in the mud' as they shifted the grime from place to place in buckets, and probed what lay underneath with rakes and shovels. The crowd was another day bigger, and another day keener. Occasionally, their expectant voices would abate when an object was turned up out of the filth, but nothing more than 'a tin kettle or two, some old jampots, and some scraps of iron' came to light. It was grim work: the water may have gone, but the mud that remained was saturated, viscous, and freezing cold. Overnight, there was a heavy rainstorm, and when the search started again on Tuesday morning, the scene was 'a wilderness of slush, and evil-smelling pools of water had gathered in the bed of the moat'.

Fell had been staying in the farmhouse with the redoubtable Scott. One newspaper thought that the experience would have been 'an eerie experience for men with less hardened nerves': the house was apparently infested with rats which cavorted merrily after dark. The policemen had awoken on the Monday to find that the eggs they had intended to eat for breakfast had been carried away or broken in the night. They may not have been aware that the apparition of 'a figure sitting by the moat's edge wringing its hands' had already been rumoured in the village. This may have been a fiction, the overactive workings of the local imagination, but, as if in sympathy for the idea, little Jack wandered up and down the banks of the moat as Fell and Scott worked in the pit below, haunting the spot in his own melancholy way as they attempted to uncover the remains of his lost mistress.

But still the earth refused to give up its secrets – if it had any. On Tuesday, Scott and Fell were joined by a 'big and burly constable from Newport', who, judging from the description, may very well have been the substantial Henry Lindsey, and together, the *Herts and Essex Observer* reported, they enjoyed 'adventures … exciting and varied'.[555] First, they attempted to drive a cattle trough into the bank in order to deepen the sluice, and to drain the residual water from the moat. Even with Scott riding in the trough as ballast, however, 'they cracked their sinews in vain'.[556] The thick mud would not give, and eventually the trough became jammed. The next scene is best described by the contemporary source:

> The plough would not budge one inch, so half-a-dozen London journalists, who had been shivering on the bank in the chilly wind, tucked up their sleeves and gave muscular assistance to the Treasury. They proved to be so desperately strong that the rope broke, and there was a cataclysm of Fleet-street on the muddy bank.

Once covered in mud, the journalists' enthusiasm hardly dimmed, for a second attempt with stronger ropes proved successful. Scott drove out gallons of mud as his vessel forced its way into the bank, although he also slipped and sank his right arm almost shoulder-deep into the filth. Fell, with grim determinism, also toppled into the morass, surfacing 'in a pitiable condition'. Undaunted by his drenching, he found a Salvation Army uniform in the farmhouse – it was supposed to belong to Harry, Dougal's long-suffering brother – and changed into it. But whatever remained of Tuesday's endeavours proved fruitless, and Wednesday dawned without any further discoveries.

✦

After the multiple soakings of the previous day, Scott may have resolved to direct his attentions – temporarily, at least – towards areas of the farm which offered comparatively firm footing. Early on Wednesday morning, Fell and PC James Field, who had also been detailed to the search, were examining a secluded spot 2 or 3 feet away from a pond, to the side of a cattle shed, hidden from view behind some old stables. They found the soil easy to turn – perhaps suggesting that it had once been disturbed. Just after ten o'clock, Fell's pick-axe met resistance, 'and hastily removing the soft loam, he drew out a long piece of bone'. The constables thought that it might have been a human femur.

Scott was not there at the time, but he was summoned at once and, peering at the bone, he instructed Fell and Field 'to lay aside their pick-axes and work with their hands only'. If he had had any intention of allowing his men to avoid the grime that morning, the plan was now abandoned. Gradually, scraping the soil away with their fingers, the men revealed ribs, half a pelvis, what looked like part of a forearm and other small parts. The bones, none of which bore any flesh, were collected in a bucket and a washing tub, and moved into the house. By 11.00a.m., with the depth of the digging at 4 feet, the excavation had to be halted – the waterline had been reached, and the bottom of the trench had filled with water. Telegrams reporting the find were sent to Superintendent Daniels and Captain Showers, and samples of the earth in which the bones were found were taken, presumably in case they contained traces of flesh. No skull had been found, and some of the small bones looked unfamiliar. The remains awaited the attention of an anatomist.

That afternoon, an unexpected visitor arrived at the Moat Farm. It was Sarah.

When Dougal had failed to make their assignation in the city, Sarah had skulked back to the suburbs, abandoning her luggage at London Bridge Station. The news of her husband's arrest followed, at the latest, the next day. She may have gone from there to South Wales, throwing herself upon the mercy of a solicitor whom she had probably consulted during the fiasco of her divorce-scheme, Frederick Stoneman Reed, since it was he who accompanied her back to the infamous house. Sarah's defence against Dougal's divorce petition had foundered on the rocks of her collusion – this was hardly the kind of credential which ought to have encouraged Reed to take her on as a client (the divorce proceedings themselves having been handled by Henry Porter, who was more conveniently located in London), but he may have been unable to resist becoming involved with a case which gathered momentum day by day, becoming more tangled, more thrilling with every new report. On the other hand, he may have enjoyed her grateful veneration of him now that she was 'dependent upon Mr Reed ... for what he can do for her'.[557] One wonders whether Reed had not put himself in something resembling Killick's unfortunate position.

Without recourse to money, Sarah had arrived in Essex to secure possession of her furniture which, she claimed, she had left in the Moat House.[558] With Reed, she was driven from Audley End Station in a dog cart, but, when they dismounted and crossed the bridge to the house, Scott stopped them, explaining that they could not enter without special permission.[559] Jack, however, scampered up to Sarah, excited by her return. 'Dear old Jack!' exclaimed Sarah as he skipped joyfully around her. When Sarah left, unable to get to her furniture without going through the magistrates, Jack 'whined pitifully'.

On Thursday, the police went back to the site of the discovery of the bones. More scrabbling around turned up a few more specimens, although one morning newspaper had already cast doubt on the idea that they had originated in a human being. The sudden rush of energy which followed their unearthing had given way to more sober consideration. None of the pieces was more than 8 inches in length.

The next target of the officers' attentions was Dougal's greenhouse – here, they found the concrete floor solid to a depth of 6 inches, and they smashed through it with a pick and a crowbar. They delved into the soil underneath, but nothing of interest was found. By the end of the day, and under the curious gaze of another crowd, many of whom had travelled out from Saffron Walden, it being early closing day in the town, Scott, Fell, Field and Lindsey had nothing but the grim obligation to return to the greenhouse the next day for more digging. The scale of the search, Scott realised, would probably have to increase. If Miss Holland's corpse did not emerge from the soil in the vicinity of the farmstead, there were about a hundred acres of outlying fields to explore. Some of these had been marked out for special attention, but the rationale was insecure – hillocks, humps and hollows lay here and there, but there was no way to determine which ones – if any – were the topological evidence of Dougal's presumed wrongdoing.

⌘

Dougal had apprehended the policemen's frustration from his cell in Cambridge Prison. The *Morning Advertiser* reported on Thursday 26 March that he regarded the quest as 'a huge joke'.[560] 'So far from being morose or ill,' they went on,

> ... he is in the best of spirits, and told his solicitor on Tuesday that the police could dig up the entire farm and pull the house to pieces if they pleased. He added, however, that he supposed someone would be responsible for the damage done.

Dougal had a couple of explanations for the fact that he had been caught with hundreds of pounds in cash about his person. One, which was hinted at but not substantiated with actual details, was that the vast sums were the proceeds of 'ordinary business transactions'.[561] According to this version, Dougal had reported the names of those with whom he had legitimately done business to his solicitor – *prima facie*, this explained why the nuts and bolts of the theory had to remain confidential, but it made its force, and even its veracity, difficult to assess. The superimposition of the second explanation – which was utterly unnecessary, supposing that the first explanation was true – made the affair seem comical: Dougal was extemporising, clutching at theories in thin air. The second account emphasised, unselfconsciously, the costs of his divorce case.[562] He suggested that he had been on his way to satisfy the state with oodles of cash.

This was all careless bravado, and typical of the man. Even his robust health seemed to mock his situation, although Friday morning's *Morning Advertiser*, in a sudden *volte-face*, now described him as 'ill'. By the time he arrived for his second magistrates' hearing at Saffron Walden Police Court, at five minutes to ten on Friday morning, under the escort of Sergeant Charles Wood and PC Nathan Minter, he looked 'very anxious and pale', according to the *Herts and Essex Observer*.[563] He wore the ubiquitous Edwardian blue serge suit and a light brown overcoat over the

top of it. The *Morning Advertiser* described him as tall and sturdily
built, with a black beard tinged with grey; 'his blue eyes,' they said,
'have a far-away dreamy look'.[564]

⚜

Dougal's solicitor was Arthur Newton, a colourful figure in his
early forties, with neatly centre-parted hair and a moustache built
for twirling in a forensic manner. Although he normally haunted
the London magistrates' courts, picking up clients in the more
interesting cases, he obviously found the Moat Farm Mystery a
temptation too rich to resist. The publicity the case had already
generated showed no sign of diminishing as the police continued
to flounder about in the grime and, with the eyes of the country watching events unfold, Newton leapt in to offer Dougal the
boon of his expertise. The opportunism of the man had already
been evidenced – in Victorian times, he had represented not only
the establishment (in the Cleveland Street Scandal, a dismal episode in which senior aristocrats, *habitués* of a homosexual brothel,
conspired in an attempt to elude public censure for their activities) but also Alfred Taylor, Oscar Wilde's co-defendant and the
broken wing of the British elite, whose prosecution was engineered by the Marquis of Queensbury. Newton's complicity
in the former action had cost him six weeks in prison for consciously jamming the machinery of justice. Later, he would be
the subject of further official displeasure when he represented
Hawley Harvey Crippen; two years after that, in consequence
of a fraud case, a further prison sentence followed, and Newton
eventually found that all he had to rely on was his fortuitous
connection with several of the most exciting legal cases of *fin de
siècle* society.[565] But telling these stories did not necessitate that
Newton stick to the truth any more than he had when in legal
practice. When he sold his recollections to the newspapers in the
1920s, the idea of Dougal's serial affiliations with the Cranwell
sisters had become, in his mind, the cross-generational orgy of
Dougal's subsequent myth. Newton found the Claveringites 'a set
of persons, of any I have met, least alive to the moralities'.[566] The
irony of this remark seems not to have struck him; instead, he
reinforced his point with a quotation, no doubt fictional, meant
to have been uttered by Emily Cranwell senior, Dougal's girls'
mother, when he mentioned to her 'how sad a thing it was':

'Ah, well!' she said, as though excusing the daughters. 'I was not unknown to Mr. Dougal myself.'

Newton would have been alarmed to find his unreal orgy missing a participant – he mistakenly remembered only 'two servant girls – sisters' who had slept with Dougal, perhaps omitting Eliza. But the shambles of his memoirs merely bookended the latter end of a career in which professional dignity and intellectual rigour were shamefully lacking. Just as Dougal and Sarah had planned to anticipate Crippen and Le Neve with their flight by boat to the Continent – a scheme interrupted only by Dougal's arrest – so Newton's tactics in the Crippen case were prefigured in his dealings in the Moat Farm case. Naturally, Dougal was a willing accomplice, cheerfully going along with Newton's intricate interweaving of lies and self-serving invention. A more self-deluded pairing than Dougal and Newton can hardly have been found in Edwardian England.

Across the courtroom stood Pearce, the Treasury Solicitor, still arguing for the credibility of the forgery charge, and seeking Dougal's ongoing remand while the policemen, seeking a body, took their dips in the stagnant waters of the Moat Farm. The schizoid character of the authorities' case had already attracted comment: proving the forgery did not depend upon the unearthing of relevant remains, but there was plenty of public enthusiasm for the idea of a prodigal Miss Holland, alive, well, and skipping lightly through her senescence, somewhere. Her reappearance remained a possibility. Likewise, there was 'little actual evidence to connect the man Dougal with a murder charge', as the *Herts and Essex Observer* reflected.[567] Worse still, the credulity of the bank clerk, Francis Bird Ashwin, who considered Dougal's missives to be the genuine output of Miss Holland's pen, threatened the integrity even of the forgery case. Nearly thirty journalists forced themselves into the spaces around the jury box, awaiting either revelation, or, supposing that Newton could land a telling blow, the collapse of the charge, and Dougal's exoneration.[568]

For these reasons, Pearce's prosecution was a study in restraint. Kate and Eliza Cranwell, the eighth and ninth of the ten witnesses to appear, brimmed with animosity towards Dougal, but their testimony was directed into areas of minimal controversy. They had never seen Miss Holland at the Moat Farm, but they had seen her accoutrements, and they had seen letters arrive for her. Against this bland backdrop, Newton was reluctant to raise the touchy issue of Dougal's relationships with them. His single interruption of Pearce's preliminary exposition – to observe that a ring found about Dougal's person at the time of his arrest was 'a gentleman's ring', and therefore unlikely to have been the property of Miss Holland – met with the most placid of replies: 'Yes, but it was worn by Miss Holland'. Ernest Legrand Holland was promptly called to prove it. Newton probably saw that specious objections on technicalities were unlikely to wash.

At the end of the hearing, Mr Reed, who had observed the affair on Sarah's behalf, requested that the deeds of Ballingarry Cottage, in Kent, be returned to her. Through him, she claimed destitution, saying that she 'had been dismissed from her recent employment in consequence of the publicity which had been given to this case'. Pearce, testing Reed's mettle, observed that, 'about twelve months ago', she had granted power of attorney, with regard to the cottage, to her husband: if Pearce's chronology was correct, this gesture fell between the commencement of Sarah's sexual liaison with Killick, and Dougal's initiation of the divorce proceedings, a curious time for Sarah to be giving up her only real asset to her spouse. But Newton advised the court that Dougal had no objection to Sarah's being granted the deeds, which was agreed by the magistrates, subject to the approval of the Treasury.

This act of easy generosity between the supposedly estranged husband and wife did not prevent Pearce from requesting Dougal's remand. Newton fought it, saying that 'if the prisoner had the smallest intention of absconding he could easily have done so when at Portsmouth' – by which he meant Bournemouth – and contending, rather against the grain of the evidence, that Dougal had been 'going about his business in the ordinary way ... when he was arrested'. Pearce's response was characteristically measured, although his contempt for the insane idea that a walking treasure chest (who, as he pointed out, *did* attempt to escape from custody as he strolled with Cox down Old Jewry) could possibly have been about 'business in the ordinary way' was unambiguous. The magistrates predictably ordered Dougal to return to prison, and he was cuffed and, before a fascinated crowd which had gathered in anticipation at the railway station, escorted to Cambridge.

This was not before what ought to have been a rather touching, perhaps even reconciliatory, scene had taken place: Sarah had
a moment to talk with her husband.[569] But she also wriggled into
the clutches of a local journalist, momentarily liberated from
Reed's cautious supervision. Her immediate assessment of events
is worth quoting in full:

> Mrs. Dougal afterwards again expressed her conviction of her hus-
> band's innocence. She stated that her husband was exceedingly
> tender-hearted and a wonderfully fascinating man. She was his third
> wife, and was his junior by over 20 years. She felt sure Miss Holland
> was alive. As for leaving her clothes and jewellery, it was just the thing
> a woman would do.

So whither the beatings, the infidelity, the secrecy of her later
portrayal of Dougal? Whither now the soft-spoken sympathy for
the missing lady? Whither the conversation with Kate under the
crystalline summer night sky – the conversation Kate, somehow,
never recalled? Sarah's confidence resembled that of her husband:
impregnable, deliberate, and, in its empty heart, unrealistic. It was
faith without proof, and against the facts. It all seemed unlikely.
But, for now, she remained below the radar, and departed Essex,
deeds in hand, with only the attention of Inspector Marden, who
had been detailed to remain in touch, to shadow her.

The day-after-day toil at the Moat Farm continued to produce
little in the way of evidence. On Saturday 28 March, the police
again attempted to encourage the moisture out of the saturated
mud of the bed of the moat, sinking a deeper channel, and trying
to guess when they might accidentally penetrate the subterranean waterline and undo the work they had done.[570] Sunday
brought a flock of visitors – it was 'a record day for sightseers' –
whose curiosity had been stimulated by police reports of Friday's
court hearing. The evidence of the Treasury's witnesses (Pryke,
Ernest Holland, the indefatigable Mrs Wisken) was written up
at length in local journals, and between 1,500 and 2,000 people
arrived to watch the ongoing search. Cyclists arrived, according
to one report, 'in battalions'. It was more and more obvious that
the story was spreading rapidly. In London, Dougal had made it

into the columns of Saturday's edition of *The Times* – this was
not his first appearance in that publication, but now his misdeeds
generated hundreds of words of newsprint, inch after inch of
coverage.[571]

On Monday 30 March, Fell and Scott abandoned the excavation of the greenhouse for good, and returned once again to
the moat, finding that their deliberate, careful digging of Saturday
had allowed the earth to dry enough for another culvert to be
driven into it, taking away the water which still pooled around
their feet. Again, large numbers of fish were exposed as the moat
drained away, and the policemen removed many of them to one
of the ponds.[572] In the so-called lower moat, which surrounded
not the house but the wooded island to its side, a similar attempt
to drain the water was begun. In the orchard behind the house,
a well was uncovered – it had been filled with earth by Dougal
a couple of years before – and Superintendent Daniels, Sergeant
William Howlett and the tireless Scott shovelled out its contents,
without turning up anything of interest. Daniels took a 'long iron
rod' and pinpricked the ground in various places, to no effect.
Morale sank again, but the policemen worked on.

Tuesday brought more of the same. The remaining water in
the lower moat was lifted out in a four-gallon bucket: this was
'a very tedious performance', according to one impatient journalist, and, when the water level eventually did begin to drop,
all the police and the visiting crowds saw was the usual wild-
life – gasping, marooned fish; occasional frogs. It was a familiar
pattern. Two areas near the drive leading up to the house were
excavated: again, nothing was discovered. The land around the
house began to take on 'the after-appearance of having been visited by an earthquake'.[573] And March ended at a low ebb – Miss
Holland was no nearer being found, and the story of the Moat
Farm 'remained as great a mystery as ever'.[574]

By Wednesday, the searchers' mood was reflected in the Moat
Farm's dreary, desolate aspect. Rain fell in a drizzle through most
of the day; mist shrouded the fields; visitors to the farm found
themselves 'ankle deep in the mire'. Another inspection of the
bed of the lower moat produced – nothing. Fell and Field dug
out a filled-in sawpit in one of the farm buildings, finding –
nothing, before they had to give up their work when they hit
water and the hole filled with fluid. Several other spots 'inside

and around the farm premises and many ditches upon the farm' were earmarked for investigation, but dozens of hours of arduous labour without success were taking their toll. A 'general feeling' had settled among the local people, and it was not an encouraging one – 'the mystery never will be unravelled', they thought.

Dougal presented in his 'usual health' and with his usual 'lively interest in the proceedings' at his next appearance at Saffron Walden Magistrates' Court, on Thursday 2 April 1903. From prison, he had been battling the ugly insinuations of the nation with threats and declamations of his own. He had apparently advised his solicitor of his intention to sue the police for the damage they had done in searching the Moat Farm; and he mocked their humourlessness and their drudgery, saying in a letter either to Sarah or to Georgina that he himself had regularly seen Miss Holland since she had last been observed by anybody else on the planet, their last meeting being 'about 9 months ago', in London.[575] Her current invisibility only reflected her indomitable *wanderlust* – she was somewhere in the world, exploring the unexplored tea rooms and end-of-pier theatricals beloved of the travelling spinster. At the Moat Farm, forks and spades continued to plumb the earth as this last statement failed to have any effect: this was a measure of the depth of the official suspicions surrounding the man. At the police court, there was no mention of any such assignations from Newton. Dougal maintained his bright-eyed public façade, chatting about the bad weather with his solicitor prior to the commencement of the formalities; but he was generally quiet during the hearing, seated in the dock, with Sergeant Charles Wood to watch over him.[576]

Pearce's holding measure of the week before – establishing a *prima facie* case for a fairly lacklustre forgery – had bought time for the police, but all their efforts in the meanwhile had failed to turn up any evidence of Miss Holland's whereabouts, dead or alive. Now, the prosecution's evidence, which was tapered to focus exclusively on the audit trails in the Birkbeck and National Provincial Banks, would be pushed harder by Newton. Putting Ashwin up first, Pearce asked him to detail the ebb and flow of money to and from Miss Holland's account. Ashwin produced document after document, a whirlwind of paper, as Pearce patiently reconstructed the chronology of Dougal's misrepresentations; Newton, in cross-examination, knew where to aim, however. Ashwin told him that the controversial Heath cheque was 'undoubtedly' endorsed in Miss Holland's hand – indeed, of all the documents he had put in evidence under examination, he only had doubts about the signatures on two.[577] He saw wish-fulfilment at play in Ernest Holland's wholesale rejection of the bank's collection of signatures, some of which were known to be genuine; he thought that Ernest and Inspector Marden had convinced themselves of the existence of a crime, each propping up the other with a zeal that the evidence did not merit. He saw variations in Miss Holland's epistolary style, with uncontested letters to the bank, dating from the years before 1899, traversing the emotional territory from starchily formal to politely personal. Pearce re-examined Ashwin, trying to contextualise his beliefs, although the clerk would not be shifted from the view that Miss Holland's 'sprained hand' – one of Dougal's more creative lies, invented to account for his unskilful early attempt to forge her signature – was a 'sufficient' explanation for the shifting shapes of her mark in the letters she sent in the summer of 1899.

The day's other witness, Isaac Newton Edwards, from the Birkbeck Bank, testified to the credits and debits on Dougal's account. It was obvious to the court that money had frequently travelled from Miss Holland's account to Dougal's – Seward Pearce added it up, coming to a total of £2,284 – and Newton found himself thwarted, unable to challenge Edwards's evidence as he had challenged Ashwin's. The magistrates again remanded Dougal to prison – Newton, his early inroads negated by the clear difficulties of Dougal's financial record, was forced to ask them for £120 from his client's account to fund the defence. This was, as Newton knew, the value of the single sale of hay that Dougal had achieved in his four years at the farm, and it put the thousands of pounds of credit which had entered his account into strange and suspicious relief. Bryans Ackland, watching the action on behalf of Miss Holland's family, made this point: the hyperbolic Newton thought Ackland 'monstrous', but he got £75, the rest being held in abeyance.[578] The bench also agreed that Dougal could have some of his jewellery returned to him, to be kept safe in Newton's office until such a time as Dougal could find some use for it.[579]

Out in Anstey, Old Pilgrim wondered. That ditch, the one which once drained the farmyard – the one which Dougal had had filled in, against local advice, and to Hell with the consequences …

⁂

Other figures from the Moat Farm's past had also begun to re-emerge. Florence Havies – now Florence Blackwell – was sought for in Stratford, in Leytonstone and even in Wanstead, before she was eventually tracked down to 7 Swanfield Road, in Waltham Cross, and interviewed by Marden.[580] As the police went, they continued to collect clues and details which needed to be carefully filtered – the foray into Leytonstone alerted Alexander Wallace, the landlord of the Two Brewers on the High Road, to the possibility that Dougal had drunk in his establishment in 1899 and 1900. Wallace checked Dougal's photograph which, by now, had found its way into the *News of the World*. But he struggled to identify the alleged miscreant with the distantly remembered customer, finally submitting (with some implied optimism) that they were indeed one and the same, but that the image in the newspaper 'may not be a good photograph'. This sounded very much as if Wallace was confused, straining to map his recollections against the incommensurate facts, but J Division of the Metropolitan Police sent a copy of his theory through to Captain Showers at Chelmsford anyway. Advice still rolled in from the public at large – a gentleman from Maidenhead named Edwin Unwin, for instance, recalled seeing a man resembling Dougal at the Queen's Hotel in Antwerp in 1900. His putative sighting was noted and filed by Scotland Yard, but the Essex force already had plenty to do in searching the hundred acres of the Moat Farm; the suggestion that the quest would become continental could only have done more to diminish the searchers' already-dwindling enthusiasm for their Sisyphean labours.

Elias Bower had continued to steer the inquiry from Scotland Yard, liaising between divisional policemen within the Metropolitan area and the Essex Constabulary. He had begun to assemble a vision of Dougal's past, including his time in Nova Scotia with the Royal Engineers, and would write to Chief O'Sullivan, an official based at Halifax, to establish whether Dougal and Bessie Stedman had been married. Could Dougal be charged with bigamy? O'Sullivan informed Bower that he could not, and added that Bessie herself was back in Canada. Even across the void of the Atlantic, she could not free herself from the stigma of her history: a reporter from the Halifax *Evening Mail* hunted her down – she was, by now, married to a civic employee in the city – and asked her what she knew of Dougal. Her initial denial of any link sounded hollow, and the reporter persisted. At length, she broke. 'May the monster get his desserts,' Bessie said. 'I have no pity for him.' [581]

Bower now arrived at the Moat Farm, attempting to drive the faltering operation towards a successful outcome. According to legend, he found Scott and his men still gazing impotently at the grime of the drained upper moat. From the bank, Bower took a great rock, and hurled it into the black abyss below his feet. It failed to penetrate the viscous slime, remaining on the surface. [582]

'The body would never have sunk under that mud if the stone wouldn't,' said Bower. 'We've got to look elsewhere for it.'

According to other accounts, Scott himself was actively leading the process in new and more logical directions. Casting about at random for places to dig had been predictably fruitless, and some means of narrowing the search was needed. The episode with the saturated sawpit provided an unlikely starting point. It had filled with water particularly quickly, it was realised, because beneath it ran a number of large pipes – inadvertently, one of these had been pierced in the course of the digging. [583] The pipes drained the overflow from the pond into the lower moat, and had been relatively recently laid. [584] Still keen to excavate the sawpit, and enthusiastic to discover what lay at the bottom of the pond, Scott saw that he had simply to re-open the drainage ditch which the pipes had replaced in order to channel the fluid away. But where had the ditch been?

Jesse thought that Scott's informant was 'a hobbledehoy lad from a neighbouring village' – by which she seems to have meant Alfred Law. [585] George Dilnot, chronicling Scott's role in the enquiry in his 1929 book, *Triumphs of Detection*, thought, instead, that it was Old Pilgrim. Old Pilgrim, he said, had mentioned a carting job he had performed for 'Muster Dougal' in the late spring of 1899:

Scott pricked up his ears and ordered another pint.

"'Twere to fill up a dyke,' Old Pilgrim explained. 'He were a-doin' away with this 'ere dyke 'cos he were a-goin' to have the farm buildings drained with pipes and all. So I takes the earth there.'

The detective got to his feet. 'You come with me,' he said, 'and I'll make it worth your while.'[586]

The ditch was described – local knowledge had come to the fore – and the police spent the week leading up to Saturday 11 April digging it out, hotly anticipating the revealed treasures of the sawpit or, if not the sawpit, then the pond.[587]

꧁꧂

Already, the widespread attention the case had generated had begun to spill over into the London lawcourts. On Monday 6 April, Ernest and Edmund Holland had applied for probate as the executors of Miss Holland's will. Representing them were Henry Bargrave Deane and Edward James Naldrett; and, on the bench, by coincidence, Sir Francis Jeune, who had heard the King's Proctor's objections to the Dougals' untidy divorce not two months before. The hearing threw new light on interesting angles of the case. Jeune and Deane fell almost to gossip: Deane commenting that, while no advertisements had been put in the newspaper asking Miss Holland to come forward, he would have expected 'the notoriety the case has obtained' to have brought the missing woman out of the woodwork; Jeune heartily agreeing, and seeking clarification on the finer details of Miss Holland's last night at the Moat Farm, as related by poor Florence Blackwell, *née* Havies. Underpinning it all was the three-cornered narrative of Miss Holland's disappearance, Dougal's arrest and the great, muddy expedition of the law – the story belonged to everyone, was on everyone's lips, had assumed folk status, at least in its basic form. As one of the detectives working on the case later remembered, 'throughout Great Britain the Moat Farm mystery was the one topic of conversation'.[588]

The multiple ownership of the matter had perhaps opened Ernest Holland's eyes to the embarrassing drawbacks of his previous histrionics at the National Provincial. Francis Ashwin had pointed out at the last hearing before the Saffron Walden magistrates that Ernest had identified authentic examples of his aunt's signature with the alleged forgeries; now, in his affidavit to the Probate Court, Ernest made a clear distinction between that part of the bank's sample dating up to April 1899 (genuine) and that part dating from June 1899 (not genuine).[589] Newspaper coverage of the whole scandal had probably caused him to rethink, remoulding his initial, florid reaction into something more considered, and something which dovetailed more neatly with the chronology of his aunt's disappearance, which, since Florence Blackwell's detection, was coming into clearer view. Jeune had heard enough, and gave the Hollands leave to presume their aunt's death on or after 18 May 1899.

Elsewhere, the newspapers themselves were batting back criticism. Their minutely detailed coverage of the Moat Farm Mystery fed the rapacious public appetite, but occasionally militated against Dougal's own inherent rights. Speculation about Miss Holland's fate in the *News of the World* and the *Daily Express* survived judicial scrutiny, but the *Star*'s allusion to Dougal's previous conviction for forgery was held to be prejudicial, and cost the editor, Ernest Parke, £50.[590] Even the smaller local newspapers suffered. The *Herts and Essex Observer*, which had recently published articles about Dougal's mistreatment of Miss Booty and, indeed, the controversial fire at the Royston Crow, found itself in similarly hot water. As the barrister Joseph Randolph Randolph observed in a hearing in the King's Bench Division, these episodes were unlikely ever to be discussed at a trial (supposing Dougal's current charge took him that far), but the reports of them could only have the effect of prejudicing the opinions of the very community from which a jury would, if necessary, be drawn.[591]

At Saffron Walden Magistrates' Court on Wednesday 8 April 1903, Seward Pearce's evidence was again pushed and prodded by a sparring Arthur Newton. Dougal's appearance had, as usual, drawn a crowd of visitors to the court; the throng, initially congregating outside, was monitored by a special detachment of police constables.[592] Dougal was driven in his cab to the back of the building, exiting handcuffed and unseen by the waiting masses.

On this occasion, the attention of the court alighted on the convoluted sale negotiations – and the transfer of ownership from Miss Holland to Dougal – of the Moat Farm. This chimed nicely with the authority Ernest and Edmund Holland had been given to assess their aunt's estate for probate, and Pearce brought up a series of witnesses, most of whom Newton tested in his various ways. Thomas Gordon Hensler, of W.H. Hart & Co., stockbrokers, testified to the multiple and lucrative raids on Miss Holland's portfolio, but Newton, not improperly, wished him to demonstrate to the court that the sales of September 1899 had been, as the prosecution suggested, driven by the dead hand of the forger. Hensler studied the signatures, but could find no way to tell whether Miss Holland or Dougal had been their author. In re-examination by Pearce, he admitted that he saw both similarities and differences in the examples, and protested that he was 'not a writing expert'.[593]

Other witnesses testified to similar drains on Miss Holland's nest-egg, all counter-signed and witnessed by Dougal; John Rutter narrated the story of the purchase of the farm, and Miss Holland's oscillating role in negotiations – starting simply as the provider of financial heft, she shortly ended up as the owner of the property, and then, again with little more than Dougal's dubious integrity to support the idea, handed it over to him, every beam, every blade of grass, every puddle. As before, Newton's initial advances seemed by the end of the hearing to have paled in the wake of Dougal's blithe financial misconduct; and the solicitor's own fiduciary disingenuity hardly improved matters. Newton asked for the balance of the £120 he had made such a fuss about at the previous session, saying that Dougal now had the added cost of fighting journalists' misrepresentations of him (although some newspapers had covered the case 'very fairly', he thought). Attempting to impose a sense of control on a defence budget which, given the resources, could easily have escalated beyond three- and into four-figure sums as Newton and Dougal sought to slay their part-imagined foes with grand and expensive legal gestures, the bench declined the request. Thinking on his feet, Newton then asked for the police to return yet more of Dougal's jewellery – 'a watch, ring, chain and pin'. But Major Biscoe, the magistrate in the chair, saw through the charade. The sudden importance of these items of jewellery to a man who had, just seconds before, been prohibited from accessing ready funds was transparently, even amusingly, mundane. 'They are in safe keeping,' Biscoe told Newton. 'The police will take care of them.' Laughter rang around the court, and Newton sloped away. It had not been his day, and, at his worst, he seemed little more morally upright than his awful client.

∽✧∽

Still the police searched and searched. The excavation of the former drainage ditch had had the effect of emptying the pond, and the mud was sifted, fruitlessly, for clues.[594] The normal intercession of the Easter holidays had passed unnoticed as the grim task went on: on the banks of the trenches, however, enormous crowds, relieved of work for the weekend, gathered to peer down at the policemen as they waded through the filth. An estimated five – perhaps even six – thousand people visited the Moat Farm over the holiday weekend. Even Newton, in his somewhat unreliable memoirs, described himself looking out across the Moat Farm's ruined landscape, gazing at the faces of the tourists, trying to read their thoughts:

> And the thousands who went must have paused in the search occasionally, to think as I did: What could a woman like Miss Holland have done in that lonely, hideous place? She was an artist, a woman of refinement, and there was not the common excuse of passionate youth either on her side or Dougal's.[595]

The policemen, according to one account, had all caught 'severe colds' from their daily wading in the freezing waters of the Moat Farm.[596] On drier land, a cat-and-mouse game had commenced among the journalists, who were no longer so willing to put their shoulder to the wheel to assist the search. Now, after weeks of frustration, they looked at one another with paranoid eyes, each thinking that his rival, writing for another paper, may have the inside line with the detectives.[597] Conspiracies, like castles in the air, were dreamed up; distrust was mutual. One journalist, an insomniac, went for a night-time stroll when he found himself wakeful; his brethren stalked after him, fearing that he had had word of a discovery. The resulting scene of collective embarrassment must have humoured the police, before the dull reality of the apparent pointlessness of their task – and the mind-altering effect it was beginning to have on Fleet Street's finest – hit again.

Pearce was forced to return to the personal, unscientific evidence of human behaviour at the next hearing at Saffron Walden, held on Thursday 16 April. Dougal had been in custody for over four weeks, and the Moat Farm had been inverted in the hunt for the missing woman, but still Dougal faced only a forgery charge. Serial remands had permitted the police to continue their hunt, but their patience, their health and their money were fast ebbing away, and no further evidence was forthcoming. Even the normally hearty Dougal had begun to look 'anxious, pale and careworn' as the legal process dragged on and on.[598] Against this agonised backdrop, Newton readied himself to pounce.

Some brief opening flurries – pitching and whirling like the snow which hung in the April air that morning – led to the much-anticipated appearance of Florence Blackwell.[599] Her evidence was necessarily circumscribed – the unwilling ghost at a particularly awful feast, her view of Dougal had taken shape and crystallised in the brief days of her tenure at the Moat Farm, four years before. There was no subsequent context with which to balance it – they had never met since. There was no possible way that she could contribute to a discussion of the Heath cheque – she knew nothing of it whatsoever. Pearce began to lead her through the chronology of her first morning at the farm, and Newton, predictably, objected.

'Are we not travelling an enormous way from the real issue?' he demanded. 'I submit with all due respect to my friend [Pearce] that nothing which happened between the prisoner and this young woman in a scullery in 1899 can have the smallest bearing on the charge of forgery. I must ask my friend to confine himself to things more to the point. What took place in the scullery in 1899 is nothing to do with this inquiry.'[600]

Pearce confessed himself to be at the mercy of the Bench. He stated, truthfully, that the court had already heard Dougal's story about his much-misunderstood nocturnal clock-winding. This had been mentioned in Pryke's evidence, back in the mists of time. Here was a chance to hear the other side of the same story. It seemed worthwhile. Major Biscoe consented to the line of questioning, but Newton peppered Florence's account with frequent sarcastic interruptions. It was a low point of the prosecution's endeavours. In 1899, Dougal had been cruel to Florence – there was little doubt about that – but the focus of the evidence had drifted, and nobody was hearing much about the forgery any more. During Florence's evidence – in fact, during her description of her master's attempt to gain access to her bedroom – Dougal had smiled, and the reporter for *The Times* had made a note of it.[601] His confidence was growing as the prosecution lost focus, and, after lunch, Dougal was again beaming, sitting in the dock twirling his moustache, stroking his beard, chatting with Newton. All the outward signs of great coolness were in place.

The next witness promised a similar excursion into the past: Mrs Florence Pollock, the boarding-house keeper of Elgin Crescent, had not seen Dougal since 1898. She was a fundamentally different character, however: assertive where the damaged Florence Blackwell was passive; uncomplicated and undaunted where Florence was delicate, deferential and shy. Pearce quizzed her about her recollections, and asked her whether she saw Miss Holland's then-visitor in the courtroom. She pointed straight to the dock.

'Yes, I think that is he,' she said. 'He is a little stouter.'

In cross-examination, Mrs Pollock claimed not to have seen any photographs of Dougal in the newspaper. Newton disbelieved her:

> Mr. Newton. – What! Surely you must have done?
>
> Witness. – I might have seen one, perhaps.
>
> Mr. Newton. – There; you see what a little persuasion will do.
>
> Witness (*angrily*). – Don't you think you can persuade me.
>
> Mr. Newton. – And when you saw it did you recognize this gentleman?
>
> Witness (*sneeringly*). – Gentleman!
>
> Mr. Newton. – Don't be rude.
>
> Witness. – I have every reason to remember him for the way he treated me in the hall. (*Laughter*)
>
> Mr. Newton. – I don't know what that was.
>
> Witness. – It made an impression upon me I have not been able to get over.
>
> (*Laughter*)
>
> Mr. Newton. – Did you look into the dock when you came in?
>
> Witness. – Where is the dock?
>
> (*Laughter*)

> Witness. – I looked all over the place. I looked there. (*Indicating the Bench*)
>
> (*Great laughter*)
>
> Witness. – I looked everywhere.[602]

This was the same desperate levity that had afflicted the newsmen. The hearing ended with another remand, and the main players due back in court on Thursday 23 April. Still the process dragged and dragged, but Dougal may have felt his exoneration, or at least his release from prison, inching closer. Newton had had his most successful hearing yet, a by-product of the prosecution's foray into something which sounded like personal spite and gossip. In the absence of new evidence, the authorities' pursuit of Dougal seemed destined to become an embarrassing, expensive mistake.

⁂

Captain Showers, Raglan Somerset and Superintendent Alexander Daniels attended the next session.[603] This was the top brass of the Essex force, their massed presence intended to silently reinforce the prosecution's ongoing desire to have Dougal remanded in custody while their officers tore up his property. The solid suggestion that the farm may not have been Dougal's at all – not legitimately, at least – did much to back their case. But the prosecution's evidence had recently become diffuse and enigmatic, and a sense of impatience on the part of the magistrates would have been natural. Between the sample charge – for forging a cheque to the value of £28 15s 0d – and the greater suspicions of multiple frauds worth thousands of pounds, there was, perhaps, space for the magistrates to exercise caution. The police hoped so, but the tolerance of Biscoe *et al* for the unfocused anti-Dougalism of the prosecution's recent witnesses would grow rapidly short. Private animosity was no substitute for the facts.

The strain had also begun to affect Seward Pearce. Newton enticed him into a particularly unpleasant early exchange in which he, Pearce, bad-temperedly described the unhelpful bank clerk Francis Bird Ashwin as Newton's 'pet witness'.[604] There was laughter in the court, but, as Newton coolly observed when it had died down, 'He was your witness, not mine'. Grumpily, Pearce examined a stream of local horticulturalists and auctioneers, all of whom had received small cheques, ostensibly from Miss Holland, covering work and goods ordered by Dougal. Again the forensic skein meandered away from the forgery of the Heath cheque; again, Newton objected. The appearances on the stand of Pryke, Harry Cox and Marden distracted, rather than informed. At last, Pearce requested a sixth remand on the basis that he had asked a handwriting expert – Thomas Henry Gurrin, who had worked on the Frankfort and Wolseley forgeries in 1895 and 1896 – to look over the bank's assortment of correspondence and cheques, filtering the authentic from the inauthentic. Gurrin had struggled with the volume of material, and was not ready to depose in court. Given a week, Pearce said, wearily, he might be. One can picture the sour expression on Newton's face, but the magistrates agreed to the remand. It had been a tiring, unsatisfactory hearing, and, at its conclusion, Dougal may once again have seen the sails of the great ship of the state's evidence burning down. As the magistrates' patience wore thinner, so the possibility of his release crept ever nearer. He was even permitted to take possession of his much-missed jewellery.

Showers, Somerset, Daniels and Pearce drove immediately over to the Moat Farm to meet with David Scott.[605] Still nothing would emerge out of the inscrutable slime, and the prospect of shutting down the search became more and more real. Pearce, in particular, must have impressed on the policemen the necessity of having something else to offer the court. His personal resources were drained, and even Newton, whose forensic style was blustery and unsophisticated, was making ground against the charge. George Dilnot, a later admirer of Scott's tenacity and good-natured common sense, saw his hero begging for time: 'Give me a few more days.'[606] In fact, it was agreed that four labourers could be brought in to assist the search – a last resort, and another cost. The men would open Pilgrim's drainage ditch to a width of 8 to 12 feet on either side, forcing more of the water out of the moat.[607] After that, if nothing was found, it was impossible to guarantee that the hunt for Miss Holland's remains would continue.

∽∾◉∾∼

Ralph Bunting was nearer sixty than fifty, and the licensee at the Three Horseshoes in Wicken Bonhunt. This was the next village along from Clavering on the road towards Newport, and, on the morning of Monday 27 April 1903, he sauntered along to the Moat Farm to watch the digging. He took his dog with him, and they stood on the bank of the precipice as, below them, the policemen and their newly employed assistants turned the thick earth. It had been an early start, and hours of digging had again yielded nothing. The rain poured continuously, but the work went on.[608]

At about midday, Bunting's dog, which had been standing beside its master, suddenly leapt into the ditch and began scratching at its muddy walls.[609] The men 'thought that it was scratching for a rat, and had some difficulty in driving it away'. Annoyances of this sort only made a difficult situation worse.

But then, a few minutes later, Thomas Barker, a twenty-year-old agricultural labourer, one of the four brought in by the police, stabbed his fork into the ground and, just where the dog had been scratching, he turned up a piece of cloth.[610] He thought it looked like part of an old coat.[611] He sunk the fork into the earth again, and, this time, it stuck on something more solid.[612] He wrenched it out and held it up in the air to examine it.[613] Attached to one of the prongs was a lady's boot; and inside the boot were the tiny bones of a human foot.[614]

CHAPTER TEN

IT WAS JUNE 1903, and the eighteenth-century surroundings of the Shire Hall in Chelmsford were being urged to adapt to the surge of public anticipation that Dougal's trial had prompted. Echoes of the clamour surrounding the 1894 trial of James Canham Read, held at the same venue, were inevitable: now, as then, tickets of admission were to be issued to try to keep the fascinated crowds back, and the representatives of the press happy.[615] Now, as then, the prosecution intended to call dozens of witnesses; for those speaking against Dougal, a special waiting room had been put aside.[616] The police busily erected barricades to control the expected swarms of sightseers outside the building. The capacity of the courtroom itself was temporarily extended by the rigging-up of a platform above the public gallery.[617] Nothing could be done to soften the garish contrasts of the 'yellow, varnished seats and staring, light greenish walls', however.[618]

There were other comparisons with Read's case. It was as if the skein of his long-since-terminated life had occasionally threatened to intertwine with Dougal's; sometimes, they missed each other only by the narrow margin of yards (and the somewhat greater margin of years). Read had lived in Jamaica Street, in Stepney, a stone's throw from the Whitechapel Road, which may have been familiar to the adolescent Dougal. He libidinously pursued his eventual victim, Florrie Dennis, through Wandsworth and Southend, both previous domiciles of Dougal's. Read and Dougal had both, apparently, forged marriage certificates. Read had slept not only with Florrie, but also with her sister Bertha. He had once sojourned to Buckinghamshire, taking Bertha with him and suggesting that she represent herself as his wife.[619] Dougal's life story remained knotted, little more than hinted at by a press now aware that too many pre-trial revelations would be countered in the civil courts, but the ghosts of Read remained.

The sense of the familiar merging with the still-to-be-discovered amplified the public's impatience for Dougal's trial to begin. The reporters readied their pens. In the infirmary at Chelmsford Prison, Dougal was busy with his own, writing to a range of correspondents in his usual bluff fashion. In his letters, he seemed remarkably unconcerned, suggesting to Georgina that she hire a trap to drive herself and her sisters from Clavering to Chelmsford for the trial.[620] Eliza and Kate were both witnesses for the prosecution, but Dougal's cheerful demeanour would not give way. He treated the forthcoming trial as if it would be a happy reunion of friends grown unfortunately distant.

⌘

We return to the scene of Thomas Barker, deep in the ditch, raising the boot with the bones in it from the earth, then to astonished eye level, and then above eye level, exclaiming his discovery to the policemen a little distance away. PC Lindsey splashed over to where Barker stood, examined the boot, and called Scott, Fell and Field.[621] With great care, a little more earth was removed from the area of the discovery. This brought up a second boot: it had slipped past the bones of the foot, which were now exposed. Throwing their shovels aside, the police now clawed at the saturated soil, working with their hands to avoid further damaging the interred owner of the boots. At length, filthy and cold, they had exposed 'the legs of a human being and the lower portion of a lady's black dress'.

Fell went to the post office in Newport to telegraph the discovery to Saffron Walden. Superintendent Daniels was away on business, but Sergeant William Howlett, who had participated in the early weeks of the search, sped to the Moat Farm, bringing with him William Carr Sprague, who was the local Police Surgeon, and a photographer, Walter Francis. From behind hastily erected canvas screens, Sprague directed the exhumation of the upper part of the body, which was found to be, as expected, a woman's, lying nearly face down in the mud, and in a state of advanced decay. When Captain Showers arrived, notified by telegram and driving from Chelmsford in his motor car, the body was manoeuvred onto a piece of board – 'an improvised stretcher' – and Francis photographed it, and the hole in the ground from which it had been extracted.[622] By the head lay a comb, some

hairpins and some twisted wires, the remains of a hair frame.[623]
These were the vain impedimenta of the deceased, whose body
was now covered in a cloth and carried through the throng of
journalists and sightseers and deposited in Dougal's conservatory, lain horizontally across a couple of chairs.[624] Sprague picked
away the mud which still adhered to the head, revealing a skull
stripped of its flesh by decomposition; a photograph was taken,
but it was decided not to perform a full examination of the
remains. Sprague reported only that, on cursory inspection, there
was nothing to reveal the cause of death. Little Jack, watching
the search, had whined as the policemen had conveyed the body
towards the house; following them into the conservatory, he now
lay by the door, and grieved.

News of the find had spread and, outside, hundreds of thrilled
visitors descended on the farm. They came by pony and trap, by
bicycle, and in great numbers on foot, scrutinising the canvas
which covered the hole in the wall of the ditch from which the
remains had been drawn and peering distantly, from the other
side of the moat, at the conservatory. Amateur photographers
took scores of snapshots; those without cameras tore twigs and
leaves from the branches of trees and pocketed them as mementos. Weeks of arduous searching had finally turned up a body:
the mystery seemed solved. The police realised that, a fortnight
before, their shovels had turned the earth within 18 inches of
the corpse, which lay not on the exact line of the drainage ditch,
which Old Pilgrim had described perfectly, but slightly to one
side of it.

Tuesday brought painful scenes as the police sought witnesses
to identify the body. Mrs Wisken was the first to view the remains,
arriving shortly after eight o'clock in the morning, escorted by
Superintendent Daniels and Sergeant Howlett. A watching journalist noticed that she was weeping as she left the Moat Farm
some time later. Ernest and Edmund Holland, Miss Holland's
nephews, arrived next. Florence Blackwell, Dougal's former servant, was the last to arrive, driven to the farm by Marden and
Bower. She suffered greatly from the experience, identifying the
body in the conservatory, as the others had, as that of Camille
Cecile Holland, but sobbing bitterly afterwards. When she had
apparently recovered her composure, she went with David Scott
and her mother, Mrs Martha Havies, who had accompanied her

to Essex, to peruse the site of the discovery of the remains; there, however, she began to collapse, and Scott and Mrs Havies supported her back to the house. Florence fell into unconsciousness, and had a hysterical fit when she awoke. Two hours passed before she was well enough to be taken to Newport Station for the journey home to Waltham Cross.

At three o'clock on Wednesday afternoon, Dr Augustus Pepper arrived at the Moat Farm to undertake the post mortem. Pepper was the pathologist of choice of the Home Office, a role which, in his time, involved him in several notable cases, perhaps the most famous of which was that of Crippen in 1910, in which Pepper worked alongside his protégé, the much more flamboyant Bernard Spilsbury. Now, with Sprague and a third doctor, Kenneth Simonds Storrs, Pepper scoured the body of Miss Holland, working with it where it lay in the conservatory. It was he who noticed that her left hand had apparently become detached, the bones missing; finding no sign of them, Fell and Scott returned to the body's former resting place and began to scrape around in the soil again. Back in the conservatory, the hand was quickly discovered – it may have been underneath the body, which was not prone but lying tilted on its right side, with the left leg drawn up.[625] Captain Showers called off the renewed search.[626]

Pepper started by taking measurements: Miss Holland was an inch over 5 feet long in the not-quite-straight position in which she lay, with her head tucked down a little towards her chest. Her femurs were 16¾ inches long, her tibiae 13⅜ inches long, her humeri 11 inches long, her tiny feet only 8¼ inches long. Decomposition had converted 'nearly all her soft structures' into adipocere, a 'repellent yellowy-white substance engendered by the stiffening and swelling of a corpse's body fats'; this had part-preserved Miss Holland, allowing her corpse to retain its shape.[627] Pepper saw no sign of physical deformity.[628] He detected traces of what he thought was blood on the left side of the neck. None of the bones was fractured; none of the vertebrae was dislocated.

On the right side of the fleshless skull, 3 inches above the mastoid process (the archipelago of bone behind the ear running parallel to the jawbone) and an inch and a quarter towards the rear, Pepper found a hole. The hole was a quarter of an inch in diameter, and had sharp, clearly defined edges. Through the hole, an equivalent circle of bone was found, split off from the inner surface of the skull. On the edge of the hole was a fine shard of lead weighing just two grains: one two-hundred-and-fortieth part of an ounce. This piece of lead was retained.

On the other side of the head, an inch and a half behind the point of the eyebrow and the same distance above the part of the cheekbone nearest the ear, there was another hole. This was a larger hole, slightly elliptical, measuring half an inch vertically and three-eighths of an inch horizontally. Fragments of bone were found near the hole. The bone at the exterior aspect of the hole had splintered slightly, particularly on the side nearest the eyebrow. Removing the top of the skull with a saw, Pepper found the brain 'wonderfully preserved': this he took to mean that the body had been buried very quickly after death had occurred, before the usual processes of putrefaction had had a chance to begin.[629]

Inside the skull, near the hole on the left-hand side, Pepper found a bullet. The bullet was elongated and weighed eighty-five grains, slightly less than one-fifth of an ounce.[630] Pepper retained the bullet. He felt that it had blasted through the skull on the right-hand side, passed through the brain, banged out the hole on the left-hand side, and fallen back inside the skull. The shot, Pepper thought, had been fired at short range, from behind, and could not have been self-inflicted. Any scorching or blackening of the skin near the entry wound, the usual signs of close-range shootings, were impossible to detect amid the decomposition of the corpse. Essential structures within the brain had been destroyed by the shot: Pepper reported that Miss Holland would have lost consciousness immediately and died, without regaining her senses, shortly afterwards.

The doctors moved to the mouth. Miss Holland was found to have had a full set of the teeth with the exception of the left upper wisdom tooth, which had been lost some years previously. She had had seven fillings to teeth which had developed cavities – three in the upper line, and four in the lower. Moving down the body again, Pepper found some of the internal organs in the chest and abdomen recognisable, and others decayed. He estimated the date of death – 'from 3 to 5 years ago'.

Early the next morning, James Day, an undertaker from Saffron Walden, arrived at the Moat Farm. With the help of his assistants, he lifted Miss Holland's body into a coffin, and there she remained, in the peace of the conservatory, while, outside, the Moat Farm prepared for further inundations by the fascinated public.[631] The inquest would begin that afternoon.

ഛൟൟഛ

In the barn near the pond, 'a very primitive court room' had been approximated. The decision to hold the inquest in a farm building must have seemed workable at the time – perhaps because the coroner's jury could more easily be taken to view the remains than could the remains, in their state of fragility, be taken to repose before the jury. It was rapidly apparent that the decision was an eccentric one, however. The Moat Farm was a detached, desolate venue for sad proceedings: the barn itself was dark, dusty, and probably cold; the day had begun with 'heavy sheets of rain pouring down, rendering everything melancholy'.[632] Through a door at the rear of the barn, the canvas tent covering the site of the discovery of the body was visible, a macabre evocation, according to one author, of more primitive times, 'when courts of justice as well as coroners' courts were held at the spot nearest to the commission of a crime, either under the open canopy of heaven, or in some rude shelter constructed out of branches of trees'.[633] In the centre of the room stood a large mahogany table, a smaller table made of oak, and a scattering of chairs.[634] The jury were to sit on wooden boards nailed to wooden boxes; opposite them, a similarly *ad hoc* arrangement was made for the crowd of journalists. The public, who turned up in droves, despite the weather, filled any vacant spaces.

Dougal had been roused from his prison cell earlier that morning, shuttling down to Newport on the train, watched closely by two guards. Driven in handcuffs to the Moat Farm, he descended from the horse-drawn cab and was led inside the old, familiar house. Crowds had attended his journey, sneering at him as he alighted from the train, running after his cab, rushing at him as he pulled into the Moat Farm.[635] Now, he stood in the sanctuary of his former drawing-room, where Alfred Marden formally charged him with the murder of Miss Holland.[636] Dougal had been informed of the finding of the body the previous evening.[637] He looked 'pale and dejected', thinner than usual.[638] But he had obviously steeled himself for this moment, and he made no comment. Then he was escorted out of the house, past the canvas tent, and into the barn, where the inquest began.

The coroner heading the session was Charles Edgar Lewis. Seward Pearce and Arthur Newton prepared to lock horns again; Bryans Ackland attended to represent the interests of Ernest Holland (who was present) and Edmund Holland (who was not); Captain Showers and Raglan Somerset represented the constabulary, and Alexander Daniels the local division; two magistrates from the Saffron Walden Police Court, Judd and Gold, were there. On the boxes which formed the jury bench perched the foreman, the Reverend Walter Landon Smith, vicar of Rickling, and fourteen other men of the communities of Clavering, Rickling and Newport upon which Dougal had preyed. Dougal, sitting next to Newton at the mahogany table, stayed wrapped inside his brown coat and kept his bowler hat on for the duration of the hearing.

Predictably, Newton, whose artillery, which had been in full boom at the previous police court hearing, and which was now silenced by the discovery of the corpse, made little ground against the initial evidence. It is possible to see Pearce luxuriating in his position, his torpor gone, offering only 'to render what assistance he could' to the inquiry, and calling Mrs Wisken and poor Florence Blackwell to recite their now-familiar evidence. Newton argued that the story of Florence's ordeal at Dougal's hands was immaterial and damaging to the ends of justice: 'What does it matter at an inquiry of this sort what Dougal did to this young woman in the scullery?' But such protests were now falling on less sympathetic ears. David Scott took his place at the table to testify to the circumstances of the disinterring of the corpse. The jury went to see Miss Holland where she lay in the conservatory. Mr Lewis adjourned the hearing, seeing that the inquest would inevitably take several attempts to complete, and one of the jury, Thomas Hunt, offered the coroner the use of the larger, lighter, warmer Parish Hall in Newport for the next sitting. A week's pause was agreed, and Dougal braved the crowds – 'about three hundred people' awaited him at Newport Station – and returned to Cambridge Prison. The next day, Seward Pearce cavorted through the scheduled police court hearing, describing the 'considerable alteration in the nature and extent of the case' against Dougal with just a hint of triumphalism. Arthur Newton was not present; he had agreed in advance to a simple remand, and the hearing of evidence was therefore postponed. This time, although Dougal had largely escaped the usual crowds on the way into the court, a fierce throng had gathered to meet him on the way out. The hearing ended at 10.30a.m., but the police, seeing the scene in the street, kept Dougal inside for fear of a 'demonstration'.[639] He spent four hours waiting for the crowd to cool off, his boredom and embarrassment punctuated only by lunch, a bottle of stout and a few cigarettes. When he did emerge, at half past two, the flames of public animosity had only been fanned by the delay. One old lady, suddenly animated by Dougal's appearance, tried to hit him on the head with her umbrella.[640] The crowd roared its approval, but the elderly assailant was restrained by the police.[641] Dougal was escorted to his cab, and driven to Great Chesterford Station to avoid similar scenes at Newport.[642]

⋙⋘

Curious tales of misery and woe began to coalesce around Dougal's story. At the moment he finally left the police court on Friday 1 May, the day of the umbrella attack, Edward King, a six-year-old spectator at the back of the crowd, fell from the box he had climbed upon to secure a better view. Initial concerns that both of his legs might have been broken proved fortunately unfounded. At the Moat Farm, visitors continued to arrive. A rainy Sunday failed to prevent one group of tourists from cycling all the way from Rotherhithe; others cycled from Newmarket. Arriving at the local railway stations were visitors from Liverpool, Bolton and Bradford. 'There was not much for them to see,' commented the *Herts and Essex Observer*. The canvas tent had been removed, and the hole filled in on the Saturday: the spot at which Miss Holland was found was now marked with a simple cross. The newspaper seemed alarmed by the number of women, including young mothers who were carrying their infants, who had come to view the scene. The weather assumed almost mythic proportions in the afternoon – 'The Farm was a quagmire, and the roads leading to it were a stream of water' – but, astonishingly, 1,000 people were unperturbed. The massed ranks of sightseers attracted orange and nut sellers to the farm, and at least one photographer set up his camera for souvenir pictures. In a startlingly modern twist, even film-makers visited the

scene: three production companies issued moving-image treat-
ments of the excitement, but the films – *The Moat Farm Mystery*
(Gaumont), *The Moat Farm Tragedy* (Harrison) and *Moat Farm
Murder* (Robert Paul) are all now lost. The Gaumont version 'was
110 feet in length, comprised four parts and showed actual foot-
age of the farm buildings where the murder took place'.[643] And
still the duller-edged stories of local misfortune rolled in: Ernest
Deeble had apparently cycled to the Moat Farm on the day of
the first inquest hearing, but had lost control of his bicycle in a
remote spot on the way home. He was discovered by the side of
the road, 'insensible and bleeding'; at Saffron Walden Hospital, it
was discerned that he had broken his arm, and lacerated his scalp.
Deeble began to feel better the next day, but his was only an early
example of the effects of an incipient curse upon visitors to the
Moat Farm.[644]

At Saffron Walden (which remained the venue for the police
court proceedings), and at Newport (to which the inquest
removed), the double-helix of concurrent hearings ran increasingly predictable courses. The deferred hearing before the
magistrates was finally held on Wednesday 6 May 1903, and consisted in the greater part of witness evidence which had already
been heard in relation to the forgery charge. The absorption of
Miss Holland's wealth into Dougal's bank account continued to
exercise the court, and the charge remained alive, but murder was
a capital offence, and it took obvious priority. Dougal continued to suffer from the antipathy of crowds, and the police had
begun to worry that an outraged sightseer might consider injuring him – on this occasion, however, there was nothing worse
than 'some hooting on the part of the large number of people'
who had, as they always would, gathered to see him depart the
scene.[645] Again the prosecution had requested and been granted
a remand. Newton, still blankly battling against the tide, managed to secure the balance of the £120 known to have been
Dougal's.[646] Dougal's defence was looking increasingly futile, and
it remained costly.

The second inquest hearing followed the next day. Two hundred and fifty people packed into Newport's higgledy-piggledy
Parish Hall – again, women formed a large part of the audience.
On the Wednesday, Augustus Pepper had given his professional
opinion to the Magistrates; he was scarcely molested by Newton,

who extracted only the dismissive detail that Pepper, when he saw an article about the Moat Farm Mystery in the newspaper, generally 'skipped it'. Now, he repeated his evidence – consistent, unambiguous – to the coroner. Newton reserved his energy for the appearance of Superintendent Pryke: he still felt that Pryke's 'friendly chat' with Dougal at the Moat Farm in early March had broken protocol. The exchange became heated, in a slightly surreal way (Newton: 'You try to shuffle things, but I am not going to be shuffled.' Pryke: 'I do not shuffle you.'), before the inquest was adjourned again until Friday 15 May. A bizarre row with Pryke was one thing, but Newton must have known that this hardly counter-balanced the weight of the evidence against Dougal.

❦

At 10.45a.m. on Tuesday 12 May 1903, Miss Holland was buried again.[647] The previous evening, her remains had been removed from the conservatory at the Moat Farm to lie overnight in the chapel at Saffron Walden Municipal Cemetery. With remarkable sentimentality, the lashing weather held off, and the day was sunny and bright, 'a delightful spring morning'. As they had gathered for Dougal, so the public now gathered for Miss Holland: about 500 people attended the funeral, all 'reverent and sympathetic'. In the chapel, Ernest and Edmund Holland, Henry Morley Hemsley (Miss Holland's solicitor), Bryans Ackland and David Scott stood among the mourners. On the bier rested the coffin, a simple affair of plain oak with brass fittings, and the inscription on its plate: 'Camille Cecile Holland, Died 19th May 1899, Aged 56 years. R.I.P.' The grave was dug near the chapel, beneath 'a very pretty silver birch tree adjoining a bed of Spanish iris, saxifrage and roses'.

Floral tributes were paid, the newspaper men who attended scribbling down the messages appended to them: 'With loving sympathy to Dear Aunt, From Edmund G. Holland,' read one; 'From Ernest. With sincere sympathy,' read another. Others came from friends and relatives, and one was sent, 'with sympathy', from Captain Showers and the Essex Police. The grieving family showed their gratitude to the police in return: at their request, Scott, Fell, Field and Lindsey, the four men who had been most directly involved in the search for Miss Holland's body, had collected hyacinths and cowslips from the Moat Farm, arranging them in the form of a cross. It was a representation of their stamina and their persistence, and a silent acknowledgement of the truth that, post-Moat Farm, the policemen's own lives would never be the same. As the coffin was lowered into the grave, Mrs Wisken placed a wreath on it. Ernest Holland considered the dignified occasion to have been quite in keeping with his aunt's character, 'for she was indeed a lady in every sense of the word'.

The next day, everyone was back in the Saffron Walden police court for another quarrel before the magistrates. Pearce's increasing confidence in the charges did little to disguise the fact that the process was now becoming an exhausting ordeal. Amid the stream of witnesses, Newton gave Kate Cranwell rather a rough time, as if out of boredom, after she had deposed to Dougal's possession of a revolver: it had been used, she said, 'for starting the races at the Clavering Coronation sports'.

'Your memory seems to get better as we go on,' observed Newton, cynically. In a bad-tempered cross-examination, he accused her of taking prompts from her sister Eliza, who was sitting in the gallery, and then of being a mouthpiece for the police's ideas, articulating a version of the case against Dougal which she had picked up 'during those few magic moments with the police officer'. Kate had admitted speaking to the police – because they had, quite properly, questioned her as a witness to Dougal's later period at the Moat Farm – but Newton's cruel implication of some sort of sexual impropriety was obvious. It was equally obviously groundless. Kate was a young, unmarried mother, an easy target for Newton, but she was not a medium for pillow talk or widely promiscuous. In the spiteful courtroom, however, casual allusions to her unconventional sexual history blended into the unedifying fabric. Seward Pearce ended the hearing promising to come to the end of the prosecution evidence as soon as he could, but another week's remand was necessary, and the case dragged on again.

The inquest, at least, sewed itself up at its third attempt. At the Parish Hall on Friday 15 May, with Dougal in his usual position, handcuffed and generally listening impassively to the evidence, Charles Edgar Lewis heard the remaining witnesses and summed up. The jury would have to consider three points. Could they be sure that the remains were those of Miss Holland? The evidence suggested that they could. Could they determine the cause of death? The autopsy evidence made their conclusion inevitable. And could they decide who had caused the fatal injury? If they could, there was really only one man in the frame.[648] The jury consulted privately for a mere five minutes before delivering the inevitable verdict – in line with their powers at the time (since revoked), they identified Dougal as Miss Holland's probable murderer.[649] Dougal, who had offered no evidence of his own, rose and said, 'Gentlemen, I am a perfectly innocent man'.[650] Mr Lewis committed him for trial at the next Assizes on the charge of wilful murder.

Still the public's excitement grew and grew. More visitors had swarmed to the Moat Farm: on Sunday 10 May; the police had been forced to bring in extra men from the surrounding villages just to keep order, so great was the crowd that gathered there.[651] Some visitors had come all the way from Manchester.[652] Others had cycled 'half the night', and fell asleep in one of the sheds when they arrived.[653] There was a touring party which had come from Woolwich, and a number of army officers drove over from Hertfordshire in a motor car. Among the crowd, one journalist spotted 'a Chinaman and several Mulattos'. Snacks and souvenirs were for sale; for those who would not pay for a photograph or a picture postcard, the vegetation which sprouted up out of the saturated turf continued to offer free mementos – some trees and shrubs had been stripped to their stumps, their leaves plucked by hungry hands. Amid these scenes, the police planned to give up possession of the Moat Farm, handing it over to a local estate agent, Henry Joshua Cheffins of Saffron Walden, who would be the interim receiver and manager of the farm and its stock.[654] Cheffins employed an ex-Royal Artillery Gunner named Champ to look after the house. Champ had been invalided out of the forces in South Africa; now, he busied himself planting scarlet geraniums in the garden around the house, pausing only to smoke the occasional pipe.[655] He had little Jack for company: Jack had initially seemed destined to go to live with Ernest Holland, but he baulked at the move, refusing to live anywhere but at the Moat Farm.

The reconvened petty sessions, held on Friday 22 May, again failed to conclude the case against Dougal. His arrival had been marked by the usual crowd at the railway station and 'some hooting and hissing', as if he were the villain in a particularly protracted pantomime.[656] Eventually, he would solicit sympathy in some quarters – in certain sentimental and agenda-led circles, at least – but now, in the bloom of his notoriety, the public simply clamoured for a view of him and expressed their limitless disdain as he scrambled into the cab which would take him to the Town Hall.

It was another peculiar hearing, a curious mixture of the immediately relevant and the distantly obscure. Newton was toothless against the evidence of William Howlett, for example, who had measured the distances from the Moat Farm to various railway stations – Audley End Station was four miles and 1,227 yards away; Newport Station three miles and 341 yards; Elsenham Station five miles and 1,341 yards; Stansted Station five miles and 866 yards. This was all incontestable, and perhaps a hint of the case tightening around Dougal – distances were being measured to the yard, train times given to the minute, bullets weighed to the grain. This level of precision now characterised the prosecution's evidence; Newton continued to challenge it with vagaries, might-not-have's.

Dougal's past returned to haunt him. Thomas Henry Gurrin, the document examiner of Holborn Viaduct, gave evidence, looking across the room at Dougal just as he had at the Old Bailey in 1895.[657] Francis Bird Ashwin had proclaimed the £28 15s Heath cheque – the first point of suspicion against Dougal if the forgery charges had to be dealt with – to be 'undoubtedly' in Miss Holland's handwriting.[658] Gurrin thought otherwise, identifying it as being in 'the handwriting of the prisoner in imitation of the handwriting of Miss Holland'.[659] Forgery followed forgery – Dougal's approximation of the magistrate Joseph Bell's signature was demolished; some letters to the secretary of the Laxey Mining Company seemed to be, lazily, in Dougal's own, undisguised, writing.[660] 'Speaking generally,' said Gurrin, not a single signature on any document dated after 19 May 1899 could be shown to be Miss Holland's own.

Cross-examined by Newton, Gurrin accepted that the analysis of handwriting was far from being a specific science. On the other hand, his years of experience, and his scientific focus on the available sample – and not on the reports of the case which had hit the newspapers – meant that his views held water. One delivery of documents which he had received from the police had consisted of a sheaf of genuine signatures, provided by Miss Holland between 19 September 1895 and 30 April 1899; Gurrin had mixed them with the alleged forgeries and then, without reference to the dates, sorted them out again.[661] In re-examination, Gurrin stressed that he had had no instructions from the Treasury *apropos* the extensive collection of signatures now produced in evidence, although he knew that the Heath cheque was presumed to have been a fake.[662] An exact science it may not have been, but the implications of Gurrin's examinations were unavoidable.

Alfred Marden's appearance was perhaps the most intriguing of the day. He testified to having collected Dougal's wife Sarah's trunk from London Bridge Station – she had left it there when their plan to flee had suddenly folded.[663] It was a large black trunk, booked in under the name of White, which Marden knew to be Sarah's maiden name. The initials on the outside, *C.C.H.W.*, were painted in white, but the *W* was of a slightly different shade, having been recently added. Inside was a fur cape which Mrs Wisken had identified as having belonged to Miss Holland. This all seems to have been received with perfect *sangfroid* by a courtroom which seems to have determinedly averted its gaze from Sarah's role in Dougal's misdeeds.

Newton, however, pressed on: had Marden not found diaries at the Moat Farm? He had, and he described them as 'general ... They contained entries referring to all matters except those connected with Miss Holland'. This remark prompted laughter in the court. And how many times had the police interviewed Sarah since Dougal's arrest?

Marden. – I cannot say definitely.

Newton. – About how many times?

Marden. – Perhaps seven or eight times.

Newton. – Have the police not pressed her to give evidence against her husband?

Marden. – No, never.

Newton. – If Mrs Dougal makes that statement in writing it is inaccurate?

Marden. – It is quite untrue. On the other hand, she has volunteered to give us information.

Newton. – Has she been offered money to do it?

Marden. – No.

Newton. – If she says in writing that she has, is it untrue?

Marden. –Yes, so far as the police are concerned.

Newton. –Where is she now?

Marden. – I cannot say.

Newton. – Do you say you really do not know her address?

Marden. – I do not, at the present time.

Newton. –Where was she last week?

Marden. – Living in Camberwell.Whenever I want to see her I see her through her priest.

Newton. – Do you say you did not know her address last week?

Marden. – It would be unfair to make it public.

Sarah had buried herself in the swarm of South London, flinging out occasional brickbats at a police force which had somehow neglected to see her complicity in its true perspective.The currents of the separate stories crossed and obliterated each other: Sarah's involvement with the suspicious trunk at London Bridge pushed her forward into the limelight, but her groundless accusations of harassment and bribery by the police had the curious effect of allowing her to recoil into the shadows. By the end of the hearing, she had acquired no definition, drifting shapelessly through the narrative of the Moat Farm, unlinked where the links ought to have been. Dougal was remanded for another week, Seward Pearce promising that the evidence for the prosecution would be completed at the next session.

In fact, it was.The grim conclusion was reached when David Scott appeared with photographs of the Moat Farm, the site of the discovery of Miss Holland's body marked with a rather mournful white handkerchief.[664] Pearce wound up his work of weeks, asking the magistrates to commit Dougal to trial on the charge of murder, and on the forgery charges which seemed, now, so remote.They formally charged him, and Dougal responded with the wide-eyed display of astonishment that the coroner's court had already seen:'I am absolutely innocent,' he remarked, before handing responsibility for his defence to his solicitor.

Pearce's prosecution had taken hours spread over days spread over months, but Newton's defence would be over in about thirty minutes. He returned to the idea that Sarah had been pressed and cajoled into giving evidence, although she had never been called to the petty sessions. He waved a signed statement at the magistrates, in which, he said, Sarah claimed that 'the police have offered me £100 if I will give evidence against him'. He argued that the careless – or vindictive – press comments on Dougal's previous conviction had undermined the balance of the judicial process, denying his client a fair trial. They had omitted to mention, he said, that Dougal, purportedly through 'want of means', had been undefended against the forgery charge at the Old Bailey in 1895; and they had neglected to mention that Dougal ended up in Cane Hill, struggling to maintain his connection to reality. And where was the proof that Dougal had murdered Miss Holland? He had 'absolutely no motive' for doing so, said Newton; and what of the evidence of commission? Whose word placed the deadly gun in Dougal's hand? Newton saw gaping holes in the prosecution's evidence – forty witnesses adding up to much less than the sum of their parts – and urged the magistrates to do the same, and to dismiss the charges against the prisoner. But three minutes' consideration was enough for the magistrates to commit Dougal to the next Essex Assizes, starting in the second half of June, where he would be tried for his life.

⋯⋯

Dougal was removed, on the same day and without returning to Cambridge, to the infirmary of Chelmsford Prison, where it was felt that he could be best supervised while he awaited his trial.[665] Marden and Scott accompanied him, the three men travelling by road to avoid the inevitable crowds of sightseers at the railway stations, and reaching the prison at about 7.00p.m.[666] Dougal had gazed at the countryside as they went along, finding it, as he would write to Georgina, 'a delightful drive through undulating country'.[667] He remained optimistic, despite the situation – one account of the departure from Saffron Walden has him snarling defiantly at his keepers, or perhaps simply advising them where to put their bets: 'It's a twenty to one chance on my getting off. I am innocent. They can't prove anything.'[668]

On reception at Chelmsford, Dougal was examined by Henry Newton, the Medical Officer. Newton found him in good health, 'of good physique, and free from organic disease'.[669] In conversation, Dougal kept his end up, and Newton could detect 'no signs of mental weakness'. This mirrored the findings of his counterpart at Cambridge, one John Buckenham, who described Dougal's behaviour while there as 'most exemplary, and his mental condition perfectly normal'.

In the clockwork of the daily routine of the prison infirmary, the time between Dougal's rising and lights out (he always slept soundly through the night) became measurable only in meals (which he ate heartily, but, now, without gaining weight). As if to relieve the monotony, Dougal settled to a short spree of letter-writing, displacing any anxieties via the eccentric medium of jovial, cheerful missives to those he had left in his wake, on the outside. Jesse remarks that his letters possessed a 'curious' and 'detached' perspective – Dougal devoted himself to trivia, the quotidian, the mundane, wishing away the very real threat of death which now hung over him.[670] The quixotic (or perhaps slightly ghoulish) Charlotte Larner, last seen – as far as can be established – in the 1890s in Northend, became a regular correspondent, offering to send cigarettes to Dougal's son Albert (who was, at the time, stationed in Aden, and serving in the Dublin Royal Fusiliers).[671] Dougal responded with his usual pedantic flatness, immersing himself in the numbing detail, but rather missing the bigger picture: 'Player's Medium are very good, sold in boxes of 50 at 1s., or Will's Gold Flake in round tins at 1s. 1½d. are also good'. Other extracts seem equally dry – in the same letter, he told Charlotte, 'Don't trouble about the spoons, they will be quite safe'. He commented on the weather: 'To-day is much better; we have a little sun after some days of rain'.[672] In a letter to Georgina, he speculated idly that the Cranwell family, who had plenty on their plate at the time, might not have gone 'to the Show at Bishops [*sic*] Stortford last week, as it was very wet'. Occasionally, he felt himself given to pronounce on world events – the assassination of Draga, the consort of King Aleksandar Obrenović of Serbia, crossed his radar, and he described it with unlikely outrage as a 'dreadful piece of business!'[673]

Rarely, casual allusions to his circumstances would appear in the texts. In one letter to Charlotte, he seems to be little more than annoyed, inconvenienced by his imprisonment: 'It is a pity I am not disengaged just now as we could have a run round together and visit some of our old haunts, friends, etc'.[674] This was, as Jesse pointed out, euphemistic in the extreme, but Dougal was now, in some ways, freer than he had ever been to indulge his fantasy world without the fear of reality crashing in. The bones of others' lives formed the architecture of his epistolary visions: besides spoons and cigarettes, other items his letters would fuss over included a watch, some slate and fawn dresses and, with dull frequency, bicycles. He would be disproportionately chipper, referring affectionately to Georgina as 'old girl' in one of his letters to her, and sending kisses to his daughter Olive, who, until her father's scandal broke, had been attending a convent school in Belgium.[675] Only once would he admit that 'the circumstances look very dark', but even then this gloomy augury was tempered by the hope that 'there will be a light cloud following' and the fact that he was 'keeping up my spirits to meet the charge'.[676] Later, he manifested a slightly sinister interest in a ballad which had been written about the Moat Farm, telling Georgina that it had apparently been performed at the Show at Bishop's Stortford by two men, 'one playing a banjo'.[677] He thought that Georgina might see a copy of the lyrics in Clavering – they were being sold for a penny each. If she did, he instructed her, 'see if there is a Printer's name at the bottom of the page, and if so, make a note of it for me, please'. Dougal plainly dreamed of the lucrative spoils of a libel case.

But things were already changing in the outside world, and, in his seclusion, Dougal was struggling to maintain contact with his past existences. Sarah, as Dougal revealed in a comment in a letter to Olive, had converted to Catholicism under the guidance of the priest – the Reverend Wright – to whom Alfred Marden had alluded, and, by early June, was preparing to be confirmed.[678] At the same time, in Clavering, Georgina was heavily pregnant: on Wednesday 10 June 1903, at her parents' house, she gave birth to a daughter. From the prison infirmary, Dougal approximated the doting father, initially misfiring with his stuffy 'allow me to congratulate you', but finally getting into the swing of things, encouraging Georgina to eat 'plenty of nourishing food' and thinking half-whimsically of names for the child, while knowing that the final choice would be the mother's.[679]

Occasional developments in his case scudded cloudily past, sometimes almost unnoticed amid the weird distractions of his remote and complex personal life. With little over a week to go before the start of the Assize sessions, Dougal wrote to Georgina mentioning that Arthur Newton had retained the barrister 'Mr. George Elliott and a junior counsel on the Chelmsford circuit' in his defence. Four days later, in another letter to the same correspondent, he was able to name Basil Watson as the junior in question.[680] But the trial now began to approach rapidly and, as it did, Dougal's fate crept up on him – suddenly, the gravity of his position was all too obvious, and his state of denial began to tremble on its useless foundations. The tedium of remand was 'a very great suspense', he declared on Tuesday 16 June – 'I shall be glad when it is over and settled'.[681] By 8.30a.m. on the subsequent Thursday, Dougal was once more pen-in-hand, writing irritably to tell Georgina that 'I go down to the Court to-day, what for I don't know'.[682] Within half an hour, with his letter finished, he was there.[683] This was the Grand Jury hearing, at the conclusion of which, as Dougal rightly supposed, musing almost to himself in his hurried letter, 'I shall know for certain when the case will be commenced'.[684]

⋇⋇⋇

Mr Justice Wright surveyed the packed courtroom – admission was by ticket only – from his position on the bench.[685] Into his middle sixties and, according to his obituary in *The Times*, equipped with some of the inflexibility common to gentlemen of his age, he was 'not altogether a man of the world' – a prototype of the socially remote judge of modern caricature.[686] These limitations were, however, neatly offset by an equally unshakeable belief in mercy and humanity, sometimes even extending to what some regarded as 'an excess of leniency'. Described as 'conscientious', 'solemn' and 'never pompous', Wright would oversee Dougal's trial: Dougal could hardly have asked for a fairer man. Indeed, Wright's summings-up were regarded as 'famously favourable to defendants' – as far as this went, which was not far, here was something to which Dougal could lash his nebulous optimism, fixing it in place against the approaching storm.[687]

Dougal's self-professed ignorance of the formalities of the Assizes was undoubtedly disingenuous. He had been through the Grand

Jury process on several previous occasions – in Hertfordshire, in Oxfordshire, in London – and must have known that the role of the Grand Jury was to ascertain the cogency of the *prima facie* case against him. The hearing itself was conducted out of his earshot, as he padded around the holding cell below the courtroom, but here was an early test of Dougal's purported claim: 'They can't prove anything'. If he had been able to perceive them, however, the urgent and *ad hoc* alterations which had been made to the courtroom, increasing its capacity to accommodate the still-hot interest of the press, might have told Dougal that someone (perhaps William Girdlestone, the keeper of the Shire Hall) was expecting the Grand Jury to shunt the case unfussily into the trial stage.

So it proved. Mr Justice Wright, whose summary of the prosecution case, vast as it was, took some hours, observed that 'he thought that it was impossible for the Grand Jury to say that there was not a strong case to send down'.[688] On balance, he reflected, 'the evidence was amply sufficient to justify them in sending the case for trial'. In the afternoon, the Grand Jury did exactly that, finding (in the jargon) a true bill against Dougal, not only on the charge of murder, but on seven specific charges of forgery which still faced him. In addition to the Heath cheque, Dougal stood accused of the approximation of Joseph Bell's signature on 27 September 1899, and of misrepresenting himself as Miss Holland on an assortment of cheques siphoning her cash, and the proceeds of the sale of her shares in the Great Laxey Mining Company, into his account. Despite all of this, the murder charge naturally remained the matter of greatest interest for the legal officials and the public alike. The trial would begin on Monday 22 June, at eleven o'clock in the morning.

Dougal faced his indictment, and then left the court in a cab, with the blinds drawn over the windows; the familiar crowd of curious townsfolk had gathered outside the Shire Hall to peer at him as he passed. Undaunted by the Grand Jury's failure to equivocate over their decision, he returned to the prison infirmary and set to his correspondence again, writing to Charlotte Larner with some of the unmerited buoyancy of before. She wrote back with more caution, hoping 'very earnestly' that 'things are not so bad as they look'.[689] 'I shall be thinking of you on Monday and all through the trial,' she pledged. So shall the nation, she might have added.

On Friday 19 June, the Essex countryside gave up its second body. This time, a mile from the scourged Moat Farm, the corpse of a man dressed in a 'good tweed suit' was discovered beside a straw stack.[690] The man had been aged between fifty and sixty, and had seemingly visited the scene of the police's quest for Miss Holland's body in late March or early April, one of the thousands of tourists the place had attracted. Returning via the Wicken road, he sought either shelter or rest in a field, and shortly died there. By the time his body was found, it was covered with a scattering of wind-blown straw, and was in bad repair. Rats had eaten the man's dead flesh, rendering the facial features unrecognisable; and his right arm – including the bones – was missing entirely. Only on closer inspection was it ascertained that the deceased had lost the arm in life, and not to the post-mortem activities of vermin.

This was the latest misfortune – it had some of the properties of a classical omen – to afflict the area; a terrible, unexpected secondary effect of the unstinting interest in the mystery of the Moat Farm. The farm itself continued to host immense crowds of the curious, and the picture postcard trade blossomed as the visitors sought mementos of their day out.[691] Elsewhere, fences were placed around the younger trees, denuded of their foliage by those hoping for a souvenir on cheaper terms; denied access to the trees, they 'plucked branches from the hedgerows … and many decorated their bicycles this way'. It remained an extraordinary scene. Excitement was tangible and, with the trial now only a weekend away, the public could sense a climax to the scandal finally nearing.

CHAPTER ELEVEN

THE HERTS AND *Essex Observer* meandered into an almost Dickensian vernacular, evoking images of the great legal scenes of nineteenth-century literature – Fagin at Newgate, Alice in the court of the Red Queen. There was a throng outside the doors of the Shire Hall in Chelmsford for 'a hour or more' before the opening of the court, it wrote.[692] This time, however, the crowd's usual target had evaded them, although only by minutes: roused early on Monday morning, Dougal had been driven, blinds drawn against the cab windows, to an entrance at the side of the building, and, by about nine o'clock, secreted in the cells below the courtroom to await the start of his trial.

Upstairs, the court was, again, crowded – 'between thirty and forty' journalists had taken their positions on the specially erected platform over the packed public gallery. To the right of Mr Justice Wright sat Colonel Richard Percival Davis, the High Sheriff of Essex; to the judge's left sat his wife, Lady Merriel Wright, who, plainly, would not have missed the event. As was so common in murder trials of the time, many of the attendees were women, in thrall to Dougal's strange enigma.

At eleven o'clock, an expectant silence settled upon the court, and the trial began. Dougal was called up from his underground quarters, striding smartly to the dock, 'in his usual health, but … nervous', according to one observer. With reference to the murder charge – the alleged forgeries would be dealt with if the capital charge failed – Dougal was asked, 'Are you guilty or not guilty?' Nervous he may have been, but his self-assurance had not dissolved. In a clear voice, without wavering, Dougal answered.[693]

'Not guilty.'

The great number of spectators – taking in the more and the less official alike – peered at a phalanx of barristers. For the prosecution, Seward Pearce had instructed Charles Frederick Gill, an industrious, driven character who was (as the *Strand* magazine put it in February 1903) 'one of the few leading counsel who stay later than half-past six at their chambers, and ... no respecter of Saturdays as a holiday'.[694] This approach to legal work was reminiscent of that of Richard Muir, but there the comparison largely ceased: philosophically, Gill had much more in common with Mr Justice Wright than he did with the pressing, urgent Muir. Gill's obituary supposed that he preferred defence cases; his inherent sympathies tended to lie with the accused, although he pursued prosecution work with 'extreme fairness' and 'essential kindliness'.[695] Apart from the dramatic Muir, Pearce could hardly have selected anyone who would have devoted such considerable time to mastering the great jigsaw of the prosecution case – such was the scale and range of the prosecution's argument, Gill's meticulous attention to detail and an ability to balance competing strands of evidence would be essential. These, rather than bursts of oratorical inspiration, were the foundation of his style of advocacy.

With Gill were Rollo Frederick Graham-Campbell and Walter John Grubbe. Grubbe was a veteran of the South-Eastern legal circuit, familiar particularly with the courtrooms of Hertfordshire and Essex. Slightly older than Gill – who was himself in his early fifties – Grubbe had accumulated nearly thirty years' journeyman experience since being called to the Bar in 1874, although he would never deal with a case more notable than Dougal's.[696] Nor would the younger Graham-Campbell, whose reputation as a barrister was described as 'sound', if not sparkling.[697] Close chums with lawyers of very senior rank, Graham-Campbell found himself appointed, in 1901, as counsel for the Attorney-General in legitimacy cases. He also undertook run-of-the-mill criminal advocacy work, but his specialism undoubtedly recommended him to Pearce. At the police court, Arthur Newton's casual forays into the territory of the Cranwell sisters' unorthodox sexual principles had suggested that their reliability as witnesses – specifically, as witnesses with personal axes to grind – might be tested at the trial. But none of the other witnesses had had quite the view of Dougal that the Cranwells had had – they were unusually vulnerable, and, at the same time, unusually valuable.

Graham-Campbell, with his particular expertise, had probably been selected to protect them from the worst predations of the barristers for the defence.

The defence itself was led by George Elliott, retained by Newton. Like Gill, Elliott was a lawyer unblessed by great rhetorical powers; instead – again like Gill – he relied on 'skill, acuteness, common sense' and a 'sympathetic mind' to achieve his results.[698] He had been involved in several causes of note, including, most recently, the springtime murder trial of George Chapman at the Old Bailey. This was Dougal's purported former acquaintance, finally called to account for the deaths of his three most recent partners. Elliott had then been, as he was now, in steadfast defence; by the time Dougal's trial began, however, Chapman had been dead for two-and-a-half months, having met his end on the gallows at Wandsworth Prison. In a case spilling over with auguries, this seemed one of the worst of them.

Supporting Elliott were Basil Watson and John Paul Valetta. Both men were new to the legal circuit, having been called to the Bar only the previous year.[699] Watson had already dabbled in criminal law at the Old Bailey, defending the son of a clergyman on charges of 'obtaining underclothing by false pretences' in October 1902; but the young man had decided to plead guilty, thereby reducing Watson's workload in the case considerably.[700] Valetta, for his part, had appeared in the High Court and before the King's Bench Division, but had never acted in criminal proceedings.[701] This was an alarmingly inexperienced defence team, particularly for a capital trial. Dougal's very existence depended on the ability of these men to unpick the great, elaborate tapestry of the prosecution's evidence.

⁂

Charles Gill's opening address was lengthy but focused, occupying the court for some time with promises of the evidence it would hear. Gill had one forensic mannerism which defied his typical straightforwardness – a 'habit of removing his eye-glasses to emphasize the particular emotion – surprise, doubt, indignation, encouragement, or incredulity – which he desired to convey'.[702] Even this trick, though, he used sparingly, preferring to start and finish with the evidence, and leaving its interpretation to the jury. Now, Gill was unambiguous about the compelling nature of the case against Dougal: he would show, he said, that 'the case against the prisoner was established – that the prisoner was guilty of the murder of Miss Holland, and that the evidence would sustain the statement he had made'.[703] One sees Gill's spectacles on his nose throughout, perhaps emphasising by their very stillness his confidence in Dougal's guilt. There would be no rhetorical flourishes; none would be required. From his seat in the dock, Dougal listened patiently to Gill's speech; at its conclusion, the first witness for the prosecution was called, and the bizarre reunion of faces from the prisoner's past could begin.

That day, twenty-one witnesses would be called to the witness box. On the bench, Mr Justice Wright kept his notes – Ernest Legrand Holland, Miss Holland's nephew, was the first man up, examined by Grubbe, cross-examined by Elliott, re-examined by Grubbe.[704] Wright made the occasional annotation, recording that two pictures of Miss Holland, produced in evidence, were nearly twenty years old; and that the Moat Farm, at the moment of Dougal's arrest, was brimming with Miss Holland's property, on open display.[705] This all tended to what Wright knew would be the crux of the case – the identification of the body, and Dougal's perceived role in its final hours in life, and in its concealment in death. Were there holes in the prosecution's argument, gaps just big enough for Dougal to crawl through?

By comparison, two subsequent witnesses, Edmund Holland and Florence Pollock, Wright considered immaterial. Mrs Pollock was once more in fine form. Her appearance before the magistrates had been a crazy departure into unplanned comedy, and so it was, for better or (probably) worse, at the murder trial. She attended in deep mourning, squinting out through swathes of crepe when Gill invited her to identify the man she had seen visit Miss Holland at Elgin Crescent. 'Do you see him in the court?' asked Gill.[706]

Mrs Pollock looked straight towards the jury box. 'Yes, I see him among those gentlemen over there,' she said. The court dissolved into laughter.

'Will you kindly remove your veil, madam?' said Gill, patiently.

Mrs Pollock did so. 'Yes,' she said. 'Oh, yes, now I can see him.' She was pointing to the same juror.[707]

'Look slowly round the court again,' said Gill.

This time, Mrs Pollock pointed at William Girdlestone, the keeper of the Shire Hall, who was sitting beside the jury box watching the trial. 'Yes, there is the gentleman,' she said.

Girdlestone stepped forward, and Mrs Pollock examined him more closely, attempting to unify him with her distant, and perhaps rather hazy, memory of Dougal in the hallway of the boarding house. Gill looked on, optimistic that Mrs Pollock would, eventually, correct her own obvious mistake; but, instead, she doggedly persisted with her identification, stubbornly describing Dougal-Girdlestone as 'very much changed since I saw him a month ago'.[708] More laughter from the public gallery greeted this remark, but the pantomime continued.

William Girdlestone returned to his seat. 'Will you do what I ask,' demanded Gill, addressing Mrs Pollock slightly more forcefully, 'and look around the court slowly, please'.[709]

Gradually, realisation dawned. Mrs Pollock's gaze reached the dock, and she exclaimed, 'That is the man sitting there!'[710] What should have been a simple matter had become a carnival of looking-glass thinking. Could Mrs Pollock's poor eyesight – or her recourse to an extemporary form of logic – have undermined her evidence? Mr Elliott leapt up to cross-examine, squeezing the last profits from Mrs Pollock's amazing testimony.

> Mr Elliott. – Are you quite sure that the prisoner is the person who called at your house?
>
> Witness. – Yes, I am quite positive. It made a great impression on me.
>
> Mr Elliott. – Have you seen the portrait of the prisoner in the papers?
>
> Witness. – I may perhaps have seen it.
>
> Mr Elliott. – Do you say that this impression has remained with you all these four years?
>
> Witness. – Yes. I feel sure he is the man. I looked all round the court when I came in, and I recognised the prisoner when I saw him.[711]

This was preposterous nonsense. Mrs Pollock was asked to stand down, and here the charade came to an end.

ᴄ⦿ᴏ

The next witness was substantially more reliable. Annie Whiting, Miss Holland's former dressmaker, and sharp as needles and pins, was the antithesis of Mrs Pollock's bumbling caricature. Annie described her own eyesight as 'very bad' – a result, perhaps, of the intense visual demands of fine embroidery work – but, asked to point him out, she struck on Dougal straight away: 'That's the man.'[712] Her recollection of the repairs and overhauls she had made of Miss Holland's wardrobe remained equally lucid. In June 1899, she had relined a skirt for her, and a portion of the same skirt was produced in evidence.[713] Likewise, Annie recognised an underskirt, dyed black and made of 'a strange material ... not sold now, and ... old-fashioned four years ago'.[714] She had made it for Miss Holland. Both garments had been found clinging to the skeleton unearthed at the Moat Farm and, although Annie accepted that, in their decayed condition, the dresses no longer bore much of her own stitching, her evidence never faltered. She had been intimately acquainted with Miss Holland's out-of-date wardrobe, and remembered its contents. Even after four years, she saw items she had once known, and knew them again, without hesitation. This went a long way towards removing any doubt about the identity of the remains.

Mrs Henrietta Wisken's memory proved similarly strong. The conclusion of the coroner's jury in May had been unambiguous, but not incontestable: in his spasm of denial at the last hearing at the police court, Arthur Newton had, on Dougal's behalf, floated the only readily available alternative explanation of Miss Holland's absence, predicated on the flimsy pretext that she was away travelling, and had been since the night of 19 May 1899. This had been Dougal's position at Cambridge Prison, voiced, probably, to all and sundry, and certainly reaching the hearing of the Governor.[715] If true, it implied that the body recovered from the Moat Farm was not Miss Holland's, and that the coroner's jury had made an awful mistake. Gill was now out to cauterise this line of defence with clear proof of the living identity of the corpse – an initial step towards the 'direct evidence of the deed' which Newton had demanded the prosecution produce.

Considerable time and energy had been spent on establishing which parts of the badly decomposed figure remained sufficiently intact to be useful in confirming its identity. Elias Bower, from the nerve centre of Scotland Yard, had travelled to Liverpool, hunting down Miss Holland's former dentists in order that they might identify their handiwork in the mouth of the corpse.[716] Unfortunately, two men firmly believed to have filled some of her teeth – Joseph and George Snape – had died within a very short period of one another in the 1880s. Their business ledgers had been lost, probably sold as scrap paper in the 1890s by William Mapplebeck, who took over some of the Snapes' trade. Only Jonathan Royston – who took over a separate part of the Snapes' business after their demise – felt confident enough to remark on the particulars of the skull's dental profile. 'I have seen the skull of the deceased,' he said – Bower had carried it with him to Liverpool.

> The stopping in the right lower wisdom tooth is in soft gold and is very characteristic of old Joseph Snape's work, it was done I should say about 30 years ago.
>
> The stopping in the right upper wisdom is very characteristic of George Snape's work and it may have a little arsenic under the stopping, which was a practice of the Snape's [*sic*]. I never knew any other dentist put arsenic in. Arsenic leaks out and causes periostitis and of the tooth and alveolar process, this is well marked in the jaw now shown me. Of course you get this from other sources of poison but this is especially well marked in this jaw.
>
> The stopping in the right upper second molar is I should say of much more recent date, probably done less than 20 years ago. The right lower first molar and bicuspid, the stopping is of still more recent date. The bicuspid was done within the past 10 years, the molar I should think was done a little earlier.
>
> The left lower wisdom has probably been stopped within the last 25 years. I know the Holland family well but I do not recollect Miss Camille Cecile Holland.
>
> All the Hollands have well marked mouths, the mouth now shown me has a marked tendency to the shape etc of that family.

This was a comprehensive tour around Miss Holland's mouth (supposing that it was Miss Holland's), which Bower augmented by divining that the more recent dental work had probably been undertaken at a London surgery 'near Praed-street or Gower-street stations', and that, at some point prior to 17 November 1895, she had had a tooth broken, painfully, by a dentist.[717] But Jonathan Royston's opinions never reached the court – probably, they were considered susceptible to the sceptical probing of the defence. Mrs Wisken, however, observing the state of things with her untrained eyes, felt that she could mention Miss Holland's teeth, as she had at Saffron Walden:

> Mr Elliott. – Have you not sworn that you could identify the body as that of Miss Holland?
> Witness. – Yes, by the shape of the head and the very nice set of teeth.[718]

Still, Mrs Wisken's primary function was not to improvise around Miss Holland's dental condition, but to further the evidentiary work begun by Annie Whiting, and to identify the clothing and accoutrements of the body as Miss Holland's clothing and accoutrements. This she did to compelling effect.

The underskirt which Annie Whiting had recognised, Mrs Wisken also knew. It was augmented with 'two rows of braid and a binding at the bottom', which Mrs Wisken herself had sewn on, during Miss Holland's stay in Saffron Walden.[719] There were the shabby remains of a bodice, peeled away from the corpse, with a silk frill at the collar and on the lapels – Mrs Wisken had added frills around the cuffs, and had relined one of the pockets. The distinctive hair frame was just like one which Mrs Wisken had seen Miss Holland wear. The tortoiseshell pin and the comb, found between the struts of the hair frame, were familiar. Even the bustle – which Miss Holland wore below her skirt, much in the manner of the oligarchs' wives of Regency England, a measure of her outmoded style – was identified by Mrs Wisken. Further, there were vests and undergarments: Miss Holland would wear two woollen vests, Mrs Wisken said, and, indeed, two woollen vests had been found on the body.[720] There were stays – the solid remains of a former corset or some similar underwear arrangement – with hooks which Mrs Wisken described attaching to Miss Holland's bloomers.[721] There were parts of a decayed elastic belt. There were the decrepit relics of a combination – an all-in-one body suit worn as the lowest layer.[722] It was a remarkable vision of a lady wrapped up not only against the evening chill of the Essex lowlands, but also against the unwanted attentions of men. If it *was* Miss Holland, the unwanted man was Dougal who was, on the evening of her disappearance, still stung by the surge of lust to which Florence Havies had refused to respond the previous evening. Miss Holland had given up her virginity for Dougal, but now the barricades were firmly up, and sex, the main lever in Dougal's psychological machine, was now out of the question.

Mr Elliott pressed Mrs Wisken closely, but Mrs Wisken's simple recollections never shuddered before the onslaught. She accepted the fact that some of the garments were unremarkable, and could be 'bought in numbers of shops', as Elliott put it.[723] She saw no initials on the clothing; she acknowledged a slight mistake she had made at the police court (Miss Holland's belt, she thought, had fastened with prongs, but the belt unearthed at the Moat Farm fastened with hooks). But, finally, Mrs Wisken's detailed appreciation of the ensemble of Miss Holland's wardrobe defied dissection. She could give details about the braids on the under-skirt, and about the frills on the cuffs of the bodice, showing how she had attached them, or emphasising the personal artistry implicit in their creation.[724] 'I can identify my own work from the general appearance,' Mrs Wisken told Gill in re-examination. By now, few could have doubted her.

Florence Blackwell, *née* Havies, was the next witness of note. Her story was familiar enough, and had been consistent throughout; she was given a rather rough time by Elliott in cross-examination, who persisted with a rather personal line of enquiry opened up by Newton at Saffron Walden:

> Mr Elliott. – You would be angry when Mr Dougal kissed you?
> Witness. – Yes.
> Mr Elliott. – Have you remained angry with him all these four years?
> Witness. – No.
> Mr Elliott. – Are you inclined to be hysterical?
> Witness. – No.[725]

In fact, she was, as newspaper accounts of her very distressed, and distressing, response to Miss Holland's disinterment had made clear. But this was the lasting effect of her mistreatment by Dougal, and a stalemate was reached in court – this was territory on which the defence dare not tread too much, for fear of making Dougal's behaviour at and around the time of Miss Holland's disappearance seem, simply, even worse. The content of Florence's evidence was, accordingly, left unharmed. She could not be sure – sure enough to swear under oath – of the colour of the dress Miss Holland was wearing on her last night at the Moat Farm, but it was 'dark', and she had identified the bodice and the skirt as being those of her lost mistress.[726] One more witness, to be called later in the same day, would complete the identification evidence, which was tightly marshalled by Gill and his colleagues – but, until then, it was time for the prosecution to turn instead to Dougal's own account of Miss Holland's absence, and to give the lie to it.

⸙⸙

On Friday 19 May 1899, Dougal had left the house with Miss Holland at 6.30 in the evening; he returned alone at 8.30p.m., announcing that Miss Holland had gone to London. He had told Superintendent Pryke that he had left her at Stansted Station, although Florence had inferred that she would be returning to Newport.[727] Dougal's account had attracted suspicion throughout the investigation – its principal features, as he explained them, did not match those remembered by poor Florence. Now, Walter Grubbe would open up Dougal's story to a fuller analysis. Could Miss Holland have caught a train to London during those two hours?

The next witness, George Maylam, showed that she could not. Maylam was the chief clerk in the timetable department of the Great Eastern Railway, and he had studied the 1899 timetable, calibrating it against Dougal's story.[728] There was one 'up' train (towards London) which had passed through Newport at 5.46p.m. and through Stansted at 6.00p.m., but Dougal and Miss Holland had left too late to rendezvous with it. The next up train did not pass through Newport until 9.25p.m., going on through Stanstead at 9.40p.m., but, by this time, Dougal had already returned home and spoken of Miss Holland's departure. None of the up timetables suited Dougal's story.

Nor did the 'down' timetables: those covering services heading away from London. Dougal had gone out for about half an hour at 9.00p.m., and then for about the same amount of time shortly before 10.00p.m., and then for a little longer shortly before midnight, each time – ostensibly – to meet a down train at the station. But the 'twelve o'clock train' he had mentioned to Florence was a fantasy; referring to his timetables, Maylam found that the last down train from Liverpool Street Station was the 10.02p.m.

service, which reached Stansted at 11.05p.m., and did not stop, except by special application, at either Elsenham or Newport.[729] There would have been no point Dougal's leaving the house to meet a midnight train – no such train was coursing through the Essex countryside that night.

The next morning, Florence had gone downstairs at seven to find that Dougal was now claiming to have received a letter from Miss Holland informing him that she was going on holiday. The same question arose – was it possible? Mr Grubbe called John Turtle, overseer of the Inland Postal Section at Mount Pleasant Post Office, to show that it was not.[730]

If Miss Holland *had* caught a train to London, it seemed that she can only have taken the 9.40p.m. service up from Stansted – or, perhaps, the same service from either Audley End (9.20p.m.), Newport (9.25p.m.) or Elsenham (9.34p.m.).[731] This service, Maylam had told the court, arrived at Liverpool Street at 10.56p.m. But Turtle explained that the mail services closed at Liverpool Street at 10.02p.m., in time for the last passenger train down, which dropped its mail at Bishop's Stortford.[732] Even if Miss Holland had attempted to send her letter from the General Post Office in St Martin's le Grand, near St Paul's Cathedral, the last post there was at 10.45p.m., eleven minutes before the up train got in (the mail in this collection was taken by passenger train to Broxbourne, and then by goods train to Bishop's Stortford). Dougal cannot possibly have had a letter from Miss Holland in his hand by seven the next morning – she could not have reached London in time for the final post.

❧

The last witness of the day was George Mold, the bootmaker of the Edgware Road whom Miss Holland patronised between 1884 and 1898.[733] He was an inveterate record-keeper and, when the remains were pulled from the earth at the Moat Farm, and the boots reunited as a pair after Thomas Barker had severed one of Miss Holland's legs with his fork, Mold rapidly produced a remarkable chain of documents and artefacts to prove the history of the footwear. Grubbe called him to the witness box as the last piece of the jigsaw of the identification evidence. The jury would adjourn for the evening with any lingering doubt about the identity of the withered remains wiped quite away.

Mold had been professionally acquainted with not only Miss Holland, but also her aunt Sarah Ann and her brother Charles, who, Mold said, went to New Orleans.[734] This was no passing contact, in the way that Annie Whiting's or Mrs Wisken's could be inferred to be – Mold had fostered a secure professional relationship with the Hollands; furthermore, he had the documentary evidence to prove it in the way that the Liverpool dentists, for example, no longer did. Shown the boots which had been removed from the body, Mold identified them as his work. Miss Holland had visited him at his shop, wishing to order a new pair of boots, on Thursday 7 January 1897; he measured her feet and wrote down her specifications, settling on a cost price of 20*s*. She had asked for a toecap, which she had never asked for before.[735] Mold found suitable lasts – wooden feet, conforming to the size and shape of Miss Holland's – for the job.[736] He delivered the boots on 21 January, and Miss Holland paid for them on 10 February.

In court, Mold pointed out his brand on the surviving leather – the word *Mold* remained visible on the right boot, and the letter *d* was just appreciable on the left.[737] Inside the right boot, he discerned traces of curly lambs' wool, matching his written record taken at the time of measuring: 'Lined curly lamb'. The heels were specified to be one and three-eighths of an inch high – Mold found the corpse's boots commensurate in this respect, too.[738] Mold pressed the lasts, which he produced in evidence, into, and out of, the boots. They were a perfect fit.[739]

Inside the Moat Farm, Superintendent Daniels had found another pair of boots.[740] These, too, had been made by Mold, and, naturally, had not been subject to the decay of the boots retrieved from the body. These boots, ordered in August 1898, were made of a slightly different leather; they were an eighth of an inch higher in the heel; they were slightly higher at the ankle; they were slightly longer.[741] Mold proved all this – with more documents, but with the same lasts – and had more evidence about other transactions with Miss Holland, all detailed meticulously in his log books. He had used the lasts five times in all, three times for Miss Holland, once for a Miss Cotman, and once for a Miss Davis, but only Miss Holland had asked for curly lambs' wool inners.[742] It was a remarkable performance of fine detail, leaving no doubt that the boots of the body were Miss Holland's. Elliott jabbed at

Mold in cross-examination, but unsuccessfully, and without the zeal with which he had attempted to counter Annie Whiting and Mrs Wisken. These 1898 boots were a little longer, he mused, hoping to find flaws in Mold's testimony; but, Mold pointed out, the extra length on the 1898 boots was not sufficient to take them from a 2½ – Miss Holland's usual size – to a 3.[743] The difference between a 2½ and a 3 was one-sixth of an inch; by implication, the extra length which Miss Holland had asked for amounted to less than this: an eighth of an inch, perhaps, or even a tenth. These were tiny, almost inscrutable, margins, and a measure of Mold's precision. At a quarter to six, Elliott desisted for the evening, Mold stepped down, and the court adjourned, twenty-one witnesses in, and with twenty-four to go.[744]

⟳⟳⟳

The pressure had apparently broken like a great wave over poor Georgina Cranwell. She had been unable to attend court on the Monday, and had stayed at home suffering from some sort of illness. Even so, she had managed to send a letter to Dougal, which he had received before the trial began.[745] On Tuesday 23 June, killing time in the infirmary before being driven to the Shire Hall, Dougal replied to her. The letter contained his usual mixture of the mundane, the delusional and the untrue, with new hints of bitterness and jealousy. Here were the thoughts of a man on trial for his life.

He looked with self-righteous envy on the freedom of others. 'I was surprised,' Dougal wrote, 'to hear the Clavering witnesses have been here since last Wednesday night; they have no doubt been having a good old time living at hotels and on the fat of the land; some of them would like to be on a similar trial again, that is, if they are being treated well. The jury were taken out for a drive after tea.' Sanctimoniously, he disdained Georgina's treatment by her sisters – a schism had developed within the Cranwell family, with Kate and Eliza on the one side and Georgina on the other. 'I am surprised at ——,' he said (the letter was edited for later publication), 'but the time may come when —— will require similar attention, and then she may know what it is to be slighted'.

He raged against the prurience of the press, losing grip of his grammar in the process: 'Anything to sell newspapers last evening on the contents bill in of course large letters, "Dougal and the servant", it was I suppose that girl's evidence about trying to kiss her'. Remorse remained outside his emotional repertoire. Even the jury – his jealousy of their evening drive (around the village of Danbury) notwithstanding – seemed 'remarkable for their youthful appearance, and appear to be drawn from the artisan class or middle class shopkeeper'.[746] He thought himself better than them: fantasies of elevated status had fuelled Dougal, and obviously fuelled Georgina, whose background was strictly working class. Then the letter skipped merrily into sudden buoyancy, and then into an attempt at honesty, his weakest suit: 'Most likely my trial on this charge will be disposed of to-day; whichever way it goes no doubt I shall be given the opportunity of writing, so that keep a good heart I am endeavouring to do so, and as far as outward appearances go, it is so'.[747] And then there were casual, even cruel, reports of Olive, and Sarah, and the unimportant saga of their slate and fawn dresses; another barbed remark about either Kate or Eliza; the bare comment that 'I am waiting to be driven down to Court'; and, lastly, 'Thank Millie for me for her kindness'. Poor Millie, the daughter of Mary Herberta Boyd; whose stepfather may have murdered her mother in Nova Scotia in 1884; who had then stood up for the same man in court in Oxfordshire in 1895; who remained unconditionally loyal, in spite of it all; who was, like Georgina herself, a living victim of this selfish, charmless individual. 'Yours very sincerely,' he signed off, 'S. Herbert Dougal'.

⁂

The second day of the trial commenced at ten o'clock on Tuesday morning – the first had belonged to the prosecution.

George Mold was briefly recalled, but the prosecution quickly moved forward with the second witness of the day. This was Edwin John Churchill, a gun, rifle and ammunition manufacturer whose premises stood on Agar Street, a road leading off the Strand, in the West End of London.[748] He described himself as a veteran of thirty-five years' experience in the gun trade and, indeed, before his death in 1910, he would touch the edges of a couple of famous shooting cases, including the mysterious death of Mrs Luard in a Kentish wood in 1908.[749] The science of ballistics was beginning to develop – after Edwin Churchill's death, his nephew Robert would drive the discipline further still, appearing in glamorous affairs alongside Bernard Spilsbury and Edward Marshall Hall, men whose names stood, and stand, for the flamboyant, dramatic character of the law courts of the twenties and thirties.

At the time of the Moat Farm case, however, ballistics remained at a fairly primitive level – Edwin Churchill's testimony was, in many ways, a world removed from the cinematic, collar-and-tie forensics of his nephew's age. He began by telling the court that he had weighed a cache of bullets found in the Moat Farm by Detective Scott; these weighed eighty-seven grains each when they were clean, or eighty-eight with the grease lubricant left on.[750] They were .32 calibre bullets, manufactured by the Union Metallic Ammunition Company, and designed for use with Smith and Wesson revolvers, although Churchill accepted that other revolvers and some rifles could also handle the ammunition.[751] He had concluded from his analysis that the bullet in Miss Holland's head had been fired from close range – within a foot of the target – by a revolver, and his reasons for this were twofold:

1. The bullet if fired from a rifle would have gone right through the head and been lost, as a bullet fired from a rifle hits harder and goes farther (about double the distance) than if fired from a revolver. The reason for this is [that] the space between the chambers of the revolvers and the barrel permits the escape of a certain amount of the gases caused by the explosion of the powder, which gases cannot escape if the cartridge is fired from a rifle.

2. My reason for stating the revolver was fired within 12 inches of the skull is because of the large amount of splintering in the skull. If the revolver had been held at some 5 or 6 yards from the skull, the bullet would have obtained a higher velocity and would have made cleaner holes (not so much splintering) and would undoubtedly have gone right through and not have stopped in the skull.[752]

Orthodox Galilean principles had absented themselves from Churchill's second hypothesis: after five or six yards, a bullet should be slowing down as antagonistic forces act upon it;

it should not be speeding up, or at a higher speed than it had attained upon leaving the gun, with the full force of the explosion of the gunpowder behind it. But the principle that the physical effects of a bullet might vary with distance appeared to stand up to scientific experiment. To test his theory, Churchill had fired four of the Moat Farm bullets into the heads of sheep, at different points of bone thickness, and examined the results. From the distances of 6 feet, 3 feet, and 2 feet, the bullets tore neatly through the skulls, and 'lost very little in shape or weight' in the course of their journey – in fact, Churchill recorded, 'only ½ a grain'.[753] But the bullet in Miss Holland's skull had been recovered in a state of disrepair, elongated, having fallen back after popping out the hole behind her left ear, and having left a fragment of itself weighing two grains by the entry wound on the right side.[754] Only at a distance of 6 inches from the target could Churchill produce significant ballistic damage: this time, he discovered, the experimental bullet was 'splintered and smashed up in a similar way to the one found in Miss Holland's skull'.[755]

In cross-examination, Churchill described some of the difficulties of the experiments. The deterioration of Miss Holland's body in the wet Essex earth had erased some of the physical evidence which Churchill would have expected to see on a gunshot wound of such proximity. Powder burns, in particular, were normally left on the skin or hair of victims shot at close range, but the skin and hair of the corpse had rotted away.[756] Churchill also excluded the use of the Quackenbush rifle found at the Moat Farm. This was a .22 calibre weapon, a bore too small to accommodate the .32 weaponry used to shoot Miss Holland.[757]

Several more witnesses – Old Pilgrim, Alfred Law, Emma Burgess, Frances Morton – appeared before the court to testify to the activity on and around the Moat Farm in the late spring and early summer of 1899. The filling-in of the drainage ditch occupied Pilgrim and Law; Burgess spoke of the arrival of Sarah on 20 May 1899, the day after Miss Holland's sudden disappearance; Mrs Morton, the vicar's wife, was the sixth witness, and the first of that day to have had the word *immaterial* written next to her name in the judge's notes.[758]

The testimony of Lucy Pittman was of more interest. She was the thirty-three-year-old unmarried assistant to her mother, the postmistress in the Quendon Post Office; this was the branch responsible for delivering letters to the Moat Farm.[759] Lucy remembered letters addressed to Miss Holland having arrived at the post office until March 1903, 'some big enough to take a banker's passbook'. Here, the prosecution touched on the question of motive, the second of Arthur Newton's demands at the police court. The court would hear more about the intricate architecture of Dougal's forgeries, every unsatisfying signature, every bank note cascaded through smaller denominations, abandoned to the receding tide of the currency.

Lucy would also sew up the evidence of the local postal arrangements. 'The prisoner,' she said, 'often met me at the gate [of the Moat Farm] and took the letters'. It was not always Lucy who delivered the letters, however: it was 'Edward Negus at first, for about a year. ... After he left off, for a short time the letters were delivered by my brother, Charles Pittman, and then by Robert Clayden for about six months, commencing in September 1900. When he ceased to deliver, I delivered the letters'. In May 1899 – when Dougal had claimed to have had the impossible overnight letter – the post office had not owned a bicycle, and Edward Negus would set out on foot to make the morning deliveries.[760] Starting at seven o'clock in the morning, and never any earlier, Lucy herself had found it impossible to reach the Moat Farm before eight; sometimes, it would be half past eight. The Moat Farm lay a little over two miles from the post office. In 1899, Negus, on the same round, starting at the same time in the morning, cannot, even if he was enthusiastic and ran all the way, have got to the Moat Farm by seven o'clock, at which hour Dougal told Florence that he had already received a letter from Miss Holland. In cross-examination, Mr Elliott, improvising around this gloomy scenario, asked Lucy, 'Do you ever have people call for letters?'

'Occasionally,' admitted Lucy.

'What time is the office open?' asked Elliott, impatient to make some headway against the rushing stream of prosecution witnesses.

'Seven o'clock,' said Lucy.

Elliott sat out the testimony of Negus and Clayden, who told the same story.

Kate and Eliza Cranwell were caught in a paradox. By contemporary standards, their reputations had been ruined by Dougal; now, they entered the witness box seeking something, perhaps, a little less satisfying than revenge. They remained forthright, challenging, but avoided personal animus in their testimony, riding, instead, a crest of moral superiority normally denied to women in their position. Kate was quizzed skilfully by Charles Gill, whose confidence in his witness's integrity was expressed in his direct approach – had she seen a revolver at the Moat Farm? Yes, Kate answered.[761] Had she seen any cartridges? Yes, said Kate. 'What sort of a revolver was it?' asked Gill.

'A bright one,' replied Kate. 'It looked like new.' This was an amateur version of Edwin Churchill's more professional analysis, but it was sufficient to suggest that Dougal had the armoury to perform the murder. Eliza, in her turn, was goaded by Mr Elliott into the admission that she had gone with Dougal to Tenby, but she did not tremble at the confession.[762] Gill assisted her in his re-examination, extracting the fact that she and Dougal had taken separate hotel rooms in the guesthouse.

A barrage of financial evidence followed, all of it familiar to anyone who had followed the progress of the proceedings at the police court. Francis Bird Ashwin was brought out, in spite of his misgivings about Ernest Holland's initially excessive response to a mixture of Miss Holland's real and purported signatures. Ashwin had decided that the National Provincial Bank had possession of only two of Dougal's forgeries; other documents suggested by the prosecution to be fakes he considered genuine.[763] George Elliott, till now starved of forensic nourishment, swarmed over Ashwin's scepticism, eliciting the accountant's experience – 'twenty-four years in the banking world' – to emphasise his credibility. Framed within the context of the evidence heard so far, however, Ashwin's confidence in the authenticity of any of the signatures post-dating Miss Holland's apparent disappearance seemed badly misplaced. Other witnesses, including Thomas Hensler and Isaac Edwards, quoted chapter and verse on Miss Holland's most suspicious transactions. It was obvious that nobody but Dougal had profited from any of the later dealings.

William Lawrence's appearance came with echoes of Dougal's 1895 conviction at the Old Bailey. Lawrence, the unfortunate cashier at the Bank of England, must have felt himself plagued by

Dougal; now, he related the story of Dougal's masquerade turn as Sydney Domville at the bank, accepting Elliott's point that Dougal had gone quietly and willingly to the secretary's office when the charade was suspected.[764] Ronald Dale and Harry Cox completed the tale of Dougal's eventful removal to the Old Jewry Police Station.

The prosecution's last witness was Detective Inspector Alfred Marden. He related the details of his involvement in his case; in cross-examination, Elliott set out on the path which Newton had cut for him, repeating the solicitor's insidious suggestion that the police had attempted to bully Sarah into giving evidence against her husband. 'She has not been pressed or offered money by the police,' said Marden, batting the idea back. 'I have spoken to Mrs Dougal about half a dozen times, or perhaps seven or eight times,' he went on, 'and other police officers have seen her in my presence. I cannot say where she is living now. Last week she was at 9 Ivanhoe Road, Camberwell'.[765] Still Sarah's role in the affair would not take shape. Was it not obvious that, having deposited a trunk in the cloakroom at London Bridge Station – a trunk with the initials *C.C.H.W.* on it, the *W* painted more recently than the *C.C.H.* – she had some sort of story to tell? These were all facts to which Marden testified under Gill's re-examination. What were her plans on the day of Dougal's arrest? No court would ever find out. Marden's six, or seven, or eight visits to her had only produced the worthless invention that was her final statement. 'I have made my statement quite voluntary [*sic*],' it reads, 'and am willing if necessary to give evidence in this matter and shall be pleased to answer any questions and give what information lies in my power'.[766] In fact, at the time of the trial, Sarah was apparently immersed in her new-found Catholicism, and was taking the confirmation name of, as Dougal put it in one of his letters to Georgina, 'Mary Magdalene – whatever that may mean, I don't know'.[767] Catholic tradition interpreted Mary Magdalene as a penitent, confessing and atoning for her sins: it is hard to believe that Sarah's choice was accidental, or, for that matter, particularly sincere. No doubt she was not so much penitent as relieved to have wriggled clear of the suspicion which, rightly, seems as if it ought to have attached to her.

⁓⊙⊙⊙⁓

It had been a rapid morning, a stream of individuals having entered and left the witness box, and, before lunch, Charles Gill closed the prosecution case. Mr Justice Wright looked over at Mr Elliott. 'Do you propose to call any witnesses, Mr Elliott?' he asked.[768]

'No,' said Elliott. Dougal would be unassisted by any friend or well-wisher he had left to him; Elliott would not risk putting Dougal before the court to speak on his own behalf. According to one description, the stress had begun to affect even the normally robust Dougal, who was 'looking haggard, his eyes sunk, and their gleam accentuated by the puffiness underneath them'.[769] There was no point exposing the man to the probing curiosity of the prosecution.

Mr Gill therefore began to deliver his closing speech. The prosecution had been a miracle of pace – Mr Justice Wright had considered no fewer than ten of its witnesses irrelevant to the case, but nearly four dozen parties had been examined in less than a day and a half. Between the excursions into the immaterial, Gill had steered the argument carefully. He accepted that he was destined to be unable to return the gun to Dougal's hand – there were no witnesses to what had happened to Miss Holland except the clinging forensics, carefully picked through by witnesses as expert as he could have wished to find. He repeated the twin pillars of his case: first – could the jury be satisfied that the corpse found in the thick earth of the Moat Farm was that of Miss Holland? He thought so.[770] He compared Miss Holland's profile in life with that of the corpse:

> The police were looking for the body of a woman somewhat over middle age, who was some 5 feet 4 inches in height, who had a well-shaped jaw and good teeth. Dr Pepper [who gave evidence on the first day of the trial] has told you that he found that the body was that of a woman of over forty years and not more than sixty. It was a well-formed body, without any deformity. In life the body would have been about 5 feet high, and the skull was that of a woman with exceptionally good teeth.

This overlooked Miss Holland's fillings, but Gill pressed on. Beyond the evidence of the autopsy, there were the layers of clothing which Annie Whiting had identified.[771] Beyond that, there was the clear evidence, as Augustus Pepper had also testified, that the gunshot wound could not have been self-inflicted. Miss Holland was clearly murdered, then. His second pillar – by whom?

Dougal 'alone had the opportunity of doing it', Mr Gill said.[772] He was also equipped with a motive. In the wake of Dougal's attempt to kiss Florence, relations in the house were 'very strange indeed'. Miss Holland was 'frequently crying', and Dougal knew that 'if she took any steps in consequence of his conduct he would revert to his original position of being a man without means. And,' Gill went on, 'on 19th May there was only this woman's life between the prisoner and the enjoyment of the property'. Outside, in the fields, supposedly on their way into town to do some shopping, Dougal and Miss Holland were finally alone, and darkness was coming on.

Then there followed the eating away of Miss Holland's bank account; and then the flight to, and very nearly from, London.[773] The facts, thought Gill, were consistent 'only with the guilt of the prisoner'.[774] With that, the prosecution rested, and the court adjourned for luncheon, 'the prisoner being provided with hot beef and potatoes sent down from the prison'.[775]

❧

George Elliott began his speech for the defence at 1.45p.m. It took him an hour and three quarters.[776]

He began by charming the jury, ushering them into 'the domain of fact' upon which his client's fortune relied.[777] He urged them, following Arthur Newton's lead, to 'ignore what has taken place since that day in March when my client came within the custody of the law. My client is conscious – alas! only too conscious – that an attempt has been made to try him by a tribunal other than this, and there have been put to the world statements with regard to him, arguments and inferences suggested to be drawn with reference to him, that have not been all of the fair, judicial nature'. The hunger of the press for news of the Moat Farm mystery had, it was true, made Dougal's public persona difficult to manage. 'It is a matter of common knowledge,' Elliott said, 'that during the months of March, April, and May this case, with all its presumed horrors and sensational incidents, formed the daily topic of conversation of the nation at large'.[778] Some of the jury, he said, may have had their 'minds warped unfavourably to the prisoner at the bar': he implored them to 'decide on the evidence alone'.

So far, Elliott's speech seemed much more archly rhetorical than Gill's had, but Elliott would now damn the prosecution with faint praise, underplaying his own talents, and mentioning that he was 'fearful somewhat lest the ability and experience of my learned friend, Mr Gill, may tell unduly against the prisoner'. Gill had been fair, no doubt, but Elliott wondered whether he had shown that the case against Dougal was 'absolute', unquestionable. A case of 'terrible suspicion ... called for the most searching inquiry', Elliott said.[779] If the jury believed that 'any possibility or shadow of doubt' remained, he said, they should not take on 'the great responsibility' of conviction.[780] In fact, Elliott knew perfectly well that the jury was not required to find an 'absolute' case against Dougal, but could convict him if the prosecution had excluded reasonable doubt – there was a very subtle difference. Still, it was not unfair to remind the jury that a wrongful conviction could result in a wrongful execution, and the risk of this was, of course, to be meticulously avoided.

So Elliott fell to the evidence. The identifying features of the remains, presented to the court by Dr Augustus Pepper and discussed by Gill in his closing address, were, Elliott said, less secure than the prosecution made out. 'The question of the identity of the dead,' he averred, 'has always been one of the most important and perplexing'.[781]

> The difficulty is sometimes great enough indeed in regard to the living. You could not have a better illustration than the comical mistake made by one of the witnesses, Mrs Pollock, the previous day, when that good lady identified the highly respectable keeper of the Court as the prisoner at the bar. Of course, this made no difference to the honest man pointed out by Mrs Pollock, but you can well imagine circumstances where a statement such as that might be fraught with the most disastrous consequences.

Dr Pepper had told the court that the 'length of the body as it lay was 5 feet 1 inch', Elliott continued; but Gill had mentioned that Miss Holland was thought to have stood 5 feet 4 inches tall.[782] 'Is not a margin of 3 inches a very considerable margin between the height of the body dead and living?' pondered Elliott.[783]

Then as regards age, Dr Pepper said that the body might be that of a lady anywhere between forty and sixty. Does that not leave considerable room for doubt as to identity? Then, Dr Pepper has said that the body was that of a woman well formed and with broad hips, whereas you have been told in previous evidence that Miss Holland was of slight build.

But Elliott was beginning to stumble over the uneven terrain of his own domain of facts. Pepper's measurement had been of the horizontal body, slightly curled, 'as it lay'. Standing erect in life, Pepper had told the court during Gill's examination, the body was likely to have been about 5 feet 4 inches tall, 'perhaps a little under or a little over'.[784] This he had ascertained by measuring her bones, and approximating her proportions – not from measuring the body in its hunched position. Likewise, although Miss Holland was, in fact, sixty-one in May 1899, the date of her presumed death, she was in good physical repair. Pepper's estimate of the age of the deceased did not preclude such a well-kept specimen as Miss Holland. As for the comment about the 'broad hips' of the corpse, this was not Pepper's at all. He had said that the remains bore 'no deformity', but he had not mentioned broad hips.[785] Elliott's attempt to disentangle Miss Holland's known physical properties from those of the corpse unravelled on its own inaccuracies.

This was a major difficulty of Elliott's defence. The sequence of events extended logically, in the direction outlined by the prosecution, unless the identity of the remains was first thrown into doubt. More effective were his lateral suggestions relating to the clothing and accessories of the corpse, although even here there were slight errors of fact. Mrs Wisken, he said, had described Miss Holland's comb, hair frame and bustle as 'very old-fashioned'.[786] In fact, Mrs Wisken had described them as 'of an unusual kind' – it was Annie Whiting who had seen Miss Holland's style as distinctly out of date.[787] The prosecution had considered the *passé* clothing to be distinctive of Miss Holland's typical get-up – Elliott objected that the same could be true of 'a body which was much older'.[788] If the jury could imagine that the corpse had been buried at the Moat Farm at any time – days or weeks, even – before half past six on the evening on Friday 19 May 1899, then it was not Miss Holland's.[789] The discovery of such outmoded clothing adhering to the remains offered theoretical support to the idea that they were not those of Miss Holland.

It was, perhaps, a blow struck back against the rout of the prosecution's evidence, and almost certainly the product of Elliott's own ratiocination, and not that of the shadowy Watson and Valetta, who had done little but watch over the course of two days; nor does it seem likely to have been lifted from Newton's initial brief. Elliott's imagination, in and around the evidence, effervesced, whereas Newton's had seemed laborious; Elliott's ideas seemed fresh and vibrant, where Newton's seemed desultory or hard-won. Another example followed closely behind: it was known that Miss Holland habitually marked her clothing with her initials – Kate Cranwell had said so in cross-examination.[790] This was, no doubt, the habit of Miss Holland's boarding-house years, intended to keep her laundry separate from that of the disparate souls who lived around her. But yet none of the garments found on the corpse bore any initials. 'It is one of those considerations that no jury can safely pass over,' said Mr Elliott.[791] This was a strong point, as far as it went, but Miss Holland's changed circumstances – she had not lived in a boarding-house for over six months – probably accounted for the absence of identifying marks: there was no longer any need for her best clothing to advertise her initials, and these may have been unpicked from older garments, and simply not applied to newer ones.

Mr Elliott disparaged Mrs Wisken's identification of her braiding, considering the handiwork 'of the commonest description possible'. Like Homer, this witness, despite her much vaunted and self-publicised memory, had nodded when she recalled the prongs on Miss Holland's belt. These had turned out to be hooks. Could the jury trust her evidence? Her controversial identification of the body by its physical features smacked of sentimentality – Dr Pepper had told the court that 'it was impossible to recognise the body from its general appearance'.[792] Suddenly, Mrs Wisken's account seemed unsteady, unsafe. Elliott had begun his deconstruction of Mrs Wisken in charming style: 'I do not desire to say one word against her,' he said, but he had proceeded to punch holes in the fabric of the dressmaker's story.[793]

Nonetheless, the cumulative effect of the mass of prosecution witnesses continued to weigh against Dougal. Elliott probably felt obliged to attack George Mold's evidence, but Mold's comprehensive record-keeping left the barrister with little room for manoeuvre. 'Is it not possible that years before Mr Mold made boots on the last for some person and has forgotten the fact?' Elliott proposed.[794] Judged against the superstructure of Mold's paperwork, however, this seemed distinctly unlikely.

And thus Mr Elliott turned to the question of motive, painting a picture of domestic bliss in the countryside of north-west Essex, interrupted only by the unfortunate episode in which the master of the house attempted to ravish the maid. Dougal and Miss Holland had, Elliott said, 'formed an intimate relationship – a relationship which was of considerable pecuniary advantage to the prisoner himself'.[795] Miss Holland doted on her man, in Elliott's romantic opinion:

> The prisoner's personal appearance, education, and behaviour were such that the lady was attracted to him, absolutely to the exclusion of her relations and friends. Does that not also show that the prisoner must have been more or less attached to her? Did not the prisoner have every desire to continue that arrangement, looking to his own circumstances and the fact that the lady was maintaining and supporting him?[796]

Mr Elliott ignored the psychological machinery of loneliness, greed and lust as he continued to elucidate his vision of Dougal's peaceful farmhouse life. 'The prisoner and Miss Holland were on the most affectionate terms, and it was not until the little incident arose in regard to the servant that we are told that the smooth current of affection was in any way disturbed.'

Elliott expressed his incredulity at the idea that Dougal would kill a goose that was freely laying golden eggs:

> Financial advantage! Here is a lady of superior birth, culture, and money, and the latter she placed at the disposal of the prisoner whenever he desired any. Her death meant an end of all her bounty to him, and it would be the worst thing that could possibly happen to him. Is there a single word of evidence to show that the prisoner was tired of the companionship of Miss Holland? Because he kissed the servant and tried to enter her bedroom – I admit with the greatest impropriety – are you going to say that he is a murderer?[797]

The scene created was a world away from the terrible truth. Elliott floated the idea that Florence could easily have seen Dougal burying the body in a spot 'visible from the bedroom window of the house'. This was a slight reworking of what Frank Whitmore, an architect, had told the court the previous day – that 'it would be possible for a person in one of the first-floor bedrooms to see the spot where the body was buried if the person leaned out of the window, but it would not be easy to see the spot from the window'. Florence, however, was cowering in the spare room, which did indeed look out onto the front of the property, fully clothed, staring out at the emptiness with (as she told the coroner) the window shut.[798] Between her and the window stood a dressing table. Even if she had, for some reason, moved the dressing table to one side, opened the window, and leaned out, she may not have seen anything. Dougal had sent her to bed at a quarter to one in the morning; he had spent the clear majority of the hours since half past six that evening outside the house, doing *something*. Florence had passed the same period in the kitchen, which was at the back of the house.

Dougal's behaviour in the period after Miss Holland's disappearance betrayed his innocence, said Mr Elliott. He had left all the furniture in the farmhouse where it was, but 'would not a man guilty of this crime afterwards remove all traces of Miss Holland's antecedents?'[799] Elliott thought he would:

> A guilty man would have desired first to remove not only from the house, but from his guilty mind, all trace of that lady whose life he had taken in this cruel, cowardly, and despicable way.

But Dougal was blasé about things of this sort, unaffected by guilt, incapable of remorse. As Elliott pointed out, he had employed Emma Burgess twice, once under Miss Holland, who was posing as Mrs Dougal, and then under the real Mrs Dougal – Sarah – following her arrival from Stansted.[800] This was an absurd risk to run, opening up the possibility that Emma would discern something not-quite-right about the suddenly different domestic arrangements; but she never did (or at least not until much later), and Dougal's nonchalant confidence in the overriding fear of intrusion which characterised the tight-lipped late-Victorian and Edwardian society he preyed upon never failed him.[801]

Elliott closed his speech in the traditional manner, transferring the great burden of the decision to the jury, in no uncertain terms:

> If you, gentlemen of the jury, say it is proved that the prisoner has the blood of that poor creature upon his hands, then your decision is final, and in a brief space he will pass to that world from which he can never return. I do not ask you to shrink from your plain duty; but I know that you will pause long, if you have any doubt in your minds, before you take on responsibility of this man's blood.[802]

They were not to be guided, he said, by 'the influences which have animated those who, to their shame, hooted this man on the streets, or have written of him as a convicted felon'.[803] Instead, he assured himself that they would examine the evidence presented to them in court without reference to the weeks of excitement the case had generated. 'If you do that,' he said:

> my client will accept your verdict as that of his fellow-men who have risen above prejudice and passion. Through me, as a last appeal, the prisoner trusts that the jury will be able to say that the case has not been proved against him, and he will feel that he has had a trial, in spite of the press and the ignoble mob, which was fair before his God and his country.

⋯⋯⋯

Mr Justice Wright gave his final instructions to the jury. He described Elliott's speech as 'eloquent', and Gill's case as 'presented with that fairness, courage and skill which always characterise the eminent counsel for the prosecution'. It was a case of circumstantial evidence, he added, so 'more than usual care was required. If there is any link missing, the apparent strength of what remains is nothing, unless it has been made out in every essential point.'[804] He acknowledged the identifications Mrs Wisken and George Mold had made of the corpse's apparel and footwear. Unless they were mistaken, he said, 'you cannot resist the conclusion that the body was that of Miss Holland'.[805] The logic of the defence was tested with an almost mathematical precision:

> If it was not the body of Miss Holland, where is Miss Holland? If it was not the body of Miss Holland, whose body was it? What have you

to go on to say that, in the face of all you have heard, it was the body of any one else?

Dougal's story of sudden travel was the only competing theory to explain Miss Holland's absence, and the evidence seemed not to be in favour of his version of events. 'If the prisoner really gave knowingly false accounts of what happened to her,' Mr Justice Wright continued, 'then that, of course, will weigh with you very heavily. There is certainly a grave case against the prisoner.'

Another point was then taken up by the judge, one which had scarcely been touched upon in the trial. The fact that the filling-in of the ditch had already been arranged by Dougal – arranged, that is, while Miss Holland was demonstrably alive and residing at the Moat Farm – suggested some days of premeditation.[806] His conduct after the alleged crime, meanwhile, might have been irresponsible, but the materiality of this was left to the jury to assess:

> The prisoner seems to have been very careless by leaving all sorts of traces of Miss Holland about the place. But you cannot expect every circumstance should exactly fit. People who commit crimes do not think of every circumstance.[807]

On the other hand, perhaps Dougal's casual attitude to Miss Holland's disappearance merely spoke of his innocence of any crime. If so, Mr Justice Wright wondered why he 'never instituted the slightest inquiry as to her whereabouts, when one would have expected that the whole country would have been disturbed'. He directed the jury to the question of motive. The progressive erosion of Miss Holland's wealth after May 1899 seemed more than suspicious. 'There is no doubt at all,' he remarked, 'that the prisoner got her fortune into his hands'.

The judge looked up from his notes. 'We have now arrived at the end of a very serious criminal case,' he told the jury. 'If you, gentlemen, have any serious doubt about it, then you must give the prisoner the benefit of it; but if you have no reasonable and serious doubt, then you must do your duty and act according to your conscience.' From the dock, Dougal examined the faces of the jury, 'as if wishing to read their innermost thoughts'.[808]

It was five minutes before four o'clock.[809] The jury retired in order to arrive at their decision. Mr Justice Wright went to his private room. Dougal was taken down to the cells below the courtroom.[810] The crowd lingered, awaiting the verdict, in a hubbub of conversation and at the pinnacle, now, of its expectation.[811]

❧

The *Daily Express* reported that Dougal exhibited 'no hint of anxiety' as he waited, silently, in the cell.[812] Others, later, saw it differently:

> There he sat, listening to the ticking of the clock, all the calmness vanished, a trembling, cowering wretch. Each instant he feared to hear the summons for him to face the court again and learn his doom, yet, while dreading, he longed for the suspense to be over. In that hour he lived almost a lifetime. Great beads of perspiration rolled down his forehead, and it was evident to those who saw him that he was suffering acutely. For him each minute seemed an hour.[813]

At eight minutes to five, the jury returned to the court.[814]

Mr Justice Wright returned from his room; Dougal was brought up from the cells. By now, he was 'very pale, but otherwise unaffected', according to one journalist. According to another, his face 'occasionally twitched'.[815] He took his place in the dock.

The Clerk of Arraigns asked the foreman of the jury whether he and his fellow jurymen had come to a verdict. They had, the foreman replied.[816]

'How do you find?' asked the Clerk. 'Do you find the prisoner, Samuel Herbert Dougal, guilty or not guilty?'[817]

Not a sound in the court.

'Guilty,' said the foreman, softly.

In the dock, Dougal blanched, and quickly pulled himself together, standing 'at "attention" like a soldier, upright and with his arms at his sides'.[818]

'And that is the verdict of you all?' asked the Clerk.

'Yes,' said the foreman.

The Clerk turned to the dock. 'Samuel Herbert Dougal,' he said, 'you have heard the verdict of the jury. Have you anything to say why sentence of death should not be passed upon you according to law?'[819]

Dougal's mouth twitched.[820] He looked towards Arthur Newton, his solicitor, and although 'he essayed to speak, for the muscles of his face moved convulsively ... to the onlookers it appeared as if [he] had lost temporarily the power of articulation'.[821] Nothing would come, and Dougal's gaze returned to the bench.

Mr Justice Wright's private secretary then placed the symbolic black cap on the judge's head.[822]

'Samuel Herbert Dougal,' said Mr Justice Wright, 'the sentence of the law is that you be taken from hence to the place from whence you came, and from there to a place of execution, and that you there be hanged by the neck until you be dead, and that your body be buried within the precincts of the prison in which you shall have been last confined after your conviction, and may the Lord have mercy upon your soul.'

'Amen,' said the Chaplain of the Court, echoed by others.

During the sentencing, the court had been hushed, but outside, in the corridor, a baby wailed.[823] The unhappy child was later said to be one of Dougal's.

But all attention was turned to the prisoner. In the dock, Dougal, who had heard the sentence 'without flinching', appeared to bow slightly to the judge.[824] Then, when he was tapped on the shoulder by one of the warders, he took his cue to leave, turned, and, pausing only to glance quickly around the yellow and green courtroom, 'as if in search of someone', descended the stairs to the cells below.[825]

CHAPTER TWELVE

DOUGAL WAS DRIVEN back to Chelmsford Prison, chased, as ever, by a hooting mob, but this time his domicile was not to be the infirmary, but the condemned cell.[826]

In fact, circumstances demanded that two cells for condemned prisoners were then required at Chelmsford: Dougal's case had not been the first that week which Mr Justice Wright had concluded by donning his ceremonial black cap. On Friday 19 June 1903, as Dougal still whiled away his long hours in the infirmary, a thirty-year-old soldier named Charles Howell had been tried for murder, an *amuse-bouche* before the popular feast of the Moat Farm case. On the evening of Monday 1 June, Howell had cut the throat of a girlfriend who had rejected him, and then given himself up peacefully to the authorities.[827] He was a damaged individual, some of whose relations had been in asylums, suggesting a hereditary tendency towards mental instability. ('If a man were to be excused from crime simply because one of his great-grandparents had been in an asylum,' said Mr Justice Wright, 'scarcely any convictions would take place, and a most dangerous state of affairs would be brought about'.) He had also – like Dougal's son Albert – served in South Africa, fighting in the Boer War. Dougal, in one of his letters, had glowed with pride about Albert's heroism – 'two-thirds of his regiment were killed; as a fact they suffered and fought over more engagements than any other'.[828] Albert had survived the war without impairment, but Howell's experience of combat had left its mark. In court, Howell's mother reported finding her son, on his return from the theatre of war, crying 'like a school child without any cause'.[829] Howell was convicted, in spite of his mental illness, and he took the permanent condemned cell at Chelmsford Prison. Dougal, upon his conviction, took a second cell, 'temporarily converted' for the purposes of housing a man facing execution.[830]

Howell's execution had been pencilled in for Tuesday 7 July; Dougal learned the day after his conviction that his own hanging was planned for Tuesday 14 July.

❧

Glimpses of Dougal in the condemned cell are predictably few. One account, slightly dubiously credited to an anonymous former prison warden, told how Dougal's history of suicidal behaviour – by which was meant the unimpressive attempt he had supposedly made to take his own life in Pentonville in 1895 – ratcheted up the stakes.[831] The man was doomed to die, but the state would not permit him to do it by his own hand. As a precaution against the anticipated execution being rendered suddenly needless, Dougal was placed 'under a strong guard of six warders ... two warders, in fact, were with him constantly'. There was another side to the state's zealous protection of the condemned man, however: those with but weeks to live, and carrying the great weight of a murder upon their obsolescent shoulders, were encouraged to relieve themselves of their spiritual burden. Dougal was reported to have attended the religious service of Sunday 28 June in the prison chapel.[832] He and Howell sat on the 'condemned pew', curtained off from the main body of the prisoners, listening to the sermon delivered by John Watson Blakemore, the prison chaplain. Blakemore and Dougal were in an odd, co-dependent position – Blakemore, working to a deadline, aimed to help Dougal repent for his sins, and Dougal, starved of society, enjoyed the chaplain's very personal attentions. With Howell, Dougal began attending chapel daily, although Dougal's motives were probably selfish ones, unlinked to the idea of repentance. He seems to have believed that his chances of a reprieve may yet have turned on the availability of positive character witnesses, and Blakemore – an ardent, zealous figure, selflessly devoted to his errant flock – must have seemed up to the task. In practice, though, Blakemore could have had no influence on Dougal's physical destiny. It was true that reprieves were sometimes granted to prisoners convicted of a capital offence, sparing their lives, but forcing upon them years of cramped living in prison instead; but when they were, the references of prison chaplains were never their animating force.

Back in London, Arthur Newton had been working, rather intermittently, on a petition to the Home Secretary. Money had been tight throughout the Dougal case – for the trial, Newton had managed to retain George Elliott, who had performed admirably in court against significant odds, but the selection of Watson and Valetta, who remained mute and in the background, suggested that cash had run short. They were inexperienced lawyers, and inapposite choices, but, probably, cheap. To pursue the case further would require more money still. However, it might also generate money. Newton was not immune to the temptations of lucre. Would he speculate to accumulate?

On 3 July, one of Newton's money-making schemes attracted the attention of the Divisional Court of the King's Bench.[833] Newton's closing remarks to the magistrates at Saffron Walden and, no doubt, his brief to George Elliott, emphasised the intrusions of the press, sections of which published details of Dougal's criminal history while the Moat Farm affair was *sub judice*. Newton had busily challenged the newspaper proprietors who had printed such material, threatening them with legal proceedings, but then suggesting, cunningly, that he would consider cash payments in lieu of satisfaction under the law. The owners of the *Herts and Essex Observer* handed over 50 guineas, but other targets felt that Newton's suggestion was improper.[834] If he had a complaint against the practice of the newspapers, he ought to have seen it through in court, they said. Newton, affecting the sort of astonished countenance of which his client would have been proud, denied the allegation that his behaviour added up to extortion. He had 'never heard that there was any objection to a compromise', he said. In the end, Newton was censured for his behaviour, but given the benefit of the doubt by a kindly judge who supposed that the solicitor had been attempting to act in Dougal's best interests. It was an undignified episode, especially if one came to wonder how some of the information had reached the papers in the first place – had Newton, by anonymous means, fed them the stories about which he later protested? It was not impossible, although, perhaps, history gives him the benefit of the doubt – the voracious appetite of the public for news of the Moat Farm, especially while the hunt for Miss Holland's body was still underway, must have opened up plenty of sources of information to the curiosity of enterprising journalists. By way of comparison to all the foregoing, the Crown's costs – covering the investigation, the prosecution, and so on – totalled £619 17s 4d. This was rather more than the public purse had spent on the fruitless prosecutions of William Gardiner at Peasenhall in 1902 (£465 19s 9d), but substantially less than had been spent on the conviction of Dougal's alleged acquaintance, George Chapman (£1,128 17s 1d).[835]

Newton's delivery of Dougal's petition, which was completed on 6 July, was a stage-managed media event, exemplifying the solicitor's push-me-pull-you relationship with the press. The petition itself, type-written in blue ink, contained one significant surprise.[836] Alongside some of the more predictable lines of assault – Dougal should be reprieved, Newton said, because of his history of madness; because he had consistently denied wilfully causing the death of Miss Holland; because he was too enervated to take the stand at the trial; because there was no evidence that he and Miss Holland were on bad terms – there came the first post-trial variation on the death of Miss Holland. On the same day that the Home Office received the petition – Tuesday 7 July – this variation splashed across the front page of *The Sun* newspaper.[837] It was in Dougal's handwriting.

The idea of an exculpatory essay had been around for a while; in a letter to Georgina, some time prior to 12 June, Dougal had mentioned the prospect of an autobiographical *apologia*.[838] 'If I have the opportunity,' he mused, 'I will write the history of this case; it will be interesting reading'.[839] But if Dougal were to give his version of events – that is, a self-formulated version, in which he took the role of the innocent party – then the difficulties implicit in attempting to get it out through the high security of a condemned cell seemed insurmountable. It may have taken until 7 July to have it published, but it seems that Newton collected the document from the infirmary while Dougal was kept there before the trial, perhaps smuggling it out at the end of his visit on the day of the Grand Jury hearing.[840] Ostensibly, the fantasy of innocence which Dougal had concocted in his dramatic, hurried, oblique handwriting had been created to contribute to a petition (supposing he would go on to need one): Dougal, at Newton's behest, was hedging his pre-trial bets. By publishing it in *The Sun*, however, Newton also ensured that the text turned a profit – we can be sure that he did not submit it to the editor *gratis*. This was big news, and had value.

In his piece, Dougal repainted the killing of Miss Holland in the shades of a gothic romance. It is worth quoting in full:

I, Samuel Herbert Dougal hereby state that on the 19th May 1899, Miss Holland and I arranged that after tea we should go for a drive.

About six o'clock I put the horse in the trap and we drove to Stansted to do a little shopping, afterwards drove slowly home stopping on the way at the Chequer's Public House and had a glass of whisky each, arriving at the Moat House at about 8 o'clock or a little after. While I was taking the horse out Miss Holland said she would not go indoors just yet as it was so fine an evening and would wait until I returned from taking the horse across the yard to the stable.

I got a box that was in the coach-house on which she sat, near the doors and which are facing the front of the Moat House.

Laying on a shelf at the side of the house was a revolver and cartridges which I had been shooting early in the afternoon. I took up the revolver which was loaded and commenced unloading by extracting the cartridges, and had lifted up the small clip of metal closing the end through which it was loaded, having the weapon in my left hand, when she said 'Come and look at the beautiful silvery moon'. I moved across towards where she sat, when the revolver accidentally exploded, and immediately I said 'I hope you are not hurt, dear', and almost at that instant her head fell forward. I supported her and spoke a few endearing words. I said, 'Speak, Cecily, dear', and thinking she had fainted placed the cushions of the trap under her shoulders and head against the trap, and ran indoors for some brandy, and was immediately confronted by the servant – (now Mrs. Blackwell) – who asked 'Where is the mistress'. I said, 'She has gone to London but is returning again to-night'. At the time I said this I thought she had only fainted and would be able to come into the house later on.

I returned with the brandy, she was still in the same position. I attempted to give her some of it but found she could not take it. I felt her pulse it was beating. I took off her hat and veil and could see no blood, and afterwards removed her cloak and still saw no blood.

At this time I became demented not knowing what I did. I took her in my arms and carried her up into the fields where there was a breeze, thinking it would revive her, and laid her on some hay close to the stacks. I knelt down beside her and again felt her pulse which was getting feeble. I went back indoors and shortly after returned to her and found her dead. I did not know what to do then. I carried her back towards the Coach-house and seeing the open ditch, which I had previously given orders to have filled up as being unsightly and to prevent the dirty water from flowing into the little Moat where some fish had recently been put. I laid her on some straw in the ditch, and returned to the house again.

I could not rest so returned to where she was. I knelt down and kissed her and placed a piece of lace over her face, and put some straw over her. I could not bury her. Afterwards I placed a branch of a thorn bush on the straw so that the fowls would not scratch the straw off the body. After that I walked about the yard backwards and forwards; then I went indoors and told the servant I was going to the Station, but in reality only walked about the Farm until nearly twelve o'clock, returning to the house and saying to the servant, 'Mistress has not returned'. I told the girl to go to bed and I retired also, but could not sleep and arose early next morning and went out and saw the straw had not been moved.

After breakfast, Alfred Law, who I had previously told to fill up the ditch commenced doing so at the spot where the straw was under the trees, and the work was afterwards continued until the trench was level, taking about a fortnight.

S. Herbert Dougal[841]

This was remarkable stuff, but it did not ring true. For one thing, as Dr Pepper's testimony had made clear, Miss Holland's corpse was discovered lying on its right side, with its left leg drawn up.[842] In Dougal's version, he abandons the body lying on its back, with a piece of lace over the face. The cause of the repositioning of Miss Holland, flipping over onto her side – she could not have done it herself – failed to manifest itself in Dougal's statement. Nor could another problem be resolved by this re-imagining of the truth. Miss Holland was found not at the bottom of the filled-in drainage ditch, but slightly to one side of it. With Old Pilgrim pointing the way, David Scott had excavated the ground along the line of the former ditch, finding nothing. It was after he had applied to widen the existing earthworks that a fork tore up Miss Holland's boot. This made it clear that Dougal had, in fact, dug a chamber in the wall of the trench, slid her body inside it, and covered the aperture with mud and debris, in order that it would not be noticed the next day. He had done this without being observed – Florence was in the kitchen, and could not have seen him – and without being heard. The distance from the house to the ditch was 173 feet – fairly close proximity – but the earth was sodden and easily moved, and Dougal's shovel slid through it soundlessly.[843]

Other parts of the statement were more craftily thought out. The difficulty of Miss Holland's missing hat and veil had been raised by Mr Elliott at the trial – Florence Blackwell had mentioned these items as part of Miss Holland's ensemble in her evidence to the court, but neither had been found on the corpse four years later.[844] There had, of course, been time, while the body reposed in the earth, for decomposition to take place, perhaps especially so for a garment of delicate fabric, such as a lace veil (it was never very clear what happened to the hat); but it was also amply clear that Dougal had pillaged the body, removing and pocketing its jewellery, for example. The veil and hat, after Dougal had finished robbing the corpse, might have finished anywhere – he may have removed them entirely, fearing that they would become obvious points of identification if the body were to surface; they may, being small and flexible objects, have concealed themselves under the detritus he threw in front of Miss Holland's improvised grave, and been buried, unseen, by the farmhands. At the trial, Elliott had attempted to subject Dougal's reprehensible actions to forensic logic: 'Assuming that the prisoner was the man who killed her, is it reasonable to suppose that he would have taken jewellery which would have been identified afterwards as having been worn on the night Miss Holland went away?'[845] The jury, quite rightly, must have thought the supposition entirely reasonable.

The publication of Dougal's statement had the Governor of Chelmsford Prison scurrying to denounce it as a forgery – it would certainly have been a major leak from a condemned cell – but the Home Office quickly came to the logical conclusion that it had emerged from the infirmary some time before the trial.[846] They were assisted in their investigation by a rather naïve clerk from Arthur Newton's Great Marlborough Street offices, who tripped down to Whitehall and mentioned to a messenger that Newton had been in possession of the statement 'for some time'. Docketing the petition and a copy of *The Sun*, several civil servants gave their opinion about the matter.

Dougal's statement, in particular, was noted as 'a very poor production', inconsistent with the facts of the case, and it was given
little more official consideration.

cҩ০৩৬

On the same day, with his worthless story plastered across the front
page of a major newspaper, Dougal's heretofore steady resolve
was observed to waver. Charles Howell had had no reprieve, and,
on Monday 6 July, William Billington, the executioner, and John
Ellis, his assistant, had arrived from Bolton and Rochdale respectively to prepare to dispatch him to the next world. In the normal
manner of things, the executioner would set up the rope the evening before the hanging, and observe the prisoner, checking on,
among other things, the sturdiness of his neck. It seems probable that Dougal, in the adjoining cell, was discreetly removed
while Billington looked around; the next day, he was taken to
the exercise yard while Howell was fetched from his cell and
hanged.[847] The sound of the tolling bell, marking the comple-
tion of the execution, 'sent thrills through him', and 'caused him
to shiver violently', and 'he returned to his quarters, after it was
all over, a wretched being'.[848] Until now, Dougal had eaten and
slept well, and smoked his pipe 'and appears to enjoy it', as one
commentator remarked.[849] That Tuesday, however, his appetite for
his usual pleasures deserted him.[850] When he was asked to remove
to Howell's now-empty cell – the 'largest and most comfortably
fitted of all the cells in the prison' but also the last home of the
condemned man – he was said to have 'betrayed some nervousness'.[851] In the circumstances, perhaps this was understandable.

cҩ০৩৬

One newspaper estimated that, over the two days of the trial,
50,000 words were telegraphed by journalists to London from
Chelmsford.[852] Dougal remained the most significant news
figure of the moment – even overseas, the press had taken up the
Moat Farm story. The *Evening World*, a New York newspaper, had
bestowed Dougal with a criminal nickname, which never caught
on: The New Bluebeard.[853] Their edition of 23 June had carried
the story, wired across the Atlantic, of Dougal's conviction, before
the morning papers in London had hit the streets.[854] In Adelaide,
Australia, the *Advertiser* had reported the trial in a couple of

paragraphs on 25 June, headlining their article *Moat Grange Murder*, declaring that Miss Holland's body had been 'buried in a cavity at the side of the moat' and that it had been 'evidently been shot first, and then battered about to prevent recognition'.[855] The latter point did not accord with the evidence of the hearing-after-hearing which had constituted the magisterial proceedings, the inquest and the trial; but Chinese whispers were at play. In the Bay of Plenty, in New Zealand, the local press initially represented Miss Holland as 'Emille', only correcting themselves in later issues.[856]

The newspaper-reading public, too, had charged their pens. While some had been keen to assist the police in their hunt for Miss Holland's remains, others saw new opportunities in Dougal's conviction and still-pending execution. From Stourbridge, one Mr Farr wrote to the Home Office, aiming to delay Dougal's hanging: 'I defy you to do so till you have seen me person aly [sic]'.[857] He demanded a special train service be laid on for him and '8 bosom friends', presumably to whisk them to the desk of the Home Secretary. But, 'we do not [want] any watchers', he added – he and his friends were 'honest hard working men and true as steel'. There is little to suggest that his request was taken particularly seriously. From Cyprus Street in Bethnal Green, William Mullens wrote in, stressing the possibility that the statement published in *The Sun* might just have been true. 'If so,' he said, 'better for a thousand murderers to go free than for one man to be hung for a crime of which he is guiltless'. The sentiment seemed the correct one, but as Mullens's letter wore on, it was obvious that he was coming round to something. He postulated the theory – one not in line with the statement in *The Sun* – that Miss Holland had suddenly felt 'the shameful infamy of her social position in her illicit liaison with her paramour', and had committed suicide. Perhaps, since he was prepared to depart from the content of Dougal's most recent account of Miss Holland's death, Mullens also considered that she had buried herself. But Mullens's empathy with the victim came from deep within – it was personal:

> I have no sympathy with criminals, and I loathe profligacy, but I feel impelled by some strange and undefinable [sic] impulse, to draw your attention to the possible mental distraction and heart agony that may

have been secretly experienced by Miss Holland which I have so
often experienced during the last 28 years, in my apparently hopeless
controversy with The Board of Trade, and I know all too well to what
such feelings lead.

Amid the chaos, a man apparently calling himself Sidford
Batcombe sent a telegram to the Home Office asking whether
Dougal's spell as an inmate at Cane Hill might affect the official thinking regarding any possible reprieve. Dougal's capacity
to understand the nature and quality of his actions was the only
aspect of Newton's petition that was considered to be worth
looking into; there were even suggestions, published in the press,
that a head injury, purportedly sustained in Dublin in 1892, had
affected his mentality.[858] As things stood, with Howell's body still
warm in the grounds of Chelmsford Prison, and Dougal checking into his room and taking up his reading material (a Bible, a
prayer book, some hymn books, *The Life of Christ*, a volume of
the *Leisure Hour* and 'a book of travels'), the official decision had
not yet been made.[859]

❧

Dougal had rebounded with renewed optimism from the dose
of reality which had been Howell's passing. He staked his hopes
on the petition, and was 'telling everyone he expected it would
meet with success'.[860] He wrote to a couple of acquaintances to
invite them to retrieve a ham which he had left to cure in the
chimney of his notorious farmhouse; when they tried to do so,
the police turned them away.[861] No matter – Dougal's positive
energies sustained themselves. He met with a handful of visitors, including his sons Charles and George, and, inevitably, the
mercenary Arthur Newton.[862] He even received, it was said, a
'pathetic' letter from his wife. He awoke anxious on Saturday 11
July, having had no further word on his fate, but the Home Office
had reached its decision, and communicated it to Chelmsford:
Dougal would die, as arranged.[863] The stress of the penalty he was
facing had already begun to impose itself on Dougal's normally
imposing features: day by day, his face had become more 'haggard and anxious-looking'.[864] Now the news was broken to him
that the petition had been rejected and, according to one source,
Dougal 'broke down like a coward ... cried like a child'.[865] Slater,

a clerk from Newton's office, visited Dougal on the Saturday afternoon, taking his last instructions and bidding him farewell. Dougal apparently begged Slater to tell Newton to petition the King, but Slater advised him of the futility of the request.[866] The unambiguous signs of Dougal's sanity – at least in the legal sense – picked up by the medical officers of Cambridge and Chelmsford Prisons outweighed his shady history in Cane Hill, an institution from which he had, at any rate, been discharged 'cured'. There was nothing left for Dougal but death, and death was expected to arrive at eight o'clock on the morning of Tuesday 14 July.

Public curiosity now surged again – how would Dougal deport himself, in the face of extinction? – but, to the outside world, facts had become difficult to obtain. Press representations of Dougal's last weekend on Earth tended to split themselves between those which perceived stoicism and acceptance, and those which saw self-pity and tearfulness. The truth probably lay somewhere in between the two positions: while the *Essex County Chronicle* had it that Dougal wept at intervals throughout Saturday and Sunday – accounting for his spasms of emotion on the basis that he detested the thought of leaving behind his ten-year-old daughter, Olive – the *Manchester Guardian* wrote that he had exhibited 'wonderful fortitude' ever since his conviction.[867] Perhaps the former source was to be preferred for its proximity, but other papers both near (the *Herts and Essex Observer*) and far (the *Irish Times*) commented on, respectively, the 'strange conflict of testimony in the Press' and 'conflicting statements as to the manner in which he had borne himself in jail'.[868] Minor details could not be agreed upon: where one article described Dougal's appetite for food, 'which had failed him since the death of Howell', abandoning him altogether, another told that 'barring the day Howell was executed his appetite has been good'.[869] One of the few areas in which the reports found common ground related to Dougal's ever-undisturbed sleep patterns – he seems to have lacked the emotional machinery to experience in dreams the guilt and shame his behaviour would have left behind in the subconscious of any normal person. Even here, however, one later source found room for speculation:

In his dreams he could hear the mournful voice of the chaplain reading the words of the burial service, he shivered at the chill of the

passage leading to the chamber of death, he could feel the hands of the executioner adjusting the noose around his neck, he could almost see that grim functionary grasp the lever, and then ——? He awoke with a start, his body bathed in perspiration, his limbs a-tremble, gasping a sigh of relief that it was but a dream.[870]

On Monday, Dougal himself put pen to paper for the last time. He wrote to Georgina, as follows, according to the transcript made for the Home Office:

No. 3891
Herbert S Dougal [*sic*]
Chelmsford Prison.

Miss Georgina Cranwell
Mile End,
Clavering,
Newport S.O.
Essex.

13th. July 1903

Dear Eina,

I have not had much opportunity to write to you before today, but as this will be my last chance, I do so with pleasure. I don't know how you may be in health, as I have not had a line from you since you mentioned the name 'Patience' to me, that I think is the only one since your illness. I do trust you have thoroughly recovered from your weakness and are now strong again.

I have had a letter from Mrs. D. stating that Olive is well and happy although she asks very often after me, poor child. Am glad to say I have arranged that she shall not be neglected as I have appointed my three brothers Trustees of a sum of money to enable them to pay her schooling for some years to come in fact until she is 'of age' so that my trouble in that direction has gone it has worried me very much as she was the only one unable to provide for herself. My jewellery has also been given to her Trustees for her benefit which ought to realise about £100 and enable her to be kept comfortably clothed as well. I asked you a question about the pieces of stuff you said was in the Cupboard at the Moat House which you thought belonged to Olive; but you have not replied to my question. In case you wish to communicate to Olive; her address is c/o The Revd. Father Wright 2 Knatchbull Road Camberwell London S.E.

You can see now I am unfortunately unable to render you any further assistance or friendship therefore dear Eina try to forget me altogether. I know it will be hard to do so, but rest assured that it is not my fault that it must be so. I cannot write more upon this point as you can quite believe it hurts me very much. I have that little motto that those little girls at Audley End Station threw into the carriage with the flowers. You remember I told you of the incident. The Head Porter's Children I think they were. If you ever see them mention 'MIZPAH' to them. I dont [*sic*] think there is anything of interest to tell you as you know all the news better than I do.

Our Chaplain the Revd J.W. Blakemore has given me great attention and from and through whom I have received great consolation and much happiness and was never better prepared for the end.

Give my regards to all your family and tell them I freely forgive them. With love and much affection,

I remain,

Your most sincere friend & now well wisher,

(Sd.) S. Herbert Dougal.

Kiss Baby for me.[871]

It was the usual self-serving stuff. Some men on the brink of death told all in a letter, or apologised for what they had done. Dougal already knew that the authorities would be waiting with hot anticipation for anything of the sort from his pen – he had been keeping the Reverend Blakemore hanging on with promises of 'a true confession ... either on the eve or morning of his execution if not before'. But this letter to Georgina was, quite deliberately, not it. Perhaps parts of it merit remark. Georgina had not written to Dougal since he had been convicted, her last letter to him having arrived on the morning his trial began.[872] But Dougal, for the second time in the course of this more and more one-sided correspondence, expressed his approval of the name she had given their daughter – Patience, which was, as a more emotionally responsive man might have been able to point out, a virtue. Georgina's choice of name, followed by the cessation of her letters, was perhaps also meant to imply that she could do no more for Dougal in this world – she would wait, instead, for the next. She may, equally, have been ill at the time and unable to write, suffering, probably, the same nervous condition that had overcome her before the trial.

Other parts of the letter were bluntly unsympathetic – Dougal's financial provision for Olive, who 'was the only one unable to provide for herself', carried a subtext. It was hardly as if Georgina was in a comfortable financial position – and nor was Kate, for that matter. Dougal's will, dispensing of the trinkets and minor investments he had left (most of which, in theory, belonged properly to Miss Holland's executors, whose own inheritance Dougal had illegally consumed), provided for his legitimate children only, plus, in a tokenistic way, the faithful Millie Dougal, his stepdaughter by his second marriage.[873] Immediately after the birth of Patience, Dougal had written to Georgina promising to 'take the will for the deed in this case', that is, to represent himself officially as the father of her child, rather than to contest an affiliation order as he had done with Kate.[874] But given that he was now about to die, he obviously saw no point in quibbling any more. Georgina – and, to her satisfaction, Sarah – may have deduced from this where his true loyalties still lay.

A few last things here: the 'pieces of stuff' in the cupboard at the Moat Farm were rough cuts of cloth which were meant to have become Olive's infernal slate and fawn dresses. Dougal, to his frustration, still could not ascertain from his correspondence whether this had been done or not. But what did it matter? Even for a letter which was consciously evasive, this was incredibly banal. And the conclusion – Dougal's last words to the outside world, in which he 'freely forgives' the Cranwells, on whom he had preyed for months, and offers them his 'kind regards' – was extraordinary, a cruel jab against a decent family who no longer had the means, or, perhaps, the spirit to reply. Dougal put down his pen, and left the letter to be found in his cell. He had less than twenty-four hours to live.

જી૭૭

Once, Dougal had hoped to become an executioner. Shortly after one o'clock on Monday afternoon, Billington and Ellis returned from Lancashire to prepare to execute him.

William Billington had followed his father James into executions; so too had William's brothers Thomas and John. In 1903, William was generally considered the superior brother, although he rapidly succumbed to the personality damage to which hangmen were almost invariably subject. By the end of the year, he had begun complaining about his fees; by 1905, he may truly have had enough, neglecting to appear at an inquest in Cork (as executioners were required to do for their victims), and subsequently losing his commission.[875] At or around the time of his final execution, Billington's estranged wife and children had been forced into the workhouse, and, that summer, he was imprisoned for failing to provide for them.[876] His life had crashed down around him, and, watching with impatient interest, was John Ellis, his erstwhile assistant.

But Ellis's capacity to deal with the unusual pressures of his profession was eventually found wanting, too. By 1923, Ellis's many years of service had seen him encounter some of the great names of true crime – the Strattons, Frederick Seddon, Crippen, George Joseph Smith and Herbert Rowse Armstrong, to name but a few. The execution of Edith Thompson at Holloway Prison on 9 January of that year, however, broke his nerve. Thompson – whose conviction was unsafe – reacted with instinctive terror when Ellis entered the condemned cell. Ellis had no option but to have her carried to the drop. She was supported there by four warders, having fainted quite away, and Ellis hanged her while she was still unconscious.[877] Situations of this sort put the executioner in a difficult position – they had to complete the job, unhappy though the circumstances were. Dealing with the fallout of these occasions was, more frequently, the trouble: Ellis had some sort of lasting shock reaction, as a result of which he 'would often sit at home staring into space'.[878] He also took to drink and, following his resignation in 1924, attempted suicide by gunshot. Failing on this occasion, he eventually succeeded in 1932, threatening his wife and daughter with a razor before cutting his throat with the same weapon.[879]

On the afternoon and evening of Monday 13 July 1903, Billington and Ellis checked the trap door over which the scaffold stood – it worked, as it had the week before for Howell – set the rope to stretch by attaching a sandbag to the end of it, and made an approximate assessment of the character of Dougal's neck.[880] They considered it 'short and thick'.[881] Based on this, and other considerations, particularly Dougal's weight (11 stones and 7 pounds, at this point), Billington proposed a drop of 6 feet and 8 inches. This would break Dougal's neck, but spare him from strangulation or decapitation.

Darkness fell. With the hours now ticking down to the execution, the urgency of the situation had begun to tell; not so much on Dougal, but certainly on the Reverend Blakemore. Dougal had taken the Sacrament at his hands in the afternoon, and they had prayed together; before retiring to bed, Dougal had scanned his prayer book and Bible.[882] This encouraged the diligent Blakemore, who still hoped to unburden Dougal's immortal soul; but Dougal fell soundly asleep without further ado, and the eve of the execution had now passed without the promised confession. Blakemore left the condemned cell, troubled by Dougal's inability, so far, to acknowledge his sin.

⁂

Dougal was woken by one of the warders at six o'clock on the morning of his death. He 'rose and dressed in a leisurely fashion', or, perhaps, with the torpor one might expect of a man with minutes to live.[883] He put on the blue serge suit he had worn through his trial.[884] There were housekeeping tasks to be done – he 'put his cell tidy, covering his bed with a brown rug and setting on one side the various articles he had used during his occupancy of the condemned cell'.[885] He 'polished his boots for the last time'.[886] He took breakfast – tea, bread and butter, and an egg, washing it down with a few sips of brandy for the sake of fortitude.[887] At half past seven, or just after, the excitable Blakemore came into the cell, and he sat with Dougal for a while.[888]

Blakemore begged Dougal to confess. 'I have made my confession,' Dougal said, casually, meaning the concoction Newton had had published in *The Sun*.[889]

This was not enough for Blakemore, who had perceived the baselessness of Dougal's written statement. 'Do you believe that any man in England will believe that confession?' he asked.

Dougal shrugged. 'Well, I don't think there is any need to alter it. There are only a few points not right.'

'Well,' Blakemore said, 'if it is a true confession will you confirm it or will you leave it unconfirmed?'

Dougal thought for a moment. 'I prefer the latter course,' he said.

Blakemore had already decided that the man was guilty of Miss Holland's murder; but Dougal's unwillingness to confirm *The Sun* story had only increased the chaplain's avid desire to extract a genuine confession from him. 'I felt that it would be a real relief to him,' Blakemore wrote later, 'not to have the false one resting on his conscience'. The probity of the published confession seemed to matter much more to Blakemore than it did to Dougal.

'His naughty spirit was hindering the operation of grace,' Blakemore complained. Since Dougal had been transferred to Chelmsford at the end of May, Blakemore had undertaken 'untiring spiritual labour on his behalf'. Now, he was 'much upset and grieved' to find that Dougal 'should have proved obdurate at the last moment'.

'My spiritual anxiety became intense,' Blakemore went on. Together, they prayed for fifteen minutes – Dougal apparently sobbed, 'but he seemed unable to unbend and make a confession'.

Then, a few minutes before eight o'clock, footsteps came through the stillness of the prison. Dougal stood up as the door to his cell opened; his eyes found William Billington, and the two men apparently shook hands. Dougal took a last drink of brandy and water to steady his nerves.[890] He co-operated while Billington pinioned his hands behind his back, and then Billington and Ellis guided Dougal to the door of his cell for the short walk to the scaffold, which stood in a shed 30 or 40 yards away.[891]

Into the main hall of the prison: the Sheriff's Marshal, the High Sheriff and the Under Sheriff of Essex, then the Governor of Chelmsford Prison, then Blakemore, then Dougal, and on either side of him a warder, in case he fell.[892] Behind them, more dignitaries, functionaries, Raglan Somerset and David Scott on behalf of the Essex Constabulary, and, of course, the press, represented by seven journalists.[893] As they walked, Blakemore began to incant the burial service, a morbid feature of executions, and an oration not normally heard, by most recipients, in advance:

'I am the resurrection and the life, saith the Lord: he that believeth in Me, though he were dead, yet he shall live; and whosoever liveth and believeth in Me shall never die.'

Out of the main hall, and into the yard. Through a cordon of prison warders, arrayed on each side.

'I know that my Redeemer liveth, and though after my skin worms destroy this body, yet in my flesh shall I see God, whom I shall see for myself, and mine eyes shall behold and not another.'

Into the execution shed, with the scaffold in the centre. Billington lined Dougal up on the chalk mark drawn on the trap-door; the lever to operate the device stood to his right.[894] He secured Dougal's legs, strapping them at the ankles.[895] He slipped the noose around Dougal's neck, adjusting it so that the knot rested behind the line of the jaw on one side. He pulled the white cap over Dougal's face, and Dougal saw nothing of the world now. No sound but the tread of the executioner on the wooden boards was heard as Billington crossed to the lever.

Suddenly, Blakemore's voice. 'Samuel Herbert Dougal, are you guilty or not guilty?' Dougal did not answer.[896]

Now the voice came closer. 'Samuel Herbert Dougal, are you guilty or not guilty?'

Blakemore was dangerously close to the trap door. Billington's hand was on the lever, and he could not let this unorthodox, last-minute inquisition go on too long.

'Guilty,' said Dougal, and the Reverend Blakemore stepped back from the trap just as Billington threw the lever. Dougal's frame plunged into the darkness of the pit below, the rope tightened above, and, instantly, there was silence.

CHAPTER THIRTEEN

AN HOUR LATER, Dougal's body was cut down, and the inquest was held. Charles Edgar Lewis, the man who had presided over the enquiry into Miss Holland's death, now presided over the enquiry into the death of her murderer. Henry Newton, the Medical Officer at Chelmsford Prison, stated that death had been due to dislocation and fracture of the second, third and fourth cervical vertebrae, and, in consequence of this injury, asphyxia linked to the instant failure of the nervous system.[897] It had been over in an instant – the soft tissue of Dougal's neck was no more than bruised, and was not split. According to the rule of law, Dougal's body was taken to a prepared grave in the prison grounds, where it was interred and covered with quicklime to destroy it. So did Samuel Herbert Dougal pass from the world, at the age of fifty-six, with the society he had left behind hastening the annihilation of his physical remains.

❦

Blakemore's zealous obsession with Dougal's spiritual health had led him into an error. Questions were asked in Parliament about the propriety of demanding confessions from men standing – quite literally – at death's door, and Blakemore was asked to explain his conduct.[898] He stressed his own anxiety, and his lack of premeditation, observing that he was motivated by 'strong impulse and quite on the inspiration of the moment'. Blakemore was apologetic, however – 'I deprecate sensation and regret any discomposure caused by this act'. The Home Office began to receive letters from disquieted members of the public: Joshua Harcourt Willson wrote to ask whether the law was not satisfied 'when a prisoner is tried & convicted without the man's feelings being harrowed in this unseemly manner'. The Home Secretary, Mr Aretas Akers-Douglas, accepted that the incident was 'to be regretted' and promised to do what he could to prevent the same thing happening again. The chaplains in other prisons in which executions then took place were sent a circular informing them of the official line.

Dougal's cell was cleared, and his letter to Georgina – for what it was worth – delivered to her.[899] Another document left for posthumous discovery – and dated 14 July, but no doubt written earlier – consisted of Dougal's objections to widespread insinuations about his first two wives.[900] Their deaths had been misfortunes, he said, not crimes. In a footnote, he lauded Blakemore, whose 'very great attention and devotion' had, he said, 'brought me face to face with my Saviour'. It was decided not to publish these last writings: they had little value, and the case needed no more oxygen breathed into it.

Out in Clavering, the Moat Farm continued to attract mobs of visitors. A sale of the farming stock on Wednesday 8 July had been attended by perhaps as many as 3,000 people, many of whom came 'not so much to buy as to see the things sold'.[901] Numerous local entrepreneurs set themselves up, selling souvenirs and refreshments, and the ballad about which Dougal had been curious was doing the rounds in great numbers. Jack and his then-owner, the ex-military man Champ, perused the event from the oasis of the well-kept garden around the house; the outlying land had returned to a primitive state, however, and bushes and dockweeds grew fecund and wild in the dark earth. The trap in which Miss Holland was reputed to have taken her last journey, just far enough away from the house to give Dougal the confidence to reach for his gun, went cheaply at £5 15s to a buyer from Saffron Walden; Prince, the pony who pulled the trap, made 18½ guineas. Many of the items were so dilapidated as to be almost worthless, but they sold on the basis of their gruesome provenance. Someone, somewhere, wanted a set of cucumber frames made by Dougal's own hands; one of his wheelbarrows, in hopeless disrepair, still raised 3s 6d. Apparently, enough barbed wire 'to enclose the whole farm' was bought up. Local pickpockets helped themselves to cash and valuables as they filtered through the throngs. It was a remarkable scene.

Later in the year, the Moat Farm itself was sold to a Mr Hubert Cowley from Wiltshire, who took it on agreement for a little less than its reserve price of £1,500.[902] This raised the problem of what to do with Jack, who had steadfastly refused to live anywhere but at the Moat Farm. Eventually, a solution to the problem was found, and, just before Christmas 1903, he was taken to Saffron Walden and offered free board and lodgings with Mrs Henrietta Wisken. The story goes that he recognised her at once and 'made himself quite at home'.[903] Shortly after this, he died, so Mrs Wisken had him stuffed.[904] He still survives in this format, his sharp eyes squinting out at you from under a glass dome.

⟨⟨⟩⟩

Arthur Newton was not done with Dougal yet. A second written confession – this one in pamphlet form and entitled *Dougal's Life Story as Related by Himself* – was on sale before the end of July.[905] Once again, it was produced through the agency of *The Sun*, in which newspaper it had shortly beforehand been serialised, and included a copy of a badly forged, extemporary 'release' form, dated 27 June, in which 'Dougal' agreed to the publication of the second confession. It was plain that Dougal had had nothing to do with this ghost-written document, but it undoubtedly went some way towards satisfying the undiminished public appetite for more Moat Farm surprises. It was full of little complaints about Miss Holland – who, apparently, was 'rather snappy at times', and suffered from fits of temper (but 'Dougal' 'didn't mind ... they gave me an opportunity of clearing out and having a good day and a game or two of billiards'). She was also, 'Dougal' said, 'naturally mean', a Scrooge to the extent that he thought it 'strange to find a woman so mean'. He was purportedly becoming more and more miserable, and drinking heavily, and had decided that to murder Miss Holland was the only solution to his ennui. She was getting in the way of his fun.

On the fatal night, 'Dougal' went on, he and Miss Holland drove into Stansted, but when he tried to sneak off to check on Sarah, whom he had stationed in a cottage there, Miss Holland had one of her spasms of temper, and sat 'jawing me all the time we were in the Chequers, the public-house where we had some whisky'. When they returned, Miss Holland clambered down off the trap and 'Dougal', who had been keeping his revolver, loaded, on a handy shelf in one of the outbuildings, shot her from slightly above and to the side. Then he pulled the body into the coach-house, galloped into the farmhouse to gulp down a steadying brandy and to tell Florence the lie about Miss Holland going to London, and returned to the body to work out what to do next.

Dragging her around the farm while he cudgelled his brains, 'Dougal' had intermittent feelings of remorse, but he eventually settled on a course of action, placing Miss Holland's body – on its back – in the bottom of the drainage ditch and covering her with straw and earth. The next morning, 'Dougal' was relieved to see Alfred Law turning barrow after barrow of debris into the ditch.

There then followed a variety of awful, if somewhat melodramatic, mental and physical repercussions, all of them animated by 'Dougal's' scarcely controlled feelings of guilt. Sometimes, for example, he would somnambulate around the farm in the night, drawn by his subconscious mind to the site of Miss Holland's burial. Once, in 1901, he attempted to leave behind the ghosts of the Moat Farm, and fled to Paris, only to return, bound by his history to remain at Miss Holland's side, despite the agony it caused him.

Of course, he had also been pilfering Miss Holland's bank account, almost as if this were meant to be a therapeutic activity. Eventually, Superintendent Pryke's visit turned out to be the beginning of the much-longed-for end. 'When the body was found,' remarked 'Dougal', 'I made up my mind to put a bold face on it, but at times as I sat in my cell I often thought that after all I was only living a life of misery, and it would be better to end it'. It must have seemed remiss to have finished on such a selfish note, however, so 'Dougal' went on:

> I am very thankful for what has been done for me, and from the bottom of my heart I thank my solicitor, Mr. Arthur Newton, for the fight he made to save my life.

This was advertising, albeit of a very peculiar kind. The pamphlet continued with three shorter tableaux which depicted, first, the scene in which 'Dougal' learned of the failure of his petition; second, the events of the trial in very broad outline; and, third, his last-gasp confession on the scaffold. The whole affair was a waste of anyone's penny, but to buy a copy today costs rather more.

This was Newton's last attempt to make money out of Dougal's misfortune. Following the rejection of his petition for clemency,

Dougal was worth more dead than he was alive. His execution gave currency to the second confession Newton had been keeping up his sleeve – the 'I did it' confession – in the way that a reprieve could not have done. What if the King, Dougal's identified locus of final appeal, had, like William Mullens of Bethnal Green, found the first confession – the 'I did it, but not on purpose' confession – weirdly compelling? Newton could not take the chance, and he let Dougal go to his death knowing that he would profit from his client's demise. The chances of Dougal being granted a royal reprieve were, of course, indescribably remote, and Newton could, realistically, have applied for this with some confidence in his ultimate failure; but, still, the principle remained. This was bad practice.

But Newton was a bad solicitor. Eight years later, he attracted the opprobrium of the authorities for deploying remarkably similar tactics when acting (theoretically) 'for' Hawley Harvey Crippen. There were false confessions, illicit deals with newspapers, and a High Court hearing found that Newton had run Crippen's defence 'for the purpose of making "copy" for the newspapers'.[906] Implicit in the making of newspaper copy was Newton's own pecuniary gain. The greatest omissions in all of this were the requirements of justice, which ought to have been Newton's primary concern. He was found culpable of misconduct and suspended from his practice for twelve months.

In the Crippen case, Newton had been following a working pattern he had established in his dealings with Dougal. Occasional slaps on the wrist, such as he received when trying to extort money from newspaper bosses, had failed, in 1903, to persuade him of the dangers of his approach (or, for that matter, the injustices of it). In 1911, one of the High Court judges had gone so far as to say that 'Crippen was not defended as he should have been', and this was a very serious statement indeed to make about a major criminal case. Dougal was similarly badly served by Newton's self-interest: the difference being that, in his case, unlike that of Crippen, very few people seemed to notice.

⟜◦⟊

With Dougal's passing from this life, so Sarah contrived her own disappearing act. Last seen in the spiritual custody of the Catholic Reverend Wright of Camberwell – referred to in Dougal's last

letter to Georgina – Sarah maintained a very low profile in subsequent years. There was only one hint of her, in fact, and this
emerged in the days soon after Dougal's execution: the Reverend
Blakemore received a letter from her, thanking him for eliciting
her late husband's confession. She knew, she said, 'how stubborn
he was': this, at least, was the story Blakemore told John Ellis
when they met again at a 1916 execution. Perhaps, after Dougal's
death, Sarah had gone to ground, a decision which might have
been attributed to the understandable shame of having been so
badly deceived and misused by her errant husband, now deceased.
However, reference to the contemporary paperwork gathered
by the Metropolitan Police, by the Home Office, by the Prison
Commissioners, by the civil courts, and so on, reveals a tale not
of innocence, but of arch complicity on Sarah's part, half-sup-
pressed by the very public attention garnered by the allegations
against her husband. Another case can be made, not for Sarah's
shame-induced descent into powerless reclusiveness, but for her
disappearance, scot-free, from an affair in which her role was conscious, her actions deliberate, and her guilt (at least by association)
tantalisingly conspicuous.

Sarah's role in Dougal's criminal activities has never been
detected, but we have traced it through the sources, from its
visible origins at Northend House to the point of her disappearance into the ether in the wake of her husband's execution.
When Sarah and her children (and her step-child by marriage)
arrived *chez* Miss Booty shortly before Christmas 1894, this was
not the conclusion of Sarah's ceaseless, painstaking attempts to
locate the previously missing Dougal, although this is exactly
how she would later paint the scene. Instead, it was an organised manoeuvre – Dougal had collected Sarah from London and
travelled back to Buckinghamshire with her. Sarah then played
Lady Muck, enjoying her unearned advantage over the unfortunate Miss Booty until Dougal's prosecution brought the charade
down. Even in this, there are whispers of Sarah's true role – was it
not she who took Miss Booty's possessions, perhaps while Dougal
was not in the house? And, if it was not, did not the controversy
of her husband's court appearance – or even the fact that he was
toting weapons in the house – give her fair warning of his true
character? Sarah said nothing to this effect in her later statements
to the police.

Next, Dublin, where Dougal stole the cheques to commit his frauds; the reader will remember that he sent Sarah the shoes he had bought in London with the proceeds. Perhaps this scarcely proves complicity – but then there was a bank account created in Sarah's name – perhaps she ought to have blocked this move – perhaps she should have seen the warning signs in the footwear. Her husband had no job, but here he was setting off for London, buying shoes and sending them home, setting up bank accounts back in Ireland. Where did she think the cash was coming from? Had she seen the sovereigns in the bag, located in the house by the police?

Following Dougal's imprisonment, and his spell in Cane Hill, the couple moved to Biggin Hill; Sarah, apparently, was none the wiser, still failing to grasp her situation. Naturally, she had walked back into the trap of her husband's aggression (attested to by others in the area at the time) and his immoral sexual behaviour (hinted at, but not quite proved by the witness statements). She moved to Croydon (perhaps via Dublin), but complained in retrospect that the violent Dougal visited her only at weekends. Nobody need doubt the practical and social difficulties encountered by Victorian women who sought shelter from the brutalising influences of their unreconstructed spouses – but Sarah's periodic rejections of her marriage ended, time and again, in reunion. If she had fled for Dublin, and the sanctuary of her mother, as she later said she had, then the urge to return to Dougal must have remained strong. The reader may consider it more likely that Sarah's vacillations, though she would later insist on their authenticity, were, in fact, often linked to Dougal's evolving plans. With Sarah in Croydon, and at a safe remove, Dougal scanned London's population of the geriatric and the lonely for a suitably wealthy spinster to prey upon.

So Miss Holland entered Sarah's story, but her recollections of her own disquiet – scattered over the course of four turbulent years at the Moat Farm – failed to chime with the impartial evidence. Had Sarah really no idea what Dougal planned to do to Miss Holland? He saw her in Croydon a few days before the murder; he made arrangements for Sarah to stay at Stansted for a while; he brought her to the Moat Farm on the day after the shooting. Nobody else in the world knew his *modus operandi* as she did, and if she was even partially ill-disposed towards him because of the beatings and the adultery she had previously alleged, he need only have given a hint of the fact that he had murdered his poor benefactress to have given Sarah cause to take the matter to the police. There had been more weapons at Biggin Hill, to add to those Dougal sported at Northend – now, at the Moat Farm, he had used one, with fatal results. One would have thought that Sarah may have feared for her own safety. Instead, her response was to adopt, without question, the false identity of Dougal's daughter while it suited her to maintain the deception, and then to go around draped in the dead Miss Holland's dresses. Only the confession of her true identity to Mrs Morton, the vicar's wife, might have betrayed a pang of conscience, but this did not go far. Sarah's confidence seemed to be rising, and she told the police that Dougal had, at this time, begun to treat her better. This seems possible, as the relationship was running smoothly on the economic engine of Miss Holland's well-fuelled bank account.

And so it went. Sarah probably imagined her late-night confessional with Kate Cranwell, in which both parties achieved epiphany, seeing, however belatedly, that Dougal had done away with Miss Holland. She certainly colluded with Dougal in the remarkable pantomime of their divorce – this was one of the reasons given by the King's Proctor for the cancellation of the action, and his decision was based on the evidence of the undercover detective, Giles. She believed – so she says – that Dougal's wealth was now derived from his sales of hay, but she enjoyed the disproportionate flood of cash which seemed to pour through the Moat Farm. She sent a small sum of money – so she says – to Miss Holland's niece, Mary Laura Mann, because she felt pity when she read in a letter of her unfortunate plight, but not because little gestures like this seemed to suggest, conveniently, that the long-absent Miss Holland was, in fact, still alive somewhere. The reader may, again, consider that Sarah's later misrepresentations in all these areas are better explained if one supposes that her actions were consciously aligned with Dougal's, and that she was complicit in his schemes. By March 1903, of course, she was ready to leave the country with him – Miss Holland's box with the extra *W*, for *White*, crudely painted on it was standing expectantly in the left luggage office at London Bridge, where she had checked it in – and only his arrest at the Bank of England prevented the plan from working. She told the press, after one of Dougal's appearances at the police court in Saffron Walden, that he was 'exceedingly tender-hearted and a wonderfully fascinating man'. She expressed her confidence in his innocence. At worst, although there is no specific proof of it, she may, in fact, have known of Dougal's intention to murder Miss Holland days before he had brought it into effect. This is the gravity of her involvement in the case, responsibility for which she proceeded to deftly elude.

So how did Sarah contrive to vanish beneath the sweep of public and legal scrutiny? Detective Inspector Alfred Marden of the Essex Constabulary emerges from the shadows of a century as Sarah's co-conspirator: a hunter collaborating with his prey, from the very centre of the police investigation. Although she went to ground on learning of Dougal's arrest, she re-emerged to find Marden awaiting her. On 22 March, he was reported to have travelled to London from the Moat Farm, tracking the elusive Sarah – tracking him, at the same time, was the special correspondent of the *Daily News*. The first sketch of Sarah as the much-wronged, devoted wife of the monstrous Dougal emerged in that organ the next day, and amid a little moral tantrum, with the sympathetic newspaperman in question invoking the obligations of journalistic ethics. 'Where she is and that she is doing is not for me to say,' he wrote. 'It is not right that a woman who has met with misfortune should be hunted out by interviewers and her situation jeopardised for the mere sake of sensationalism.' This seemed almost monastically self-denying for a press in the thrilling grip of the year's greatest crime sensation. Further remarks, however, shone a dim light on Sarah's quickly circumscribed role in the police's reconstruction of events: 'She is not, and never has been, a protégé of the police. They know where she is, and all about her, but beyond that there is no connection between her and the officers of the law'.

Marden was to liaise with Sarah from this point – late March 1903 – through to at least the time of the trial in mid-June, and, as he told the court, they were to see each other at least six – and possibly as many as eight – times over that period. He was also a man in the first throes of the professional misconduct which would see his career fizzle out before the First World War. When he was reduced in rank in November 1912, it was from the responsible and senior post of Superintendent of the Southend Division, but his offences were known to go back as far as 1903. He seemed to have set out on a collision course with official displeasure at this time, and his behaviour, through the years, had become worse: this led eventually to the inevitable disciplinary tribunal. He had illegally questioned prisoners, it was said; he had lied and sworn; he had failed to show the proper respect to the Chief Constable, to principal officers and to the Standing Joint Committee of the Constabulary; and there were other serious charges which were not taken into account by the tribunal.[907] One wonders what these may have been. No Hyde was visible in the lauded Jekyll of his early career, but, by its end, the former had come to dwarf the latter. Even after his retirement from the police force in 1913, Marden found his maverick urges difficult to control – the built-in temptations of his self-defined role, as a self-employed private investigator, cannot have helped. In 1920, he was fined £5 plus court costs for impersonating a policeman; the masquerade was apparently for the benefit of one Miss Wakefield, the mother of an illegitimate child. Bearing all this in mind, what action or actions of Marden's can be considered to account for Sarah's casual immunity from the police interest in her husband's crimes – and what, if anything, motivated Marden? Two possible explanations are available.

The first is a Masonic theory. Dougal and Marden had, apparently, been members of the same Freemasons' Lodge: St Andrew's, number 1817, Shoeburyness, Essex. Dougal had, history says, joined the lodge during his fleeting spell in Southend. Had an acquaintance developed between Marden and Dougal – one which, thirteen years later, Dougal used to his advantage, enlisting Marden to protect Sarah? It seems unlikely: Dougal was clearly in Hornsey, in north-west London, on 18 February 1891, at the time of the birth of his daughter Gladys; Marden was not initiated at the lodge in Shoeburyness until 26 February 1891, suggesting that the two men never met each other in a Masonic context. Nor is Dougal's membership of the Freemasons an unequivocal fact in itself – no record of his own initiation into the Masonic fraternity at Southend has been found. In the probable absence of their hinted-at personal acquaintance, could Marden's sense of brotherly loyalty to Dougal have been so strong? In shielding Sarah from the police enquiry, he would hold all the risk, with nothing to gain. And what had Dougal to gain? The fraud charge against him held fast until the discovery of Miss Holland's body, and his confidence in the untraceable corpse never diminished until his victim's foot emerged from the earth. This was little upon which to stake a high-risk strategy, betraying the possibility of something worse than a few forged cheques in his desire to invoke Marden's Masonic allegiance: better to let fate take his course, ride out the accusations of forgery, and hope that the body never disinterred itself. The idea of Masonic devotion does little to explain Sarah's peculiar invisibility to the police. There were, besides, other temptations to which Marden was, later, known to be susceptible. The Masonic conspiracy depends upon the flashing of a secret sign from the holding cell, or from the dock, but the flashing eyes of Dougal's wife, experienced privately in their multiple rendezvous, may have been sufficient to tempt Marden into transgression. A second theory diffuses the conspiratorial smokescreen, and what is left behind, more plausibly, is sex.

Sarah was known to be a woman of prepossessing physical attractions, and, morally, she was not beyond sleeping with men for ulterior purposes – this is what she had done with Dusty Killick, with the adulterous nature of their liaison forming the conspired-for pretext for Dougal's divorce action. Could Marden have fallen under a similar spell? Was he an adulterer? His marriage – to Mary Weekes Newbury, the wedding taking place in Devon in the mid-1880s – never seems to have faltered. But yet Marden may be the co-respondent named in a 1908 divorce case, the man who, it was said, slept with one Annie Bowden in Torquay in March, April or May 1906. What would Marden, then a service police officer in the Essex force, be doing in Torquay in 1906 – unless he and his wife were visiting her mother, elderly and suffering from hemiplegia, and probably seizures, in Sidmouth, a few miles away to the north-east?

Then, fourteen years on, did Marden's illegal impersonation of a policeman, in an attempt to improve the mysterious Miss Wakefield's prospects, imply that he had been somehow persuaded by her, too; and, if so, are these later examples enough to sustain the idea that Marden may not have been averse to Sarah's persuasions in 1903? The reader may find that there is cause to stop and wonder. Following her early appearance in the *Daily News*, a second manipulated portrayal of Sarah's innocence splashed in *The Sun* on 14 April. This depiction fairly closely prefigured Sarah's final statement to the police, which extended to nearly four-and-a-half pages of typed text, recounting her version of her life with Samuel Herbert Dougal, disingenuous detail by disingenuous detail. The statement itself referred to Marden only as convention demanded, in the third person; but logic dictates that he and Sarah must have written it – and the potted history which appeared in *The Sun* – together. Their fraudulent narratives read as if they were consciously constructed to distance Sarah from the most damaging features of the case against her husband – their studious architecture argues for the involvement of Marden, a man professionally versed in the laws of evidence, and one following the case, in his professional capacity, very closely, with all the access to official files and unofficial gossip that that implied. Even the suddenly remembered detail about the divorce which closes the police statement – 'The Decree Nisi has been rescinded by the King's Proctor's intervention. I have never lived with him [Dougal] since.' – echoes with legalese, more readily accessible to Marden, one would have thought, than to Sarah, who, back in 1895, appeared to have been unable even to write her own letter to the Governor of Holloway Prison requesting Dougal's pension papers. It might also be mentioned here that Sarah told *The Sun* that, among the papers which had been taken into police custody since their trawl of the Moat Farm, there was a little literary effort of her own: an autobiography in draft form, written since she had come to realise that her life was an eventful one, and one which merited formal documentation.[908]

Dougal's execution marked the end of the Moat Farm Mystery: Marden was of no use to Sarah after this time, and there is little doubt that their liaisons – professional and personal – ended quite abruptly. Her protection had, in the meantime, been guaranteed by his subterfuge, and, in spite of any residual feelings of rejection he may have experienced in the wake of their fling's dismal end, he was unable to expose her true role in the case without endangering – or, more realistically, destroying – his own career. One of his rewards for his perceived diligence in the case was a promotion to Superintendent – times had never been better for Marden, and to have confessed to his misuse of power would have been to have brought his run of luck to a juddering end.

Dougal, following what he could of this from his prison cell, was similarly double-bound. Although he had sneeringly suggested to Pryke, way back at the beginning of the Moat Farm investigation, that Sarah knew as much or more than he did about the disappearance of Miss Holland, he never repeated this statement, or anything similar. To implicate Sarah was to implicate himself, and there was no sense in doing that. There seems little point attempting to redeem Dougal now, but, with young Olive joining her mother in London as his case splashed across the global media, his thoughts may have turned to the ongoing welfare of his remaining legitimate daughter. Olive was remembered in his will, and his determination not to draw Sarah into his affairs may have been a strange last beneficence on the part of this terrible, selfish man. He found murder easy, and set it against a separate, distorted moral standard to which you and I have, happily, no access at all; but he might not have been able to countenance taking any action which he felt liable to impair his daughter's prospects. One of the most peculiar features of of Dougal's eccentric behavioural repertoire, when seen in the context of his criminality, was his more-or-less authentic feelings of affection and duty towards most of his direct and legitimate descendants: blood ran thick, for him – at least, it did sometimes.

By these means, Sarah Henrietta Dougal skipped neatly around the prospect of legal accountability for the money she had spent, for the clothes she had worn, and perhaps even for the death of the rightful owner of that money and those clothes, Miss Holland. She is one of the great lost criminal personalities of the early twentieth century. More vigorous and creative than Ethel le Neve, Crippen's passive mistress, she seems more like a prototype Grace Duff. In 1928, Duff (who lived in Croydon, on Birdhurst Rise, which joins, at its northern end, Birdhurst Road, which joins, at its northern end, Coombe Road, where Sarah once lived) poisoned three members of her own family with arsenic and evaded the law when the inquests into the deaths could not identify a suspect. There was something dashing about Duff's escape, marred only by the appearance on her doorstep, years later, of the true crime writer Richard Whittington-Egan, who confronted her with her misdeeds. Duff, by then an old woman, maintained a stoic silence in the face of this provocation, although the psychological impact of Whittington-Egan's sudden arrival thrills the imagination. Sarah, however, was never hunted down in the same manner, and seems to have drifted out of life without returning to the unforgiving limelight. Still, she ought to be remembered in parallel with her husband, his equal, possibly his muse; together, they choreographed the awful dance which led to his death on the gallows, and her evaporation into living oblivion.

Dougal's star shone after his death, and then waned again. One assessment of his significance, offered in the immediate aftermath of his execution, had it that 'since Charles Peace was hanged we have only had one notable criminal, Samuel Herbert Dougal'.[909] Peace was put to death in 1879, so this view elevated Dougal's case – if *elevated* is the right word – above the great cases of the late Victorian and early Edwardian periods. George Lamson, an advocate of aconitine, an unusual poison which he fed to his nephew, Percy Malcolm John; John Babbacombe Lee, the man they couldn't hang; the sad, damaged Mary Pearcey; Thomas Neill Cream, the Lambeth Poisoner; Severin Klosowski, otherwise George Chapman, the Borough Poisoner and Dougal's supposed former acquaintance; all stood in Dougal's criminal shadow. Dougal was quickly replicated in wax and introduced to Madame Tussaud's Chamber of Horrors; his name became a byword for a particularly unashamed form of criminal decadence, and he was assumed to be understood as a cultural icon, part of the social fabric. Reflecting on May Sinclair's *Uncanny Stories* for the *Fortnightly Review* in February 1924, S.M. Ellis mentioned the names of a subset of great criminals of the past, relying upon his readers to appreciate his allusions without further explanation:

> Miss Sinclair here condenses into one or two pages all the horror of many famous murder stories – the pig-like slaughter of Weare by Thurtell, and the victims of Jack-the-Ripper; the unusual end of the Brides in the Bath; the butcherly cutting-up of the body of her mistress by Kate Webster at Richmond, and of Mrs. Crippen by her husband; and all the mystery of Dougal at the Moat Farm after the disappearance of his victim.[910]

But here already were the signs of Dougal's gradual relegation to the second tier of British murders. In 1903, Crippen had been an ordinary salesman of quack remedies, and George Joseph Smith – the killer of the Brides in the Bath – was only months out of prison, where he had been sent for two years for receiving stolen goods, and looking for ways to make his compulsive deceptions pay off. By the end of the First World War, both were great, classic names in true crime – Dougal was being superseded.

In 1928, Dougal was inducted into the *Notable British Trials* series, published by William Hodge of Edinburgh. His case was edited by the writer Fryniwyd Tennyson Jesse, and her introduction remains the standard account of Dougal's life. But his trial itself had been largely unexceptional and here, again, Dougal suffered. Crippen's case had been illuminated by greater performances *in camera* – the legendary testimony of Bernard Spilsbury being one obvious example. The evidence in Dougal's case – as far as it went, omitting Sarah's role – had been overwhelmingly one-sided.

Between the wars, more cases blew up, forcing Dougal backwards in the reckoning. Bywaters and Thompson was one; Rattenbury and Stoner was arguably another. In both examples, the developing role of women in British society framed the events, making them seem ultra-modern in comparison to Dougal's almost 'feudal' legend of naked, cycling farm girls.[911]

Not all authors saw progress in the same way, of course. In February 1946, writing in the *Tribune*, George Orwell lamented the decline of British murder, perceiving a golden age of homicide lasting from about 1850 to 1925. Here, Dougal met the outline criteria, but, in truth, he had been long forgotten, or at least demoted to a lower grade. Orwell mentioned William Palmer of Rugeley, Jack the Ripper, Cream, Florence Maybrick, Crippen, Frederick Seddon, George Joseph Smith, Herbert Rowse Armstrong and Bywaters and Thompson as the blue riband of Victorian and Edwardian malfeasance, and complained that one contemporary case – the so-called Cleft Chin Murder – had, by comparison, 'no depth of feeling in it'. Orwell did not know it, but Neville George Clevely Heath would emerge, later in the same year, with a particularly gruesome crime which would do much to restore conservative opinions of the British murderer as a villain *sans pareil*. But Dougal was nowhere to be seen. In less than half a century – admittedly set over a period of great social and technological change, but, whichever way one looks at it, less than the average lifetime – Dougal's glamour and intrigue, which had once captivated the nation for months on end, had largely gone.

It was particularly ironic, then, that, by virtue of his prodigious sex drive, Dougal's was probably the only Edwardian case some of whose cast survived to walk the Earth in the last years of the twentieth century. Let us take the story of the baby crying in the corridor at Chelmsford Shire Hall, just as Mr Justice Wright intoned the death sentence. It seems unlikely to have been Patience Cranwell, Georgina's daughter, since Georgina was at home in, we presume, a state of nervous collapse – by the by, Patience Cranwell married a gentleman named Griffin, and she died in Devon in 1993. The wailing child in the corridor may just have been Herbert George Cranwell, however, clutched in Kate's arms; he passed away in Bishop's Stortford in 1987. It seems extraordinary to think that anyone who attended court on the day that Samuel Herbert Dougal was sentenced to death might have survived to see, for instance, the Challenger Space Shuttle Disaster.

So Dougal *was* still with us, but, as it turned out, not in his original shape. He was occasionally the inspiration for imaginative literature – *The Smartest Grave*, by R.J. White, first published in 1961, uses the Moat Farm case as a springboard for its fiction, and begins:

> It was getting dark when Henry Pilgrim drove into Market Street. Mrs. Whiffen, watching at the window, saw the lights of the trap before she heard the pony's hoofs on the cobbles. She was on the doorstep when the little tub jolted to a standstill. The shafts strained upward, as if they would lift the pony off its feet, when the big man jumped out.
>
> 'Mrs. Whiffen? How do you do? We are late, I fear. A thousand apologies.'[912]

It seems redundant to mention the name of the true-life model on whom the 'big man', mentioned above, was based: in the book, he is Captain Dugdale.

There have been other literary efforts: a novel by Douglas G. Browne, *Rustling End*, published in 1948; a play by Michael Voysey, *The Amorous Goldfish*, published in 1960. Most recently,

Andrew Taylor, whose great-great-grandparents, he says, once owned the Moat Farm, has immortalised the case (with one or two adaptations) in his novel *Bleeding Heart Square* (2009).[913] His grandmother – a repository of historical minutiae, like all grandmothers – gave him the details, and, intriguingly, he recalls seeing a photograph of her and his great-aunt as children, holding hands in an evocative-looking garden. His interest in Dougal's case being thus piqued, he acquired a copy of Jesse's *Notable British Trials* edition and, flicking through it, found a name which sang to his writer's ear: Lydia Faithful. In *Bleeding Heart Square*, the main character is Lydia Langstone. One cannot help but feel that this is a touching, part-accidental, tribute to a vulnerable young lady horribly brutalised by Dougal in the spring of 1899.

❧

Perhaps, in time, Dougal will find a secure place in the hierarchy of great British murderers. With a little more luck – a less alert cashier than William Lawrence at the Bank of England on 18 March 1903 ought to have been enough – Dougal and Sarah would have fled the country: a train to the coast, and away, much in anticipation of Crippen and le Neve, who got away – temporarily successfully – seven years later. Then there would have ensued an international search for the living, as well as the sticky, filthy search in the grounds of the Moat Farm for the dead. He came within a whisker of much greater notoriety.

But it was not to be. Perhaps Dougal's milieu does seem antiquated: the hangmen, the training ships, the shares in the Uruguayan railway – these seem a world away. But the oak and lath Hertfordshire pubs, the Moat Farm itself – some things remain. It is said that, late at night, in the perfect darkness of the Essex countryside, Miss Holland's ghost can still be heard in the old Elizabethan farmhouse, tinkling on the grand piano. And, sometimes, Dougal's ghost can, too, be heard, re-enacting his hurried business of the night of Friday 19 May 1899. Apparently, he slams the front door when he comes in, and he slams it when he goes back out again.[914]

BIBLIOGRAPHY

Arthur, H., *All the Sinners*, London, 1931

Baker, J.H., *An Introduction to English Legal History*, London, 1971

Chapman, P., *Madame Tussaud's Chamber of Horrors*, London, 1984

Church, R., *Murder in East Anglia*, London, 1993

Cyriax, O., *The Penguin Encyclopedia of Crime*, Harmondsworth, 1996

Dilnot, G., *Triumphs of Detection*, London, 1929

Donnelley, P., *Essex Murders*, Barnsley, South Yorkshire, 2007

Ellis, S.M., 'Current Literature' in *Fortnightly Review*, February 1924

Evans, S.P., *Executioner – the Chronicles of James Berry, Victorian Hangman*, Stroud, Gloucestershire, 2004

Feather, F., & Lockwood, M., *A Life of Dougal*, Essex, 2010

Fielding, S., *The Executioner's Bible*, London, 2007

Furniss, H. (ed.), *Famous Crimes*, London, n.d.

Gawsworth, J., *The Life of Arthur Machen* (ed. R. Dobson), Tartarus Press, Leyburn, North Yorkshire, 2005

Glazebrook, P.R., 'Wright, Sir Robert Samuel (1839–1904)' in *Oxford Dictionary of National Biography*, Oxford, 2004-2008

Goodman, J. (ed.), *The Daily Telegraph Murder File*, London, 1995

Gribble, L., *Triumphs of Scotland Yard*, London, 1955

Herber, M., *Legal London – A Pictorial History*, Chichester, West Sussex, 1999

Honeycombe, G., *The Murders of the Black Museum*, London, 1988

Jesse, F.T., *Trial of Samuel Herbert Dougal*, London and Edinburgh, 1928

Jobb, D., *Crime Wave – Con Men, Rogues and Scoundrels from Nova Scotia's Past*, Nova Scotia, 1991

Lewis, R.H., *Edwardian Murders*, London, 1989

Machen, A., *The Three Impostors; or, the Transmutations*, California, USA, 2001

'My Murderer' in *Avallaunius – The Journal of the Arthur Machen Society*, No. 13, Spring 1995

Piers, H., *The Evolution of the Halifax Fortress, 1749–1928*, Halifax, Nova Scotia, 1947

Piper, L., *Murder by Gaslight*, London, 1991

Puttick, B., *Ghosts of Essex*, Newbury, 1997

Reynolds, A. & Charlton, W., *Arthur Machen*, Oxford, 1963 & 1988

Smith, David James, *Supper with the Crippens*, London, 2005

Sugden, P., *The Complete History of Jack the Ripper*, London, 2002

Taylor, A., *Bleeding Heart Square*, London, 2009

Wallace, E., *The Secret of the Moat Farm and Other True Tales of Suspense*, London, n.d.

White, R.J., *The Smartest Grave*, London, 1961 & 1974

Whittington-Egan & Whittington-Egan, R. & M., *The Bedside Book of Murder*, Newton Abbot, 1988

Wood, W. (ed.), *Survivors' Tales of Famous Crimes*, 1916

Woodgate J., *The Essex Police*, Lavenham, Suffolk, 1985

The Moat Farm Mystery, Daisy Bank Publications, Manchester, n.d.

Web Sources

Higginbotham, P., 'Training Ships', www.workhouses.org.uk/training-ships, retrieved 28 May 2009

Old Bailey Proceedings Online (www.oldbaileyonline.org, version 6.0, retrieved 28 August 2011), December 1895, trial of Samuel Herbert Dougal (t18951209-66)

Toumlin, V., 'An Early Crime Film Rediscovered: Mitchell and Kenyon's 'Arrest of Goudie' (1901)', www.jstor.org/stable/3815558, retrieved 22 October 2011

www.british-history.ac.uk/report.aspx?compid=22522

www.gov.ns.ca/nsarm/cap/royalengineers

Newspapers, Periodicals, etc. (UK unless stated)

Abingdon Herald

Advertiser (Adelaide, Australia)

Banbury Guardian

Bay of Plenty Times (Bay of Plenty, New Zealand)

Berks and Oxon Advertiser

Daily Express

Daily Mail

Essex County Chronicle

Essex Newsman

Evening World (New York, United States of America)

Glasgow Herald

Henley Advertiser

Hertfordshire Mercury
Herts and Essex Observer
Herts Guardian
Irish Times
Jackson's Oxford Journal
Liverpool Mercury
Manchester Evening News
Manchester Guardian
Oxfordshire Weekly News
Penny Illustrated Press
People's Journal
Police Gazette
Saffron Walden Weekly News
The Scotsman
The Star
The Strand
The Sun
Thomson's Weekly News
The Times

Files in Public Archives, etc.

Essex Record Office [ERO]: J/P 2/9
Hertfordshire Archives and Local Studies [HALS]: DE/L 4731
The National Archives / Public Record Office [PRO]: HO 144/212/
    A48697D
HO 144/662/X57181
J 77/750/2824
MEPO 3/159B
PCOM 8/38
TS 29/5
WO 97/2689
WO 117/40

Private Collections

Culpeper Archive (Author's collection)
Evans / Skinner Crime Archive

NOTES

Epigraph

1   One of Miss Holland's lyrics, quoted in the *Daily Express*, 24 March 1903

2   From 'As Your Hair Grows Whiter', words and music by Harry Dacre, which Dougal would sing in the fields of the Moat Farm, amending the pronouns along the way: 'As her hair grows whiter, I shall love her more' (*The Star*, 24 March 1903)

Chapter One

3   Wallace, 7; Chapman, 128

4   Honeycombe, 135; Lewis, p.7

5   Jesse, 6; Honeycombe, 135; Gribble, 75

6   Wallace, 7; Donnelley, 47

7   Lewis, 32

8   PRO, WO 97/2689

9   PRO, WO 97/2689; PRO, HO 144/662/X57181

10 Lewis, 32

11 Jesse, 6

12 PRO, HO 144/662/X57181

13 *Liverpool Mercury*, 12 March 1869

14 Lewis, 32

15 PRO, HO 144/662/X57181

16 *Liverpool Mercury*, 9 June 1871

17 PRO, WO 97/2689

18 HALS, DE/L 4731/8

19 PRO, HO 144/662/X57181

20 www.gov.ns.ca/nsarm/cap/royalengineers

21 HALS, DE/L 4731/8

22 Jobb, 54

23 PRO, WO 97/2689

24 HALS, DE/L 4731/8

25 PRO, WO 97/2689

26 Jobb, 54

27 Jesse, 7

28 PRO, HO 144/662/X57181

29 HALS, DE/L 4731/15

30 Piers, 57

31 Jesse, 7

32 Donnelley, 47; Honeycombe, 136

33 Jobb, 54; Jesse, 7

34 PRO, HO 144/662/X57181

35 Chapman, 129; Cyriax, 135

36 Jobb, 55
37 Jobb, 49
38 Wallace, 7
39 PRO, WO 97/2689
40 Feather & Lockwood, 2
41 Feather & Lockwood, 2; Wallace, 7; PRO, HO 144/662/X57181
42 Jobb, 54
43 Goodman, 125
44 Goodman, 126
45 Wallace, 7
46 PRO, HO 144/662/X57181
47 Lewis, 33
48 Wallace, 7
49 PRO, HO 144/662/X57181; Lewis, 33
50 Jesse, 7
51 PRO, WO 97/2689
52 PRO, HO 144/662/X57181
53 Wallace, 7
54 PRO, HO 144/662/X57181
55 HALS, DE/L 4731/8
56 Lewis, 33
57 Jobb, 55
58 Jesse, 7
59 Wallace, 8
60 Jobb, 55
61 PRO, WO 97/2689
62 PRO, WO 117/40
63 PRO, WO 117/40; PRO, WO 97/2689
64 PRO, WO 97/2689
65 PRO, HO 144/662/X57181
66 Higginbotham, 'Training Ships'
67 HALS, DE/L 4731/8
68 HALS, DE/L 4731/1
69 *The Times*, 12 April 1889
70 Evans, 81–2
71 *The Times*, 13 April 1889
72 Cyriax, 156
73 *The Times*, 7 August 1889
74 HALS, DE/L 4731/12

Chapter Two

75 *Herts and Essex Observer*, 13 July 1889
76 HALS, DE/L 4731/13
77 *Herts Guardian*, 13 July 1889
78 *Herts and Essex Observer*, 13 July 1889
79 HALS, DE/L 4731/13
80 *Herts Guardian*, 7 December 1889; *Hertfordshire Mercury*, 7 December 1889
81 HALS, DE/L 4731/9
82 *Herts and Essex Observer*, 7 December 1889
83 PRO, HO 144/212/A48697D
84 Evans, 369
85 PRO, HO 144/212/A48697D
86 www.british-history.ac.uk/report.aspx?compid=22522
87 Jesse, 7
88 Wallace, 8
89 Jesse, 205
90 PRO, J 77/750/2824
91 PRO, MEPO 3/159B; PRO, HO 144/662/X57181
92 PRO, MEPO 3/159B
93 PRO, HO 144/662/X57181
94 PRO, MEPO 3/159B
95 PRO, HO 144/662/X57181
96 PRO, MEPO 3/159B
97 Jesse, 197

98   *Jackson's Oxford Journal,*
      14 April 1895
99   Jesse, 197
100 *The Times,* 20 October 1894
101 Reynolds & Charlton, 37;
      PRO, MEPO 3/159B
102 Gawsworth, 124
103 Machen (2001), 102
104 Machen, (2001), 113
105 Machen (1995), 11
106 Jesse, 55
107 Jesse, 197
108 PRO, MEPO 3/159B
109 *Jackson's Oxford Journal,*
      13 April 1895
110 *Abingdon Herald,* 2 March
      1895
111 *Jackson's Oxford Journal,*
      13 April 1895; *Banbury
      Guardian,* 11 April 1895
112 *Oxfordshire Weekly News,*
      17 April 1895
113 *Oxfordshire Weekly News,*
      17 April 1895; *Banbury
      Guardian,* 11 April 1895
114 *Abingdon Herald,* 2 March
      1895
115 *Oxfordshire Weekly News,*
      17 April 1895
116 *Banbury Guardian,* 11 April
      1895
117 *Jackson's Oxford Journal,*
      13 April 1895
118 *Banbury Guardian,* 11 April
      1895
119 *Abingdon Herald,* 2 March
      1895
120 *Banbury Guardian,* 11 April
      1895

121 Jesse, 197
122 *Banbury Guardian,* 11 April
      1895
123 Jesse, 198
124 *Oxfordshire Weekly News,*
      17 April 1895
125 *Banbury Guardian,* 11 April
      1895
126 *Henley Advertiser,* 20 April
      1895
127 *Oxfordshire Weekly News,*
      17 April 1895
128 *Henley Advertiser,* 20 April
      1895
129 Jesse, 9
130 *Berks and Oxon Advertiser,*
      17 May 1895; Machen
      (1995), 11
131 *Old Bailey Proceedings Online*
      (t18951209-66); Jesse, 205
132 *Old Bailey Proceedings Online*
      (t18951209-66)
133 *Old Bailey Proceedings Online*
      (t18951209-66); PRO,
      MEPO 3/159B
134 PRO, MEPO 3/159B
135 *Old Bailey Proceedings Online*
      (t18951209-66)
136 PRO, MEPO 3/159B
137 *Old Bailey Proceedings
      Online* (t18951209-66)
138 PRO, MEPO 3/159B
139 *Old Bailey Proceedings Online*
      (t18951209-66)
140 *Old Bailey Proceedings Online*
      (t18951209-66); PRO,
      MEPO 3/159B
141 *Old Bailey Proceedings Online*
      (t18951209-66)

142 PRO, MEPO 3/159B

143 *Old Bailey Proceedings Online*
(t18951209-66)

144 PRO, MEPO 3/159B

145 *Old Bailey Proceedings Online*
(t18951209-66)

146 PRO, MEPO 3/159B

147 *Abingdon Herald*,
23 November 1895

148 *The Times*, 10 December
1895

149 *Old Bailey Proceedings Online*
(t18951209-66)

150 PRO, MEPO 3/159B

151 *The Times*, 14 January 1896

152 PRO, MEPO 3/159B

153 Cyriax, 530

154 PRO, MEPO 3/159B

155 PRO, HO 144/662/X57181

156 PRO, PCOM 8/38

157 PRO, MEPO 3/159B

158 PRO, HO 144/662/X57181

159 PRO, MEPO 3/159B

160 PRO, HO 144/662/X57181

Chapter Three

161 Jesse, 204

162 Jesse, 11

163 Jesse, 205–6

164 Jesse, 206

165 Jesse, 11

166 PRO, HO 144/662/X57181

167 PRO, HO 144/662/X57181;
PRO, MEPO 3/159B

168 PRO, HO 144/662/X57181

169 PRO, MEPO 3/159B

170 Jesse, 1

171 Jesse, 4

172 Lewis, 35; PRO, HO

144/662/X57181

173 Jesse, 4

174 Jesse, 1

175 PRO, MEPO 3/159B

176 *Penny Illustrated Press*,
18 April 1903

177 Jesse, 1

178 Jesse, 2

179 Jesse, 213

180 PRO, MEPO 3/159B

181 PRO, HO 144/662/X57181

182 *The Times*, 19 July 1898

183 *The Times*, 23 July 1898

184 *The Times*, 30 July 1898

185 PRO, MEPO 3/159B

186 Jesse, 13

187 PRO, MEPO 3/159B

188 PRO, HO/144/662/
X57181

189 PRO, MEPO 3/159B

190 Jesse, 213

191 PRO, MEPO 3/159B

192 Jesse, 56

193 PRO, MEPO 3/159B

194 Jesse, 14

195 PRO, HO 144/662/X57181

196 Jesse, 14

197 PRO, MEPO 3/159B

198 Jesse, 14

199 PRO, MEPO 3/159B

200 PRO, MEPO 3/159B; HO
144/662/X57181

201 PRO, MEPO 3/159B

202 PRO, MEPO 3/159B; Jesse, 74

203 PRO, MEPO 3/159B

204 Jesse, 73; 14

205 Jesse, 163

206 PRO, MEPO 3/159B

207 Gribble, 72

208 Jesse, 75

209 Jesse, 15

210 Jesse, 75

211 Jesse, 16-7; Chapman, 133

212 Jesse, 16-7

213 PRO, MEPO 3/159B

214 Jesse, 77, 75

215 Jesse, 77

216 Jesse, 17

217 Jesse, 15

218 Jesse, 16

219 Wood, 2; 4-5

220 Wood, 7; 5

221 PRO, MEPO 3/159B

222 Wood, 3

223 Jesse, 17; *The Times*, 28 April 1899

224 Wood, 7

225 PRO, MEPO 3/159B

Chapter Four

226 Jesse, 17; *Daily Mail*, 21 March 1903

227 *Daily Mail*, 21 March 1903

228 *Daily Mail*, 21 March 1903; *The Sun*, 24 March 1903

229 Jesse, 17

230 PRO, MEPO 3/159B

231 PRO, HO 144/662/X57181

232 National Archives, HO 144 662 X57181

233 PRO, MEPO 3/159B

234 PRO, HO 144/662/X57181

235 Jesse, 166

236 PRO, HO 144/662/X57181

237 PRO, HO 144/662/ X57181; Wood, 6

238 PRO, HO 144/662/X57181

239 Jesse, 82

240 PRO, HO 144/662/ X57181; Jesse, 82

241 Jesse, 85

242 PRO, MEPO 3/159B

243 Jesse, 166

244 PRO, HO 144/662/X57181

245 PRO, HO 144/662/ X57181; Jesse, 20

246 PRO, MEPO 3/159B

247 PRO, HO 144/662/X57181

248 Jesse, 185

249 Jesse, 84

250 PRO, HO 144/662/X57181

251 PRO, MEPO 3/159B; Jesse, 83

252 PRO, HO 144/662/X57181

253 Jesse, 80

254 PRO, MEPO 3/159B

255 Jesse, 82

256 PRO, HO 144/662/X57181

257 Jesse, 82

258 PRO, HO 144/662/X57181

259 Jesse, 83

260 PRO, HO 144/662/X57181

261 Jesse, 84; 22

262 PRO, HO 144/662/X57181

263 Jesse, 186

264 Jesse, 83-4

265 Jesse, 82

266 PRO, MEPO 3/159B

267 Jesse, 81

268 Jesse, 167

269 PRO, MEPO 3/159B

270 *The Moat Farm Mystery* (Daisy Bank), 8

271 PRO, HO 144/662/X57181

272 PRO, MEPO 3/159B

273 PRO, HO 144/662/X57181

274 PRO, MEPO 3/159B

275   Jesse, 104

276   Jesse, 105

277   PRO, MEPO 3/159B; PRO, HO 144/662/X57181

278   PRO, HO 144/662/X57181

Chapter Five

279   Jesse, 159

280   Jesse, 215

281   PRO, MEPO 3/159B

282   Jesse, 216

283   PRO, HO 144/662/X57181

284   Jesse, 114

285   Jesse, 216

286   PRO, MEPO 3/159B

287   Jesse, 114

288   PRO, HO 144/662/X57181

289   PRO, MEPO 3/159B

290   Jesse, 105; *The Star*, 21 March 1903

291   Jesse, 177

292   PRO, HO 144/662/X57181

293   PRO, MEPO 3/159B

294   Jesse, 125

295   Jesse, 217

296   Jesse, 165

297   PRO, MEPO 3/159B

298   Jesse, 217

299   Jesse, 105

300   Jesse, 106; PRO, HO 144/662/X57181

301   Jesse, 106

302   Jesse, 188

303   PRO, HO 144/662/X57181

304   PRO, MEPO 3/159B

305   Jesse, 164

306   Jesse, 113

307   Jesse, 217

308   PRO, MEPO 3/159B

309   Jesse, 218

310   PRO, HO 144/662/X57181

311   PRO, MEPO 3/159B

312   Jesse, 26

313   *The Star*, 24 March 1903

314   Jesse, 225

315   PRO, HO 144/662/X57181

316   PRO, MEPO 3/159B

317   PRO, HO 144/662/X57181

318   PRO, MEPO 3/159B

319   *The Times*, 2 March 1900

320   *The Times*, 16 December 1901

321   PRO, MEPO 3/159B

322   PRO, MEPO 3/159B; Jesse, 218

323   PRO, MEPO 3/159B

324   PRO, HO 144/662/X57181

325   Wood, 9

326   Whittington-Egan & Whittington-Egan, 140

327   Wood, 9

328   Wood, 9-10

329   Wood, 10

330   PRO, HO 144/662/X57181

331   PRO, HO 144/662/X57181; Jesse, 125

332   PRO, HO 144/662/X57181

333   PRO, MEPO 3/159B

334   Jesse, 26

335   Wood, 6

336   Jesse, 15

337   Sugden, 444

338   Jesse, 27

339   Honeycombe, 144

340   Church, 101

341   Jesse, 13

342   Lewis, 37

343   Jesse, 27

344 Church, 101

345 Lewis, 38

346 Honeycombe, 144

347 *Herts and Essex Observer*, 25 April 1903

348 Jesse, 104-5

349 Jesse, 108

350 PRO, MEPO 3/159B; Jesse, 28

351 Jesse, 28

Chapter Six

352 PRO, MEPO 3/159B

353 Jesse, 116

354 Jesse, 120

355 PRO, MEPO 3/159B

356 Jesse, 108

357 *The Star*, 23 June 1903

358 Jesse, 108

359 PRO, HO 144/662/X57181

360 PRO, MEPO 3/159B

361 PRO, J 77/750/2824

362 PRO, MEPO 3/159B

363 PRO, HO 144/662/X57181

364 PRO, HO 144/662/X57181; PRO, MEPO 3/159B

365 Jesse, 109-10

366 Jesse, 110

367 Jesse, 29

368 PRO, J 77/750/2824

369 Jesse, 190

370 Jesse, 28

371 Jesse, 110

372 PRO, HO 144/662/X57181

373 Jesse, 110

374 Jesse, 109-10

375 PRO, MEPO 3/159B

376 PRO, HO 144/662/X57181; Jesse, 110

377 Jesse, 108

Chapter Seven

378 *Essex Newsman*, 9 May 1903

379 Jesse, 28

380 Jesse, 28-9

381 Jesse, 29

382 PRO, J 77/750/2824

383 *The Times*, 10 April 1905

384 *The Times*, 10 April 1905; PRO, J 77/750/2824

385 PRO, J 77/750/2824

386 PRO, HO 144/662/X57181

387 Jesse, 29

388 PRO, HO 144/662/X57181

389 *Manchester Evening News*, 20 July 1903

390 Jesse, 153

391 Jesse, 118

392 *Herts and Essex Observer*, 28 March 1903

393 *Essex Newsman*, 28 March 1903

394 PRO, MEPO 3/159B

395 Baker, 270

396 PRO, TS 29/5

397 Jesse, 30

398 Jesse, 110

399 *Herts and Essex Observer*, 17 January 1903

400 *Herts and Essex Observer*, 28 March 1903

401 *Saffron Walden Weekly News*, 7 December 1900

402 *Saffron Walden Weekly News*, 16 January 1903

403 *Herts and Essex Observer*, 17 January 1903

404 *Saffron Walden Weekly News*,

16 January 1903

405   *Saffron Walden Weekly News*,
       16 January 1903; *Herts and*
       Essex Observer, 17 January
       1903

406   *Herts and Essex Observer*,
       17 January 1903

407   *Saffron Walden Weekly News*,
       16 January 1903

408   *Herts and Essex Observer*,
       17 January 1903

409   *Saffron Walden Weekly News*,
       16 January 1903

410   *Herts and Essex Observer*,
       17 January 1903

411   *Saffron Walden Weekly News*,
       16 January 1903

412   *Herts and Essex Observer*,
       17 January 1903

413   *Saffron Walden Weekly News*,
       16 January 1903

414   *Herts and Essex Observer*,
       17 January 1903

415   *Saffron Walden Weekly News*,
       16 January 1903

416   *Herts and Essex Observer*,
       17 January 1903

417   *Herts and Essex Observer*,
       31 January 1903

418   *The Times*, 1 February 1956

419   *Herts and Essex Observer*,
       28 March 1903

420   *Herts and Essex Observer*,
       31 January 1903

421   Jesse, 30

422   *Herts and Essex Observer*,
       31 January 1903

423   Jesse, 110

424   PRO, MEPO 3/159B

425   PRO, TS 29/5

426   Honeycombe, 145

427   Jesse, 30-1

428   Woodgate, 63

429   *The Times*, 16 December
       1925

430   *The Times*, 6 January 1902

431   Woodgate, 63

432   Woodgate, 92

433   Evans, 126-7

434   Evans, 76-7

435   Evans, 77

436   Evans, 79

437   Evans, 77-8

438   Woodgate, 56-8

439   Woodgate, 58

440   *Herts and Essex Observer*,
       5 July 1902

441   Jesse, 31, 157

442   Jesse, 85

443   Jesse, 85-86

444   PRO, HO 144/662/X57181

445   Jesse, 86

446   Jesse, 86; *Herts and Essex*
       Observer, 27 June 1903

447   Jesse, 86

448   Jesse, 86; PRO, HO
       144/662/X57181

449   Jesse, 86

450   PRO, HO 144/662/
       X57181; Jesse, 87

451   Jesse, 87

452   Jesse, 87; PRO, HO
       144/662/X57181

453   Jesse, 87

454   PRO, HO 144/662/X57181

455   Jesse, 87

456   Jesse, 87; PRO, HO
       144/662/X57181

457 Jesse, 87; PRO, HO 144/662/X57181

458 Jesse, 87

459 Jesse, 88

460 PRO, HO 144/662/X57181

461 Jesse, 88

462 Jesse, 89-90

463 Jesse, 90

464 Jesse, 89

465 Jesse, 90

Chapter Eight

466 PRO, HO 144/662/X57181

467 PRO, MEPO 3/159B

468 Jesse, 33; PRO, HO 144/662/X57181

469 *The Star*, 20 March 1903

470 Jesse, 33

471 Jesse, 90, 170

472 PRO, MEPO 3/159B

473 PRO, MEPO 3/159B; Jesse, 112

474 PRO, MEPO 3/159B

475 Jesse, 70

476 Jesse, 118

477 Jesse, 161

478 Jesse, 118

479 Jesse, 113, 118

480 Jesse, 118

481 Jesse, 192

482 PRO, MEPO 3/159B

483 *The Times*, 10 March 1903

484 PRO, MEPO 3/159B

485 PRO, HO 144/662/X57181

486 PRO, MEPO 3/159B

487 Jesse, 135

488 *The Times*, 16 March 1903

489 PRO, HO 144/662/X57181

490 PRO, MEPO 3/159B

491 PRO, MEPO 3/159B; Jesse, 69

492 PRO, MEPO 3/159B

493 PRO, HO 144/662/X57181

494 Jesse, 123

495 PRO, HO 144/662/X57181

496 Jesse, 207; PRO, HO 144/662/X57181

497 PRO, HO 144/662/X57181

498 Jesse, 135

499 *Herts and Essex Observer*, 28 March 1903

500 PRO, HO 144/662/X57181

501 PRO, MEPO 3/159B

502 PRO, HO 144/662/X57181

503 Jesse, 130

504 Jesse, 131

505 PRO, MEPO 3/159B

506 *Thomson's Weekly News*, 6 October 1906

507 Jesse, 132

508 PRO, MEPO 3/159B

509 Jesse, 132

510 PRO, MEPO 3/159B

511 *Thomson's Weekly News*, 6 October 1906

512 *Herts and Essex Observer*, 21 March 1903

513 Jesse, 132

514 *Thomson's Weekly News*, 6 October 1906

515 PRO, MEPO 3/159B

516 *Thomson's Weekly News*, 6 October 1906

517 *Herts and Essex Observer*, 21 March 1903; Furniss, Vol. 2, No. 24, 247

518 *Thomson's Weekly News*, 6 October 1906

519 Jesse, 132

520 *Police Gazette*, 3 April 1903

521 Jesse, 207

522 *Herts and Essex Observer*, 21 March 1903

523 Furniss, Vol. 2, No. 24, 248

524 Jesse, 133

525 *Herts and Essex Observer*, 21 March 1903

526 Jesse, 133

527 *Herts and Essex Observer*, 21 March 1903

528 Furniss, Vol. 2, No. 24, 248; *Herts and Essex Observer*, 21 March 1903

529 *Herts and Essex Observer*, 21 March 1903

530 Furniss, Vol. 2, No. 24, 248

531 PRO, HO 144/662/X57181

532 PRO, HO 144/662/X57181; *Daily Express*, 20 March 1903

533 *Daily Express*, 20.03.1903

534 Jesse, 91

535 PRO, HO 144/662/X57181

536 *Herts and Essex Observer*, 21 March 1903

537 PRO, MEPO 3/159B

538 Jesse, 34-5

539 *Herts and Essex Observer*, 28 March 1903

540 PRO, MEPO 3/159B

541 PRO, MEPO 3/159B; *Herts and Essex Observer*, 28 March 1903

542 *Herts and Essex Observer*, 28 March 1903

543 *Herts and Essex Observer*, 21 March 1903

Chapter Nine

544 PRO, MEPO 3/159B

545 *The Sun*, 31 March 1903; PRO, MEPO 3/159B

546 PRO, MEPO 3/159B

547 Culpeper Archive (Author's collection)

548 Jesse, 36

549 Jesse, 36

550 Culpeper Archive (Author's collection)

551 PRO, MEPO 3/159B

552 *Herts and Essex Observer*, 28 March 1903

553 *The Star*, 21 March 1903

554 *Herts and Essex Observer*, 28 March 1903

555 *Herts and Essex Observer*, 21 March 1903; 28 March 1903

556 *Herts and Essex Observer*, 28 March 1903

557 PRO, MEPO 3/159B

558 PRO, MEPO 3/159B

559 *Herts and Essex Observer*, 28 March 1903

560 PRO, MEPO 3/159B

561 *Herts and Essex Observer*, 28 March 1903

562 PRO, MEPO 3/159B

563 *Herts and Essex Observer*, 28 March 1903

564 PRO, MEPO 3/159B

565 Smith, 251

566 Evans / Skinner Crime Archive (by permission)

567 *Herts and Essex Observer*, 28 March 1903

568 *Herts and Essex Observer*,

4 April 1903

569 *Essex County Chronicle*, 3 April 1903

570 *Herts and Essex Observer*, 4 April 1903

571 *The Times*, 28 March 1903

572 *Herts and Essex Observer*, 4 April 1903

573 Arthur, 165

574 *Herts and Essex Observer*, 4 April 1903

575 Arthur, 165; PRO, PCOM 8/38

576 *The Sun*, 2 April 1903; *Herts and Essex Observer*, 4 April 1903

577 *Herts and Essex Observer*, 4 April 1903

578 *Herts and Essex Observer*, 4 April 1903; *Herts and Essex Observer*, 11 April 1903

579 *Herts and Essex Observer*, 4 April 1903

580 PRO, MEPO 3/159B

581 Jobb, 55

582 Jesse, 37

583 *Herts and Essex Observer*, 11 April 1903; 2 May 1903

584 *Herts and Essex Observer*, 4 April 1903

585 Jesse, 38

586 Dilnot, 222

587 *Herts and Essex Observer*, 11 April 1903

588 *People's Journal*, 4 October 1919

589 *Herts and Essex Observer*, 11 April 1903

590 *Herts and Essex Observer*,

591 *Herts and Essex Observer*, 25 April 1903

592 *The Times*, 9 April 1903

593 *Herts and Essex Observer*, 11 April 1903

594 *Herts and Essex Observer*, 18 April 1903

595 Evans / Skinner Crime Archive (by permission)

596 *People's Journal*, 4 October 1919

597 Evans / Skinner Crime Archive (by permission)

598 *The Times*, 17 April 1903

599 *Daily Mail*, 17 April 1903

600 *Herts and Essex Observer*, 18 April 1903

601 *The Times*, 17 April 1903

602 Jesse, 168; *The Times*, 17 April 1903

603 *Herts and Essex Observer*, 2 May 1903

604 *Herts and Essex Observer*, 25 April 1903

605 *Herts and Essex Observer*, 2 May 1903

606 Dilnot, 222

607 *Herts and Essex Observer*, 2 May 1903

608 PRO, MEPO 3/159B

609 *Herts and Essex Observer*, 2 May 1903

610 *Herts and Essex Observer*, 2 May 1903; *The Times*, 28 April 1903

611 *The Times*, 28 April 1903

612 *The Times*, 28 April 1903;

11 April 1903; PRO, MEPO 3/159B

PRO, MEPO 3/159B

613 *The Times*, 28 April 1903
614 *The Times*, 28 April 1903;
     Herts and Essex Observer,
     2 May 1903

Chapter Ten

615 *Glasgow Herald*,
     13 November 1894
616 *Herts and Essex Observer*,
     20 June 1903
617 *Herts and Essex Observer*,
     27 June 1903
618 Jesse, 44
619 Piper, 11–28
620 Jesse, 226
621 *Herts and Essex Observer*,
     2 May 1903
622 *The Times*, 28 April 1903;
     Herts and Essex Observer,
     2 May 1903
623 Furniss, Vol. 2, No. 25, 273;
     Herts and Essex Observer,
     2 May 1903; *The Times*,
     28 April 1903
624 *Herts and Essex Observer*,
     2 May 1903
625 *Herts and Essex Observer*,
     2 May 1903; PRO, HO
     144/662/X57181
626 *Herts and Essex Observer*,
     2 May 1903
627 PRO, HO 144/662/
     X57181; Cyriax, 8
628 PRO, HO 144/662/X57181
629 Furniss, Vol. 2, No. 26, 290;
     PRO, HO 144/662/X57181
630 PRO, HO 144/662/X57181
631 *Herts and Essex Observer*,

632 Furniss, Vol. 2, No. 26, 290–1
633 Furniss, Vol. 2, No. 26, 291
634 *Herts and Essex Observer*,
     2 May 1903
635 Furniss, Vol. 2, No. 26, 290–1
636 *Herts and Essex Observer*,
     2 May 1903; Furniss, Vol. 2,
     No. 26, 290–1
637 Furniss, Vol. 2, No. 26, 290
638 *Herts and Essex Observer*,
     2 May 1903
639 *Herts and Essex Observer*,
     9 May 1903
640 *Herts and Essex Observer*,
     9 May 1903; Furniss, Vol. 2,
     No. 26, 292
641 Furniss, Vol. 2, No. 26, 290
642 *Herts and Essex Observer*,
     9 May 1903
643 Toumlin, 45 & n.33
644 *Herts and Essex Observer*,
     9 May 1903
645 *The Sun*, 6 May 1903; *Herts
     and Essex Observer*, 9 May
     1903
646 *Herts and Essex Observer*,
     9 May 1903
647 *Herts and Essex Observer*,
     16 May 1903
648 *Herts and Essex Observer*,
     23 May 1903
649 *The Times*, 16 May 1903
650 *Herts and Essex Observer*,
     23 May 1903
651 *Herts and Essex Observer*,
     16 May 1903
652 *Herts and Essex Observer*,
     23 May 1903

653 *Herts and Essex Observer,* 16 May 1903

654 *Herts and Essex Observer,* 23 May 1903

655 *Herts and Essex Observer,* 23 May 1903; 11 July 1903

656 *Herts and Essex Observer,* 23 May 1903

657 Jesse, 127

658 Jesse, 117

659 *Herts and Essex Observer,* 23 May 1903

660 Jesse, 128

661 Jesse, 129

662 Jesse, 129-30

663 *Herts and Essex Observer,* 23 May 1903

664 *Herts and Essex Observer,* 30 May 1903

665 *Herts and Essex Observer,* 20 June 1903

666 *Herts and Essex Observer,* 6 June 1903

667 Jesse, 226

668 Furniss, Vol. 2, No. 26, 294

669 PRO, HO 144/662/X57181

670 Jesse, 41

671 Jesse, 223

672 Jesse, 225

673 Jesse, 224

674 Jesse, 41, 221

675 Jesse, 224, 222

676 Jesse, 221

677 Jesse, 225

678 Jesse, 222

679 Jesse, 224

680 Jesse, 225

681 Jesse, 226

682 Jesse, 227

683 *Herts and Essex Observer,* 20 June 1903

684 Jesse, 227

685 PRO, MEPO 3/159B

686 *The Times,* 15 August 1904

687 Glazebrook, 'Wright, Sir Robert Samuel (1839–1904)', *ODNB*

688 *Herts and Essex Observer,* 20 June 1903

689 Jesse, 228

690 *Essex Newsman,* 20 June 1903

691 *Herts and Essex Observer,* 6 June 1903

Chapter Eleven

692 *Herts and Essex Observer,* 27 June 1903

693 *Herts and Essex Observer,* 27 June 1903; Furniss, Vol. 2, No. 26, 294

694 *The Strand,* Vol. 25, No. 146, February 1903, 143

695 *The Times,* 23 February 1923

696 *The Times,* 18 March 1926

697 *The Times,* 4 June 1946

698 *The Times,* 28 October 1916

699 *The Times,* 21 January 1941; 20 December 1943

700 *The Times,* 23 October 1902

701 *The Times,* 20 December 1943

702 *The Times,* 23 February 1923

703 *Herts and Essex Observer,* 27 June 1903

704 Jesse, 70

705 PRO, HO 144/662/X57181

769 Furniss, Vol. 2, No. 26, 295

770 Jesse, 135-6

771 Jesse, 136

772 Jesse, 137

773 Jesse, 138-9

774 Jesse, 139

775 *Herts and Essex Observer*, 27 June 1903

776 PRO, HO 144/662/X57181

777 Jesse, 139

778 Jesse, 140

779 *Herts and Essex Observer*, 27 June 1903

780 Jesse, 140

781 Jesse, 141

782 Jesse, 94

783 Jesse, 142

784 Jesse, 96

785 Jesse, 94

786 Jesse, 142

787 Jesse, 78

788 *Herts and Essex Observer*, 27 June 1903

789 Jesse, 142

790 Jesse, 109

791 Jesse, 142

792 Jesse, 97

793 Jesse, 141

794 Jesse, 143

795 *Herts and Essex Observer*, 27 June 1903; Jesse, 143

796 Jesse, 143

797 Jesse, 144

798 PRO, HO 144/662/X57181

799 Jesse, 145

800 Jesse, 104-5

801 Jesse, 145

802 Jesse, 145-6

803 Jesse, 146

804 Jesse, 146-7

805 Jesse, 147

806 Jesse, 147-148

807 Jesse, 148

808 *Hertfordshire Mercury*, 27 June 1903

809 *The Times*, 24 June 1903

810 *Herts and Essex Observer*, 27 June 1903

811 *Manchester Guardian*, 24 June 1903

812 *Daily Express*, 24 June 1903

813 Furniss, Vol. 2, No. 26, 295

814 *Manchester Guardian*, 24 June 1903

815 *Weekly News*, 4 October 1919 (Evans / Skinner Crime Archive, by permission)

816 *Herts and Essex Observer*, 27 June 1903

817 *The Scotsman*, 24 June 1903

818 *Herts and Essex Observer*, 27 June 1903

819 *The Scotsman*, 24 June 1903

820 *Herts and Essex Observer*, 27 June 1903

821 *Hertfordshire Mercury*, 27 June 1903

822 *Herts and Essex Observer*, 27 June 1903

823 *The Scotsman*, 24 June 1903

824 *Herts and Essex Observer*, 27 June 1903

825 *Hertfordshire Mercury*, 27 June 1903; *The Scotsman*, 24 June 1903

Chapter Twelve

826   *Herts and Essex Observer*,
        27 June 1903

827   *The Times*, 20 June 1903

828   Jesse, 223

829   *The Times*, 20 June 1903

830   *Herts and Essex Observer*,
        4 July 1903

831   *Weekly News*, 4 October
        1919 (Evans / Skinner
        Crime Archive, by
        permission)

832   *Herts and Essex Observer*,
        4 July 1903

833   *The Scotsman*, 4 July 1903

834   *Manchester Guardian*, 4 July
        1903

835   Furniss, Vol. 7, No. 100, 128

836   PRO, HO 144/662/X57181

837   PRO, HO 144/662/X57181;
        The Sun, 7 July 1903

838   Jesse, 42

839   Jesse, 42

840   *Herts and Essex Observer*,
        20 June 1903

841   PRO, HO 144/662/X57181

842   Jesse, 94

843   Jesse, 81

844   Jesse, 82, 145

845   Jesse, 145

846   PRO, HO 144/662/X57181

847   *Herts and Essex Observer*,
        11 July 1903

848   *Herts and Essex Observer*,
        11 July 1903; *The Scotsman*,
        15 July 1903

849   *Herts and Essex Observer*,
        4 July 1903

850   *The Scotsman*, 15 July 1903

851   PRO, MEPO 3/159B

852   *Essex Newsman*, 27 June 1903

853   *Evening World*, 23 June 1903

854   *Evening World*, 23 June 1903

855   *Advertiser*, 25 June 1903

856   *Bay of Plenty Times*,
        23 March 1903

857   PRO, HO 144/662/X57181

858   *The Star*, 28 March 1903

859   PRO, HO 144/662/X57181

860   *The Scotsman*, 15 July 1903

861   *Daily Express*, 29 June 1903

862   *The Scotsman*, 15 July 1903

863   *Herts and Essex Observer*,
        18 July 1903

864   *The Scotsman*, 15 July 1903

865   PRO, HO 144/662/X57181

866   *Irish Times*, 15 July 1903

867   PRO, HO 144/662/
        X57181; *Manchester
        Guardian*, 15 July 1903

868   *Herts and Essex Observer*,
        18 July 1903; *Irish Times*,
        18 July 1903

869   PRO, HO 144/662/
        X57181; *The Scotsman*,
        15 July 1903

870   Furniss, Vol. 3, No. 1, 12

871   PRO, HO 144/662/X57181

872   Jesse, 228

873   PRO, HO 144/662/X57181

874   Jesse, 224

875   Fielding, 50, 52, 54–5

876   Fielding, 55

877   Fielding, 57

878   Fielding, 58

879   Fielding, 89–91

880   *Herts and Essex Observer*,
        18 July 1903